WONDERSCIENCE

Volume 2

Elementary
Science Activities

American Chemical Society

In association with

American Institute of Physics

American Mathematical Society

WADSWORTH

THOMSON LEARNING

Australia • Canada • Mexico • Singapore • Spain
United Kingdom • United States

WADSWORTH

THOMSON LEARNING

Education Editor: Dan Alpert
Associate Development Editor: Tangelique Williams
Marketing Manager: Becky Tollerson
Marketing Assistant: Ingrid Hernandez
Project Editor: Trudy Brown
Print Buyer: Barbara Britton
Permissions Editor: Joohee Lee
Production Service: Black Dot Group

Wonder Science Editor: James Kessler
Copy Editor: Amy J. Schneider
Illustrator: Jim Wizniewski
Text and Cover Designer: Peggy Corrigan
Cover Printer: Phoenix Color
Compositor: Black Dot Group
Printer: Quebecor World

Printed in the United States of America

1 2 3 4 5 6 7 04 03 02 01 00

For permission to use material from this text, contact us by
Web: http://www.thomsonrights.com
Fax: 1-800-730-2215
Phone: 1-800-730-2214

Library of Congress Cataloging-in-Publication Data

Kessler, James H.
   The best of WonderScience: elementary science activities /
James H. Kessler, Andrea Bennett.
      p. cm.
   Includes index.
   ISBN 0-8273-8094-1
      1. Science—Study and teaching (Elementary)—United States.
2. Science—Study and teaching—United States—Activity programs.
I. Bennett, Andrea T. II. Title.
LB1585.3.K47 1996
372.3'5—dc20   96-19106

   ISBN 0-537-59031-4 (Volume 2)

Wadsworth/Thomson Learning
10 Davis Drive
Belmont, CA 94002-3098
USA

For more information about our products, contact us:
Thomson Learning Academic Resource Center
1-800-423-0563
http://www.wadsworth.com

International Headquarters
Thomson Learning
International Division
290 Harbor Drive, 2nd Floor
Stamford, CT 06902-7477
USA

UK/Europe/Middle East/South Africa
Thomson Learning
Berkshire House
168-173 High Holborn
London WC1V 7AA
United Kingdom

Asia
Thomson Learning
60 Albert Street, #15-01
Albert Complex
Singapore 189969

Canada
Nelson Thomson Learning
1120 Birchmount Road
Toronto, Ontario M1K 5G4
Canada

DESCRIPTIVE CONTENTS

Section 1   Science through Your Senses 1

Use your senses to make observations and classify information.
Also do some fun experiments to learn about your senses of smell,
taste, and touch.

Section 2   Chemical Tests 49

Discover similarities and differences in the ways substances react.
Test substances and record the results so that these experiences can
be used to identify chemicals.

Section 3   Materials 85

Perform tests to learn about the qualities and structure of polymers
and paper. Create and test a variety of materials, and then use your
results to build a strong bridge. Learn about density by testing
whether substances float or sink in various liquids.

Section 4   Measuring 133

Use the metric system to measure length and to do simple calculations using scale drawings. Build devices that measure time.
Learn how to use a compass, and then make a simple one.

Section 5   Math Skills 181

Introduce concepts in math by doing a series of hands-on activities.
Gain experience with graphing, volume, probability, and symmetry
in ways that help students develop real understanding.

Section 6   Physics 229

Learn about the science of movement. Conduct experiments to
discover the power of levers and identify what causes friction.
Calculate speed and explore concepts of design.

Section 7   States of Matter 277

Conduct investigations to identify characteristics of gases, and
learn about the gases that make up our atmosphere. Explore
features of solids, liquids, and gases while noticing that substances
can sometimes possess qualities from more than one of these states
of matter.

Section 8   Earth & Space Science 313

Make models to learn about the earth-changing qualities of erosion
and the inner workings of volcanoes. Conduct tests on water and
on soil. Notice patterns in the length of shadows and in the shape
of the moon over time so that you can make reasonably accurate
predictions.

CONTENTS

Preface / vii

UNIT		PAGE

Section 1 SCIENCE THROUGH YOUR SENSES

1	Use Your Powers of Observation	1
2	Smell and Taste	13
3	The Sense of Touch	25
4	Classification	37

Section 2 CHEMICAL TESTS

5	Chemistry and Color	49
6	Investigating a Chemical Unknown!	61
7	Chemistry Mystery Solvers	73

Section 3 MATERIALS

8	Polymers	85
9	Parade of Paper	97
10	Materials: Test for the Best!	109
11	Float and Sink	121

Section 4 MEASURING

12	Millimeters, Centimeters, and Beyond!	133
13	Measuring Time	145
14	Understanding Scale	157
15	Finding Your Way with the Amazing Compass	169

Section 5 MATH SKILLS

16	Let's Graph It!	181
17	Volume: Full of Surprises!	193
18	Probability	205
19	Symmetry: Two Sides to the Story	217

Section 6 PHYSICS

20	The Force of Friction!	229
21	The Clever Lever	241
22	Structure and Function	253
23	The Essence of Speed	265

	UNIT	PAGE

Section 7 STATES OF MATTER

24	States of Matter	277
25	Gases	289
26	The Atmosphere	301

Section 8 EARTH & SPACE SCIENCE

27	Erosion! Go with the Flow	313
28	Soil Science	325
29	Volcanoes: What a Blast!	337
30	Water: Clearly Wonderful!	349
31	Looking at the Moon	361
32	Shadows	373

Appendix: Safety in the Elementary (K–6) Science Classroom / 385

Activity Index: The Best of Wonder Science, Volume I / 390

Activity Index: The Best of Wonder Science, Volume II / 409

Keyword Index / 417

PREFACE

Welcome to *The Best of WonderScience, Volume 2.* This volume of *The Best of Wonder-Science* is a compilation of the last thirty-two topics from *WonderScience* magazine, the hands-on physical science activity magazine published by the American Chemical Society, the American Institute of Physics, and the American Mathematical Society. When they combine this volume with *The Best of WonderScience, Volume 1* (covering sixty-five topics), elementary school teachers now have the opportunity to access over 600 hands-on activities spanning ninety-seven different science topics. The two volumes of *The Best of Wonder-Science* provide a comprehensive resource for elementary school teachers to enrich the study of many different science topics in the elementary curriculum. The books cover many topics generally taught in grades three to six in physical science, earth and space science, and some life science.

The activities in both *The Best of WonderScience* books focus on the *process* of doing science. The importance of establishing an experimental control; changing and controlling variables; observing, measuring, and recording data; and drawing reasonable conclusions are all emphasized. Whenever possible, mathematics is incorporated into activities so that math and science skills are developed together. Careful attention has also been paid to the sequence of the activities within each unit; the more general introductory activities come first, followed by more focused activities that build on each other to gradually develop student understanding.

In addition to the new science topics with over 200 new activities, *The Best of WonderScience, Volume 2,* has several features that make it a useful companion to *The Best of WonderScience, Volume 1.*

Keyword Index

The most significant of these features is a comprehensive keyword index covering both Volumes 1 and 2. The entries for Volume 1 are presented in regular type, and the entries for Volume 2 are in bold. Now it is easy to search for a concept or substance and discover its application in many activities across several topic areas.

Activity Index

The Best of WonderScience, Volume 2, also contains a separate index listing all ninety-seven topics covered in both volumes, with a short description of each activity within each topic and the page on which it can be found in either volume.

Expanded Teacher's Guides

The Best of WonderScience, Volume 2, contains information for the teacher on the science covered in each unit. The teacher information pages suggest introductions and modifications to activities as well as expected results and activity extensions.

Links to the National Science Education Standards

Each Teacher's Guide includes a section explaining how the activities in that unit connect to the content and process goals of the National Science Education Standards.

Student Activity Sheets

The Teacher's Guides also include Student Activity Sheets, which can be easily photocopied so that each student can record observations and answer questions during the activities.

Science Classroom Safety Guide

The Best of WonderScience, Volume 2, also includes an appendix entitled *Safety in the Elementary (K–6) Science Classroom.* This guide covers general safety considerations for students, including eye protection, fire and heating safety, and safe handling of laboratory equipment and other materials.

Internet Link

We're also on the Web! For science activities and information based on *The Best of Wonder-Science,* go to *WonderNet: Your Science Place in Cyberspace!* at www.acs.org/wondernet.

If you have any questions or comments or need additional information about any of the activities, please feel free to call the ACS Office of K to 8 Science at 1-800-227-5558, extension 6165.

This unit on Observation offers students many opportunities to think about and explore the importance of observation in the study of science. Students will observe a chemical reaction, human behavior in the school cafeteria, cold and hot water containing food coloring, the details of an "ordinary" peanut, and more!

The skills of observation are central to all the sciences. All the theories of science are simply theories until they are tested through actual experimentation, where observation can determine whether or not the theory is valid. In biology, the major theories of the cellular basis of life, evolution, and the structure and function of the human brain have been confirmed and refined through observation. In earth science, the breakthrough theory of plate tectonics was proven through painstaking observation. In physics, theories concerning relativity and the speed of light have been validated through observation. In chemistry, the theory that all matter is composed of atoms has also been substantiated through observation.

Peanut Particulars

In this activity, students begin to realize that very close observation can reveal a surprising amount of detailed information about an "ordinary" object. Students should be encouraged to closely observe the peanut visually as well as to explore the textures and sounds of the peanut. Students will also practice making drawings based on their observations. This is a skill that scientists use on a regular basis. By the end of the activity, students may become very attached to their peanuts, so students should be able to keep them if possible.

Water—Watch and Wonder!

Students observe the movement of food coloring in hot and cold water to draw conclusions about the behavior of water molecules at different temperatures. Although students are not actually observing the water molecules directly, they should understand that as a result of observing the movement of food coloring, certain conclusions about the water molecules can reasonably be drawn. A somewhat analogous form of indirect observation is regularly practiced in astronomy. Because it is not possible to sample material from the surface of a distant star, scientists draw conclusions about the composition of the star based on the indirect method of observing the wavelengths of light the star emits.

Chemistry and Colors—Mix and Match

Students use an indicator, an acid, and a base to observe and modify the color change in a chemical reaction. Students will discover how their eyes can discern very subtle variations in color and will learn how to modify these colors using small amounts of simple chemicals. (Note: Alka-Seltzer® contains aspirin, which is a form of acid. This acid contributes to the color change in cup A but does not need to be taken into account for the purposes of the color-matching activity with lemon juice and baking soda in cup B.)

Food for Thought

Students observe their colleagues eating in the cafeteria to determine eating patterns and preferences. The activity exposes students to a type of observation often used to collect data in the social sciences. You could discuss with students the advantages and disadvantages of observing students eating compared with using survey questions about their eating habits. You could also mention that observing behavior is a valuable means of gaining information about the characteristics of animals and human infants who cannot answer survey questions.

Think in a Wink!

Students must get as much information as they can from observing a very detailed drawing for a short period of time. Students should realize that when they concentrate on observing a particular detail, such as types of objects or the color of objects, they should be able to notice more about that aspect of the picture than when they observed in a more general way.

Unit 1
Observation

Activity Answers and Extenders

Here are answers and some additional ideas you can use to extend your students' experiences with observation.

Peanut Particulars

If for some reason peanuts are unavailable, other objects—such as leaves, rocks, or sticks—can be substituted for peanuts. The point is for students to observe the details of an object very closely to distinguish it from similar objects. A fun variation of this activity is for students to cut an index card in half and to put one thumbprint on each card. They should keep one print and put the other into a pile with other prints. When the group to choose from is large enough, the finer details of the print become increasingly useful in finding the match. It is easy to make the connection between this detailed observation and a practical application of crime solving or fingerprint-based ID systems.

Water—Watch and Wonder!

Students should notice that the food coloring moves and mixes much more in warm water than in cold water. You can try using ice water, but the outside of the glass usually has so much condensation on it that it is difficult to observe the food coloring. If you are in a low-humidity environment, you may get away with using ice water, which results in a very dramatic difference between the two cups.

Chemistry and Colors—Mix & Match

After placing 5 drops of Alka-Seltzer® solution into cup A, the solution should appear purple compared with that in cup B.

This is because the Alka-Seltzer® solution is slightly acidic. When students attempt to match this purple color by adding 1 drop of lemon juice to cup B, the solution should turn pink. This pink color is produced because the 1 drop of lemon juice is even more acidic than the Alka-Seltzer® solution. Students counteract the effect of the extra acidity by adding small quantities of baking soda (a base) to eventually achieve the matching color of the Alka-Seltzer® solution in cup A.

Food for Thought

As mentioned in the activity, it is best if students can observe the eating behavior of other students while staying as inobtrusive as possible. You might accomplish this if students can observe subjects with whom they do not ordinarily eat. The subjects may be less likely to ask questions and joke around with students they are less familiar with.

Think in a Wink!

Encourage students to focus their concentration as much as possible in preparation for viewing the picture. After observing the picture, students may describe their observations very loosely, such as "There was a guy on a bridge fishing." Instead, have students record their observations according to the three categories in the chart. Under **Type of Object,** they might put man, fishing pole, and bridge. Under **Description,** for the man, they could describe the man's clothes, that he had a mustache and hat. Finally, under **Relates to Other Objects,** they could write that the man was holding the fishing pole with both hands while his arms were extended over the bridge railing. This method of data recording should produce significantly more detail than the looser description method.

Observation

NATIONAL SCIENCE EDUCATION STANDARDS

The activities in this unit can be used to support the teaching of the following standards:

✔ **Unifying Concepts and Processes**

Evidence, Models, and Explanation

Evidence consists of observations and data on which to base scientific explanations. *(All activities)*

Using evidence to understand interactions allows individuals to predict changes in natural and designed systems. *(All activities)*

✔ **Science as Inquiry**

Abilities Necessary to Do Scientific Inquiry

Design and conduct a scientific investigation.
   Food for Thought

Develop descriptions, explanations, predictions, and models using evidence.
   Water—Watch and Wonder!   *Chemistry and Colors—Mix and Match*

Think critically and logically to make the relationships between evidence and explanations.
   Water—Watch and Wonder!   *Chemistry and Colors—Mix and Match*

✔ **Understandings about Scientific Inquiry**

Some investigations involve observing and describing objects, organisms, and events. *(All activities)*

Scientific explanations emphasize evidence; have logically consistent arguments; and use scientific principles, models, and theories. *(All activities)*

✔ **Physical Science**

Properties and Changes of Properties in Matter

Substances react chemically in characteristic ways with other substances to form new substances (compounds) with different characteristic properties.
   Chemistry and Colors—Mix and Match

STUDENT ACTIVITY SHEET

NAME ______________________________ **DATE** __________

Food for Thought

Use the chart below to record your observations about the food chosen and the amount eaten by different subjects in the cafeteria.

Food Item	Subject	Subject	Subject	Subject

STUDENT ACTIVITY SHEET

AME ______________________________ **DATE** __________

Think in a Wink!

se the chart below to record your observations about the picture you see.

Type of Object	Description	Relates to Other Objects
EXAMPLE Car	Yellow with black top facing this way →	In front of store Two people in it

Peanut

YOU WILL NEED:

peanuts in the shells
paper
pencils

Scientists must observe the things they study very closely in order to learn a lot about them. Sometimes scientists may need to observe the smallest details of an object. Other times they need to observe a process, such as a chemical reaction or a falling object. Sometimes they may need to observe things over a long period of time such as plants growing or the way animals behave. The activities in this *WonderScience* unit should give you some practice for improving your powers of observation!

1 Divide students into groups of four or five. Give a peanut to each student. Ask students to observe their peanut very closely. Is it long or short, skinny or chubby? Does it have pointed or rounded ends? Does it make a sound when shaken? Does it have a pattern of markings or any other special features?

2 When students are very familiar with their own peanuts, have each group of students place their peanuts in a pile in the middle of the group. Someone should mix up the peanuts. Each student in the group should then pick out his or her peanut based on their original observations.

3 Now that students have a good idea about the details that help tell one peanut from another, have them draw a detailed picture of their peanut. Have each student sign his or her drawing. The peanuts should be placed in a pile again. Students should trade drawings so that no one has his or her own drawing.

4 Students should use the drawing to find the peanut that matches that drawing. Once they believe they have the correct peanut, they should see if they are right by asking the person who signed the drawing. Students should continue looking until each drawing is matched with its correct peanut.

Particulars

5 After all peanuts are correctly identified, students should tell the student who drew the peanut what helped them find the peanut and how the drawing could be improved. All pictures and peanuts should be returned to their original owners.

6 Students should now make as accurate and detailed a drawing of their peanut as possible and again sign their drawing. They should take into account things about their peanut they did not notice before, as well as suggestions from their classmates.

7 Next, have two groups get together and mix all their peanuts in a pile. Challenge students to find their peanut. Students should know their own peanuts pretty well by now. After all peanuts are found by their owners, students should trade drawings among each other as in step 4. Challenge students to find the peanut that matches the drawing.

8 Put all groups together. Place all peanuts in a pile. See if students can locate their peanut. Trade drawings for the last time. See if students can find the peanut from the drawing.

WATER
Watch and Wonder!

YOU WILL NEED:

2 clear plastic cups
hot water (from tap)
cold water
food coloring (blue and yellow)
white sheet of paper

Sometimes you can observe one thing to learn about something else you cannot observe. Scientists call this **indirect observation**. For example, although water molecules themselves are too small to observe, you can observe the way food coloring moves in water to try to learn more about the movement of water molecules. Let's try it!

BE CAREFUL WITH HOT TAP WATER— IT CAN BE **VERY** HOT.

1 Fill one cup about 3/4 full with cold water and the other cup about 3/4 full of hot water. Allow the cups to stand for about 1 minute so the water is very still.

2 Gently, place 1 drop of blue and 1 drop of yellow food coloring in the very center of the surface of each cup.

3 Hold a white piece of paper behind the cups so that you can observe the food coloring very clearly.

4 Describe what the food coloring looks like in each cup.

5 Based on your observation of the food coloring, what do you think is the difference between the way water molecules act in cold water compared with hot water?

Chemistry and Colors— Mix and Match

Sometimes when scientists do an experiment, such as a chemical reaction, they may be very interested in the colors produced during the reaction. Scientists may need to observe the color very closely to compare it with another color. In the activity below, you can use your powers of observation to try to create an exact color match using a chemical reaction.

1 Tear up two or three red cabbage leaves into small pieces. Place the pieces into a zip-closing plastic bag. Add 1 cup of warm water to the bag and seal it tightly.

2 Squeeze the leaves in the bag until the water turns a dark blue color. This is your **indicator** solution. An indicator can change color when certain substances are added to it. Use masking tape and a pencil to label two of your cups A and B. Pour 1/4 cup of the indicator into each of the two cups.

3 In a separate cup, add 1/4 cup of water. Place 1 Alka-Seltzer tablet in the water. Wait for the tablet to dissolve completely. Use your straw to place 5 drops of Alka-Seltzer solution into cup A. Swirl the cup. What do you observe? How does the color in cup A compare with the color in cup B?

4 Look at the ingredients on the package of Alka-Seltzer. Aside from aspirin, the ingredients are sodium bicarbonate and citric acid. Sodium bicarbonate is baking soda, and citric acid is the acid in citrus fruits such as lemons and oranges.

CHALLENGE! See if you can add the right amounts of lemon juice and baking soda to the indicator in cup B to produce the exact color that the 5 drops of Alka-Seltzer solution produced in cup A. Here's how to do it!

Add one drop of lemon juice to the indicator solution in cup B. Swirl the cup. If this does not match the color of the solution in cup A, use your toothpick to add a small amount of baking soda to cup B and swirl again. Keep track of the exact amounts of lemon juice by drops and baking soda by toothpicks you are adding. Observe the colors in the two cups very closely.

5 When you think you know the right amounts of lemon juice and baking soda, rinse out cups A and B to get ready to test your results! Place 1/4 cup of indicator in cups A and B. Add 5 drops of Alka-Seltzer solution to cup A as before, and swirl. All at once, add the exact amount of lemon juice and baking soda that you think will match the color in cup A, and swirl. How did you do?

Food for thought

Scientists also study the behavior of humans and other animals. A lot can be learned about animals and people by studying the way they behave in different environments. In the following activity, you will observe your fellow humans in the school cafeteria to learn about the types of food these humans prefer to eat.

1 As a class, decide the best way to divide student observers around the cafeteria for the most efficient observation and data recording. You might want to have a master plan of all the cafeteria tables, and label each table A, B, C, etc. The subjects eating at each table can be numbered 1, 2, 3, etc. This gives each subject a code name such as B-3 or C-6. Observers should decide in advance which subjects they will be responsible for observing. The number of subjects for each observer should probably be limited to four or five.

2 Each observer should make a chart (like the example below) of all the individual food items offered for lunch on the day of observation. The chart should also include the subjects to be observed by table letter and seat number. You could also include whether the subject is a boy or a girl.

3 Emphasize that the observers should interfere as little as possible with the subjects they are observing. It is best if the subjects being observed do not notice the observers so the subjects' eating will be as natural as possible.

4 Observers should record the types of foods and drinks that subjects choose as well as the amount they eat or drink. After students bring back their observations, all the data could be compiled in a large chart or on the board.

5 What can you learn from the data? Do students seem to choose one food over another? Do boys and girls seem to choose different foods? Does there seem to be a difference based on grade level? Are there foods that subjects choose but do not finish or eat very little? What are some possible reasons for this behavior? Is this different between boys and girls?

6 Of food brought from home, what were the most common items? How did the amount of food eaten from home compare with the amount of food eaten from the cafeteria? Based on your observations, are there any recommendations you could make to the cafeteria?

	A–1 Boy	A–2 Girl	A–3 Boy	A–4 Girl
Spaghetti	ATE ALL			
Hamburger		ATE ALL		
Broccoli	ATE ONLY THE TOPS			ATE ONE PIECE. ONLY THE TOP
Salad	ATE LETTUCE BUT NO TOMATO			ATE ONLY CUCUMBER SLICES
Roll				2 ROLLS WITH BUTTER. ATE ALL
French Fries				
Milk	DRANK ALL		DRANK 2 MILKS	
Juice		DRANK 1/2		2 JUICES. DRANK ALL
Food from home			PEANUT BUTTER & JELLY. ATE 1/2, GAVE AWAY 1/2. 2 CHOCOLATE CHIP COOKIES	2 CUPCAKES. ATE 1, GAVE 1 AWAY

Think in a Wink!

YOU WILL NEED:

picture on front of this *WonderScience* unit

paper

pencil

Sometimes the things that scientists observe happen very quickly. Scientists need to get a lot of information about what they are observing in a short period of time. It's kind of like being a witness to a traffic accident or a close play in a baseball game. If there is no instant replay, you need to be a very good observer while the action is taking place. Also, if you know what you are looking for ahead of time, the information you get from your observations should be more detailed and complete.

1 Tell students ahead of time that they will need to observe the picture very closely for about 3 seconds to get as much information as possible about what they see. They should look for details in the following three categories:

- Different types of objects (such as people, cars, animals, buildings, plants)
- Details of objects (such as blue car, brick house with red door, etc.)
- How objects relate to each other (person in car, dog in front of tree, etc.)

Type of Object	Description	Relates to other objects
Car	Yellow with black top facing this way ------>	In front of store Two people in it

2 Students should make a chart like the one at right to better organize their observations according to the three categories above.

3 Have students sit close enough to see the full open picture well. Show the picture for about 3 seconds. Have students write down their observations in the chart. Discuss what students observed. Did they see more or less than they thought they would?

4 Show the picture again for another 3 seconds. Have students record their observations. Discuss whether it was easier to get more detail the second time and why.

5 Now divide the class into groups of at least three students per group. Each student in the group should concentrate on observing one of the three categories and recording his or her observations quickly.

6 Have each group report on their observations, and have the class judge which group made the most complete and accurate observations.

Learning about smell and taste usually occurs in the context of the other senses: vision, hearing, and touch (covered in other units of *The Best of WonderScience*, Volumes 1 and 2). When teaching about any of the senses, an important point to stress with children is the involvement of the brain. The sense receptors for taste and smell, as well as those for touch, vision, and hearing, would all be useless without their nerve connections to the brain. It is only when the nerve message is received and interpreted by the brain that we actually have the sense of smelling or tasting or any other sense.

The Nose Knows!

You can begin a discussion of the sense of smell by letting students know that when they smell something, molecules from what they are smelling actually go up their nose. This will be a revelation for most students and can lead to a spirited exchange in which some students may not be willing to accept this seemingly bizarre idea. You can make an analogy with the other senses. Light has to enter the eyes to see, sound has to enter the ears to hear, and molecules have to enter the nose to smell. In "The Nose Knows!," students investigate the different ways molecules get into the air in order to be smelled.

Results:

I. After poking through the plastic wrap and immediately smelling over the hole, students may detect a faint smell. But after waiting just two or three minutes, they should be able to smell the perfume much more distinctly.

II. Scratching the outer surface of the peel of a citrus fruit allows the molecules that are in the peel to be exposed to the air, to evaporate, and to go up the nose.

III. The candy mint has a faint odor, but when it is placed in water and partially dissolved, the odor becomes much stronger.

Sniffing Out Good Taste

Ask students if they have ever tried to taste something while holding their nose. Or if food tastes different when they have a cold and their nose is all stuffed up. The point is that the sensation we commonly refer to as taste is really a combination of the sense of taste and the sense of smell. While you are eating, some molecules from the food in your mouth travel in the air behind your mouth and nose and attach to the smell receptors way up in your nose. So while you are tasting, you are also smelling.

Results:

When the M&M is being chewed with the nose closed, a sensation of sweetness is recognizable, and maybe a hint of chocolate. But when the nose is released, the taste of chocolate is much stronger. Similar results occur with the Reese's Piece. With the nose closed, it tastes sweet, but with the nose open, the peanut flavor is much more recognizable.

How Sweet It Is!

The setup for this activity might be a little confusing. Each *student* needs to have about $\frac{1}{4}$ cup of standard (sweetened) solution and four empty Dixie cups. Each *group* needs to have 8 ounces of unsweetened solution and four empty Dixie cups. Working together, the group will make a different concentration of sweetened solution in each of the *group's* four Dixie cups. A small amount of these solutions will be poured into each *student's* four Dixie cups for tasting and comparing with the standard.

Results:

The standard recipe for Kool-Aid is one packet of drink mix plus 1 cup of sugar in 64 ounces of water. One cup of sugar is the same as 16 tablespoons. Sixteen tablespoons in 64 ounces is the same as 1 tablespoon in every 4 ounces. This is the same as $1\frac{1}{2}$ teaspoons in every 2 ounces. So the $1\frac{1}{2}$ teaspoons of sugar in 2 ounces of unsweetened Kool-Aid should taste closest to the standard solution.

Get the Skinny on Low-Fat Cookies!

Many students may be unaware of the existence of low-fat cookies or low-fat food in general. You might want to begin a discussion of the reasons why people might want to limit their fat intake. Fats are high in calories per gram, and certain types of fats have been implicated in raising blood cholesterol levels. Students should also be aware that there is always a trade-off. To reduce the fat and still have a taste that people will like, cookie and cake makers almost always increase the amount of sugar or other sweetener in the recipe.

Results:

When scraping the white cream from one of the wafers of each cookie, students should notice a definite difference in the feel and even the look of the cream. The creams also have a different feel in the mouth and a different taste. It is a little more difficult to detect a difference in the taste of the wafers, but there is a difference.

Assessment/Integration:

Challenge students to write an advertisement for any food they choose. The ad can be for radio, television, or a newspaper or magazine. The ad must mention as many senses as possible.

NATIONAL SCIENCE EDUCATION STANDARDS

The activities in this unit can be used to support the teaching of the following standards:

✔ **Unifying Concepts and Processes**

Evidence, Models, and Explanation

Evidence consists of observations and data on which to base scientific explanations. *(All activities)*

✔ **Science as Inquiry**

Abilities Necessary to Do Scientific Inquiry

Design and conduct a scientific investigation. *(All activities)*

Develop descriptions, explanations, predictions, and models using evidence. *(All activities)*

Think critically and logically to make the relationships between evidence and explanations. *(All activities)*

✔ **Life Science**

Structure and Function in Living Systems

Specialized cells perform specialized functions in multicellular organisms.

Making Sense of Smell and Taste

The Nose Knows

I. Perfume

1. When you smelled over the hole for the first time, did you smell anything?

    _____

2. After you waited two or three minutes and smelled again, was the smell stronger, weaker, or about the same?

    _____

3. If the smell was stronger, what do you think caused the increased smell?

    _____

    _____

    _____

II. Citrus Fruit Peel

1. When you first smelled the fruit peels before one of them was scratched, did you detect an odor?

    _____

2. When you smelled the scratched peel, was the smell stronger, weaker, or about the same?

    _____

3. If the smell was stronger, what do you think caused the increased smell?

    _____

    _____

    _____

III. Hard Candy

1. When you first smelled the candy, before you put it in water, did you detect an odor?

    _____

2. When you smelled the candy after it had dissolved a little in water, was the smell stronger, weaker, or about the same?

    _____

3. If the smell was stronger, what do you think caused the increased smell?

    _____

    _____

    _____

NAME _____   DATE _____

Sniffing Out Good Taste

M&M

1. When you had the M&M in your mouth with your nose closed, did it seem as if you were tasting the normal flavor of an M&M?

    _____

2. When you opened up your nose, did you notice any change in the flavor?

    _____

3. If the flavor did seem to change, describe what you tasted with your nose closed compared to what you tasted with your nose open.

    _____

    _____

4. When you opened your nose, did you notice that the taste seemed stronger when you breathed in or when you breathed out?_____

    _____

    How do you explain why this might be?

    _____

    _____

Reese's Piece

1. When you had the Reese's Piece in your mouth with your nose closed, did it seem as if you were tasting the normal flavor of a Reese's Piece?

    _____

2. When you opened up your nose, did you notice any change in the flavor?

    _____

3. If the flavor did seem to change, describe what you tasted with your nose closed compared with what you tasted with your nose open.

    _____

    _____

4. When you opened your nose, did you notice that the taste seemed stronger when you breathed in or when you breathed out?

    _____

    How do you explain why this might be?

    _____

    _____

The Nose Knows!

Believe it or not, your sense of smell works because tiny bits of the thing you are smelling actually go up your nose! WHAT??!! Say it's not so!! But—it's true. It's as plain as the nose on your face. When you smell something, the molecules from the thing you are smelling (we will call them "smell molecules") are getting sucked right up your nose. Whether it's a peeled banana, freshly mowed grass, frying bacon, or someone's perfume, if you can smell it, the molecules from these things have gotten into the air and into your nose.

But how do the molecules get into the air to begin with? Here are a few examples to think about and to try out:

I. Some things that we smell are made up of molecules that go up into the air faster than the molecules of other things. Perfume is a good example. In perfume, the smell molecules get into the air quickly and can be smelled very easily.

YOU WILL NEED:

paper cup

inexpensive perfume or eau de cologne

dropper

plastic wrap

rubber band

pushpin

1 Place one drop of perfume into the center of a cup. Cover the cup immediately with plastic wrap and a rubber band.

2 Carefully use a pushpin to poke a small hole in the center of the plastic wrap. Try not to squeeze the cup. Just after you have made the hole, smell directly over the hole. Can you smell the perfume?

3 Wait two or three minutes and smell again. Does the smell seem any stronger? If it does seem stronger, what do you think has happened to cause the increased smell?

4 While smelling over the cup, gently squeeze the cup to force a little air from the hole. Do you notice a difference in the strength of the smell? If so, what do you think causes this?

II. Sometimes the molecules you are smelling don't just fly up into the air on their own. They might need a little help as in the activity below.

1 Place two pieces of citrus peel on a paper towel. Smell each of them. Now carefully use your pushpin to poke and scrape the outer surface of one of the peels.

2 Smell each peel. Why do you think the scratched peel smells stronger than the unscratched one?

3 Try testing grapefruit, lemon, or lime peels in the same way.

Do not eat the foods
you are using in your experiment.

III. Here's another way that smell molecules can get into the air.

1 Place a peppermint candy in each of two cups. Smell the candies in each cup.

2 Add water to one of the cups so that it is 1/4 to 1/3 full. Swirl the cup so that the candy begins to dissolve. Now smell both cups. What do you notice? Based on what you have learned so far, why do you think one smells more than the other?

Making Sense of Smell and Taste

Let's take a look at how the senses of smell and taste work. We'll look at smell first. As you learned in "The Nose Knows," in order to smell something, the molecules from the thing you are smelling need to go up your nose. But what happens up there in your nose that actually causes you to smell stuff? The answer starts with two little areas of skin way up inside your nose, just under your eyes. This area of inner nose skin contains tiny structures called **smell receptors**. The job of a smell receptor is to recognize a smell molecule from the thing you are smelling and then to send a nerve message about it to your brain.

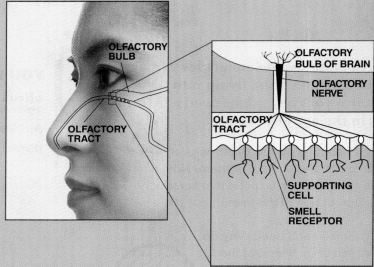

Here's how it works: At one end of the receptors are some very thin hair-like structures that are right at the surface of the inner nose skin. Attached to the other end of the receptor is a nerve going up to the brain.

When the right kind of molecule goes up your nose, the molecule attaches to the receptor. This causes a nerve message to travel along the nerve to the brain. Based on the message received by the brain, you get the sense of a particular smell.

The sense of taste works in a similar way. On the tongue, there are little bumps that are covered with taste buds. A taste bud is like a little sack containing the **taste receptors**. A taste receptor works a lot like a smell receptor. The job of a taste receptor is to recognize a taste molecule from what you are tasting and to send a nerve message about it to your brain.

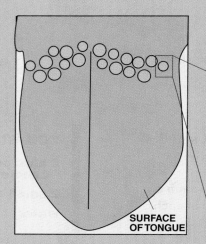

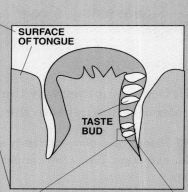

At one end of the taste receptor are some long hair-like structures. These thin structures are right at the surface of the taste bud. Attached to the other end of the receptor is a nerve going to the brain.

When the right kind of taste molecule reaches a taste receptor, the molecule attaches to the receptor. This causes a nerve message to travel along the nerve to the brain. Based on the message received by the brain, you get the sense of a particular taste.

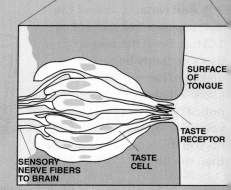

But the sense you get when you eat food is not all caused by the action of your taste buds. When food is in your mouth, it's not just taste that's going on—smell is happening too. From your mouth, where the food is, smell molecules from the food make their way to the smell receptors. Although you don't realize it, the sensation you have when you eat is a combination of tasting and smelling.

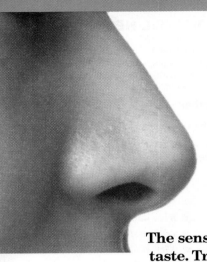

Sniffing Out Good Taste

To taste something,
it is very important to have
your smeller working also.
The sense of smell is very much involved in the sense of
taste. Try the following activity to see if this smell/taste
combination makes sense to you.

YOU WILL NEED:

M&Ms®
Reese's Pieces®

**Wash your hands
before doing
this experiment.**

1 Hold your nose closed and place an M&M in your mouth. While keeping your nose closed, chew the M&M but don't swallow yet.

2 While the chewed-up M&M is still in your mouth, let go of your nose and see if the taste seems to change. What do you notice? Repeat the same activity and concentrate on the taste you sense with your nose closed compared with the taste you sense with your nose open.

3 Repeat steps 1 and 2 with a Reese's Piece. What do you taste with your nose closed? How about with your nose open?

4 Repeat steps 1–3. This time, when you are ready to open your nose, breathe IN through your nose and then breathe OUT through your nose to see which has more effect on taste. Do you notice a difference? How can you explain it?

How Sweet it is!

At factories that make food or soft drinks, one of the most important tests done on the product is the taste test. A person, who knows what the product should taste like, takes a taste to be sure all the ingredients are of good quality and combined correctly. Let's see if you're ready to become a professional taster!

Teacher Preparation:
Prepare 64 oz of Kool-Aid by adding Kool-Aid powder, sugar, and water according to the directions on the package. This is the **standard solution**.

Then prepare another 64 oz of Kool-Aid, but this time do not add any sugar. This is the **unsweetened solution**.

Pour about 1/4 cup of the standard solution into 8-oz cups and distribute one to each student. Each student will also need four empty Dixie cups. Each group of students will need 8 oz of the unsweetened solution and four empty Dixie cups.

The students will make Kool-Aid samples with different amounts of sugar. The object of the activity is for students to use their sense of taste to identify the sample that most closely matches the taste of a standard solution.

You will need at least four students in each group to make the test solutions so that each student can taste each test solution and compare each with the standard.

Wash your hands before doing this experiment.

1 First, each **student** should label his or her own 8-oz cup **standard** and the Dixie cups **1/2, 1, 1 1/2,** and **2**.

EACH STUDENT HAS THESE CUPS

2 Next, one student from each group should label **the group's** four Dixie cups **1/2, 1, 1 1/2,** and **2** and pour the unsweetened solution evenly among these four cups so each is about 2/3 full.

EACH GROUP HAS THESE CUPS

3 A second student should add 1/2 teaspoon of sugar to the cup labeled **1/2**, and 1 teaspoon of sugar to the cup labeled **1**, and so on according to the labels on the cups. These are the test solutions.

4 A third student should carefully stir the test solutions until as much sugar is dissolved as possible.

5 A fourth student should pour the test solution labeled **1/2** evenly among the students' cups labeled **1/2**, and then pour the test solution labeled **1** evenly among the students' cups labeled **1**, and so on according to the labels on the cups.

EACH STUDENT HAS THESE CUPS

EACH STUDENT HAS THESE CUPS

Your job, as a group, is to figure out which test solution tastes the most like the standard. Your sense of taste will be your guide.

Scientists do not normally taste their experiments; but trained taste testers, under very controlled conditions, do need to taste.

6 Each student should take a small sip of the standard solution and concentrate on the taste. After considering the taste of the standard, take a sip of the test solution labeled 1/2. Does it seem similar to the standard? Talk it over with your group to see if anyone thought the **1/2** teaspoon test solution tasted similar to the standard.

7 Take a sip of the standard again so that you know the taste. This time, take a sip of the test solution labeled **1**. Does it seem similar to the standard? Talk it over with your group to see if anyone thought the 1 teaspoon test solution tasted similar to the standard.

8 Repeat the taste test comparing the standard with the test solution cups marked **1 1/2** and **2**.

What is the group's final decision? Which test solution was closest to the standard?

Get the Skinny on Low-Fat Cookies!

YOU WILL NEED:

chocolate sandwich cookie with white cream in the middle

low-fat chocolate sandwich cookie with white cream in the middle (same variety as above but low-fat)

paper towels

plastic spoons or Popsicle sticks (clean and unused)

Do not use cookies with the fat substitute "Olestra"

Have you tried low-fat cookies?
Do they taste different from the regular version? Do they feel different in your mouth? What part of the cookie tastes the most different? Let's find out!

1 Place two paper towels on your work surface. Label one of them **Low-fat** and the other one **Regular**. Place one regular cookie on the towel marked Regular and place a low-fat cookie on the towel marked Low-fat. Carefully pull each cookie apart so that the two chocolate wafers are separate.

> **Wash your hands before doing this experiment.**

2 Use a plastic spoon or Popsicle stick to scrape the white cream completely off one of the wafers from each cookie. You should now have a wafer with cream and a wafer without cream for each cookie. Describe anything that seemed different about the creams while you were scraping them. Save the cream from each cookie.

3 Take a taste of the regular cookie wafer with no cream. Chew it and move it around in your mouth so you really get a good sense of the taste. Now take a taste of the low-fat wafer with no cream. Can you tell any difference? Does one seem more sweet, more bitter, more chocolate?

4 Now taste the cream from the regular cookie. Move it around in your mouth and let it melt. Now try the same thing with the cream from the low-fat cookie. What differences do you notice? Do they feel different or taste different? In what way?

5 Taste the regular cookie wafer that has some cream on it. Get a good sense of its taste. Now taste the low-fat cookie wafer with the cream on it. What is your decision about what causes the difference in taste between the two types of cookies? Is it the wafer, the cream, or a combination?

The sense of touch gives us a lot of useful information about our environment, and it also protects us from minor and more serious harm. Students will experiment with several features of the sense of touch, including our ability to sense temperature and pressure and to differentiate between objects and textures.

Get in Touch with Your Feelings

Ask students to imagine what it would be like to have *only* their sense of touch to provide information about their surroundings. What would a typical morning be like? Could they decide which clothes to wear based only on their sense of touch? Could they make their own breakfast or find their way to the bus stop? How would they use their sense of touch to accomplish these routine activities?

Results:

Expect students to find it somewhat difficult to describe different feel sensations in a single word such as *smooth* or *rough*. Allow them to describe their touch sensations in phrases or sentences rather than in a single word. Encourage students to make the most detailed observations they possibly can.

Sandpaper Scraper

In the first activity, students use their sense of touch to try to identify objects that are very different in shape and texture. In this activity, students use their sense of touch to recognize subtle differences between materials that are very similar.

Results:

Students become more aware of the fine distinctions their sense of touch can provide between textures. To make this activity more challenging, add a fourth or even a fifth sandpaper sample. Using another part of the hand or a finger other than the index finger may provide more sensitivity than the index finger. One reason for the increased sensitivity may be that other fingers or parts of the hand may not be as callused as the index finger.

Temperature Touch-o-Meter

This activity focuses on the body's temperature receptors, which allow us to sense changes in hot and cold. Ask students how it feels to go from a hot day outdoors into an air-conditioned room or a pool of cool water. Although the room and the pool may not be very cold, they will feel very cold at first. The reason is that the brain interprets temperature on a relative scale instead of an absolute or actual scale. In other words, the brain senses the large difference in temperature resulting in a sensation of cold that is more extreme than the actual temperature warrants. The body soon becomes accustomed or adapted to the new temperature, however, and you feel comfortable. The actual temperature in the room has not changed, but your body's perception of the temperature changes. The reason for this is that once certain receptors and nerves have generated impulses to the brain for a period of time, the impulses are generated less frequently and the brain interprets this as a less powerful stimulus or a less extreme temperature.

Results:

When the finger is in the ice water for only 5 seconds and then is placed in room-temperature water, the finger feels as if it has been placed in warm water. When the index finger from the other hand is placed in the same room-temperature water, it feels much cooler than the other finger. When the finger is in the ice water for 20 seconds and the same activity is repeated, the finger should take a significantly longer time to experience a sense of warming when placed in the room-temperature water. For some students, the sense of warming may be apparent only when the index finger from the other hand is placed in the same room-temperature water and feels cooler.

Unit 3
The Sense of Touch

Let's Give a Big Hand for the Sense of Touch!

In this activity, students determine whether different parts of the hand and arm have different levels of sensitivity to touch. Ask students to predict which parts of the hand and arm would be most sensitive and why.

Results:

In this activity, subjects were able to distinguish the difference between one and two points much more readily on the fingertips than on other areas of the hand and arm. The farther the points were from the fingertips, the less accurately subjects could tell the difference between one and two points.

The second part of the activity demonstrated that the greater the distance between the points, the greater the ability to distinguish between one and two points.

Read It with Feeling

Start this activity by supplying examples of Braille from the school, the local library, or a local organization for the visually impaired. Students will most likely be amazed that the different arrangements of such tiny bumps can be detected well enough to be interpreted as letters, words, and sentences.

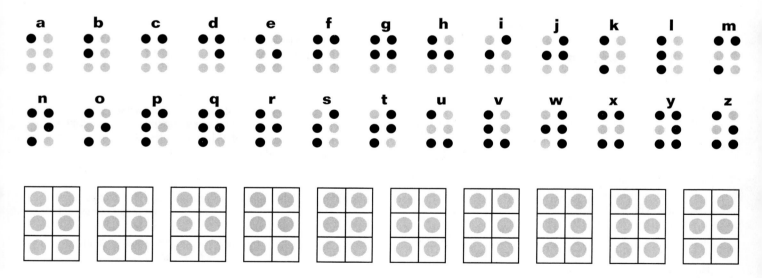

NATIONAL SCIENCE EDUCATION STANDARDS

The activities in this unit can be used to support the teaching of the following standards:

✔ **Unifying Concepts and Processes**

Evidence, Models, and Explanation
Evidence consists of observations and data on which to base scientific explanations.
   A Temperature Touch-o-Meter
   Let's Give a Big Hand for the Sense of Touch!

✔ **Science as Inquiry**

Abilities Necessary to Do Scientific Inquiry
Design and conduct a scientific investigation. *(All activities)*
Think critically and logically to make the relationships between evidence and explanations. *(All activities)*

✔ **Life Science**

Structure and Function in Living Systems
Specialized cells perform specialized functions in multicellular organisms.
   A Touchy Subject
   Let's Give a Big Hand for the Sense of Touch!

STUDENT ACTIVITY SHEET

NAME _____ **DATE** _____

Get in Touch with Your Feelings

You and your partner should each use one of the charts below to make your touch observations and guesses.

Touch Observation Chart					
Object 1	**Object 2**	**Object 3**	**Object 4**	**Object 5**	**Object 6**
Observations	Observations	Observations	Observations	Observations	Observations
Guess	Guess	Guess	Guess	Guess	Guess

Touch Observation Chart					
Object 1	**Object 2**	**Object 3**	**Object 4**	**Object 5**	**Object 6**
Observations	Observations	Observations	Observations	Observations	Observations
Guess	Guess	Guess	Guess	Guess	Guess

NAME _____   DATE _____

Let's Give a Big Hand for the Sense of Touch!

Use the picture of the hand below to record "Y" or "N" to see how accurately you can tell the difference between one and two points on different areas of your hand and arm. (Be sure to mark answers in pencil so they can be erased and the same picture can be used for your partner's answers.)

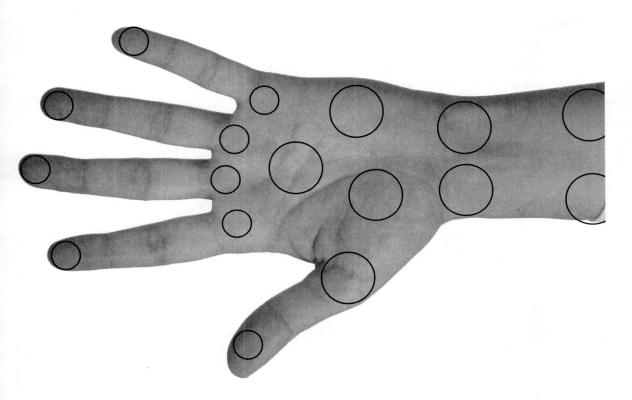

Use the chart below to record your answers for steps 1–4 at the bottom of the page.

Area touched	Answers															
	1/2 cm				1 cm				1 1/2 cm				2 cm			
Fingers																
Palm																
Wrist																
Arm																

Get in Touch with Your Feelings

YOU WILL NEED:

shoe box (with lid)	pen cap	eraser
tape	paper clip	candle
marble	piece of sponge	sea shell
cotton ball	crayon	bottle cap
cotton swab	rubber band	small battery

When people talk about the five senses, they almost always list sight and hearing as the two most important. But the human sense of touch is also an important sense. Touch is very sensitive and can communicate a lot of information. Try the activity below and see if you can get a feel for what we mean.

TEACHER PREPARATION:

Have students bring in shoe boxes so that there is one box for each pair of students. Cut a hole in the end of each box that is big enough or a student's hand and arm to fit in but not so big that they can see into the box when their hands are inside. Place an assortment of 6 to 10 small items from the above list into each box. Place the lid on each box and tape it down securely.

1 Make a chart like the one shown or use the chart in the Student Activity Sheet. This is your **Touch Observation Chart.**

2 Do not look inside the box. Place your hand into the box and begin touching some of the objects inside. Pick one item and feel it until you can tell certain things about it such as whether it is hard or soft, smooth or rough. Write down your touch observations in the chart. Use descriptive words such as crinkly, fuzzy, jagged, bumpy, round, long and thin, short and fat, spongy, pointy, flat, greasy, stretchy, bendable.

3 When you think you have enough information about the object, write down what you think the item is in the "Guess" box on the chart. Do not let your partner see your answers.

4 Continue feeling each item and writing down your observations and answers until you think you have identified all of them. Now give the box to your partner, who should try identifying the items in the same way.

5 When you are both done, look at your charts to see how many objects you both thought were in the box. Then compare your observations. Did you have observations that were different, but you guessed the same object? Did you have observations that were the same, but you guessed different objects?

6 Open up the box to see what the objects are and to see how many you each got right!

Touch Observation Chart

Object 1	Object 2	Object 3	Object 4	Object 5	Object 6
Observations	Observations	Observations	Observations	Observations	Observations
Guess	Guess	Guess	Guess	Guess	Guess

A Touchy Subject

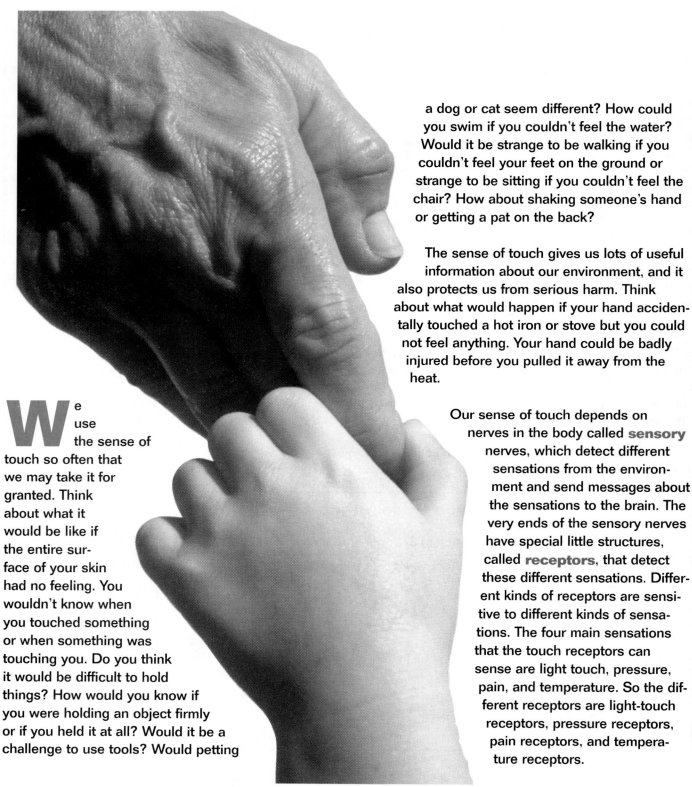

a dog or cat seem different? How could you swim if you couldn't feel the water? Would it be strange to be walking if you couldn't feel your feet on the ground or strange to be sitting if you couldn't feel the chair? How about shaking someone's hand or getting a pat on the back?

The sense of touch gives us lots of useful information about our environment, and it also protects us from serious harm. Think about what would happen if your hand accidentally touched a hot iron or stove but you could not feel anything. Your hand could be badly injured before you pulled it away from the heat.

We use the sense of touch so often that we may take it for granted. Think about what it would be like if the entire surface of your skin had no feeling. You wouldn't know when you touched something or when something was touching you. Do you think it would be difficult to hold things? How would you know if you were holding an object firmly or if you held it at all? Would it be a challenge to use tools? Would petting

Our sense of touch depends on nerves in the body called **sensory** nerves, which detect different sensations from the environment and send messages about the sensations to the brain. The very ends of the sensory nerves have special little structures, called **receptors**, that detect these different sensations. Different kinds of receptors are sensitive to different kinds of sensations. The four main sensations that the touch receptors can sense are light touch, pressure, pain, and temperature. So the different receptors are light-touch receptors, pressure receptors, pain receptors, and temperature receptors.

Sandpaper Scraper

YOU WILL NEED:

tape

3 different grades of sandpaper (fine, medium, and coarse)

cardboard or paper

blindfold

Teacher Preparation:
Cut each piece of sandpaper into equally-sized squares so that each pair of students will get one square of each type of sand paper.

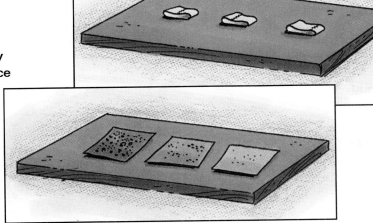

1 Loop three pieces of tape so the sticky side is on the outside of the loop. Place the tape in a row on a piece of cardboard or paper as shown. Your partner should wear a blindfold or look away. While your partner is not looking, stick the three squares of sandpaper on the pieces of tape in any order.

2 Have your partner feel each piece of sandpaper with his/her index finger and decide which piece is fine, medium, and coarse.

3 As your partner makes a decision, write the number 1 under the one he/she thinks is the finest sandpaper, a 2 under the medium, and a 3 under the coarsest. Have your partner remove the blindfold to see the results.

4 Now switch roles so that your partner arranges the sandpapers in a different order and you do the touching.

Some other ideas:

Is it easier to tell the difference between the sandpapers if you touch them very lightly or if you press down a little harder? Why do you think this is?

Try rearranging the sandpapers and feeling them with your pinky or another finger. Does one finger seem more sensitive than another? If so, why do you think this is?

Try feeling the sandpapers with the fleshy part of your hand beneath your thumb. Is it easier or harder to figure out which is fine, medium, and coarse?

Temperature Touch-o-meter

One important aspect of the sense of touch is the ability to detect and distinguish between different temperatures. Most people are pretty sensitive to room temperature and can detect a change of only one or two degrees. Explore how your body senses temperature in the activity below!

YOU WILL NEED:

cup of ice water

cup of hot water
(from the tap)

cup of water at
room temperature

1 Place your index finger in a cup of ice water for about 5 seconds. Now take your finger out and place it immediately into a cup of room-temperature water. Notice how your finger feels as soon as you put it in the room temperature water. Don't take it out yet.

2 Leave your finger in the cup for a minute or two and describe how the temperature of the water feels. Does the water feel warmer or cooler than you thought it would? Does the temperature seem to change while your finger is in the water? If so, how?

3 While your index finger is still in the water, place your index finger from the other hand into the room-temperature water also. What do you notice? How could you explain what you feel?

4 Now place your original finger back in the ice water, but this time, leave it in for about 20 seconds. Then move it into the room-temperature water as you did before. Notice how your finger feels as soon as you put it in the room-temperature water. Don't take it out yet.

5 Leave your finger in the cup for a minute or two and describe how the temperature of the water feels. How does the temperature feel compared with how it felt when your finger was in the ice water for only 5 seconds? If it seems to be different, why do you think this might be?

6 While your index finger is still in the water, place your other index finger from the other hand into the room-temperature water also. What do you notice? Do your two fingers feel any different from the way they felt before?

7 Repeat steps 1–6 but instead of using ice water, use hot water from the tap. The water should feel hot but not so hot that it hurts. See if you can predict the changes and differences in temperature that you think you will feel.

Let's Give a Big Hand for
the Sense of Touch!

Your touch receptors are spread all over your body. These receptors are closer together in some areas of your body than in others. Here's a way you can tell where they are close together and where they are farther apart.

YOU WILL NEED:

large paper clip

photocopy of the hand and arm

metric ruler

TEACHER PREPARATION:
Photocopy the picture of the hand and arm in the Teacher's Guide so that there is one for each student.

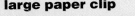

1 Carefully unbend a large paper clip. Form it into a "U" shape as shown. Squeeze the ends of the paper clip together so they are about 1/2 centimeter (cm) apart. You will be touching the fingers, palm, and arm of your partner with one or both tips of the paper clip.

2 Ask your partner to look away as you gently touch the areas on your partner's hand that match the areas circled on the picture. For each area, touch the skin with either one or both ends of the paper clip. Ask your partner whether he/she feels one or two points. For a correct answer, write a "Y" for yes in the circle. For an incorrect answer, write an "N" for no.

3 When you are finished, look at the results of your testing. Where did your partner have the most correct answers? Where were there a lot of incorrect answers? What does this tell you about how close together the touch receptors are in the fingers, palm, and arm. Where do you think they are closest together? Why? How about farthest apart? Why?

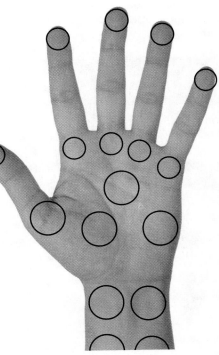

Let's try something different.

1 Start off with the paper clip ends close together as before (about 1/2 cm apart). Have your partner look away as you gently touch four fingers with one or two points. Use the chart below to keep a record of the number of right and wrong answers for 1/2 cm.

2 Now spread the ends of the paper clip 1 cm apart. Repeat the testing as you did in step 1. Record the right and wrong answers for 1 cm.

3 Repeat these tests for 1 1/2 cm and for 2 cm. At what distance did your partner get most of the answers right? Does this tell you anything about how far apart the touch receptors are?

4 Repeat the activity using the palm, wrist, and arm. Then switch roles so that your partner tests you!

Area touched	Answers							
	1/2 cm		1 cm		1 1/2 cm		2 cm	
Fingers								
Palm								
Wrist								
Arm								

Read It with Feeling

For people who cannot see, the sense of touch can be used to get information by reading a special alphabet code called Braille. In Braille, different arrangements of tiny raised dots are used for each letter of the alphabet. In the activity below, you can make your own Braille dots and begin to feel what it's like to read using your sense of touch.

TEACHER PREPARATION:
Check with your school or local library for books in Braille so that students will have some samples to see and feel. Photocopy the strips of Braille cells from the student activity sheet. Each student should get a strip of 10 cells.

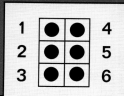

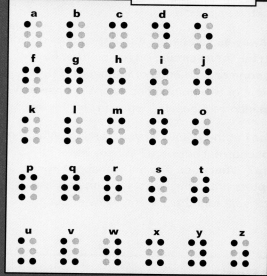

In Braille, dots within the basic six-dot pattern shown at right are raised into little bumps that can be sensed by the finger tips. The arrangement of raised dots stands for a letter of the alphabet. At right is the Braille alphabet. The black dots show which dots would be raised for each letter.

1 You have 10 Braille cells to work with. Look at the Braille alphabet at right and find the letters for your first name.

2 Put some glue in a cup. Dip a toothpick into the glue and put a dot of glue on the first cell where the dots would be raised to make the first letter of your first name. Place a little round seed on each dot of glue.

3 Repeat step 2 for each letter of your name in order. Allow the glue to dry for a few hours or overnight. Put a mark on your paper (not your name) to identify it.

4 Exchange papers around the room so that no one knows whose name they have. Make sure you are holding the paper in the right direction and look at the Braille alphabet above while you feel the letters. Try to figure out what name is spelled.

ILLUSTRATIONS BY JIM WISNIEWSKI/STEVE EDSEY & SONS UNLESS OTHERWISE INDICATED

Classification

This unit features classification activities in biology, chemistry, and earth science. Students will be introduced to the basics of a taxonomic key, to the periodic table of the elements, and to a method for classifying rocks. The point should be stressed that classification is not an end in itself but is used to organize information to make the study of new organisms, objects, and substances more efficient and to more easily lead to new discoveries.

Systems of classification are used in many aspects of our daily lives. In a grocery store, the milk, cheese, and yogurt are all placed together in the dairy aisle because of their similar characteristics. Spaghetti, macaroni, and lasagna noodles are grouped and arranged together, as are napkins, paper towels, tissues, and toilet paper. At home, you probably have one drawer for socks and another for shirts. Your silverware is probably grouped together in one place, but subgrouped as forks, knives, and spoons. There may even be subgroups within these subgroups, for example, butter knives and steak knives or teaspoons and tablespoons.

Grouping items with similar characteristics is the key to the concept of classification. Each scientific discipline has its own classification system, but all are based on this fundamental concept.

Classification helps scientists learn more about what they study, because when discovering something new, scientists can see if and where the object, substance, or organism fits into their classification system. Depending on where the item fits, scientists can make certain assumptions about it and begin analyzing it accordingly. This creates a continuous system of more efficient experimentation, discovery, new experimentation, and potential new discoveries.

Classification—All SORTS of Fun!

This activity shows students that classification works in two ways: Organisms with similar characteristics are grouped together higher up the chart, but they can also be separated into subgroups based on differences in characteristics lower down the chart. This is how a classification system goes from a large group with general similarities to smaller and smaller groups with more specific similarities.

Periodic Table of the Elements

Using the instructions on the last page of this unit, students search through the periodic table to locate elements near each other that are used to produce similar products. You could color-photocopy one periodic table for each group of students. Students should see that the elements, like the organisms in biology, are grouped according to certain similar characteristics. The activity also offers a chance to introduce students to the periodic table in a fun and unique way. If students ask why each atom has a certain number, the answer is that this atomic number is the number of protons in the atom's nucleus or center. If students ask why the symbol for some elements does not seem to match the element name, such as Pb for lead, the reason is that some of the symbols are based on Latin, Greek, or German words.

Start Your Own Rock Group!

Students perform five different tests on common rock samples to try to place rocks into several groups based on similar characteristics. Many rocks may appear very similar at first, so students will need to observe the results of their tests very closely to note any minor differences that can be used to sort rocks into two or more groups. Because there are five tests for each of twelve samples, this activity should probably be done over several class periods.

Unit 4
Classification

Classification—Extra-Credit Activity

A grocery store is like a giant classification system. Just look down any aisle and you will see classification at work. For example, look at the dairy section. Among the items in the dairy section are milk and cheese. Within the milk area, there are skim, 1%, 2%, whole, and half-and-half. Next to whole milk, you may see chocolate milk. There is also special milk without lactose, with its own variations. You may also see whipping cream and heavy cream. In the cheese area, there are traditional cheeses such as American, swiss, and cheddar. There are also cottage cheese, cream cheese, and ricotta. Within cottage cheese, there are large curd, small curd, low-fat, and no-fat varieties.

Some of this classification can be pictured in a flow chart like this:

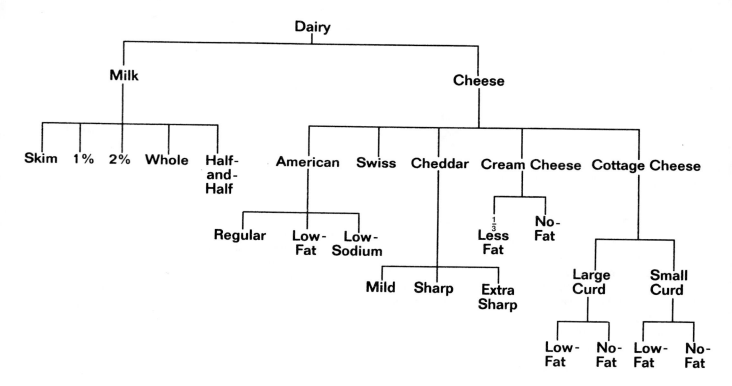

For an extra-credit activity, have students go to a local grocery store, accompanied by an adult, and create a classification flow chart like the one above of items within an area of the store. The dairy aisle works well, and so do the meat and deli sections.

NATIONAL SCIENCE EDUCATION STANDARDS

The activities in this unit can be used to support the teaching of the following standards:

✔ **Unifying Concepts and Processes**

Systems, Order, and Organization

Types and levels of organization provide useful ways of thinking about the world. *(All activities)*

Types of organization include the periodic table of elements and the classification of organisms. *(All activities)*

✔ **Science as Inquiry**

Abilities Necessary to Do Scientific Inquiry

Design and conduct a scientific investigation.
  Start Your Own Rock Group!

Use appropriate tools and techniques to gather, analyze, and interpret data.
  Classification—All SORTS of Fun!
  Start Your Own Rock Group!

Think critically and logically to make the relationships between evidence and explanations.
  Start Your Own Rock Group!

✔ **Understandings about Scientific Inquiry**

Some investigations involve observing and describing objects, organisms, and events. *(All activities)*

✔ **Physical Science**

Properties and Changes of Properties in Matter

Substances are often placed in categories or groups if they react in similar ways.
  A Periodic Table Game!

More than 100 known elements combine in a multitude of ways to produce compounds, which accounts for the living and nonliving substances that we encounter.
  A Periodic Table Game!

✔ **Life Science**

Structure and Function in Living Systems

Important levels of organization for structure and function include organisms.
  Classification—All Sorts of Fun!

STUDENT ACTIVITY SHEET

NAME _____   **DATE** _____

Classification—All SORTS of Fun!

Look at the mystery bugs below. Although they look pretty similar, a key can be used to identify which bug is which. Each numbered step in the key gives you two choices, either a or b. You have to pick one and do what the key says.

Here's how it works: Look at bug A and start with step 1 of the key. Bug A has foot pads, so you go to 2. It has antennae, so you go to 3. It has a dot on its rear section, so Bug A is Spot. Try each bug until you have identified each bug by name.

Then try a similar activity with flower classification.

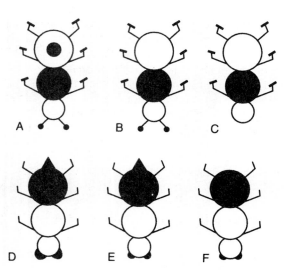

1a. Has foot pads ....go to 2

1b. Does not have foot pads ....go to 4

2a. Has antennae ....go to 3

2b. Does not have antennae..........................Bugsy

3a. Has dot on rear section ....Spot

3b. Does not have dot on rear section ....Rover

4a. Has rear stinger......................................go to 5

4b. Does not have rear stinger.......................Milo

5a. Has big eyes ....Robin

5b. Does not have big eyes............................Lily

1a. Has 6 petals ....go to 2

1b. Has 5 petals ....go to 4

2a. Has large center ....go to 3

2b. Has small center ....*Florus dotus*

3a. Has lines on petals ....*Florus lineus*

3b. Does not have lines on petals ....*Florus blanca*

4a. Has thorns on stem ....*Stemius stickerus*

4b. Does not have thorns on stem ....go to 5

5a. Has one set of leaves ....*Leafus singularus*

5b. Has two sets of leaves ....*Leafus doublus*

STUDENT ACTIVITY SHEET

NAME ______________________________ **DATE** __________

Start Your Own Rock Group!

Use the chart below to record the results of the five different tests on your twelve rock samples.

Rock Sample	Break Test	Color Test	Texture Test	Streak Test	Hardness Test
1					
2					
3					
4					
5					
6					
7					
8					
9					
10					
11					
12					

Classification—

Scientists who study biology place the plants, animals, and other living things they study into groups according to the similarities among them. This process of sorting things based on their similar characteristics is called classification.

Classifying organisms according to their similar characteristics helps scientists understand how groups of organisms are related and helps to identify newly discovered organisms. The activity below gives an idea of the way biologists classify living things. Let's see how it works.

If you had to divide the living things below into just two groups, how would you do it?

FISH   DOG   COW   BIRD   TURTLE   HUMAN

You could start by putting the ones that lay eggs in one group and the ones that don't lay eggs in another.

LAY EGGS

DO NOT LAY EGGS

You could then divide the ones that lay eggs into those with feathers and those without feathers.

You could divide the ones that do not lay eggs into those with four legs and those with two legs.

FEATHERS

WITHOUT FEATHERS

FOUR LEGS

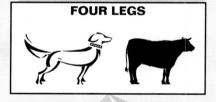

TWO LEGS

Divide the ones without feathers into those with legs and those with no legs.

Divide the ones with four legs into those that eat meat and those that do not eat meat.

LEGS

NO LEGS

EATS MEAT

DOES NOT EAT MEAT

If you take any organism and move up the chart, you can find the characteristics of that organism. Try the dog: it eats meat, has four legs, does not lay eggs.

Fill in the characteristics for these organisms.

Turtle:_____, _____, _____.

Bird: _____, _____.

Human: _____, _____.

All SORTS of fun!

The classification system pictured on the previous page uses a **flow chart** to group and organize the organisms. Biologists also use a numbered system like the one below, called a **key**, in a similar way. It uses the same information as the flow chart but presents it in a different way. A key helps scientists identify the organisms they discover. Here's an example of how it works.

If you observed some fish and had never seen fish before and didn't know what a fish was, the key could help you identify the new organisms as fish. Each step in the key gives you two choices, either a or b. You have to pick one and then do what the key says. Let's try it:

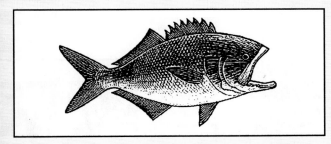

After observing the fish and learning a few things about them, you start with step 1: They lay eggs, so you go to 2.
They have no feathers so you go to 3.
They have no legs…They are fish.

Try each of the other organisms from page 2 to practice using the key.

Look at the mystery bugs below. Although they look pretty similar, a key can be used to identify which one is which. Look at one of the bugs, and begin with step 1 of the key. Work through the key until you have identified that bug by name. Try each bug until you have identified all six bugs. (Answers are given on the bottom of the last page of the unit.)

BUG A

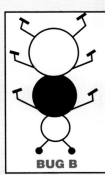
BUG B

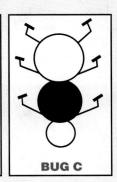
BUG C

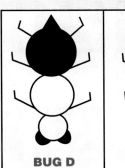
BUG D

BUG E

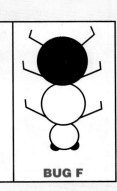
BUG F

1a. Lays eggs _____ go to 2

1b. Does not lay eggs _____ go to 4

2a. Has feathers _____ Bird

2b. Does not have feathers_____ go to 3

3a. Has legs_____ Turtle

3b. Does not have legs _____ Fish

4a. Has two legs _____ Human

4b. Has four legs _____ go to 5

5a. Eats meat _____ Dog

5b. Does not eat meat _____ Cow

1a. Has foot pads _____ go to 2

1b. Does not have foot pads_____ go to 4

2a. Has antennas _____ go to 3

2b. Does not have antennas _____ Bugsy

3a. Has dot on rear section_____ Spot

3b. Does not have dot on rear section _____ Rover

4a. Has rear stinger _____ go to 5

4b. Does not have rear stinger_____ Milo

5a. Has big eyes_____ Robin

5b. Does not have big eyes _____ Lily

43

For instructions on how to play a fun Periodic Table ga

PERIODIC TABLE

1

H — Hydrogen 1
- o Rocket fuel
- o Hydrogenation of fats
- o Petroleum desulfurization
- o Water, ammonia
- x 1.0079

2

Li — Lithium 3
- v Lubricant additive
- o Pacemaker batteries
- + Alloys used in space
- v Glass and Pharmaceuticals
- x 6.941

Be — Beryllium 4
- o X-ray tube windows
- + Watch springs
- + Sparkfree tools
- v heat conducting ceramics
- x 9.01218

Na — Sodium 11
- o Street lights
- + Nuclear reactor coolant
- + Batteries
- v Kitchen salt, soda, glass
- x 22.9898

Mg — Magnesium 12
- + Racing Bikes
- + Airplanes
- v Bricks for fireplaces
- v Pigments, fillers
- x 24.305

At room temperature the element is:

YELLOW	Gas
RED	Liquid
WHITE	Natural Solid
GREEN	Man-made Solid

Appearance in Na

- Unshaded
- Shaded
- Half-Shaded

3 4 5 6 7 8 9

K — Potassium 19
- v Fertilizer
- v Glass lenses
- v Matches, gun powder
- v Salt substitute
- x 39.0983

Ca — Calcium 20
- o Metallurgy
- + Cable insulation, batteries
- v Fertilizer
- v Concrete, Plaster of Paris
- x 40.08

Sc — Scandium 21
- o Leak detectors
- v Large Screen TV's
- v Stadium lighting
- x 44.9559

Ti — Titanium 22
- o Heat exchanger
- + Airplane motors
- + Bone pins
- v Pigments for paint and paper
- x 47.88

V — Vanadium 23
- + Construction materials
- + Tools
- + Springs
- + Jet engines
- x 50.9415

Cr — Chromium 24
- o Plating for car parts
- + Tools, knives
- v Lasers, camouflage paints
- v Stereo, video tapes
- x 51.996

Mn — Manganese 25
- + Steel for rail switches
- + Tools, axles
- v Safes, plows
- v Batteries
- x 54.9380

Fe — Iron 26
- o Bikes, cars, bridges
- + Magnets, machines
- + Nails, tools
- + Tin cans
- x 55.847

Co — Cobalt 27
- o Gamma radiation source
- + Razor blades
- + Permanent magnet
- v Catalytic converters
- x 58.9332

Rb — Rubidium 37
- o Photoelectric cells
- o Gas scavenger in vacuum tubes
- o Heart muscle research
- x 85.4678

Sr — Strontium 38
- v Nuclear batteries in buoys
- v Beta radiation source
- v Phosphorescent paint
- v Fireworks (crimson)
- x 87.62

Y — Yttrium 39
- v Color TV screens
- v Radar, lasers
- v Superconductors
- v Fireproof bricks
- x 88.9059

Zr — Zirconium 40
- o Nuclear fuel rods
- o Catalytic converters
- v Zircon gemstone
- v Furnace bricks
- x 91.224

Nb — Niobium 41
- + Cutting tools
- + Pipelines
- + Superconducting magnets
- + Welding rods
- x 92.9064

Mo — Molybdenum 42
- o Filament in electric heaters
- + Rocket motors
- v Lubricants
- o Source of radio isotopes
- x 95.94

Tc — Technetium 43
- o Radiation source for medical research
- x (98)

Ru — Ruthenium 44
- o Eye treatment
- o Thickness meters for eggshells
- + Fountain pen point
- + Electrical contacts
- x 101.07

R — Rhodium 45
- o Headlight reflectors
- o Telephone relays
- o Catalytic convertors
- + Airplane sparkplugs
- x 102.906

Cs — Cesium 55
- o Photoelectric cells
- o Gamma radiation source
- o Atomic clock
- v Scintillation counters
- x 132.905

Ba — Barium 56
- + Spark plugs
- + Gas scavenger in vacuum tubes
- v Fireworks (green)
- v Fluorescent lamps
- x 137.33

La — Lanthanum 57
- + Lighter flints
- + Battery electrodes
- v Catalytic converters
- v Camera lenses
- x 138.906

Hf — Hafnium 72
- o Nuclear submarines
- o Controls nuclear reactions
- o Gas scavenger in vacuum tubes
- x 178.49

Ta — Tantalum 73
- o Capacitors
- + Vacuum tube filaments
- + Cutting tools
- + Weights
- x 180.948

W — Tungsten 74
- o Welding electrode
- o Lamp filaments, TV
- + Rocket nozzles
- v Cutting and boring tools
- x 183.85

Re — Rhenium 75
- + Oven filaments
- + Jewelry plating
- + Electrodes
- + Thermocouples
- x 186.207

Os — Osmium 76
- + Decorations
- + Compass needles
- + Fountain pen points
- + Clock bearings
- x 190.2

Ir — Iridium 77
- o Satellite thruster engine
- + Hypodermic needles
- + Standard one meter bar
- + Helicopter sparkplugs
- x 192.22

Fr — Francium 87
- Seldom found in nature
- x (223)

Ra — Radium 88
- v Neutron source
- v Antique Glow in the dark paint
- x 226.025

Ac — Actinium 89 (ALPHA RAYS, NEUTRONS)
- o Neutron source
- x 227.028

Rf: Rutherfordium* 104
- *Proposed name
- x (261)

Ha: Hahnium* 105
- *Proposed name
- x (262)

Sg: Seaborgium* 106
- *Proposed name
- x (263)

Ns: Nielsbohrium* 107
- *Proposed name
- x (262)

Hs: Hassium* 108
- *Proposed name
- x (266)

Mt: Meitnerium* 1
- *Proposed name
- one atom observed during discovery

Ce: Cerium 58
- + lighter flints
- + Catalytic converters
- v Kluge lights
- o Self-cleaning ovens
- x 140.12

Pr: Praseodymium 59
- + Cryogenic refrigeration
- + Permanent magnets
- v Search lights
- v Ceramic coloring
- x 140.908

Nd: Neodymium 60
- + High strength magnets for disc drives
- + Coloring for eye glasses
- v Ceramic capacitors
- v Glass for lasers and lenses
- x 144.24

Pm: Promethium 61
- v Nuclear batteries
- v Thickness gauge
- v Starter for fluorescent lights
- x (145)

Sm: Samarium 62
- v Ceramic capacitors
- v High temperature permanent magnets
- v Lasers
- x 150.36

Eu: Europium
- v Color TV tubes
- v X-ray intensifier screens
- v Mercury lamps
- v Energy saving trichromat fluorescent lights
- x 151.96

Th: Thorium 90
- o Coating on filament wire
- v Fuel for breeder reactors
- v Gaslight mantles
- v Crucibles
- x 232.038

Pa: Protactinium 91
- x 231.036

U: Uranium 92
- o Breeder reactor fuel
- o Nuclear reactor fuel
- + Gyro compasses
- v Glass coloring
- x 238.029

Np: Neptunium 93
- x 237.048

Pu: Plutonium 94
- v Nuclear batteries-pacemakers
- v Nuclear reactor fuel
- v Film cleaner
- x (244)

Am: Americium
- v Crystal research
- v Smoke detectors
- v Glass thickness meters
- v Neutron source
- x (243)

OF THE ELEMENTS

Helium 2
- Balloons, blimps
- Diving bell atmosphere
- Lasers, leak detectors
- Nuclear plant coolant
x 4.00260

Used As:

Calcium 20
- .... Name and Atomic Number
o .... Elemental Form
v .... Alloy, Blend, or Mixture
/ .... Compound
x .... Raw Material for Atomic Weight

Copyright: Gelest, Inc. 1991, 1994
Copyright: Association of the Dutch Chemical Industry

mpound Form

emental Form

emental and
mpound Form

13

Boron 5
- v Regulator in nuclear plants
- **v Tennis rackets**
- v Heat resistant glass
- v Eye disinfectant
- x 10.81

14

Carbon 6
- o Diamond, **pencils**
- o Tire colorant, steel
- v Controls nuclear reactions
- v Plastics, life
- x 12.011

15
Nitrogen 7
- o **Cryogenic surgery**
- o Coolant (liquid nitrogen)
- v Ammonia production
- v Rocket fuels
- x 14.0067

16

Oxygen 8
- o **Combustion**
- o Steel production
- o Water purification
- v Sand, water, cement
- x 15.9994

17
Fluorine 9
- v Uranium enrichment
- v Refrigerator coolants
- o **Toothpaste additives**
- v Teflon
- x 18.9984

Neon 10
- o Neon lights
- o Fog lights
- o TV tubes, lasers
- o Voltage detectors
- x 20.179

Aluminum 13
- o Window frames, doorknobs
- o Tube, cable, foil
- o Fireworks, flash bulbs
- + Cars, rockets, **planes**
- x 26.9815

Silicon 14
- o Micro chips, **solar cells**
- v Tools
- v Quartz, cement, glass
- v Silicone rubbers and oils
- x 28.0855

Phosphorus 15
- v Fireworks, **matches**
- v Fertilizers, detergents
- v Toothpastes
- v Pesticides
- x 30.9738

Sulfur 16
- o Matches, fireworks
- o Batteries
- o Vulcanization of rubber
- v **Permanent wave lotion**
- x 32.06

Chlorine 17
- v **Water purification**
- v Bleach, hydrochloric acid
- v Plastics (PVC)
- v Stain removers
- x 35.453

Argon 18
- o Light Bulbs
- o Gas discharge tubes
- o Lasers, Geiger counters
- o Welding blanket gas
- x 39.948

10
Nickel 28
- **Coins**
- Knives, forks, spoons
- Crucibles, white gold
- Rechargeable batteries
- 58.69

11

Copper 29
- o Cable, wire, **water pipe**
- + Pennies, bronze sculpture
- + Statue of Liberty
- + Bells, carillons
- x 63.546

12
Zinc 30
- o Corrosion resistant coating
- o Batteries, **gutters**
- + Water and gas valves
- v White pigments in rubber
- x 65.39

Gallium 31
- o **Quartz thermometers**
- v Computer memory
- v Transistors, laser diodes
- v Used to locate tumors
- x 69.72

Germanium 32
- o Infrared night vision
- o **Wide-angle lenses**
- v Fiber optics
- v Dentistry
- x 72.59

Arsenic 33
- o Shotgun pellets
- o Metal for mirrors
- v Glass, lasers
- **v Light emitting diodes=LED**
- x 74.9216

Selenium 34
- o **Light meters**
- o Copy machines
- o Solar cells
- v Anti-dandruff shampoos
- x 78.96

Bromine 35
- v Tear gas
- v Fire retardants
- v Disinfectants
- v **Photographic film**
- x 79.904

Krypton 36
- o **Fluorescent bulbs**
- o Flash bulbs
- o Wavelength standard
- o UV lasers
- x 33.80

Palladium 46
- Catalytic converters
- Hydrogen separation
- **Dental crowns**
- Anti-tumor agents
- 106.42

Silver 47
- o Mirrors, batteries
- + **Silverware**
- v Photographic film and paper
- v Photosensitive glass
- x 107.868

Cadmium 48
- o **Rechargeable batteries**
- o Plating of screws, bolts
- v Regulator in nuclear reactors
- + Red and yellow pigments
- x 112.41

Indium 49
- o Solar cells, mirrors
- o Regulator in nuclear power
- v Photo cells, **transistors**
- v Blood and lung research
- x 114.82

Tin 50
- + Coins, cups and plates
- + **Organ pipes**
- v Opalescent glass, enamel
- v Weather resistant vinyl siding
- x 118.71

Antimony 51
- + Solder, type for printing
- + Lead batteries
- v Fire Retardants
- **v Ceramic glazes**
- x 121.75

Tellurium 52
- o Percussion caps
- o **Vulcanization of rubber**
- o Battery plate protector
- + Electrical resistors
- x 127.60

Iodine 53
- o **Disinfectant**
- v Halogen lamps
- v Ink pigments
- v Salt additive
- x 126.905

Xenon 54
- o UV lamps, **sun lamps**
- o Paint testers
- o Projection lamps
- o Electronic flashes
- x 131.29

Platinum 78
- o Catalyst for nitric acid prod.
- o **Crucibles**
- o Dental crowns
- o Anti-tumor agents
- 195.08

Gold 79
- o Precious metal
- o **Jewelry**
- + Electrical contacts
- + Dental crowns
- x 196.967

Mercury 80
- o **Barometers**, thermometers
- o Street lights
- v Dental fillings
- v Seed protection
- x 200.59

Thallium 81
- o Thermometer filling
- v Infrared detectors
- v Heart muscle research
- v **Insecticides**
- x 204.383

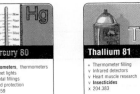
Lead 82
- o Radiation protection
- + Roof coverings, **batteries**
- + Solders, ammunition
- v Gasoline additives
- x 207.2

Bismuth 83
- o Catalyst in rubber production
- + **Fuses**
- + Fire Sprinklers
- v Antiacids, Antidiarrheals
- x 208.980

Polonium 84
- o **Nuclear batteries**
- o Neutron source
- o Antistatic agents
- o Film cleaner
- x (209)

Astatine 85
- + Seldom found in nature
- x (210)

Radon 86
- o **Earthquake prediction**
- o Health threat in homes built on granite
- o Seldom found in nature
- x (222)

110
*No name proposed
UPAC interim name:
Jnununium

111
*No name proposed

Gd: Gadolinium 64
- v Diagnosing osteoporosis
- v Permanent magnets
- v X-ray tubes
- v Computer memory
- x 157.25

Tb: Terbium 65
- + Magneto-optic alloys for CD's
- v X-ray screens
- v Fluorescent lamps
- + Magneto-strictive alloys for submarine transducers
- x 158.925

Dy: Dysprosium 66
- + Magneto-optic alloys for CD's
- v Color TV tubes
- v X-ray screens
- v Mercury lamps
- v Neutron scavenger
- x 162.50

Ho: Holmium 67
- v Glass coloring
- v Eye-safe lasers
- x 164.930

Er: Erbium 68
- v Glass coloring
- v Infrared fiber optics
- v Coating for sunglasses
- v Pink simulant gemstones
- x 167.26

Tm: Thulium 69
- v Lasers
- x 168.934

Yb: Ytterbium 70
- v Dentures
- v Portable X-ray source for blood treatment
- v Carbon arc lamps
- x 173.04

Lu: Lutetium 71
- v Temperature sensing optics
- x 174.967

Cm: Curium 96
- x (247)

Bk: Berkelium 97
- x (247)

Cf: Californium 98
- v Neutron source
- x (251)

Es: Einsteinium 99
- x (252)

Fm: Fermium 100
- x (257)

Md: Mendelevium 101
- x (258)

No: Nobelium 102
- x (259)

Lr: Lawrencium 103
- x (260)

Start Your Own Rock Group!

YOU WILL NEED:

safety glasses for all participants

empty egg carton (1 per group)

12 rock samples (per group)

masking tape

pens

sheets of paper

old rags

small hammer

magnifying glass (optional)

unglazed porcelain tile (back of porcelain bathroom tile)

nail

penny

glass marble

Scientists who study **geology** have a classification system for rocks and minerals. These geologists test samples of the rocks and minerals to find out about their characteristics. Samples that have similar characteristics are grouped together. Try the tests below on your own rock samples and see if you can group your rocks according to their similar characteristics.

1 Divide students into groups of four to six. Have each student bring in three or four different looking rocks that can be found around the house, park, or school.

2 Have each group decide which 12 rock samples to test. Place each sample in its own compartment in an egg carton. Use small pieces of masking tape to number the compartments from 1 to 12.

3 On a separate sheet of paper, make a chart like the one below. Use the whole page, and make the spaces large enough to record your observations for each of the following tests on each rock sample:

Rock Sample	Break Test	Color Test	Texture Test	Streak Test	Hardness Test
1					
2					
3					
4					
5					
6					
7					
8					
9					
10					
11					
12					

BREAK TEST

Wrap a rag around one of your rock samples. Place it on a hard surface outdoors and tap it with the hammer until it breaks. Do not hit the rock so hard that it smashes into many pieces—two or three pieces are good enough. If the rag tears, use another. Place the pieces back into their compartment in the egg carton. Repeat with each sample.

Under **Break Test** in the chart, describe the way the rock broke.

Did it break in a smooth or jagged way? How hard was it to get the rock to break? Did it crumble or break cleanly?

COLOR TEST

Describe the color of your rock on the inside and outside surfaces. Record your observations in the chart.

Is it all one color or a mixture? If it is more than one color, are the colors in blotches in different parts of the rock, in streaks, dots, or some other form?

TEXTURE TEST

Look at each rock very closely. Describe the texture of the outside and inside surfaces.

Are the surfaces rough or smooth, shiny or dull? Does it look like it is made of one kind of material or more than one? Are there any little crystals or shiny flakes? If you have a magnifying glass, describe how the surfaces appear when magnified.

STREAK TEST

With each rock sample, try to draw a line on a piece of unglazed porcelain.

Which rocks made a streak? What does the streak look like?

HARDNESS TEST

Use the tests in the hardness scale for each rock sample. The greater the number on the scale, the harder the rock. Record the hardness number in the chart for each rock sample.

HARDNESS TESTS	HARDNESS SCALE
Can be scratched with a fingernail	1
Can be scratched with a penny	2
Can scratch a penny	3
Can scratch a glass marble	4
Can be scratched with an iron nail	5
Can scratch an iron nail	6

Look at your chart. Do some rocks seem to have more in common with each other than with other rocks? Work with your partners to put the rock samples in groups based on similar characteristics you observed in the different tests. This is classification!

A Periodic Table Game!

Scientists who study **chemistry** have their own system of classification. Chemists need to know about the different atoms that make up all the different living and nonliving things on Earth. Just as biologists place animals that have similar characteristics together into groups, chemists place atoms that have similar characteristics together into groups. All these groups are organized into a big chart called the "**periodic** (peer-ee-ah-dik) **table**."

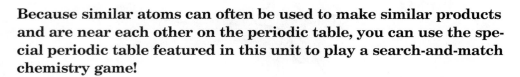

Because similar atoms can often be used to make similar products and are near each other on the periodic table, you can use the special periodic table featured in this unit to play a search-and-match chemistry game!

Divide students into groups of two or three.

The object of the game is to find two or more elements that are next to each other on the periodic table and are used to make the same or similar products. They can be side by side, up and down, or diagonal. For instance, strontium (38) is used in fireworks and so is barium (56), which is directly below it. Another example is lead (82), which is used in batteries, and diagonally up from lead is antimony (51), which is also used in batteries. Just to the right of antimony is tellurium (52), and below tellurium is polonium (84), both of which are also used in batteries.

You can set up a point system to keep score of who finds more elements found in similar products, that are next to each other. Two such elements and products next to each other are worth 5 points, three next to each other are worth 10, four are worth 15, and so on.

You might also want to encourage students to use their own knowledge to make connections among the elements. For example, silver (47) and gold (79) are next to each other, but jewelry is only listed for gold. Students could list jewelry as common to both silver and gold and score 5 points.

Have fun and good luck!

Answers to Mystery Bugs Activity:

BUG A	BUG B	BUG C	BUG D	BUG E	BUG F
Spot	Rover	Bugsy	Robin	Lily	Milo

Chemistry and Color

Paints, dyes, inks, and natural pigments all depend on chemicals to give them their wide variety of colors. But aside from the role that chemicals play in coloring our natural and human-made environment, color itself often plays a very important part in chemistry experimentation. The color of a substance can help scientists determine what the substance might be. Color changes also give scientists important information about whether a particular chemical reaction may have taken place and what the reactants and products might be. In this unit, students focus on this role that color plays in chemical investigations.

Gold Paper Insert:

For a class set of gold color-changing paper, call 1-800-227-5558, extension 4600.

Colors on the Moooove

You could explain to students that sometimes scientists need to be able to tell the difference between substances that are very similar. Sometimes adding a test chemical to the substances can help scientists tell them apart. In this activity, food coloring is the test chemical. It is used to help tell the difference between skim milk, whole milk, and half-and-half.

Results:

The drop of food coloring should spread out the most in skim milk, the least in half-and-half, and somewhere in between in whole milk.

The investigation is taken one step further when another test chemical (dishwashing detergent) is added to each color dot. The detergent should cause the color to move and spread quickly away from the center and toward the edge of the bowl. There may also be some swirling of the colors. The reason for the movement of the food coloring in the milks is not well understood. One possible explanation has to do with the way detergent molecules surround the tiny fat globules in milk. Detergent molecules are long. They have a charged end and a neutral end. The neutral ends of many detergent molecules surround the fat globules. All the charged ends stick out and repel each other, causing the spreading action. The food coloring is just pushed along.

Show Your True Colors

This simple process of chromatography should separate the different-colored food dyes in the food coloring drops. Several chemical principles are involved in separating substances based on chromatography. The degree to which a substance attaches to water or to the filter paper plays a part in determining how far it travels up the paper. The size, weight, and shape of the color molecule also help determine how it moves on the filter paper and where along the paper it attaches. These factors usually cause enough separation that you can tell which colors were combined to make the original mixture.

Go for the Gold

This unit features the use of a special sheet of goldenrod paper. This is not just any goldenrod paper. Students see in the activity that the paper changes color from gold to red when a base such as baking soda, laundry detergent, or soap is applied to it. It also changes back from red to gold when an acid such as vinegar or lemon juice is applied to it.

Results:

Step 4: When water, baking soda, soap, and laundry detergent solutions are rubbed on separate sections of the paper, everything except water turns the paper red. Students should realize that since these substances cause a similar color change, they may have something in common. They should also see that the red color was not the same intensity for all samples. This should suggest that the samples have both similarities and differences. This is a way that chemists can begin to categorize substances.

Step 5: The vinegar turned the red back to gold.

In the second part of the activity, the gold paper is used to make a solution.

Results:

Step 4: Both the laundry detergent solution and the baking soda solution turn the yellow test liquid red, but the detergent turns it a darker red. Students should conclude that there is something "stronger" about the detergent than the baking soda.

Step 5: The one drop of vinegar turns both solutions yellow, but even more yellow than the original test solution (control).

Step 6: If the detergent solution is in some way stronger than the baking soda solution, students should predict that it will take fewer drops of the detergent solution than it does of the baking soda solution to turn the test solution back to its original color.

Step 7: That is indeed what happens. This means that there is either a stronger base in the laundry detergent than in the baking soda or that the base itself is about the same strength, but is higher in concentration.

Vitamin C Testing—Chemistry's Clear Solution!

This activity calls for using biodegradable starch pellets used as packing material. This material has become very common as an alternative to Styrofoam "peanuts." If you or your students do not have any starch pellets from a recently opened box, try a mailing supply store.

If startch packing pellets cannot be found, an alternative is using 1 Tablespoon instant mashed potatoes to 1/4 cup water and filtering.

After making the starch solution and adding the diluted tincture of iodine, the starch and iodine solutions in all cups should be blue. To these three samples of blue solution, students add drops of vitamin C, Tang, and orange juice. When the amount of vitamin C reaches a certain level, the solution changes from blue to clear. The key to the test is for students to understand that the *more* drops of Tang or orange juice needed to turn the blue solution clear, the *less* vitamin C the Tang or orange juice has. The converse is also true: The *fewer* drops it takes to turn the blue solution clear, the *more* vitamin C the Tang or orange juice has.

Results:

Step 5: The vitamin C solution should turn the blue solution clear in the fewest number of drops. It has the highest concentration of vitamin C.

Step 7: The Tang solution should turn the blue solution clear in fewer drops than it takes the orange juice. It has a higher concentration of vitamin C than orange juice.

Step 8: The orange juice requires the most drops to turn the solution clear. It has a lower concentration of vitamin C than the Tang solution.

Color & Chemistry—(An Artful Solution!)

This activity gives students an opportunity to have some more fun with the color-changing paper. In addition to the activities suggested, you could have students write on the dry paper with a white candle and then use a cotton swab to rub the paper with a baking soda solution. This will reveal the hidden writing.

Chemistry and Color

NATIONAL SCIENCE EDUCATION STANDARDS

The activities in this unit can be used to support the teaching of the following standards:

✔ **Unifying Concepts and Processes**

Evidence, Models, and Explanation

Using evidence to understand interactions allows individuals to predict changes in natural and designed systems. *(All activities)*

✔ **Science as Inquiry**

Abilities Necessary to Do Scientific Inquiry

Design and conduct a scientific investigation. *(All activities)*

Develop descriptions, explanations, predictions, and models using evidence. *(All activities)*

Think critically and logically to make the relationships between evidence and explanations. *(All activities)*

✔ **Physical Science**

Properties and Changes of Properties in Matter

A substance has characteristic properties, all of which are independent of the amount of the sample.

Colors on the Moooove

A mixture of substances often can be separated into the original substances using one or more of the characteristic properties.

Show Your True Colors

Substances react chemically in characteristic ways with other substances to form new substances (compounds) with different characteristic properties.

Go for the Gold!

Vitamin C Testing—Chemistry's Clear Solution!

Color & Chemistry—An Artful Solution!

Go for the Gold

Go for the Gold I

Record your observations after placing water and the solutions of soap, baking soda, and detergent on the gold paper. Include as many details as you can about what happened with each solution. Also point out the similarities and differences between the results for the solutions.

Water: _____

Soap: _____

Baking soda: _____

Laundry detergent: _____

What did you notice when you put vinegar on each sample? _____

_____

Go for the Gold II

Record your observations after placing 1 drop each of baking soda solution and laundry detergent solution into their separate cups of yellow solution. Record the color of these solutions compared with the color of the control. Also note how the colors compare with each other.

Baking soda: _____

_____

Laundry detergent: _____

_____

What happens when you add a drop of vinegar to the baking soda and the laundry detergent test cups?

_____

Baking soda and laundry detergent solutions can change the color of the test solution back to the color of the control. Make a prediction about which solution can do it in the fewest number of drops. Explain why you picked the one you did.

_____

After adding drops of baking soda and laundry detergent to their cups, which one changed back to the color of the control in the fewest number of drops? Was your prediction correct?

_____

NAME _____   DATE _____

Vitamin C Testing—Chemistry's Clear Solution!

1. After dissolving the starch pellets in water and then filtering the water, what color is your final filtered starch solution?
_____

2. After adding 1 drop of iodine solution to each cup of starch solution, what is the color of the solutions?
_____

3. How many drops of vitamin C solution did it take to change the color of the starch/iodine solution from blue to clear?
_____

   The more vitamin C a solution has, the fewer drops it takes to turn the starch/iodine solution from blue to clear. Does this mean that the vitamin C solution has a lot of vitamin C or a little? _____

4. Would you expect Tang to have more or less vitamin C than the vitamin C solution you tested?
_____

5. Do you think it will take more or fewer drops of Tang than it did of vitamin C solution to change the starch/iodine solution from blue to clear? _____

6. How many drops of Tang did it take to change the test solution from blue to clear?_____

7. Does Tang have more or less vitamin C than the vitamin C solution?_____

8. Would you expect orange juice to have more or less vitamin C than the vitamin C solution and the Tang you tested?
_____

9. Do you think it will take more or fewer drops of orange juice than it did of vitamin C solution or Tang to change the starch/iodine solution from blue to clear? _____

10. How many drops of orange juice did it take to change the test solution from blue to clear?_____

11. Does orange juice have more or less vitamin C than the vitamin C solution and the Tang?
_____

Colors on the Moooove

Color is used all the time and in many different ways in chemistry. Color can help us figure out what a substance is, can help us tell when a substance has changed, and can be used to help tell us how strong or weak a substance is. Try the activity below and see that chemistry and color can be an exciting combination!

YOU WILL NEED:

milk (skim, whole, and half & half)

3 shallow bowls

liquid dish detergent

food coloring

cotton swabs

masking tape

pen

small paper cup

1 Use your masking tape and pen to label your three bowls **skim milk**, **whole milk**, and **half & half** as shown. Add about 1/4 cup of skim milk, whole milk, and half & half, each to its labeled bowl. Look at the milks closely. What differences do you notice about them? What do you think might cause these differences?

2 Gently add one drop of food coloring to the center of the milk in each bowl. DO NOT STIR OR DISTURB THE BOWLS. What do you observe about the way the food coloring looks in each bowl? Does this observation make sense with what you observed about the milks before you put in the food coloring?

3 Dip a cotton swab in your detergent. Carefully touch the center of each food coloring drop in each bowl. Do not stir. Use a different cotton swab tip for each bowl. What do you observe? Do you notice a difference in the way the color looks in each of the bowls? What do you think might cause these differences?*

* For an explanation of the color movement in the milk, see the Teacher's Guide.

Show Your True Colors

YOU WILL NEED:
coffee filters
food coloring droppers (red, blue, green, and yellow)
cotton swab
metric ruler
pencil
tape
small cup (3 oz)
big clear plastic cup (8 oz)
water

Sometimes chemists need to know what is in a mixture of chemicals. If different colors are mixed together and you need to figure out what the colors are, you can use a method like the one that chemists use. The colors can be separated using chromatography. (kro-ma-tah-gruh-fee). Try it and see!

1. Cut a strip from a coffee filter that is about the same height as your tall clear plastic cup and about 2 cm wide.

2. Place one drop each of two different food colors together in your small 3-oz cup so that they mix. Even though the colors are mixed, a little chemistry can make them come apart again!

3. Use your cotton swab to soak up the food color from the cup. Touch your coffee filter strip with the cotton swab to make a dot of color about 2 cm from the bottom of the strip. Allow the strip to dry for 3–5 minutes.

4. Place a little water in the bottom of your large clear plastic cup. Wrap the top of the strip around a pencil and tape it down as shown. Place the pencil on the cup but be sure that only the very bottom of the paper strip touches the water. **Do not allow the dot to go into the water.**

5. Watch the color dot as water moves up the strip. What do you notice? How many colors do you see? If you see more than two colors, what do you think could cause that?

6. If you mixed three or four colors, do you think you could see them *all* as they moved up the strip? Try it and see! How about trying just one color. There may be more to that one color than you think!

Go for the

A color change can tell us that a chemical reaction has occurred. It can also give us some hints about the type of chemicals that are causing the color change reaction. Check out these activities using a special gold-colored paper to see chemistry and color go for the gold!

TEACHER PREPARATION:
Cut gold paper into pieces about 4 × 8 cm long. (An 8.5 × 11 in sheet should make 18–20 pieces.) Each group of students should get two pieces.

1 Use your masking tape and pen to label your four cups **water**, **soap**, **baking soda**, and **detergent**. On a sheet of paper, use your plastic knife to scrape up and down on the edge of the soap to make some soap flakes.

2 Place 1/2 teaspoon of each powder into its labeled cup. Add 2 tablespoons of water to each cup and swirl to mix. Put only water in the cup labeled water.

3 Use your pen to divide the piece of gold paper into four sections. Label the sections **water**, **soap**, **baking soda**, and **detergent**.

4 Dip one end of a cotton swab into the water. Rub the water in its area on the gold paper to make a dot a bit smaller than a dime. Repeat for each solution with a clean end of a cotton swab. Do you notice any difference between the dots? Describe what you see. Put the paper aside to dry.

5 After about 5 minutes, put one drop of vinegar on each dot. What do you notice?

Wash your hands when you are done experimenting.

Gold

This gold paper is pretty amazing. In the last activity, you saw that some substances produce a darker colored red when they react with chemicals in the paper. You also saw that vinegar could make the color go back to gold. Here's another way to use the gold paper to learn more about your baking soda and detergent solutions.

1 Cut up three pieces of gold paper into very thin strips. Place the strips into a zip-closing plastic bag. Add about 1/4 cup warm water. Push the air out of the bag and seal it tightly. Squish the paper and the water for 3 or 4 minutes until the water is very yellow. Open a corner of the bag and pour all the yellow solution into your large cup. Do not drink any solutions.

2 Use the masking tape and pen to label two small cups **baking soda** and **detergent**. Place 1/2 teaspoon of baking soda and 1/2 teaspoon of laundry detergent into their labeled cups. Add 1 tablespoon of water to each cup. Swirl to mix.

3 Now label your three remaining small cups **control**, **baking soda test**, and **detergent test**. Divide the yellow solution evenly among these three cups.

4 Add one drop of baking soda solution to the baking soda test cup and swirl. Using a clean dropper, now add one drop of the detergent solution to the detergent test cup and swirl. Do not add anything to the control cup. What do you observe? How do the colors in the two cups compare to the color in the control? Does one solution make a darker color than the other?

5 Using a clean dropper again, add one drop of vinegar each to the baking soda test cup and to the detergent test cup. Swirl each cup. What happens?

6 You can add drops of baking soda solution and detergent solution to their test cups to turn them back to the color of the control. Which do you think would take more drops to change back to color of the control? Why?

7 Try it by adding one drop at a time of baking soda solution to its test cup and swirling after each drop. Count the drops as you go. Stop adding solution when the color stays the same as in the control. Now try the same thing by adding drops of detergent solution in its test cup. Which took more drops to reach the color of the control? Was that what you predicted?

TEACHER PREPARATION:
Cut gold paper into pieces about 4 × 8 cm long. Each group of students should get three pieces.

Vitamin C Testing—

YOU WILL NEED:

4 starch pellets (biodegradable starch "packing peanuts" available at mailing supply stores)

water

coffee filter

Tang® breakfast drink

vitamin C tablet

tincture of iodine solution

plastic cups (two 8-oz and five 3-oz)

measuring spoons

3 droppers

orange juice

masking tape

pen

Do not drink any solutions.

Which has more vitamin C: Tang® drink mix or orange juice? Chemistry and color can help you find the answer!

CAUTION:
Be careful when using tincture of iodine. Read and follow all directions on the label. When finished activity, rinse out all cups and throw them away.

TEACHER PREPARATION:
Make a solution by adding 1 teaspoon of tincture of iodine to 1 tablespoon water. Place about 1/4 teaspoon of this iodine solution into labeled cups so that each group gets one.

1 Use the two 8-ounce cups to make your *starch solution*: Dissolve 4 starch pellets in 1/2 cup of water. Set up a coffee filter in the other cup as shown. Pour the starch solution through the filter. Label this cup **starch solution**.

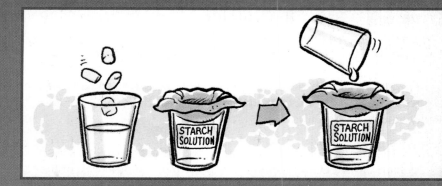

2 Label three of the small plastic cups **vitamin C test**, **Tang test**, and **orange juice test** as shown below. Add 1 tablespoon of starch solution to each cup.

3 Now add 1 drop of iodine solution to each labeled test cup.

4 Label your fourth cup **vitamin C solution**. Crush your vitamin C tablet and add it to 2 tablespoons water in this cup. Stir.

Chemistry's Clear Solution!

The more vitamin C a solution has, the fewer drops it takes to turn the starch/iodine solution clear. So the fewer drops it takes, the more vitamin C the solution must have. Let's see whether Tang or orange juice has more vitamin C.

5 Now place 1 drop of the **vitamin C solution** in the **vitamin C test** cup and swirl. What do you observe? If nothing happens, try adding another drop.

6 Mix up some Tang® by adding 3/4 teaspoon of Tang® powder to 2 tablespoons of water in your fifth cup. Label this cup **Tang Drink**.

7 Try adding 1 drop of Tang® drink to the **Tang test** cup. If it takes more than 1 drop to clear the solution, that means there is less vitamin C in 1 drop of Tang® than there is in 1 drop of your vitamin C solution. How many drops does it take?

8 Now try adding 1 drop of orange juice to its test cup. What do you observe? How many drops of orange juice does it take for the solution to become clear? Which has more vitamin C, Tang® or orange juice?

CHALLENGE
Try testing some other drinks for vitamin C, such as orange soda pop, lemon-lime soda pop, cranberry juice, or apple juice.

Color & Chemistry—
An Artful Solution!

Chemistry and color can make for some interesting art work. Try these next three activities to express yourself as a *WonderScience* chemistry and color artist!

1 Place 1/2 teaspoon of laundry detergent in one tablespoon of water. Swirl to mix.

2 Dip a piece of gold paper in water. Shake off any excess water and place the paper on the back of the index card.

3 Dip a cotton swab in the detergent solution and gently place one drop in the center of the gold paper. What do you observe?

4 Use a piece of Ivory® soap to draw a design on the wet paper.

5 Take a tiny bit of detergent between your thumb and index finger and sprinkle it from about 30 cm above the paper.

Experiment with these activities to make other *WonderScience* chemistry and color art!

YOU WILL NEED:

gold paper (insert) (see Teacher's Guide)
large index card (5 in x 8 in)
water
laundry detergent
Ivory® soap
small plastic cup
cotton swab
vinegar

Wash your hands when you are done experimenting.

ILLUSTRATIONS BY JIM WISNIEWSKI/STEVE EDSEY & SONS UNLESS OTHERWISE INDICATED

Investigating a Chemical Unknown!

In this unit, students perform a variety of simple tests on six different white powders: salt, sugar, Epsom salt, baking soda, cornstarch, and laundry detergent. The activities demonstrate that the various properties of the different substances can be tested and that the test results can be used to help identify an unknown combination of substances. There are many basic and sophisticated tests that chemists do to determine the characteristics of a wide variety of chemicals, but the core concept of developing and using tests to understand more about a substance is common to all of them.

A WonderScience Chem-Vestigation!

In this activity, students create a reusable testing chart on which to conduct experiments throughout the issue. Instructions call for using $\frac{1}{8}$ teaspoon of each powder on the chart, but it is not important that it be exactly $\frac{1}{8}$ teaspoon. If you want to use Popsicle sticks to measure out a little bit of each powder, that will be fine. (Be sure to use separate spoons or sticks and separate straws for each powder to avoid cross-contamination.) Students can use the observation chart provided on the Student Activity Sheet or make their own charts, but the chart should be large enough so that detailed observations can be written in each block.

Put Chemistry to the Test!

This page gives students some background information about each test they will perform. The information should help students understand why a particular test can demonstrate certain distinguishing characteristics of the different substances. The page also presents students with the challenge of the entire issue: to use all the information from all the tests to identify a mystery powder at the end of the unit.

Dissolve It and Solve It!

Students place 2 teaspoons of each substance in separate cups. They add 1 tablespoon of water and swirl, and then add another tablespoon and swirl. These amounts were chosen so that much of the soluble material would dissolve but would be in high enough concentration to crystallize in the evaporation test. Adding more water to make the substances dissolve further would render the evaporation test less effective.

Color Clues You Can Use!

Dilute grape juice indicator is dripped onto the different powders to see whether any distinctive color change occurs. Grape juice indicator changes color when combined with a base. Of the powders tested, baking soda and laundry detergent should cause the greatest color change.

Drop a Hint

This activity encourages very close observation of some subtle differences between the way a drop of food coloring behaves in each solution made from the different powders. Be sure students do not mix the solution after adding the drop. They should simply observe. Some things to look for are the way the drop spreads out on the surface of the solution and whether the drop floats or sinks. Have students make particularly detailed observations, because some of the differences may not be as obvious as others.

Discover the Unknown!

The two powders that work well together as a mystery substance are baking soda and cornstarch. Be sure to tell students that there are two, and only two, powders in the mystery unknown. Because the powders are mixed, the results of the tests may not be as distinctive as they were with the individual powders, but there should be enough of an indication to determine which powders are present.

The following are the results we observed when doing all the tests described in the issue.
Of course, some of your results may be somewhat different.

	Salt	Sugar	Epsom salt	Baking soda	Cornstarch	Laundry detergent	Mystery powder
Vinegar test	Got wet.	Got wet.	Got wet.	Bubbled. More bubbly than detergent.	Got wet.	Bubbled. Foamy thick bubbles.	Bubbled. Foamy thick bubbles.
Iodine test	Wet.	Wet.	Wet.	Wet.	Turned dark purple.	Wet.	Turned dark purple.
Dissolving test	A lot left that did not dissolve. Cloudy liquid.	Almost all dissolved. Clear liquid.	More dissolved than regular salt, but not as much as sugar.	A lot did not dissolve. Even more than salt.	Most looks like it is floating around in the water. Liquid looks milky.	Most dissolved, but there is a film of white on the top.	Not much dissolved. Looked kind of milky but also had a lot left on bottom of cup.
Evaporation test	Several large crystals. Many tiny ones— smaller than original salt.	Gooey, blob-like, sticky syrup.	Long crystals. Still wet beneath the surface.	Many small crystals. Rim of built-up crystals around the outside.	White, smooth. No visible crystals.	White crystals around the outside. Grayer on the inside.	White and transparent crystals. No definite shapes. Mixed together.
Indicator test	Wet.	Wet.	Wet.	Dark gray-greenish.	Wet.	Green.	Greenish.
Color Drop test	Kind of granular. Brownish-red. Broke apart.	Spread out quickly on the surface. Defined edges.	Spread out slowly. Hazy and wispy around the edges.	Lots of lines on the surface.	Most sinks straight to the bottom.	Stays in a small tight circle on the surface.	Spreads out slowly. Wispy around the edges. Some sinks.

Investigating a Chemical Unknown!

NATIONAL SCIENCE EDUCATION STANDARDS

The activities in this unit can be used to support the teaching of the following standards:

✔ **Unifying Concepts and Processes**

Evidence, Models, and Explanation

Evidence consists of observations and data on which to base scientific explanations.
(All activities)

✔ **Science as Inquiry**

Abilities Necessary to Do Scientific Inquiry

Design and conduct a scientific investigation. *(All activities)*

Use appropriate tools and techniques to gather, analyze, and interpret data. *(All activities)*

Develop descriptions, explanations, predictions, and models using evidence.
   Discover the Unknown!

Think critically and logically to make the relationships between evidence and explanations.
(All activities)

✔ **Physical Science**

Properties and Changes of Properties in Matter

A substance has characteristic properties, such as solubility, that are independent of the amount of the sample.
   Dissolve It and Solve It!
   Drop a Hint
   Discover the Unknown!

Substances react chemically in characteristic ways with other substances to form new substances (compounds) with different characteristic properties.
   A WonderScience Chem-Vestigation!
   Color Clues You Can Use!

STUDENT ACTIVITY SHEET

NAME _____ **DATE** _____

Use this chart to record detailed observations of the results of your tests on the different substances.

OBSERVATION CHART

	Salt	Sugar	Epsom sa
Vinegar test			
Iodine test			
Dissolving test			
Evaporation test			
Indicator test			
Color Drop test			

aking soda	Cornstarch	Laundry detergent	Mystery powder

YOU WILL NEED:

- **salt**
- **sugar**
- **Epsom salt**
- **baking soda**
- **corn starch**
- **laundry detergent** (white powder)
- **tincture of iodine**
- **vinegar**
- **6 plastic cups**
- **6 plastic spoons**
- **sheet of white paper**
- **black construction paper**
- **blank overhead transparency**
  (1 for each group)
- **plastic straws**
- **masking tape**
- **pen**

TEACHER PREPARATION:
Prepare the iodine test solution by adding 10 drops of tincture of iodine to 1/4 cup of water in a plastic cup. Divide the solution evenly among student groups. Also cut 3 plastic straws in half so that each student group has 6 half-straws. The Testing Chart and Observation Chart should be saved for use throughout this *WonderScience* unit.

Substances have their own characteristics that make them different from other substances. Scientists have come up with different kinds of tests for these characteristics that help them tell one substance from another. In the following activities, you and your partners will test 6 substances to see some of the characteristics that make each substance unique. In the last activity, you can use these tests to identify an unknown combination of these substances!

This column is for the last activity.

1 Use the masking tape and pen to label your plastic cups **salt, sugar, Epsom salt, baking soda, corn starch, and laundry detergent**. Place 2 tablespoons of each substance into its labeled cup.

2 Use a black sheet of construction paper and masking tape to make a chart like the one shown. Place a blank overhead transparency over the chart and tape it down to the construction paper as shown. This is your **Testing Chart**.

3 Now make a chart like the one shown or use the chart in the Student Activity Sheet. This is your **Observation Chart**. After doing each test, record your observations in the observation chart. You will use the Testing Chart and Observation Chart throughout the unit.

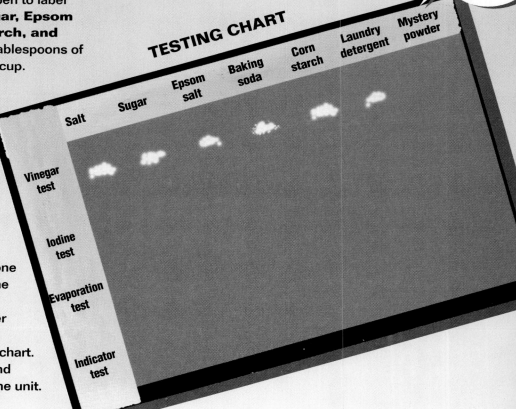

TESTING CHART

	Salt	Sugar	Epsom salt	Baking soda	Corn starch	Laundry detergent	Mystery powder
Vinegar test							
Iodine test							
Evaporation test							
Indicator test							

Chem-Vestigation!

VINEGAR TEST

4 Place about 1/8 teaspoon of each powder under its name along the vinegar area of the testing chart as shown. Use a straw to drip 2 or 3 drops of vinegar on each powder. Observe the powders closely and record your observations in the observation chart.

If you now had the 6 powders in front of you without labels, which powders do you think you could identify using the vinegar test and your notes from your observation chart? Explain.

CAUTION:

- Be very careful when using tincture of iodine.
- Read and follow all directions on the label.
- When you have finished the activity, rinse out the iodine cup and the straw and throw them away.

IODINE TEST

5 Place about 1/8 teaspoon of each powder under its name along the iodine area of the testing chart. Use a straw to drip 2 or 3 drops of iodine solution on each powder. Observe the powders closely and record your observations.

If you had the 6 powders in front of you without labels, which do you think you could identify using the iodine test and your notes from your observation chart? Explain.

JIM WISNIEWSKI

OBSERVATION CHART

	Salt	Sugar	Epsom salt	Baking soda	Corn starch	Laundry detergent	Mystery powder
Vinegar test							
Iodine test							
Dissolving test							
Evaporation test							
Indicator test							
Color Drop test							

Put Chemistry to the Test!

Read this page for a better idea of how the tests throughout this *WonderScience* unit will help you figure out the unknown mystery powder on the last page!

The first test you did was a vinegar test. Vinegar contains a weak acid called **acetic acid**. One of the most common reactions with vinegar causes bubbling and the release of carbon dioxide gas. You may have seen this bubbling in one or more of your powders. If you see bubbling in the unknown, you will have some idea of what might be in the unknown powder.

The second test was the iodine test. Iodine bonds very well with starch. In fact, one of the statements in the **caution** on the iodine label says: "If accidentally swallowed, give starch." This is because the starch bonds with the iodine, making it more difficult for the iodine to harm you by bonding to other chemicals in your body. The dark blue color seen when iodine is added to starch is caused by the way light reflects off the new compound made up of the iodine and starch. The iodine test will help you figure out if starch is in the mystery powder.

In *Dissolve It and Solve It!*, you added water to the powders to compare them on the basis of how well each dissolved. The tendency of a substance to dissolve is called its **solubility**. The most common liquid in which substances dissolve is water. The interaction of the water molecules with the atoms and molecules of the substance determines if and how much of the substance will dissolve. Therefore, different substances will dissolve differently. You may have noticed that one or two substances dissolved almost completely while others appeared to dissolve very little. You can use this information to help you figure out what is in your unknown powder.

The evaporation test is the opposite of the dissolving test. Instead of seeing what happens when water is added to the different powders, you can observe what happens when the substances lose the water that was added. As water evaporates from some substances, they tend to appear similar to how they looked before they were dissolved. Other substances may look very different. The evaporation test may help you identify the mystery powder.

In the indicator test, the liquid made from grape juice and water is added to each of the six powders. When grape juice is added to certain substances, the mixture changes color. Materials like grape juice that change color when added to certain substances are called **indicators**. Different substances cause different color changes when mixed with grape juice. That's why grape juice may be able to help you figure out what your unknown substance might be.

The color drop test is not a standard chemical test but can be used to see differences between solutions made from your six powders. The test depends on how the drop of food coloring interacts with the solution in which it is dropped. Because the solutions are made from different substances, the drop tends to act differently in each one. That's why you may be able to use the drop test to help you figure out your unknown.

Dissolve It and Solve It!

Another test that scientists can do to help them identify a substance is to see how well it dissolves in water. Some substances dissolve very easily, others do not dissolve at all, and still others are somewhere in between. By slowly adding water to your powders, you may be able to tell one powder from another based on how well each dissolves.

DISSOLVING TEST

1 Use the masking tape and pen to label your plastic cups **salt, sugar, Epsom salts, baking soda, corn starch**, and **laundry detergent**. Place 2 teaspoons of each substance into its labeled cup.

2 Add 1 tablespoon of water to each cup. Swirl each cup for about 10 seconds, then go back to the first cup and swirl each one again for another 10 seconds.

3 Observe the cups carefully. Which powders appear to have dissolved the most? How about the least? Is there anything else about the solutions that you notice? Record your observations in the chart.

4 Add one more tablespoon of water to each cup. Swirl each cup for 10 seconds. Have any of the substances dissolved completely? Save your plastic cups with the solutions in them for use in the final two activities.

If you now had the 6 powders in front of you without labels, which powders do you think you could identify using the dissolving test and the notes from your observation chart? Explain.

EVAPORATION TEST

1 Get your plastic-covered testing chart from the first activity. Take the 6 solutions you made in step 4 above. Use a straw to place 2 or 3 drops of solution from each cup along the **evaporation** area of the testing chart.

2 Allow the drops to evaporate over night. The next day, observe what is left from each solution. Record what you observe in your observation chart.

Color Clues You Can Use!

Scientists may also identify a substance by testing it with another chemical and observing a color change. One type of chemical scientists often use to test substances is called an **indicator**. In the following activity, you can use grape juice as an indicator to help you tell the difference between your substances.

1 Add one teaspoon of concentrated grape juice to 1/4 cup of water.

This is your *indicator* solution; it will change color when added to certain substances.

This column is for the activity on page 72

2 Get your plastic-covered testing chart. Place about 1/8 teaspoon of each powder under its name along the indicator area of the testing chart. Use a straw to drip 2 or 3 drops of indicator on each powder. Observe the powders closely and record your observations.

If you now had the 6 powders in front of you without labels, which powders do you think you could identify using the indicator test and the notes from your observation chart? Explain.

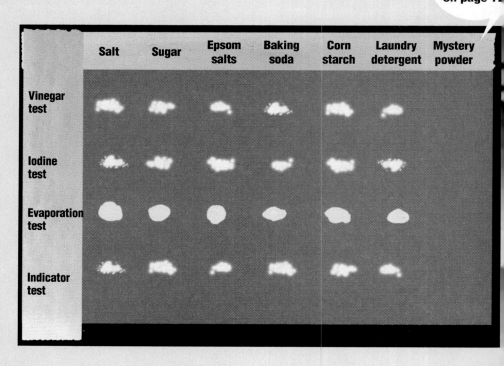

	Salt	Sugar	Epsom salts	Baking soda	Corn starch	Laundry detergent	Mystery powder
Vinegar test							
Iodine test							
Evaporation test							
Indicator test							

Drop a Hint

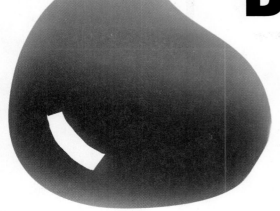

YOU WILL NEED:

solutions from previous activities

food coloring (not yellow)

white paper

You can also do the *"WonderScience color drop"* test to help you tell the difference between your solutions.

COLOR DROP TEST

1 Very carefully place one drop of food coloring in the center of each solution from the dissolving test.

2 Observe the drop very closely. Watch the way it spreads out on the surface of the solution.

3 Crouch down and look at the solution from the side to see beneath the surface. Does the colored drop stay on the surface or does it sink below? Does it sink quickly or slowly?

4 Repeat steps 1–3 for each of your solutions, and record the results in your chart.

If you now had the 6 solutions in front of you without labels, which do you think you could identify using the color drop test and the notes from your observation chart? Explain.

JIM WISNIEWSKI

Discover the Unknown!

YOU WILL NEED:

mystery substance from your teacher

all testing materials from previous activities (vinegar, iodine, water, straw, grape juice indicator, food coloring, spoons, cups)

Let's use all the information you have gathered so far to see if you can identify an unknown substance by doing the tests you have done throughout this *WonderScience* unit.

TEACHER NOTE:
See Teacher's Guide for instructions on making the mystery substance.

1 You and your partner should decide which tests and in what order to do them to find out what is in your mystery substance.

HINT 1: The mystery substance contains TWO of the powders you have been working with.

HINT 2: Because the mystery substance contains a combination of two powders, the test results may not look exactly the same as if you ran the tests on the individual powders.

HINT 3: Don't let hint 2 scare you. If you made good observations in the previous activities and make good observations now, you should be able to figure out which two powders make up the mystery substance.

GOOD LUCK!

In this unit, a scenario is presented in which students are introduced to a series of different chemical tests to solve a mystery. The scenario is intended to add interest and motivation for students in performing the tests. Each test involves a systematic approach to discovering an unknown substance that may lead to discovering which snack shop worker swiped the secret bing bong recipe. You will need to refer to this *Teacher's Guide* before setting up each activity to find out the identity of each mystery substance.

Solve a Powderful Mystery!

In this activity, students test four different known powders with four different test liquids. They also test a mystery powder with the same four liquids. By comparing how the mystery powder reacts with the four liquids, to the way each known powder reacted, students will be able to identify the mystery powder as one of the known powders. Be sure to explain to students that each known powder will give a different set of reactions when tested with the four liquids. Students should look down a column under the powder's name and then try to match up that set of reactions with the reactions of the mystery powder. You could use any of the known powders as the mystery powder, but we suggest baking powder.

A Colorful Caper

In "A Colorful Caper," students use a process called paper chromatography to separate the colors in the coatings of three different candies. They then compare the colors on their paper strips to the colors produced on a strip on which *you* have done chromatography of the mystery candy in advance. We recommend using a brown M&M as the mystery candy. You should do chromatography ahead of time on three or four brown M&Ms and post the resulting chromatography strips around the room so that students will have a sample to compare their own chromatography strips to. When they match one of their known strips to the mystery strip, they will know the identity of the mystery candy.

Soda Solutions

In this activity, students test three different known liquids and one mystery liquid. This time each known sample will produce a different color when added to some freshly made red cabbage juice indicator solution. When the mystery liquid is then tested with red cabbage indicator, its color will match one of the known liquids. Your mystery liquid can be any of the known liquids, but we suggest using Zinger. For the different liquids, use water, Sprite, and Zinger ($\frac{1}{2}$ Sprite and $\frac{1}{2}$ vinegar).

Going, Going, Gone!

In "Going, Going, Gone!," students check three known liquids for their evaporation rate from brown paper. They then check the evaporation rate of the mystery liquid. Students should be able to match the evaporation rate of the mystery liquid with one of the known liquids, thereby discovering the identity of the mystery liquid. You could use any of the liquids as the mystery liquid, but we suggest alcohol.

NOTES

NATIONAL SCIENCE EDUCATION STANDARDS

The activities in this unit can be used to support the teaching of the following standards:

✔ **Unifying Concepts and Processes**

Evidence, Models, and Explanation

Evidence consists of observations and data on which to base scientific explanations. *(All activities)*

✔ **Science as Inquiry**

Abilities Necessary to Do Scientific Inquiry

Design and conduct a scientific investigation. *(All activities)*

Think critically and logically to make the relationships between evidence and explanations. *(All activities)*

Recognize and analyze alternative explanations and predictions. *(All activities)*

✔ **Physical Science**

Properties and Changes of Properties in Matter

A substance has characteristic properties, all of which are independent of the amount of the sample. *(All activities)*

Substances react chemically in characteristic ways with other substances to form new substances (compounds) with different characteristic properties.

Solve a Powderful Mystery!
A Colorful Caper
Soda Solutions

STUDENT ACTIVITY SHEET

NAME _____   DATE _____

Solve a Powderful Mystery!

Testing Chart

	Baking soda	Baking powder	Corn starch	Cream of tartar	Mystery powder
Water					
Vinegar					
Iodine					
Red cabbage					

STUDENT ACTIVITY SHEET

NAME _____   DATE _____

Solve a Powderful Mystery!

Observation Chart

	Baking soda	Baking powder	Corn starch	Cream of tartar	Mystery powder
Water					
Vinegar					
Iodine					
Red cabbage					

Solve a Powderful

The local snack shop sells doughnuts, soda, candy, ice cream, and other yummy food. One day, around lunchtime, the secret recipe for the famous chocolate bing bongs was suddenly gone! Who could have taken it? Only three snack shop workers, Daniel, Jack, and Elliana, know that the recipe is hidden under the baking powder container. They are trusted workers, but now they are all suspects! Let's do some investigating to see which one, if any, committed this dastardly deed.

All three workers were at the snack shop the day the recipe disappeared, but only Daniel had white powder on his sleeve after lunch! If the powder turns out to be baking powder, Daniel may be our culprit! Let's check it out!

The powders used in the snack shop bakery are baking soda, cornstarch, cream of tartar, and baking powder. We can test these powders and see how they act when certain liquids are added to them. Then we can test the powder that was found on Daniel. Your teacher will give you a small sample of the mystery powder taken from Daniel's clothes.

Mystery!

YOU WILL NEED:

sheet of white paper

pen

wax paper

masking tape

baking soda

corn starch

baking powder

cream of tartar

tincture of iodine

water

vinegar

red cabbage

9 plastic cups

4 droppers

zip-closing plastic bag

TEACHER PREPARATION: Prepare the iodine solution by adding about 10 drops of tincture of iodine to 1 tablespoon of water. Prepare the red cabbage solution by tearing up 1 or 2 leaves of red cabbage. Place the pieces in a zip-closing plastic bag. Add about 1/2 cup warm water. Seal the bag and squish the cabbage for about 3–5 minutes until the water turns a medium to dark blue.

Label 5 plastic cups **baking soda**, **baking powder**, **corn starch**, **cream of tartar**, and **mystery powder**. Place about 1 tablespoon of each powder into its labeled cup. See Teacher's Guide for the identity of the mystery powder. Label another 4 cups **water**, **vinegar**, **iodine solution**, and **red cabbage**. Place about 2 teaspoons of each solution into its labeled cup.

1 Make two charts like the one shown or use the charts from the Student Activity Sheet. One is your Testing Chart, and the other is your Observation Chart. Tape a piece of wax paper over your testing chart as shown.

2 Place about a 1/8 teaspoon sample of each white powder under its name. You will have four samples of each powder under each name.

3 Use a separate dropper to place two or three drops of each liquid on each white powder in its row. Observe closely and write down your observations in the Observation Chart.

4 Based on your observations, what was the mystery powder found on Daniel's clothes? Do you think he could be the culprit? Why or why not?

	Baking soda	Baking powder	Corn starch	Cream of tartar	Mystery powder
Water					
Vinegar					
Iodine					
Red cabbage					

A Colorful Caper

YOU WILL NEED:

M&M® (brown)

Reeses Piece® (brown)

Skittles® (dark purple)

water

3 cotton swabs

clear plastic cups

pencil

coffee filter (white cone type)

scissors

Our investigators also noticed a brown candylike smudge on the baking powder container. This could be more evidence! Each suspect was seen eating candy that day during a lunch break. Daniel was eating Reeses Pieces; Jack was eating Skittles; and Elliana was eating M&Ms. Luckily, we saved the smudge by transferring it to some white strips of paper. Your teacher can give you the mystery smudge we saved and show you how to test it.

TEACHER PREPARATION:

See the Teacher's Guide for the identity of the mystery candy. With the mystery candy, follow steps 1–4 below to create one mystery candy-testing strip for each group.

1 Cut three strips from the coffee filter so that each is about as tall as your cup and about 3 centimeters (cm) wide. For each candy, use a pencil to write its name on a separate strip as shown.

2 In a small cup, add a little water. Dip a cotton swab in the water and gently wet one side of a candy.

3 Gently rub the candy's wet side onto its labeled filter strip about 2 cm from the end. This should make a dark dot on the paper.

4 Use a pencil or pen to make a small hole in the strip at the opposite end from the dot. Make the hole about 2 cm from the end. Slip your pencil through the hole and lay the pencil on the cup as shown.

5 Carefully pour water into the cup so that the water just reaches the bottom of the paper strip. Watch as the water soaks up into the strip. As the water moves up through the colored dot, what do you observe?

6 Repeat steps 2–5 for the other two candies. Compare the chromatography strips of the three known candies to the chromatography strip of the mystery candy supplied by your teacher. Based on your observations, who do you think left the mystery smudge on the baking soda container? Are you convinced that this person is the culprit? Why or why not?

Soda Solutions

YOU WILL NEED:

Sprite®

vinegar

red cabbage

water

zip-closing plastic
  bag

9 plastic cups

tablespoon

4 droppers

We also found an empty cup that had been knocked over near the recipe hiding spot. There was a little spilled liquid near the edge of the cup. Daniel likes water, Jack likes Sprite, and Elliana likes Zinger. If we can figure out what the spilled liquid is, maybe we can use it as evidence against one of our suspects! You can do a chemical test to help figure out what the spilled liquid might be. Your teacher will give you a sample of the mystery liquid found at the crime scene.

TEACHER PREPARATION: Label four plastic cups **water**, **Sprite**, **Zinger**, and **mystery liquid**. See the Teacher's Guide for ingredients of liquids and of the identity of the mystery liquid sample. Place about 1 tablespoon of each liquid in its labeled cup. Give a set of cups to each group.

STUDENT ACTIVITY:

1 Prepare the red cabbage solution by tearing up one or two leaves of red cabbage.

Place the pieces in a zip-closing plastic bag. Add about 1/2 cup warm water. Seal the bag and squish the cabbage for about 3–5 minutes until the water turns a medium to dark blue.

2 Label five plastic cups **control**, **water**, **Sprite**, **Zinger**, and **mystery liquid**. Divide the blue solution evenly between these five cups.

3 Place three drops of each liquid in its labeled cup of blue test solution. Do not put anything in the cup labeled **control**. You will use the color in the control cup to compare with the colors in the other cups.

4 Swirl the solutions to mix. Did you notice any change in color in any of the cups? Based on your observations, what is the mystery liquid spilled at the crime scene? Does this evidence prove who committed the crime? Why or why not?

Going, Going, Gone!

YOU WILL NEED:
mineral oil
water
alcohol
4 small cups
4 cotton swabs
brown paper
    from paper bag

During our investigation, we noticed a few drops of clear liquid on the floor of the snack shop kitchen. If it turns out to be oil, the culprit might be Daniel since he carries an oil can to oil the machinery. But Jack was using water to clean some equipment so if it is water, Jack may be the recipe thief. But then again, Elliana was putting a little alcohol on a scratch on her elbow that same day, so maybe the liquid is alcohol, and Elliana grabbed the recipe. We saved a sample of the mystery liquid so we could test it. Your teacher will give you a sample.

TEACHER PREPARATION:
Label four cups **oil**, **water**, **alcohol**, and **mystery liquid**. Place about 1/2 teaspoon of each liquid into its labeled cup. See the Teacher's Guide for the identity of the mystery liquid.

1 Use a pencil or pen to divide the brown paper into four areas as shown. Label the areas **oil**, **water**, **alcohol**, and **mystery liquid**.

2 Dip a cotton swab into the oil and swipe it across its area on the brown paper.

3 Dip a separate cotton swab into each liquid and swipe each one across its area of the brown paper.

4 Observe the streaks on the paper. Different liquids are absorbed into paper differently. Also, each liquid evaporates at a different rate. Based on your observations, who do you think dripped the liquid found on the kitchen floor? Do you think this was the worker who nabbed the recipe?

No one swiped the secret bing bong recipe.
The workers borrowed it together to make a yummy chocolate birthday bing bong for their boss, Jane!

Plastic, rubber, cellulose (which makes up plant roots, stems, and leaves), proteins, DNA, and synthetic fibers such as polyesters are all polymers. A polymer is a long chain of repeating molecules. The characteristics of the polymer depend upon the molecules of which it is composed, how they are bonded to each other, and the length of the chain. This unit focuses on the observable characteristics of a few different polymers but does not try to explain these characteristics on the molecular level. As usual, most activities concentrate on the process of experimenting with materials to learn about their properties.

Plastic Insert:

For a class set of special plastic film, call 1-800-227-5558, extension 4600.

A Plastic Film Festival!

You could begin the activity by asking students to name some of the qualities of the very familiar plastic film used in plastic grocery bags, sandwich bags, and plastic wrap. You could hand out samples of the three types of plastic and see if students can come up with their own tests to compare the plastics. We suggest six different tests in the activity, but students may think of others. As students perform the different tests, be sure that they record their observations accurately and completely so they can report them to the rest of the class.

The activity makes use of a special piece of plastic called polyvinyl alcohol. The plastic has some interesting characteristics when compared to the other plastics in the first five tests, but its uniqueness is revealed in the last test using water. When polyvinyl alcohol is placed in water, it will dissolve. Ask students for possible uses of a thin film that dissolves in water. Some of its uses are discussed on the page after the activity.

Goop to Go!

In "Goop to Go!," students make two different polymers. One is made of glue, water, and laundry detergent; the other is made from glue and liquid starch. The laundry detergent that we used was Tide without added bleach. The kind with bleach might work, but we did not try it. You might want to try different laundry detergents to see if any others work better. For the other polymer, we used liquid starch in a plastic bottle with a screw-on squeeze-trigger sprayer top. You can simply unscrew the

sprayer top and pour out the starch solution into cups for students. Do not attempt to use liquid starch in aerosol cans—it will not work. If you cannot find liquid starch, simply make the first polymer from glue, water, and laundry detergent and allow students to vary the concentrations of the ingredients to see if they can make polymers with different characteristics.

Diapers—The Inside Story

You can ask students to guess what makes disposable diapers so absorbent. You could take a disposable diaper, unfold it, and place it in water. When it is full, take it out and pass it around the room. Students will be amazed at how heavy it is and at how much water it must have absorbed.

When students are getting the sodium polyacrylate powder out of the diapers, it may at first seem difficult to separate the powder from the cotton material simply by shaking. After shaking for a while, students should tilt the bag so that the powder moves to one lower corner. Then each student should reach into the bag and move the other diaper material away from the powder, keeping everything in the bag. The bag should then be resealed and grasped in the middle, keeping the other diaper material separate from the sodium polyacrylate powder. Students should then shake the bag some more, and the powder should fall down into the lower part of the bag.

In the first part of the experiment, it should only take 4 to 6 drops to reach the cup edge on the paper towel with no sodium polyacrylate. On the paper towel that *does* have the powder, it should take more than 100 drops. The volume of the powder should increase as it absorbs water and becomes a gel.

Sodium polyacrylate is sold at gardening stores as a medium for growing plants. It holds a lot of water and then releases it gradually to the plant roots.

Poke but Don't Soak

You could fill a plastic bag with water and hold a sharpened pencil up and ask students what they think will happen if you push the pencil into and then through the bag. After getting their answers, you could hold up an inflated balloon and a long wooden skewer and ask the same question.

When students push the pencil through the bag, very little if any water should leak out. This is due to the flexibility and water-proof qualities of the plastic. The plastic molds around and squeezes against the pencil, making a water-resistant seal. After students have done this activity, you could demonstrate a similar phenomenon with an inflated balloon. Carefully poke through the thick, unexpanded rubber near the knot of the balloon. Twist the skewer as you move it through the balloon and then poke the skewer through the thickest part at the other end of the balloon.

Polymers

NATIONAL SCIENCE EDUCATION STANDARDS

The activities in this unit can be used to support the teaching of the following standards:

✔ **Unifying Concepts and Processes**

Evidence, Models, and Explanation
Evidence consists of observations and data on which to base scientific explanations.
   (All activities)

Form and Function
The form or shape of an object or system is frequently related to its use, operation, or function. *(All activities)*

✔ **Science as Inquiry**

Abilities Necessary to Do Scientific Inquiry
Design and conduct a scientific investigation. *(All activities)*
Develop descriptions, explanations, predictions, and models using evidence.
   Goop to Go!
Think critically and logically to make the relationships between evidence and explanations.
   Diapers—The Inside Story
   Poke but Don't Soak

✔ **Physical Science**

Properties and Changes of Properties in Matter
A substance has characteristic properties, all of which are independent of the amount of the sample. *(All activities)*
Substances react chemically in characteristic ways with other substances to form new substances (compounds) with different characteristic properties.
   Goop to Go!

✔ **Science in Personal and Social Perspectives**

Science and Technology in Society
Technology influences society through its products and processes.
   Pondering Polymers

STUDENT ACTIVITY SHEET

NAME _____   **DATE** _____

A Plastic Film Festival!

Use the chart below to record your observations.

	Crumple/ Wrinkle test	Stretch test	See-through test	Stick-to-itself test	Tear test	Water test
Plastic wrap						
Shopping bag						
Film insert						

NAME _____ **DATE** _____

Goop to Go!

Use the chart to record your observations for the three different polymers that you made.

	Observations
Polymer I	
Polymer II	
Polymer III	

Diapers—The Inside Story

1. On the paper towel *without* the diaper granules (sodium polyacrylate), how many drops of colored water did it take for the water to travel to the edge of the cup? _____

2. On the paper towel *with* the diaper granules (sodium polyacrylate), how many drops of colored water did it take for the water to travel to the edge of the cup? _____

3. How does the sodium polyacrylate look as water is added to it?

_____

_____

4. What do you think the sodium polyacrylate is doing to the water as water is added to it?

_____

_____

5. In step 10, how many teaspoons of water did your last cup of sodium polyacrylate soak up? _____

6. Now that you see what sodium polyacrylate can do, can you think of any other uses for it, aside from its use in diapers?

_____

_____

YOU WILL NEED:

plastic wrap

plastic shopping bag

plastic film insert (See Teacher's Guide)

scissors

3 cups (plastic or paper)

water

paper towel

A Plastic Film Festival!

Polymers are chemicals that make up lots of common and very useful materials. One important material made from polymers is plastic. One of the great things about plastic is that it can be molded into almost any shape. In this activity, you can test different plastics that have been molded into very thin films. Be prepared for some surprises!

Make a large chart like the one shown or use the one from the Student Activity Sheet. You will use the chart to record your observations about the plastics for each test.

TEACHER PREPARATION

Cut each type of plastic into pieces that are about 8 cm × 10 cm. Each group should get 1 piece of each type of plastic.

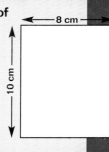

CRUMPLE/WRINKLE TEST

Crumple each piece of plastic into a ball as small as you can make it. Let the pieces uncrumple. Record your observations for each plastic.

STRETCH TEST

While holding the plastic firmly, pull it until it stretches. Try to stretch it without tearing it. Now hold it in a different place, and pull in a different direction until it stretches. Record your observations.

SEE-THROUGH TEST

Hold each piece up and look through it toward a light in the room. How well were you able to see through it? Record your observations. Put each piece down on a page from a book or magazine. How well were you able to see through it? Record your observations.

STICK-TO-ITSELF TEST

Fold the piece of plastic over on itself and rub the two halves together. Did you notice any difference between the way the different plastics stuck to themselves? Record your observations.

TEAR TEST

At this point, your pieces of plastic are a little beaten-up, but you can still do the tear test on them. Use your thumb and index finger from both hands to tightly grasp the edge of the plastic as shown. Tear each plastic and compare what you notice about each one. Record your observations.

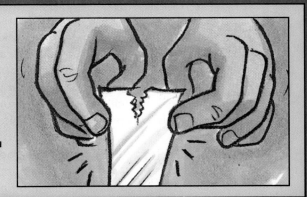

WATER TEST

Place a paper towel on your work surface. Fill three cups about half-full with water. Dip each piece of plastic into its own cup so that the plastic goes under the water. Take the pieces out and put them on the paper towel. What do you notice about how the water and the plastic look? Record your observations.

	Crumple/ Wrinkle test	Stretch test	See-through test	Stick-to-itself test	Tear test	Water test
Plastic wrap						
Shopping bag						
Film insert						

Pondering Polymers

A polymer is a very long chemical made up of repeating little chemical units all hooked together in a very long chain. Polymers are found almost everywhere in nature. Some natural polymers are the **proteins** that make up hair, feathers, fur, cartilage, beaks, nails, and horns. Another natural polymer, called **cellulose**, makes up wood, leaves, and other plant parts. Cotton, starch, silk, and rubber (from rubber trees) are also made of natural polymers.

There are also polymers made in factories, or **synthetic** polymers. The most common synthetic polymer is plastic. The great thing about plastics is that they are lightweight, can be rigid or flexible, can be molded into almost any shape, and can last a very long time. This quality is a problem when it comes to the disposal of plastics. Because they do not break down in nature, plastics take up a lot of room in landfills. But these days, plastics are being recycled more and more to save our resources and to reduce the amount of plastic in landfills.

In "A Plastic Film Festival," you saw that the different plastic films had different characteristics. The plastic included in your *Wonder-Science* is made of a polymer called **polyvinyl alcohol**. This plastic film is very unusual because it dissolves in water. Dissolving plastic film is used to package substances in exact amounts to be dissolved in water. The entire packet can simply be placed in the right amount of water and be mixed up and ready to go! The plastic is also used to make hospital laundry bags. Laundry is placed in the bag, which is then sealed and thrown right in the washing machine, bag and all!

In "Goop To Go," you used Elmer's® glue and laundry detergent to make a polymer. Elmer's glue has its own polymer already in it called **polyvinyl acetate**. Like other polymers, polyvinyl acetate is a long chain. These strands of polyvinyl acetate slide past each other as the glue flows. A chemical in Tide® is able to connect the strands together, forming a polymer with different characteristics. This new polymer will be soft or stiff based on the amounts of glue, water, and laundry detergent you use. In the glue and liquid starch polymer, a chemical in the starch solution binds the polyvinyl acetate molecules together.

In "Diapers—The Inside Story," you looked at a polymer made up of granules found inside disposable diapers. This polymer is called **sodium polyacrylate**. This is called a super-absorbent polymer because it can absorb hundreds of times its weight in water. After water is absorbed, the polymer changes from a powder to a gel. Exactly how the water gets absorbed by this polymer to create a gel is not completely understood. One thing we know is that salt will cause the gel to become a liquid. Try sprinkling a little salt on the gel and stirring to see what happens.

In the last activity, you should be able to poke a pencil all the way through a plastic bag of water and cause no leaks. Can you think of how the long, flexible chains of polymers in the plastic bag might work to allow you to do this?

Dissolving plastic is provided by Chris Craft Industrial Products.

ILLUSTRATION BY STEVE MCENTEE

Goop to Go!

YOU WILL NEED:

Elmer's® glue

Tide® powdered laundry detergent

liquid starch (not aerosol can)

paper towels

measuring spoons

water

small plastic cups

straws or spoons for stirring

In "A Plastic Film Festival," you made a solid polymer dissolve using a liquid (water). In this activity, you can combine two liquids to create a polymer that is more solid!

POLYMER I

1 Make a chart like the one shown or use the chart in the Student Activity Sheet. Place 1 teaspoon of Elmer's glue and 1 teaspoon of water into a small cup. Stir to mix.

2 Place 1 teaspoon of Tide powdered laundry detergent into a different small cup. Add 1 tablespoon of water. Stir to mix.

3 While stirring the glue–water solution with a straw, your partner should slowly add the Tide–water solution until a white glob forms in the cup. (This may take between half and all of the detergent solution.)

4 Remove the glob and place it on a paper towel. Cover it with another paper towel and press down gently to soak up some of the excess liquid. Pick up the glob and see what it feels like. Does it stretch, wiggle, or bounce? Can it be molded? Record your observations.

	Observations
Polymer I	
Polymer II	
Polymer III	

POLYMER II

1 Place 1 teaspoon of Elmer's glue into a small cup.

2 While stirring with a straw, your partner should slowly add liquid starch until a white glob forms in the cup. (This will probably take between 2 and 3 tablespoons of liquid starch.)

3 Remove the glob and place it on a paper towel. What do you notice about this polymer compared to the first one you made? Take it off the paper towel and move it between your hands. Record your observations.

POLYMER III

The third polymer you make is up to you! Using Elmer's glue, Tide detergent, water, and liquid starch, see if you can come up with a combination that makes a polymer that has characteristics somewhere between Polymer I and Polymer II. Good Luck!

Wash hands after handling materials.

Diapers—

Polymers come in many different forms. In "A Plastic Film Festival," you used a polymer that was made into thin flat film. In "Goop To Go!" you used liquids and came up with a thick putty kind of polymer. These different polymers had different characteristics.

In the following activity, you will use a polymer that is in a powdered form. It has some special characteristics of its own! Let's investigate them.

1 Use a pair of scissors to cut off the paper or plastic edge around the entire diaper. Place the remaining padded middle part of the diaper into the zip-closing plastic bag.

2 Reach into the bag with both hands and separate the cotton, paper, and plastic layers of the diaper. Leave all material in the bag. Seal the bag and shake it for about 1 minute. Look at the bottom of the bag as you tilt it to one side. You should notice white granules collecting in the corner of the bag.

3 Now, without opening the bag, move the cotton, plastic, or other large pieces of material toward the top of the bag. Keep the material up there as you shake the bag again. This will allow the granules to fall down to the bottom without getting picked up by the cotton again.

4 After you have about 1/2 teaspoon of granules in the corner of the bag, slowly open the bag and remove the large pieces of material. Throw them away. Now, carefully pour the granules into a small cup. Wash your hands.

5 Take two empty cups. Cut a paper towel into two pieces that will fit over your cups as shown. Hold the paper towel pieces down over the cups with a rubber band around the rim of each cup.

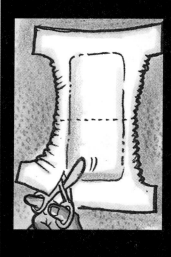

The Inside Story

6 Place a small amount (about 1/8 teaspoon) of the white granules onto the center of one of the paper towels.

7 Place about 1/4 cup of water into a small cup. Add one drop of food coloring and swirl to mix.

8 Add one drop of the colored water to the center of the paper towel on one cup and one drop to the granules on the other cup. Continue to go back and forth, adding one drop to the paper towel on one cup, and then one drop to the granules on the other.

What do you observe? Which towel is getting wetter? What do the granules appear to be doing? How many drops can you add to the granules before the water spreads to the rim of the cup?

9 Take the rest of your granules and divide them as evenly as you can among three clear plastic cups. Add 1 tablespoon of water to one cup and swirl to mix. Allow the cup to sit still. Watch what happens. What do you observe?

10 Do you think the granules will absorb 2 tablespoons of water? Try it in your next cup and see. How much more do you think it can absorb? Use your last cup to find out!

Poke But Don't Soak

The flexibility of plastic makes it useful for many different purposes.

1 Fill the plastic bag about 3/4 full of water. Seal the bag. Hold the bag over a sink or bucket or over the ground outside.

2 While you hold the bag, your partner should slowly push the point of the pencil through one side of the plastic bag and into the water. Did any water spill? Don't take the pencil out.

3 Why do you think very little or no water spills? Look closely at the plastic bag surrounding the pencil. How would you describe the way the plastic bag fits around the pencil?

4 Do you think the pencil can go all the way through the water and out the other side of the bag with no water spilling? Ask your partner to slowly push the pencil all the way through the other side of the bag. What happened? Is there anything about long thin polymers that might help explain why the pencil can do this?

ILLUSTRATIONS BY JIM WISNIEWSKI/STEVE EDSEY & SONS UNLESS OTHERWISE INDICATED

96

In this unit, the characteristics of three different types of paper are explored through various simple tests. For many students, this will be the first time they have ever thought seriously about paper, which we all tend to take for granted as part of our everyday life. As is the case with most activities in *The Best of WonderScience*, the experimental process is emphasized rather than the expected outcomes. Students should see that they can learn a lot about the properties of paper by testing the different samples each in the same way. This "scientific" approach to learning about paper can hopefully be carried over and applied to learning about the characteristics of other materials and substances in future science activities.

Tear . . . and Compare!

You could start this activity by asking students if they have any idea what paper is made from. After discovering that it is made from trees, ask students how they think the trees might get processed to eventually become something so different-looking as paper. You could then introduce the "Tear . . . and Compare!" activity as a way of looking closely at the characteristics of paper, which could lead to ideas about how paper is made.

For each type of paper, the tear should be straighter and cleaner when torn down the length as opposed to across the width. This is true because the majority of the fibers that make up the paper are oriented lengthwise as a by-product of the paper manufacturing process. Also, the ends of the fibers are frayed and intertwined in a lengthwise direction. This makes tearing *along* the fibers cleaner than tearing *across* them.

In the pull test, the opposite is true. It is harder to pull the paper until it snaps in the lengthwise orientation than it is to pull it until it snaps across the width. This is because it is more difficult to break the fibers themselves and their intertwined connections than to separate them from each other when they are side by side widthwise.

The Path to Paper

This is a ten-step explanation of the paper-making process. Step 7 is where the liquid paper slurry flows onto a moving wire screen. The screen moves at about 60 miles per hour. Because the slurry is over 90% water, the movement of the screen tends to orient the fibers in the slurry in the direction of movement of the screen. This fiber orientation helps account for some of the phenomena students observe in "Tear . . . and Compare!" and "Flex Finder."

Flex Finder

You might want to ask students if the flexibility of a type of paper might have anything to do with the purpose of the paper. Ask students to think about the uses of paper towels, newspaper, and notebook paper. Is there anything about the intended use of these papers that might cause them to be designed with different amounts of stiffness or flexibility? After getting answers from students, introduce the activity as a way to compare the flexibility of the different papers, using numbers.

Our results showed that the paper towel was the most flexible, notebook paper was the least flexible, and newspaper was in the middle.

In all cases, the strip cut from the width was more flexible than that cut from the length. This result is consistent with the results from "Tear . . . and Compare!"

Soak It Up!

Absorbency is an important characteristic of different types of paper. You could start by asking students which paper is probably the most absorbent and which is the least. Ask them how the absorbency matches the purpose of the paper. You might also want to ask students how they think paper manufacturers make one paper absorbent and another not. (Absorbent papers have fibers that are more loosely spaced and are not coated.)

Our results showed the paper towel to be most absorbent and notebook paper the least, with newspaper in between.

Unit 9
Parade of Paper

Seeing Is Believing!

The extent to which you can see through a paper affects the way it is used. When you are reading or looking at pictures, it can be very distracting to see words or pictures from the other side of the page. Ask students which papers should guard against this the most.

Our results showed that when held up to the light, the paper towel was most transparent, the notebook paper was the least, and the newspaper was in between.

When placed on printing, our results showed that the notebook paper and paper towel were easiest to read through. The newspaper was more opaque.

The Art of Recycling

This is a fun activity where students can be creative in making paper and become introduced to a very rudimentary model of the paper-making process.

Parade of Paper

NATIONAL SCIENCE EDUCATION STANDARDS

The activities in this unit can be used to support the teaching of the following standards:

✔ **Unifying Concepts and Processes**

Evidence, Models, and Explanation
Evidence consists of observations and data on which to base scientific explanations.
(All activities)

✔ **Science as Inquiry**

Abilities Necessary to Do Scientific Inquiry
Design and conduct a scientific investigation. *(All activities)*
Think critically and logically to make the relationships between evidence and explanations.
  Tear . . . and Compare!
  Flex Finder

✔ **Physical Science**

Properties and Changes of Properties in Matter
A substance has characteristic properties, all of which are independent of the amount of the sample. *(All activities)*

✔ **Science in Personal and Social Perspectives**

Science and Technology in Society
Technology influences society through its products and processes.
  The Path to Paper

STUDENT ACTIVITY SHEET

NAME ______________________________ **DATE** __________

Tear . . . and Compare!

TEAR TEST: Use the chart below to record your observations for the tear test.

	Length	Width
Newspaper		
Notebook paper		
Paper towel		

1. Look very closely at the torn edge of the papers. What do you see sticking out along the torn edge? ________________

2. What might these little fibers have to do with the way the papers tear differently down the length and across the width?

____

____

____

PULL TEST: Use the chart below to record your observations for the pull test.

	Length	Width
Newspaper		
Notebook paper		
Paper towel		

3. How do you think the arrangement of fibers in the papers might explain why the papers are easier to pull apart in one direction than another?

____

____

____

STUDENT ACTIVITY SHEET

NAME ______________________________ **DATE** __________

Flex Finder

In this activity, you can compare the flexibility of three different kinds of paper. You will be comparing the flexibility of papers cut along the length and those same papers cut across the width.

After doing steps 1 and 2, look at the example that describes how to use a protractor to measure the angle of bend for the paper samples. Now use the chart below to record your observations for steps 3–6:

	Angle of bend (L)	Angle of bend (W)
Newspaper		
Notebook Paper		
Paper Towel		

1. Do your observations seem to make sense with what you discovered in the first activity, "Tear . . . and Compare!"? Why or why not?

____

____

____

2. In what way do you think the flexibilities of these papers match the different ways they are used?

____

____

____

Tear...

There is a lot more to paper than people usually realize. Let's do a quick investigation of three common kinds of paper to begin to learn more about this very useful stuff.

YOU WILL NEED:
1/4 sheet newspaper
notebook paper
paper towel
metric ruler
scissors
magnifying glass

TEACHER PREPARATION: Each student should have one piece of newspaper, notebook paper, and a paper towel.

TEAR TEST

1 Make a chart like the one shown, or use the chart from the Student Activity Sheet. Using scissors, cut each piece of paper in half lengthwise. Label one half "**length**" and the other half "**width**."

2 Tear the piece marked "length" down the length of the paper and tear the piece marked "width" across the width. What difference did you notice between the way the papers tore? Record your observations in the chart.

3 Repeat the tear test with the other two types of paper. Did you notice any difference in the way these papers tore when you tore them down the length and across the width? What do you think might cause this difference?

You can get an idea of what might be going on here by looking more closely at each type of paper to see what paper is made of.

4 Look very closely at the torn edge of the papers. Use a magnifying glass if you have one. What do you see sticking out along these torn edges? Record what you see.

Could these have anything to do with why the paper tears differently down the length than it does across the width? Let's investigate these papers a little more.

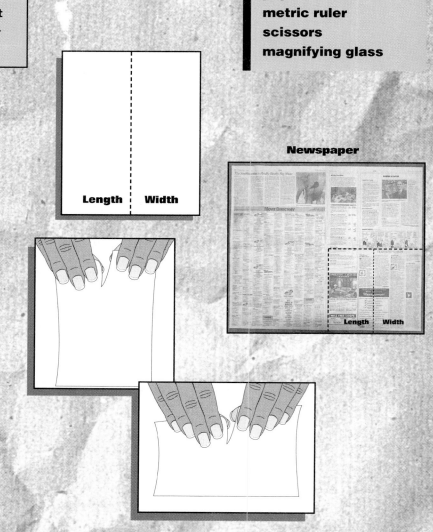

Newspaper

	Length	Width
Newspaper		
Notebook paper		
Paper towel		

and Compare!

PULL TEST

5 Use your scissors to cut two strips from each type of paper. Each strip should be 1 cm wide and 15 cm long. Cut one strip along the length of the paper and mark it "**L**." Cut the other strip along the width of the paper and label it "**W**."

6 Firmly hold the "L" strip from one kind of paper at the top and bottom. Begin to pull the paper to try to break the strip. Pull harder and harder until the paper snaps.

7 Now use the "W" strip from the same kind of paper. Pull the paper until it snaps. Did you notice any difference between how hard it was to break the "L" strip compared to the "W" strip? Record your observations.

8 Repeat steps 6 and 7 for the other two kinds of paper. Did you notice any difference between how hard it was to break the "L" strip compared to the "W" strip for these papers?

Since you saw that paper is made of many tiny fibers, how might this help explain the results of the tear test and the pull test?

Length   **Width**

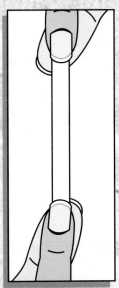

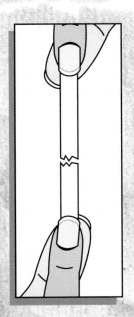

	Length	Width
Newspaper		
Notebook paper		
Paper towel		

103

The Path to Paper

Newspapers, magazines, books, paper towels, tissues, toilet paper, napkins, paper bags, wrapping paper, art paper, packaging, and money are all made of paper. Photocopying machines and computer printers also use huge amounts of paper. Where does all this paper come from and how is it made? Below is the basic manufacturing process for making paper:

1 Paper starts with wood. Logs from trees are put into a machine that strips off the bark.

2 The debarked wood is then placed in a machine that breaks the wood up into small wood chips.

3 The wood chips are placed under pressure in a heated vat with chemicals to soften the wood and to begin to separate the fibers that make up the wood. This is done by breaking down a natural glue called **lignin**, which helps hold the fibers together.

4 The wood is then shredded some more and rinsed, bleached, and pressed to get rid of the excess chemicals. The wood is now **pulp**.

5 The pulp is beaten to flatten out the fibers and to split the fiber ends so they can join together better in the paper-making process.

6 The pulp is mixed with water in big tanks where a substance called **sizing** is added. Sizing helps the tiny fibers connect to each other during the rest of the paper-making process.

7 When the pulp is mixed with the right amount of water, sizing, and other chemicals, it is called **slurry**. The slurry is then fed onto a quickly moving wire screen. As the slurry is laid down on the moving screen, the fibers tend to arrange themselves lengthwise onto the screen.

8 The slurry on the screen is then pressed between felt presses to flatten the new paper and to get rid of more water.

9 The paper then moves to big drying rollers where almost all the water is removed.

10 The paper is then pressed between polished rollers where it is finally smoothed, dried, and ready to be sold.

In some paper-making plants, the time it takes for the slurry to be poured on the moving screen to the time the paper is rolled and ready to be shipped is less than one minute!

Flex Finder

The flexibility of paper is often important in how the paper will be used. In the following activity, a protractor can be used as a paper flex finder!

1 From each piece of paper, cut two strips. The strips should be 15 cm long and 5 cm wide. Cut one strip along the length of the paper and the other along the width as shown. Mark the one cut along the length "**L**" and the one cut along the width "**W**."

2 Tape each "L" strip to the table. Make sure that only 1 cm of each piece is taped to the table. The amount of bend in the paper gives you an idea of how stiff or flexible the paper is. Which paper is the most stiff? Which is the most flexible?

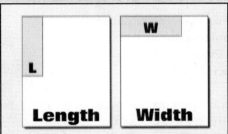

Length   Width

Here's an example of how you could measure the amount of bend in the paper by using a protractor. Hold the protractor against the table as shown. If any paper was completely stiff, it would cross the protractor at the 90° mark. The example here crosses at 70°. Therefore, the paper is bending at an angle of about 90–70, or 20°.

3 Make a chart like the one below, or use the chart from the Student Activity Sheet. Measure the angle of bend of each "L" strip with the protractor. Record the angles in the chart.

4 You have already seen that there are some differences between the way paper acts along its length compared to across its width. What do you think will happen when you tape the "W" strips to the table? Do you think they will bend more, less, or the same as the "L" strips? Why?

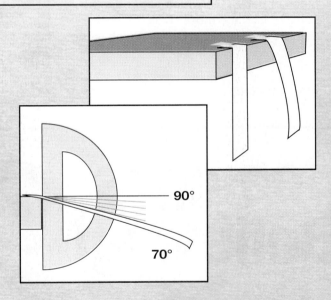

5 Tape the "W" strip next to the "L" strip of the same type of paper. Make sure only 1 cm of each strip is taped to the table.

6 Use your protractor to measure the angle of bend of the "W" strips, and record them in the chart. Do your observations tell you anything about the way the fibers might be arranged in the different papers?

	Angle of bend (L)	Angle of bend (W)
Newspaper		
Notebook paper		
Paper towel		

Soak It Up!

Some papers are made to soak up water well. These papers are **absorbent**. For others, it's better if they don't soak up much water. How easy it is to see through paper is another quality that is important for different papers. Investigate both in the activities below!

ABSORBENCY

1 Cut a strip from each type of paper. Each strip should be about 10 cm long × 5 cm wide. Place them on a sheet of wax paper.

2 Carefully squeeze one drop of food coloring onto the center of each piece of paper. On which paper did the color spread the most? Do you think this is the most absorbent? Which is the least?

Seeing Is Believing!

1 Hold your three papers up to the light. Which one lets the most light through? How about the least?

2 Place your three papers on a printed page. Can you read through all three? Which is the easiest to read through? Which is the most difficult?

3 Was the one that let the most light through also the one that was easiest to read through?

The Art of Recycling

You can use the paper we have been testing to make your own special recycled paper. By adding color, glitter, colored confetti, cut-up thread, or even dried flower petals, you can make your own recycled paper art! Let's try it and see what you can create!

1 Students should work in pairs. Each pair of students should tear up one sheet of notebook paper, one paper towel, and 1/4 sheet of newspaper into pieces about 2 cm × 2 cm.

2 Place all of the paper pieces in one cup of water. Push the pieces down into the water and stir them so they become well soaked. Put your and your partner's names on the cup and give it to your teacher.

TEACHER INSTRUCTIONS: Place the water and paper mixture in the blender and blend until smooth. This water and paper blend is called a **slurry**. Place each group's slurry back into the cup.

DO NOT ALLOW STUDENTS TO USE THE BLENDER.

3 Place several layers of newspaper on your work area. Lay a paper towel down on the newspaper. Now place one piece of screen on the paper towel. Add some colorful ingredients to your slurry and stir to mix well. Pour the slurry onto the center of the screen.

4 Lay the other piece of screen on top of the slurry. Use a sponge to flatten down the slurry and to absorb some of the water. Turn the screens over, and use the sponge on the other side in the same way.

5 Using a rolling pin, slowly flatten out the slurry in all directions. Turn the screens over and use the rolling pin on the other side.

6 Place a paper towel on top and use the rolling pin again to flatten the paper and to soak up more water. Turn the screens over and repeat.

7 Pull the screens apart and carefully peel the paper from the screen and allow it to dry overnight on a piece of paper towel.

YOU WILL NEED:

BASIC RECYCLED PAPER:

newspaper

notebook paper

paper towels

measuring cup

water

blender or food processor
(for use by teacher)

2 pieces of screen (about 30 cm × 30 cm)

sponge

rolling pin

ADDITIVES:

food coloring
glitter
crayon shavings
colored thread
confetti
dried flower petals
colored tissue paper

Look at this page and see how many examples of paper you can find.

ILLUSTRATIONS BY
JIM WISNIEWSKI/STEVE EDSEY & SONS
UNLESS OTHERWISE INDICATED

Materials: Test for the Best!

Wood, stone, ceramics, metal, glass, textiles, and plastic are all materials we see or use every day. Scientists have also been able to produce many different combinations of these materials or totally different materials for a wide variety of uses. The basic principles behind making and using any material are the same: both the nature of the material itself and how it is shaped determine its usefulness for a particular purpose. In this unit, students begin to investigate these two major principles of materials with the goal of using materials they create and test to build a bridge.

Get the Scoop on Goop!

You could ask students if they have ever thought about why certain materials are chosen for certain uses. Why is wood a good building material? Why not use it for skyscrapers? Why are containers for liquid often made of plastic instead of glass? The activities are intended to get students thinking about the characteristics of materials and their usefulness.

"Get the Scoop on Goop" is designed for students to work in six groups to make three different materials per group. The eighteen final materials are placed on one large class chart, and tests are conducted on each sample with all the students looking on. Another approach would be to modify the activity so that each group makes and tests all eighteen different materials. This requires more materials and greater coordinated distribution, but students get more direct experience making and testing a variety of materials. Students should wash hands after this activity.

Test for the Best!

As students test the materials, you should emphasize that a particular test should be done as much as possible in exactly the same way for each material tested. Actual material testing equipment is designed to do the test in exactly the same way every time. This gives a more accurate idea of the characteristics of each material for the purposes of comparing the materials. Ask students whether it is possible to perform the tests in the activity the same way for every material. Can they think of ways to be sure that the same test is done as much as possible in the same way every time? Also, be sure to remind students that they will be using this material to build a bridge. You could begin taking suggestions of how the different materials might be used for this purpose.

Pasta Power!

Spaghetti is used as a model for a building material that is long and thin, such as a beam or board. The activity shows, in a quantitative way, that short things are hard to bend and long things are easier to bend. A 10-cm length of spaghetti should break much more easily than a 2-cm length. After students fill in the chart, they can make a graph of their results. Given the results of the test, you could ask students how the spaghetti might be used as a bridge-building material.

Results:

(Many other possibilities exist, but they should have the same general trend.)

Number of cm off table	10	8	6	4	2
Number of pennies before it breaks	10	11	16	21	42

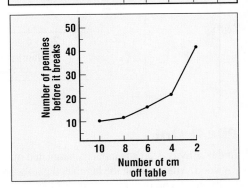

Unit 10
Materials: Test for the Best!

Strength in Numbers?

In the previous activity, students investigated whether the length of a piece of spaghetti affects its strength. In this activity, students investigate whether the number of pieces of spaghetti affects strength. Therefore, the length is kept constant as different numbers of spaghetti strands are tested. After students fill in the chart, they could make a graph of their results. You could ask students how they would use the information from their tests on number and length of spaghetti to make a decision about how to use spaghetti in bridge construction.

Results:

(Many other possibilities exist, but they should have the same general trend.)

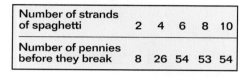

Number of strands of spaghetti	2	4	6	8	10
Number of pennies before they break	8	26	54	53	54

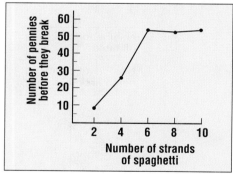

Pile It On!

In this activity, students model a laminated material such as plywood. After making the laminated planks and allowing them to dry overnight, they may warp, even if you temporarily put a book on them to flatten them out. If the planks warp while drying, place the book on them to straighten them out.

After conducting the activity, students will see that the more layers used to make a laminated board, the more weight it can support. After running the tests and recording the data, students can graph their results. You might also ask students

to place each board on edge between their thumb and index finger. If students squeeze the board gently, then harder, they will see the relative strengths of the boards when placed under stress in this different dimension. This may give students some ideas of various ways to use the boards in their bridge-building challenge.

Results:

(Many other possibilities exist, but they should have the same general trend.)

Number of layers	2	4	6	8	10
Number of pennies for 1 cm sag	2	6	18	38	45

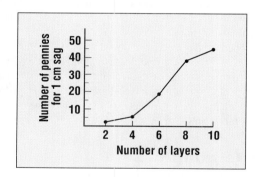

The Ultimate Materials Challenge!

Students should probably work in the same groups as they have been to design and build a bridge. Encourage students to use the information they have gained throughout the issue to build the strongest bridge possible. Different materials may be better suited as the foundation, the vertical supports, and the road bed. Encourage students to combine materials if they think it will make a better bridge. An example might be to incorporate spaghetti lengths across the width of the planks to add strength to the planks. Encourage students to be creative, to have fun, and to use the results of their activities to guide them.

NATIONAL SCIENCE EDUCATION STANDARDS

The activities in this unit can be used to support the teaching of the following standards:

✔ **Unifying Concepts and Processes**

Evidence, Models, and Explanation

Evidence consists of observations and data on which to base scientific explanations. (*All activities*)

Models help scientists and engineers understand how things work. (*All activities*)

Form and Function

Form and function are complementary aspects of objects, organisms, and systems in the natural and designed world. The form or shape of an object or system is frequently related to its use, operation, or function. (*All activities*)

✔ **Science as Inquiry**

Abilities Necessary to Do Scientific Inquiry

Design and conduct a scientific investigation. (*All activities*)

Use appropriate tools and techniques to gather, analyze, and interpret data.

> *Pasta Power!*
> *Strength in Numbers?*
> *Pile It On!*

✔ **Physical Science**

Properties and Changes of Properties in Matter

A substance has characteristic properties all of which are independent of the amount of the sample.

> *Get the Scoop on Goop!*
> *Test for the Best!*

✔ **Science and Technology**

Abilities of Technological Design

Identify appropriate problems for technological design.

> *The Ultimate Materials Challenge!*

Design a solution or product.

> *The Ultimate Materials Challenge!*

Implement a proposed design.

> *The Ultimate Materials Challenge!*

STUDENT ACTIVITY SHEET

NAME _____   DATE _____

	Flour only	Flour and Salt	Flour and Sugar
Water			
Milk			
Egg White			

Flour and Sand	Flour and Gelatin	Flour and Baking Soda

We make houses, clothes, cars, artwork, televisions, and all the other products around us from the substances in nature. We take these substances and combine them in different ways to make different kinds of materials. These different materials are good for different uses.

In the following activities, you will create and test different materials for building a model bridge. You will make a cement-like material with flour as the base, a beam-like material from uncooked spaghetti, and a plywood-like material from paper and glue. Then you will figure out the best way to use these materials to make the strongest bridge possible.

TEACHER PREPARATION:

Make a large chart like the one shown or use the chart from the Student Activity Sheet in the Teacher's Guide. Students can place their finished samples on the chart to dry. Also, make a copy of the chart for each group to record their observations.

The basic recipe for all material samples is **2 teaspoons of flour and 2 teaspoons of either water, milk, or egg white**. For most samples, you will also be adding 1 teaspoon of either **salt, sugar, fine sand, gelatin, or baking soda,** as shown in the chart.

Divide students into six groups. Each group will have its basic ingredients. The groups will be (1) Flour only, (2) Flour and Salt, (3) Flour and Sugar, (4) Flour and Sand, (5) Flour and Gelatin, and (6) Flour and Baking soda. Each group will use its basic ingredients and water, milk, and egg white to make three different samples of material. When all groups are finished making their materials there will be 18 different samples.

YOU WILL NEED:

flour

water

milk

pasteurized egg white product (such as Egg Beaters)

salt

sugar

fine sand

unflavored gelatin

baking soda

6 plastic cups

measuring spoons

plastic spoon for mixing

18 disposable paper or Styrofoam cups (3 per group)

scissors

6 observation charts

chart for samples

Do not eat or drink any substances.

	Flour only	Flour and Salt	Flour and Sugar	Flour and Sand	Flour and Gelatin	Flour and Baking Soda
Water						
Milk						
Egg White						

Scoop on Goop!

In this activity, you will create different materials that can be molded and that harden. You will then test your different materials to see what characteristics they have. You should also begin to think about which material you might use for your bridge and how you would use it.

1 To make your group's first sample, place 2 teaspoons of flour and 1 teaspoon of your group's other ingredient into your plastic cup. Then add 2 teaspoons of water. Mix very thoroughly.

Some materials become very thick, so the plastic spoon used for mixing should be strong. You will want your material to be pretty thick—somewhere between a thick paste and a thin dough. If the material is too thin, add extra flour, about a teaspoon at a time, and mix well.

2 Use your scissors to cut away the top part of a paper cup so all that's left is the very bottom shallow part, about a centimeter tall. This is your sample container.

3 Scoop out the material you have mixed and place it in the container. Smooth and flatten the material with the spoon or your fingers until it is level with the top of the container. Wash the extra material from your plastic cup and spoon.

4 Repeat steps 1–3 to make your group's next two materials, but use milk in one and egg white in the other, instead of water.

5 Place all finished materials on a large chart. Begin filling in your observation chart with anything that you have already noticed about the different samples. Allow the samples to sit for 24 hours before doing the tests on the next page.

Be careful using scissors.

This activity is continued on the next page-->

Test for the Best!

Testing the Different Materials:
After 24 hours

A. Drying time:
Touch each sample very lightly with your fingertip. Note which are moist, tacky, almost dry, and dry.

B. Surface features:
Look at the surface of each sample. Describe the way it looks. Is it cracking, bulging, smooth, rough, lumpy, coming out of the container, shrunken, expanded, or something else?

C. Scratch test:
Take a serrated plastic knife and gently saw back and forth two or three times on the surface of each sample. Do not saw in the direct center of the sample. Try to press down with the same force on each one. Record what effect the knife has on the surface: no cut, light cut, average cut, or major cut.

D. Hardness:
Take a sharpened pencil and push it through a paper cup from the inside as shown. Wrap a piece of masking tape a few times around the pencil under the cup so that the cup cannot be pushed down the pencil. Place the pencil point gently on the sample away from the center. Do not push down. Your partner should add two pennies at a time while you watch the pencil point from the side. Continue adding pennies until the point of the pencil pierces the surface. Count the number of pennies and record.

After 48 or more hours

A. Flexibility:
Touch each sample and push down to see if the material seems flexible or stiff. Record your results: very flexible, somewhat flexible, or not flexible.

B. Hardness:
Place each sample on a roll of toilet paper as shown. Place the point of a ballpoint pen in the center of the sample. Have your partner lift the hammer about 3 centimeters above the pen. Let the hammer drop onto the top of the pen (do not swing the hammer). Lift the hammer to the same height and let it fall again. Repeat and count the number of hits until the pen breaks through the bottom of the container. Record the number of hits for each sample.

Begin thinking about the best material for making your model bridge.

Pasta Power!

One of your bridge-building materials is raw spaghetti. Let's investigate spaghetti in two different ways. First you'll see how much weight different lengths of spaghetti can hold. Then you'll see how much weight different *numbers* of spaghetti strands can hold. After learning more about spaghetti, you can think about how it could be used as a bridge-building material.

1 Take a piece of spaghetti and bend it very gently, trying not to break it. Now bend it again until it breaks. Would you say that spaghetti is flexible or brittle?

Let's run a test on spaghetti to learn about some of its qualities as a building material.

2 Make a chart like the one at right. Use a pencil to carefully poke two holes on opposite sides of a Dixie cup. Use a piece of string to tie a handle on the cup to make a little bucket as shown.

3 Place a little piece of masking tape on the end of a piece of spaghetti as shown. Place the piece of spaghetti on the table so that there is a length of 10 centimeters of spaghetti between the edge of the table and the piece of tape.

4 Tape the spaghetti down just behind the edge of the table and again further down the spaghetti. Hang the cup handle on the spaghetti up against the tape.

5 Gently place pennies one at a time into the cup. Continue to add pennies until the spaghetti breaks. Record the number of pennies in the chart under 10 cm.

6 Repeat steps 4–6 on a new piece of spaghetti. This time have 8 cm of spaghetti between the edge of the table and the tape. Record the number of pennies it took to break the spaghetti. Was it more, fewer, or about the same as for 10 cm?

7 Repeat the experiment for 6, 4, and 2 centimeters. Be sure to record your results. What did you notice? Could this be important for bridge building?

YOU WILL NEED:

raw spaghetti (regular thickness)	**string**
Dixie cup	**pennies**
pencil	**masking tape**
metric ruler	**safety glasses**

Number of cm off table	10	8	6	4	2
Number of pennies before it breaks					

10 cm

Strength in Numbers?

You have checked to see how much weight different lengths of spaghetti can hold. Now lets see how the *number* of spaghetti strands affects strength.

1 Pour water into the pan until the water is about 2 centimeters deep. Place 2 pieces of spaghetti in the water and immediately take them out again. Move your fingers up and down the spaghetti until the two pieces stick together. Lay the stuck spaghetti down on wax paper to dry.

2 Repeat step 1 for 4, 6, 8, and 10 pieces of spaghetti. Leave the stuck spaghetti strands to dry overnight. You should have beams of 2, 4, 6, 8, and 10 pieces of spaghetti.

Testing your beams:
This time, you will test all your beams at the same distance off the edge of the table.

3 Make a chart like the one at right.

4 Place a piece of masking tape on the end of the two-spaghetti beam as shown. Place the beam of spaghetti on the table so that there is a length of 10 centimeters of spaghetti between the edge of the table and the piece of tape.

Number of strands of spagetti	2	4	6	8	10
Number of pennies before they break					

5 Make a "bucket" from a paper cup and string as you did in step 3 of "Pasta Power!" Hang the cup handle on the spaghetti up against the tape. Gently place pennies one at a time into the cup. Continue to add pennies until the spaghetti breaks. Record the number of pennies in the chart under 2 strands.

6 Repeat steps 4 and 5 for the beams made of 4, 6, 8, and 10 strands. What did you notice? Which seems to have the greatest effect on strength, the length of spaghetti hanging off the table, or the number of strands stuck together? Does this give you any bridge-building ideas?

Pile It On!

One way to make a thin flat material stronger is to stick several layers of it together. This is called laminating the material. Layers of wood can be laminated to form plywood. The lamination process makes plywood strong enough to be used in many different ways in construction. In the following activity, you can laminate some paper to see how much strength laminating gives.

1 Put your paper strips into piles of 2, 4, 6, 8, and 10 strips each. These piles will become your laminated planks. Cover your desk with newspaper. On top of the newspaper put a piece of wax paper.

2 Make a laminating mixture by mixing 2 teaspoons of white glue with 1 teaspoon of water in a small cup.

3 To make your first plank, lay a paper strip on the wax paper. Paint the surface of the strip with the laminating mixture. Place the second strip on top of the first. Slide the strips between your thumb and index finger to press them together. Write a small 2 on the top strip and place it on another piece of wax paper to dry.

4 Repeat step 3 until you have made planks of 4, 6, 8, and 10 strips. Mark all five planks and place them on the wax paper to dry. Place another piece of wax paper on top of the planks. Put a book on top of everything to flatten the planks. In about 10 minutes, take the book off, remove the top layer of wax paper, flip the planks over and allow them to air dry overnight.

Testing:

1 Make a chart like the one at right. Place two identical stacks of books about 10 cm apart. The stacks need to be about 5 cm high. Lay the 2-strip plank across the books as shown. Have your partner place the ruler behind the plank. Note where the plank crosses the ruler and record that number.

2 Stack pennies, one at a time, in the middle of the plank. Look at the ruler and continue adding pennies until the middle of the plank has dropped 1 centimeter. Record the number of pennies in the chart.

3 Repeat steps 1 and 2 for the other planks and record your results. How do you think these planks might be useful in building your model bridge?

Try turning the planks sideways and squeezing them between your thumb and index finger. Any bridge building ideas there?

YOU WILL NEED:

paper (30 strips)	wax paper
small Dixie cup	newspaper
teaspoon	water
paintbrush	metric ruler
white glue	pen or marker
	pennies

TEACHER PREPARATION: Prepare 30 strips of paper for each group by cutting strips about 2.5 cm wide and about 21.5 cm long.

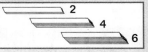

Number of layers	2	4	6	8	10
Number of pennies for 1 cm sag					

119

The Ultimate Materials Challenge!

Use the materials that you have worked with throughout this issue of *WonderScience* to make the strongest bridge you can build. The bridge should be strong enough so that toy cars and trucks loaded with weight can actually travel across it. The bridge that carries the most weight from end to end is the winner!

Here are the rules:

The bridge needs to be at least 60 cm long, 15 cm tall, and 10 cm wide. You may use only the cement-like, beam-like, and board-like materials you have learned to make in your *WonderScience* activities. No tape, string, rubber bands, or any other material may be used.

You can combine any of the *WonderScience* materials in new and different ways.

Send us a drawing or photograph of your bridge and we may put it on the Internet at WonderNet, the Website containing *WonderScience* activities and more! www.acs.org/wondernet

Remember to include the names of the kids in your group, your teacher's name, and the name and address of your school.

GOOD LUCK!

Float and Sink

The reason an object sinks or floats in water has to do with the weight of the object compared with the weight of a volume of water equal to the volume of the object. An object of a particular volume will sink in water if the object weighs more than the weight of an equal volume of water. The object will float if it weighs less than the weight of an equal volume of water. This relationship between weight and volume is the key to understanding sinking and floating. This unit focuses on comparing the weight of equal volumes of two different substances to predict whether one substance will sink or float in the other. The substances are then combined to test the prediction. The practice of comparing the weight of equal volumes of substances is a way of comparing the densities of the substances. The concept of density is discussed in "Density Does It!" within the context of the activities.

Water and Wax—The Sink-and-Float Facts!

In this first activity, two little aluminum foil cups are molded around a candle so that equal volumes of wax and water can be placed on opposite ends of a balance. You could also use tea lights, in which the candles can easily be removed from the lightweight metal containers. On the basis of their observations, students predict whether wax will float or sink in water. They then test their prediction. The plastic wrap called for in the materials is used as a liner to prevent leakage from the aluminum foil cups. You can try making the cups without the plastic wrap; if the aluminum foil cups don't leak, you will not need the plastic.

Float or Sink . . . What Do You Think?

Here, equal volumes of clay and water are placed at opposite ends of a balance. On the basis of their observations, students make a prediction about whether clay will sink or float. They test their prediction by placing a ball of clay in water. Students also flatten out the ball of clay and form it into a little boat to test whether the boat sinks or floats.

Density Does It!

In the preceding activities, floating and sinking are discussed in terms of a comparison between the weight of equal volumes of a substance and water. In *Density Does It!*, this relationship between weight and volume is explained in terms of density. Density is simply a shorthand way of saying weight per unit volume. If an object's density is greater than that of water, the object will sink. If the object's density is less than that of water, the object will float.

Floating Fluids!

Equal volumes of water and mineral oil are placed on opposite ends of a balance. Students observe the movement of the balance and then predict whether the oil will sink or float. Students will see that the same sink-and-float rules that apply to a solid and a liquid also apply to two liquids. The addition of the candle is interesting because wax is more dense than oil but less dense than water.

Go Nuts with Sink and Float!

We've designated this activity for take-home use to encourage parental involvement. Feel free, however, to use it in the classroom if you choose. In the previous activity, students discovered that mineral oil is less dense than water. They also observed that wax, which floats in water, sinks in the less dense oil. In this activity, students use saltwater, which is more dense than water. Students observe that a peanut sinks in fresh water and predict whether the peanut could possibly float in the more dense saltwater.

Activity Answers and Extenders

Water and Wax—The Sink-and-Float Facts!

The water side of the balance should go down, which indicates that water weighs more than an equal volume of wax. This is another way of saying that water is more dense than wax. This makes sense because wax is made from oil, which is less dense than water. When students place the wax in the water, the wax floats. Regardless of how large or small a piece of wax is, it will always float because density is an integral characteristic of the wax that does not change with size.

Float or Sink . . . What Do You Think?

The clay side of the balance should go down, which indicates that clay weighs more than an equal volume of water. When the clay ball is placed in water, students see that it sinks. When the clay is flattened out and shaped into a boat, students observe that the clay boat floats. The boat floats even though the volume of the clay itself, in the clay ball and in the clay boat, is the same. What is different is the volume of the *overall object*. The volume of the clay boat is greater than the volume of the clay ball because the boat includes the large open space occupied by air. Because the volume of the overall object has increased— even though the weight and density of the clay itself remain the same—the density of the *overall object* has decreased, enabling the clay boat to float.

Density Does It!

In "*Density Does It!*," the relationship between weight and volume that students have been working with in the activities is, for the first time, discussed in terms of density. Density is defined as mass per unit volume. It is discussed as weight per unit volume to avoid a digression into the difference between mass and weight. Students may ask whether the density of a material can be changed. This is a tricky question. The density of a material is thought of as the mass per unit volume of the material in its "normal" state. For example, the density of a particular brand of white bread might be 0.5 g/cm³, but it could be compressed so that the compacted piece has a much higher density. That brand of bread, in general, would still have a density of 0.5 g/cm³, but the particular compressed piece would have a higher density.

Floating Fluids!

The water side of the balance should go down, which indicates that mineral oil is lighter than water. When combined, the oil floats in a layer on top of the water. Since wax is more dense than oil but less dense than water, the candle sits right at the interface between the oil and the water. One small variable is not accounted for in this setup: the wick in the candle has a different density than the wax. But for the purposes of the activity and the nice observations it produces, this variable is negligible.

Go Nuts with Sink and Float!

Students discover that a peanut, which sinks in fresh water, will float in the more dense saltwater. This activity also works with a piece of carrot in place of the peanut halves. You could relate this saltwater floating phenomenon to pictures of people floating high in the water in the Dead Sea, which has a very high salt concentration

NATIONAL SCIENCE EDUCATION STANDARDS

The activities in this unit can be used to support the teaching of the following standards:

✔ **Unifying Concepts and Processes**
Evidence, Models, and Explanation
Using evidence to understand interactions allows individuals to predict changes in natural and designed systems. *(All activities)*
Constancy, Change, and Measurement
Evidence for interactions is often clarified through quantitative distinctions—measurement.\
  Water and Wax—The Sink-and-Float Facts!
  Float or Sink . . . What Do You Think?
  Density Does It!
  Floating Fluids!

✔ **Science as Inquiry**
Abilities Necessary to Do Scientific Inquiry
Design and conduct a scientific investigation.
  Float or Sink . . . What Do You Think?
  Floating Fluids!
  Go Nuts with Sink and Float!
Develop descriptions, explanations, predictions, and models using evidence.
  Float or Sink . . . What Do You Think?
  Floating Fluids!
  Go Nuts with Sink and Float!
Think critically and logically to make the relationships between evidence and explanations.
  Float or Sink . . . What Do You Think?
  Floating Fluids!
  Go Nuts with Sink and Float!

✔ **Physical Science**
Properties and Changes of Properties in Matter
A substance has characteristic properties, such as density, which are independent of the amount of the sample. *(All activities)*

NAME _____   **DATE** _____

Water and Wax—The Sink-and-Float Facts

1. After water is added to the empty cup on the ruler, which weighs more, the water or the wax? _____

2. On the basis of this observation, do you think the wax will sink or float in the water? _____
Why? _____
_____
_____
_____

3. When you put the wax in the water, did the wax sink or float? _____

4. If you had a huge block of wax as big as a house and you placed the wax in a giant pool of water, do you think the wax would sink or float? _____
Why? (Try to explain your answer by comparing the weight of the wax to the weight of water.)
_____
_____
_____
_____

5. If you had a piece of wax the size of a grain of sand, do you think it would sink or float? _____
Why? (Try to explain your answer by comparing the weight of the wax to the weight of water.)
_____
_____
_____
_____

6. Almost all wood floats. If you had a block of wood on one end of a balance and an equal amount of water at the other end, which would weigh more, the water or the wood? _____

NAME _____   DATE _____

Float or Sink . . . What Do You Think?

1. After water is added to the empty cup on the ruler, which weighs more, the water or the clay? _____

2. On the basis of this observation, do you think the clay will sink or float in the water? _____
Why? _____
_____
_____
_____

3. When you put the clay in the water, did the clay sink or float? _____

4. If you had a piece of clay the size of a grain of sand, do you think it would sink or float? _____
Why? (Try to explain your answer by comparing the weight of the clay to the weight of water.)

_____
_____
_____
_____

5. If you had a huge block of clay as big as a house and you placed the clay in a giant pool of water, do you think the clay would sink or float? _____
Why? (Try to explain your answer by comparing the weight of the clay to the weight of water.)

_____
_____
_____
_____

6. How could you reshape this giant block of clay to make it float?

_____
_____
_____
_____

Water and Wax—
The Sink-and-Float Facts!

Everybody has had some experience with sinking and floating. Even the most simple examples of sticks floating and rocks sinking raise some very big questions. Namely: Why does one sink and the other float? It can't just be the weight because a tree trunk weighing thousands of pounds will float while a grain of sand, weighing very little, will sink. What's going on here? In the activities that follow, let's try to find out!

Students will first need to use aluminum foil and plastic wrap to form two little cups as close to the size of the candle as possible. The plastic wrap prevents the cups from leaking.

1 Cut a square of aluminum foil and a square of plastic wrap to the same size and large enough so that the sides can be folded up around the candle as shown.

2 Lay the plastic wrap on top of the foil. Lift both pieces up around the candle and squeeze them against the candle to create a little cup the same size as the candle. Fold down the extra aluminum foil and plastic. You can trim the extra off with scissors if you want.

3 Remove the candle from the cup by gently pushing the candle out of the cup from the bottom. Repeat steps 1 and 2 to make another cup but leave the candle in this cup.

JIM WISNIEWSKI

126

4 Tape a pencil to a table as shown. Cut two pieces of masking tape to the same length (about 5 cm). Loop each piece of masking tape so it is sticky on both sides. Place a piece of tape on opposite ends of the ruler. Place the ruler on the pencil so that the ruler is as balanced as possible.

5 Place the candle in its cup at one end of the ruler. Place the empty cup at the other end. Make sure the ruler stays where it is on the pencil. Push the cups down so that they stick well to the tape.

6 Very slowly and carefully, add water to the empty cup until it is full. How did your balance move? Which weighs more—the candle or the same amount of water?

7 Let's see if the candle floats or sinks in water. What do you think it will do? Why? Fill a large cup or bowl with water. Take the candle out of its cup and place it in the water. Does it sink or float?

8 If the candle weighed more than an equal amount of water, what do you think would have happened?

127

Float or Sink...

In the first activity, you saw that if a piece of wax weighed less than an equal amount of water, the wax would float. How about if something weighs *more* than an equal amount of water—what happens then? Let's see!

YOU WILL NEED:

2 small paper Dixie® cups

clay

ruler

masking tape

pencil

water

large cup or bowl

pennies

1 Take a ball of clay about the size of a Ping Pong ball and press it down into the bottom of one of your cups. Be sure that the clay is pressed down evenly so that the surface of the clay is flat.

2 Look at the side of the cup to see how high the clay is in the cup. If you cannot see the surface of the clay through the side of the cup, hold the cup up to the light.

3 Use a ruler to measure from the bottom of the cup to the level of the clay as shown. Now measure this same height and mark it on the other cup.

128

What Do You Think?

4 Tape a pencil to the table as shown. Cut two pieces of masking tape to the same length (about 5 cm). Loop each piece of tape so it is sticky on both sides. Place a piece of tape on opposite ends of the ruler. Place the ruler on the pencil so that the ruler is as balanced as possible.

5 Place the cup with the clay at one end of the ruler. Place the empty cup at the other end. Push the cups down so that they stick well to the tape.

6 Very slowly and carefully, add water to the empty cup until the water reaches the mark you made. There should now be the same amount of water in the water cup as there is clay in the clay cup. Which weighs more—the clay or the same amount of water?

7 Do you think the clay will float or sink in water? Why? Fill a large cup with water. Tear the cup away from the clay and place the clay in the water. Does it sink or float? Was your prediction correct?

JIM WISNIEWSKI

Here's something you might not expect:

Remove the clay from the water and flatten it as much as you can into a pancake. Pinch the clay together at the front and back to form a kind of little boat as shown. Place the boat on the water. Does it sink or float?

How does your little boat act like an ocean liner made from steel? How much cargo do you think your boat could hold? Try putting some pennies in it to find out! (An explanation of why a clay boat can float is found in the Teacher's Guide.)

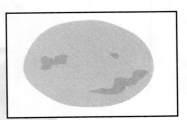

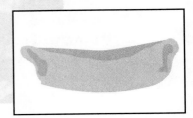

Density Does It!

In *Water and Wax—The Sink-and-Float Facts!*, you saw that if an object weighs less than the same amount of water, the object will float in water. In *Float or Sink…What Do You Think?*, you saw that if an object weighs more than the same amount of water, the object will sink in water.

Scientists who need to know if a substance will sink or float need to know how much a standard amount of the substance weighs. Scientists often use a cubic centimeter (cm^3) as this standard amount. A cm^3 is a cube that is 1 cm long, 1 cm wide, and 1 cm deep. It looks like this:

The following examples show how knowing the weight of a cm^3 of a substance can tell you if the substance will sink or float.

EXAMPLE 1:

If you weighed 1 cm^3 of **lead**, it would weigh 11.3 grams.

If you weighed 1 cm^3 of **water**, it would weigh 1 gram.

According to what you know from your *WonderScience* activities, will lead sink or float in water?

EXAMPLE 2:

1 cm^3 of **oak** wood weighs .76 grams. Will oak sink or float in water? How do you know?

EXAMPLE 3:

1 cm^3 **of mineral oil** weighs .85 grams. Will it sink or float in water? Would a piece of oak float or sink in mineral oil?

The weight in grams of a cm^3 of a substance is called the density of the substance. It is the density of a substance that tells you whether something will sink or float. The density of lead is 11.3 grams per cm^3, the density of water is 1 gram per cm^3, and the density of oak is .76 grams per cm^3.

Floating Fluids!

When you talk about sinking and floating, most people think of a solid object floating or sinking in water. But there are also liquids that sink or float in other liquids. There are also solid objects that sink or float differently in liquids other than water. Try the activity below to see what we mean!

YOU WILL NEED:

water
food coloring
mineral or baby oil
masking tape
tablespoon
baby food jar
piece of birthday candle
  (about 2 cm long)
ruler
pencil
2 Dixie® cups (3 oz)

1 Tape a pencil to the table as shown. Cut two pieces of masking tape to the same length (about 5 cm). Loop each piece of tape so it is sticky on both sides. Place a piece of tape on opposite ends of the ruler. Place the ruler on the pencil so that the ruler is as balanced as possible.

2 Place a cup at each end of the ruler. Press the cups down so that they stick to the tape. Add 3 tablespoons of baby oil to one of your cups.

3 Very slowly and carefully, add 3 tablespoons of water to the empty cup. Which weighs more—the oil or the same amount of water? Do you think the oil will float or sink in the water? Why?

4 Pour the water from your cup into the baby food jar. Add 1 drop of food coloring and swirl to mix. Very carefully pour the oil on top of the water. Look at your jar from the side. Did the oil float or sink on the water? Is this what you expected? Why?

5 Take a piece of birthday candle and place it on the oil. What happens? Look at the jar from the side. Is the candle sinking and floating at the same time? If you put wax on one end of a balance and an equal amount of baby oil on the other end, which do you think would weigh more? Why?

JIM WISNIEWSKI

Go Nuts with Sink and Float!

YOU WILL NEED:

water
salt
tablespoon
fresh unsalted peanuts in shells
2 clear plastic cups (about 8 oz)
masking tape
ballpoint pen

In *Floating Fluids!*, you saw that mineral oil weighs less than an equal amount of water. Now let's look at a liquid that weighs *more* than an equal amount of water. If an object sinks in water, is there a chance it will float on this liquid? Let's find out!

1 Use your masking tape and pen to label one cup salt and the other cup fresh. Add water to each cup until they are about 3/4 filled.

2 Add 2 tablespoons of salt to the cup labeled salt. Stir until no more salt will dissolve.

3 Take one peanut out of the shell. Separate the peanut in half. Place one of the halves in fresh water and the other half in saltwater. In which liquid does the half-peanut sink? In which liquid does the half-peanut float?

4 Based on the activities you have done throughout your *WonderScience*, do you think fresh water weighs more or less than the same amount of peanut? Explain your answer. Do you think saltwater weighs more or less than the same amount of peanut? Why?

JIM WISNIEWSKI

WONDER SCIENCE

Millimeters, Centimeters, and Beyond!

The most important metric units of length are the millimeter, the centimeter, the meter, and the kilometer. These units are related to each other by powers of 10. For instance, 1 centimeter is 10 millimeters, 1 meter is 100 centimeters, and 1 kilometer is 1,000 meters. These ratios make it easy to convert from one unit to another. To find the number of centimeters in a kilometer, for instance, you only need to multiply 1,000 by 100. It's easy.

Scientists all over the world use the metric system, and that promotes effective communication among scientists. When a scientist publishes results, other scientists use these results to design new experiments and to create new theories. That's how science moves ahead. Having one standard measurement system promotes the good communication that helps scientists everywhere build on each other's work.

Measure Yourself in Metric!

Students measure their height in centimeters using a string. If you want, you can place a mark on the string and have the students stand on the string so the mark is just under the edge of the student's shoe. Students should realize that they will need to control the tightness of the string to get an accurate measurement. For heights greater than 1 meter, the height can be written as 1 meter plus the remaining number of centimeters. This conversion from centimeters to meters plus centimeters brings out the basic process of measuring length: counting how many times the distance unit goes into the length, and then adding the remainder. It's division!

Students also carry out similar activities that introduce the unit of millimeters.

English vs. Metric—And the Winner Is . . .

There is a powerful advantage of the metric length units. The centimeter is subdivided into only one unit, the millimeter. Ten millimeters make one centimeter. Now compare that simplicity with the division of the inch. There's half an inch, one quarter of an inch, an eighth of an inch, and a sixteenth of an inch. Adding fractions of an inch requires converting to a common denominator, such as eighths or sixteenths. It's a lot of work. Students will need to work with both systems, but working in metric does have its advantages. You could create other math problems involving the metric system in calculating cost to give students extra problem-solving practice.

Metric Map Maneuvers

It's easy to get mixed up in converting miles to kilometers or vice versa. Here's how to do it. To convert 8 kilometers to miles, for example, you need to know how many miles in 1 kilometer, and then you'll multiply that number by 8. One kilometer is about six-tenths (0.6) miles. Now let's figure it out:

1 km = 0.6 mi

8 km = 8 × 0.6 mi = 4.8 mi

So we get the relationship 8 km = 4.8 mi. For a given distance, which is greater, the number of miles or the number of kilometers? The number of kilometers is always greater, because the kilometer is the smaller unit. So that's an easy way to check your conversion.

Let's go the other way and convert 5 miles to kilometers. One mile is about 1.6 kilometers. Now, to convert 5 miles to kilometers:

1 mi = 1.6 km

5 mi = 5 × 1.6 km = 8 km

Again, let's check: the number of kilometers (8) is greater than the number of miles (5), just as we expect.

Keep Metric in Mind!

The estimating performed in this lesson helps students understand how the metric length units are related. Also, if students can estimate well, they can catch many measurement errors.

Teacher Answer Key

English vs. Metric—And the Winner Is . . .

4. After getting used to the metric system, students should notice that in certain situations, it is easier to use than the English system. The divisions of the centimeter are tenths, whereas the divisions of the inch are halves, quarters, eighths, and sixteenths. Multiplying and dividing by 10 is a snap!

5. The silver chain costs $10 per centimeter. Because there are 10 millimeters in 1 centimeter, each millimeter costs $1. The length of the silver chain is 13 cm, 5 mm.

The cost of the centimeters = 13 cm $\times$ $10 per centimeter = $130 plus the cost of the millimeters = 5 mm $\times$ $1 per millimeter = $5.

The cost of the whole chain = $135.

Metric Map Maneuvers

1. The distance on the map from Atlanta to Columbia is 3 cm (rounded off to the nearest centimeter). Each centimeter represents 100 km. So the distance from Atlanta to Columbia is 3 cm $\times$ 100 km per cm = 300 km.

2. Since the distance is 300 km and the speed is 100 km per hour, the time it would take would be 3 hours.

time = 300 km $\div$ 100 km per hour = 3 hours

3. The distance on the map from Madison to Richmond is 11 cm (rounded to the nearest centimeter). Because 1 cm represents 100 km, 11 cm represents 1,100 km. If the speed is 100 km per hour, the time it would take would be 11 hours.

1,100 km $\div$ 100 km per hour = 11 hours

4. 1 cm represents 100 km.

1 cm = 10 mm.

Because 10 mm represents 100 km, 1 mm represents 10 km.

5. The distance on the map from Boston to Providence is 7 mm (some students may measure this as 6 mm, which is correct). On the map, 7 mm represents 7 $\times$ 10 km or 70 km.

Extension Ideas

Here are some additional ideas you can use to extend your students' experiences with observation.

History

The first length units were created in antiquity and were based on the human body. These include the cubit—the distance from the elbow to the fingertip—and the foot. Because it was inconvenient to use one particular forearm or foot for all measurements, these distances were transferred to standards made of some sturdy material. Then someone, such as a merchant, who made frequent measurement could make a copy of the standard. This process is called **calibration**. The meter, a more modern unit, was devised in France at the end of the seventeenth century. It is a certain fraction of the circumference of the Earth.

Challenge students to use the library to research other information about the origin of length units.

Technology

Ask students to visit a hardware store, accompanied by an adult, and find out whether fasteners, such as screws, nuts, bolts, and washers, are sold in English or metric sizes.

Ask students to check the speedometer of a car to find out what units are used for the speed and also to find the range of speeds displayed.

Millimeters, Centimeters, and Beyond!

NATIONAL SCIENCE EDUCATION STANDARDS

The activities in this unit can be used to support the teaching of the following standards:

✔ **Unifying Concepts and Processes**

Constancy, Change, and Measurement

Scientists usually use the metric system. (*All activities*)

An important part of measurement is knowing when to use which system.
  English vs. Metric—and the Winner Is . . .

✔ **Science as Inquiry**

Abilities Necessary to Do Scientific Inquiry

Students should develop general abilities, such as . . . making accurate measurements. (*All activities*)

Measure Yourself in Metric!

Use the spaces below to record the different lengths you measured:

1. Your height in centimeters: _____ .

   Your height in meters and centimeters: _____, _____.

2. The distance in centimeters from the tip of your thumb to the tip of your little finger, with your fingers spread as far as they can go (include millimeters beyond the last centimeter mark if necessary): _____, _____.

3. Width of your little finger in millimeters: _____.

4. Approximate thickness of your thumbnail in fractions of a millimeter: _____.

5. Total distance of your three jumps in meters, centimeters, and millimeters: _____, _____, _____.

Now see if you can FACE these metric measurements!

6. Distance between your partner's eyebrows in centimeters and millimeters: _____, _____.

7. Distance from the tip of your partner's nose to the tip of your partner's chin in centimeters and millimeters: _____, _____.

8. Width in fractions of a millimeter of one of your partner's hairs (measured while still in your partner's head): _____.

9. Width of your partner's earlobe in centimeters and millimeters: _____, _____.

10. Distance from the bottom of the nose to the top of your partner's upper lip in centimeters and millimeters: _____, _____.

STUDENT ACTIVITY SHEET

NAME _____   DATE _____

Metric Map Maneuvers

Use the chart below to record your answers to the Challenge in step 6.

City Names	Centimeters	Kilometers	Total Kilometers
Columbus, OH, to Charleston, WV	2	200	
Charleston, WV, to Hartford, CT	7.9	790	

Measure Yourself in Metric!

YOU WILL NEED:
metric tape measure
  or metric ruler
meter stick
paper
pencil
string (about two meters)
scissors
calculator

Suppose you wanted to measure your height. You would probably measure yourself with a yard stick or measuring tape, and the answer would be in feet and inches. Let's try a different way of measuring using the Metric System and see what happens.

To help you get started, look at the metric ruler printed on this page. Each numbered mark is one centimeter. Notice the small marks between each centimeter mark. These small marks are millimeters. One centimeter is made up of 10 millimeters.

1 Have your partner take the string and mark it at your foot and head to show your height. To measure your height, just measure the length of the string one mark to the other! How many centimeters is it? It's probably more than 100!

2 If you are taller than 100 centimeters, you can write your height in two ways. One way is just to give the total number of centimeters. Here's another way: If your height is 122 centimeters, you can also write that as 1 meter, 22 centimeters. To get the 22 centimeters, just subtract 100 centimeters from your total height. Then write your height as 1 meter and the remaining number of centimeters.

3 If your height is 153 centimeters, how could you write it using meters and centimeters? A very tall person might be 205 centimeters tall. How would you write this height using meters and centimeters?

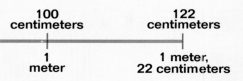

100 centimeters — 1 meter

122 centimeters — 1 meter, 22 centimeters

4 Spread one hand as far apart as you can. Press it down on your metric ruler. Measure the distance from the tip of your little finger to the tip of your thumb. How many centimeters is it? If your fingers don't land exactly on centimeter marks, you will have to count the millimeters beyond the last centimeter mark. One possible answer could be 15 centimeters, 6 millimeters.

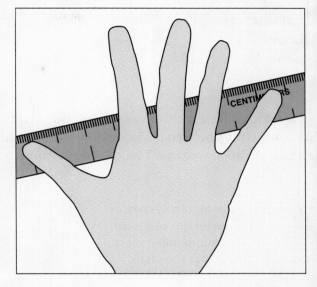

5 Measure the width of the fingernail on your little finger. This is probably less than 1 centimeter so you will need to count the millimeters. How many millimeters is it?

6 Now look at your thumb from the side. Try to measure the thickness of your thumbnail. It's probably less than 1 millimeter. Does it look like 1/2 millimeter or 1/4 millimeter or even less?

If you measure a long distance, it can be a very large number if you use centimeters. Often it's easier to understand a measurement when is it given in meters and centimeters, instead of just in centimeters. Try the following activity to see what we mean.

7 Find a space where you can jump across a room. Set up a starting line. Take three jumps and make a mark to show how far you went. Now measure this total distance with the meter stick. First measure off whole meters until you are close to the mark. Then measure the remaining distance to the mark in centimeters.

8 If the mark is not exactly at a centimeter line, you will also need to count the millimeters beyond the last centimeter mark. Your answer might be something like 2 meters, 43 centimeters, 3 millimeters. Use a separate sheet of paper to record the distances for you and your partner in _____ meters, _____centimeters, _____ millimeters.

YOU WILL NEED:

ruler with centimeters and inches

calculator

paper

pencil

Now let's make the same measurement with English and metric units to see which is easier! Pretend that you are a biologist who just discovered two new worms. You need to measure the length of these worms. You decide to measure in both inches and in centimeters.

1 First use the metric system. Measure the length of Worm #1 in centimeters and millimeters. Record your result in the chart.

2 Now try the English system. Look at the inch ruler. The numbered lines are inches. Now look at all the different ways that the other lines divide up an inch. There's a line for a half inch, for a quarter inch, for an eighth inch, and for other fractions too. Now measure Worm #1 in inches and fractions of an inch. Record the result in the chart.

3 Now measure Worm #2 in the metric and the English systems. Record your measurements for Worm #2 in the chart.

There are different ways to write the lengths of Worm #1 and Worm #2 in the metric system.

For #1, you could write 105 millimeters or 10 centimeters, 5 millimeters. If you know decimals, you can write this number as 10.5 cm.

For #2, you could write 16 millimeters or 1 centimeter, 6 millimeters. If you know decimals, you can write this number as 1.6 cm.

4 Which system was easier to use, English or metric? What made one easier than the other? Now measure worms #3 and #4 using both systems. If you haven't already, you will soon become a metric measuring master!

	Worm #1	Worm #2	Worm #3	Worm #4
length in centimeters and millimeters				
length in inches and fractions of an inch				

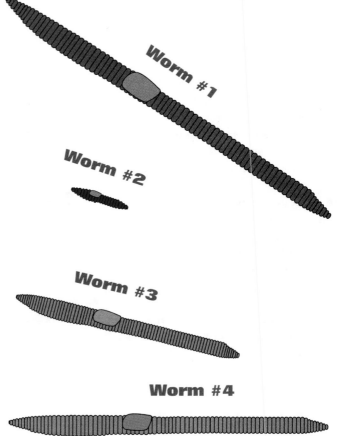

AND THE WINNER IS. . .

You can also use the metric system to help you figure out how much something costs. Suppose you want to buy a gold chain. The jeweler says the chain costs $20 per centimeter if measured in centimeters or $50 per inch if measured in inches. Let's first use the metric system to figure out the cost of the chain.

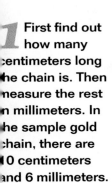

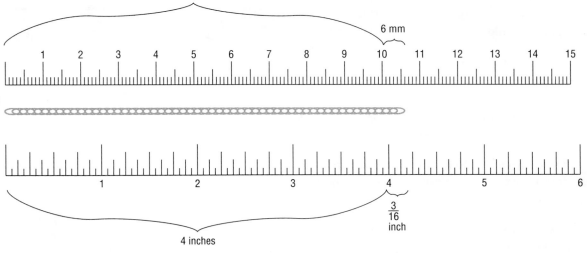

1 First find out how many centimeters long the chain is. Then measure the rest in millimeters. In the sample gold chain, there are 10 centimeters and 6 millimeters.

2 Next, you need to know the cost of each centimeter and each millimeter. You already know that each centimeter costs $20, but how much does each millimeter cost?

Because it's in metric, it's easy! If one centimeter is $20, and there are 10 millimeters in a centimeter, to find the cost of 1 millimeter, just divide by 10! $20 divided by 10 equals $2. So each millimeter costs $2.

3 So the cost of the centimeters equals: 10 cm x $20 per centimeter = $200
and the cost of the millimeters equals: 6 mm x $2 per millimeter = $12
so the cost of the whole chain equals: $212

4 Now let's figure out the cost using inches. The gold chain is $4\frac{3}{16}$ inches long. You already know that each inch costs $50, but what about the $\frac{3}{16}$ of an inch? You will need to divide $50 by 16 because there are 16 sixteenths in one inch. Then you will need to multiply your answer by three to get the cost for $\frac{3}{16}$ ths of an inch.

5 Use your metric ruler to help you find the cost of the silver chain below. It costs $10 per centimeter. What is its total cost?

Metric Map Maneuvers

YOU WILL NEED:

pencil and paper
metric ruler

Suppose you used the metric system to measure the distance from your home to your school or from your school to a school in another state. If you measured the distance in meters, it would probably be an awful lot of meters to count. A larger unit would be much easier to use. A better unit for measuring these longer distances is the **kilometer**.

One kilometer is 1,000 meters. A kilometer is a little longer than half a mile; in fact, it's about six-tenths of a mile.

On the map at the right, 1 centimeter represents 100 kilometers. This is called the **scale** of the map. For example: if the distance between two cities on the map is 2 centimeters, in real life, the cities are 2 x 100 or 200 kilometers apart. Use your metric ruler to answer the questions below.

_____ 1 mile

_____
$1 \text{ km} = \frac{6}{10} \text{ of a mile}$

1 How many kilometers is it from Atlanta, Georgia, to Columbia, South Carolina?

2 If you drove at 100 kilometers per hour, and could travel in a straight line, how long would it take you to travel from Atlanta to Columbia?

3 If you drove 100 kilometers per hour, and could go in a straight line, how long would it take you to drive from Madison, Wisconsin, to Richmond, Virginia?

4 If 1 centimeter represents 100 kilometers, how many kilometers does each millimeter represent?

5 How many kilometers is it from Boston, Massachusetts, to Providence, Rhode Island?

6 CHALLENGE: See how many trips you can plan that will take you to three cities with a total travel distance of as close to 1,000 kilometers as possible. You cannot use any city more than once. Example: Columbus, Ohio, to Charleston, West Virginia (200 kilometers), and then from Charleston to Hartford, Connecticut (about 790 kilometers), for a total of 990 kilometers—Not Bad! See How Many You Can Find!

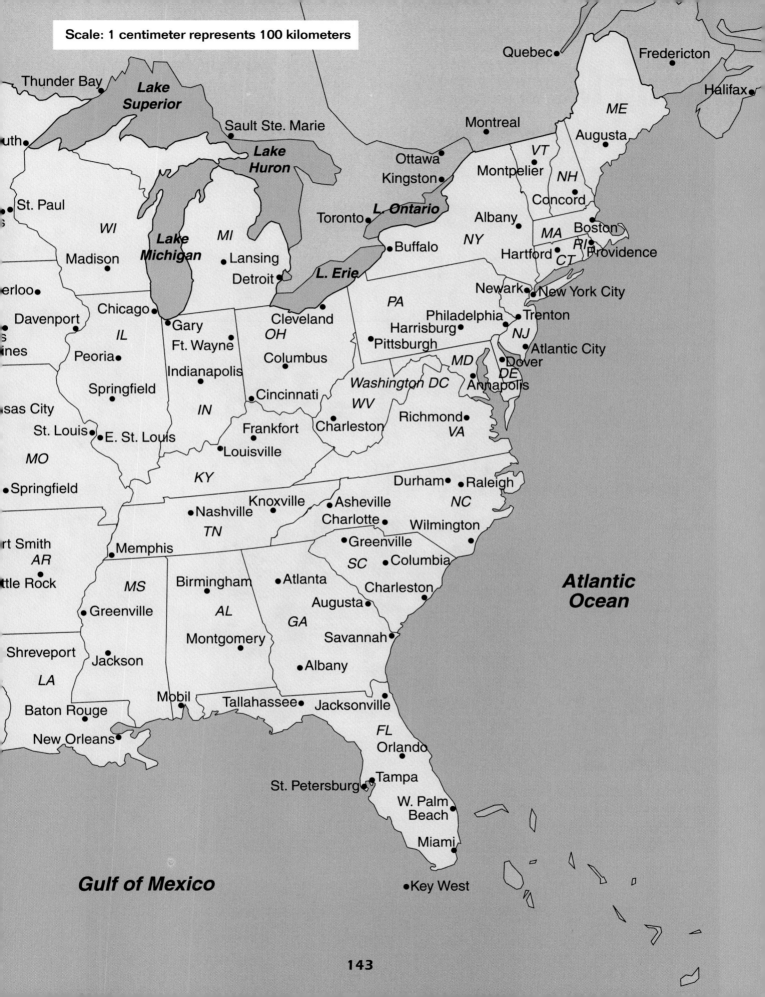

Keep Metric in Mind!

Now that you have worked with the metric system for a while, let's see how well you can estimate the length of some common objects in millimeters, centimeters, and meters.

YOU WILL NEED:

metric ruler
pencil
paper (to record estimates)
paper clip
straw
button
shoe
tooth pick
period from a printed page
pen cap

1 Divide the class into groups of two or three. Place an object such as those listed above on a desk in the middle of the group.

2 Each student should write down the name of the object and also record an estimate of its length in centimeters and millimeters.

3 After everyone has written down an estimate, one person in the group should measure the object. The student whose estimate was closest gets a point. Repeat the metric estimating game for five or six objects.

You can expand the estimating game to include larger objects in the classroom!

4 Have students estimate the length of the chalk board. After all estimates are written, have a student measure the actual length with a meter stick and see who was closest! You can suggest estimating all the way to millimeters for the most accurate estimates.

5 Repeat step 4 with the width of the room, width of a window, height of a chair, width of a bulletin board, or other structures in the room that can be measured.

Do not use chairs, desks, stools, or anything to climb on in order to measure.

WONDERSCIENCE

Time measurement is as old as civilization itself. In ancient times, farmers predicted when to plant crops by observing the moon and stars. Later, inventors made timekeeping devices, such as hourglasses and water clocks, to measure shorter periods of time, such as portions of days, hours, and minutes. Through the activities in this issue, students will create timekeeping devices and learn to get a sense of time from the sun, moon, and stars.

It's Swing Time!

To introduce this activity, hold up a piece of string with a washer tied to one end and let the washer swing back and forth. Ask students where else they have seen this kind of motion (a swing on a playground, a tire hanging from a rope, etc.). Explain that all these are examples of **pendulums,** and that students will be exploring the different factors that affect the motion of pendulums. The length of the pendulum determines the number of swings the pendulum makes in a given amount of time. The greater the length, the slower the pendulum swings and the fewer swings it makes in a given amount of time (length is measured from the pivot point of the string to the middle of the washer.) Also, as long as the pendulum is pulled back only a short distance (about 10 degrees from vertical), the distance pulled back will not affect the swing time. The amount of weight on the end of the pendulum also will not affect the swing time.

Results:

Steps 3 through 5: The number of swings in 20 seconds does not depend on the number of washers.

Observations

Length of Pendulum (cm)	Number of Swings in 20 Seconds
10	30
40	15
Challenge Answer	
21	20

Water Clock: Set It and Wet It!

Ask students to describe what happens if a boat has a hole in it and water leaks in (it settles lower and lower in the water and then sinks). Do the size and number of holes affect how fast the boat sinks? Does the amount of weight in the boat matter? Explain that these same principles are used to make a clock by letting water leak slowly into a floating cup containing one or

more marbles. The important variables in determining the time it takes to sink are the size of the cup, the size and number of holes, and the number of marbles.

Results:

Students determine a combination of number of holes, hole size, and number of marbles to make the cup sink at different rates. In general, the smaller and fewer the holes and the smaller the number of marbles, the slower the sinking rate. Conversely, the larger and more numerous the holes and the greater the number of marbles, the faster the sinking rate.

Secondhand Sand!

Ask students if they have ever seen an hourglass. Explain that the hourglass was invented to help the officers of sailing ships know when to change the crew on deck (this crew is called the "watch," not to be confused with the timepiece). Ask students how they might go about building something similar to an hourglass. The challenge in building sand timers is to have the sand run out slowly enough without getting clogged. When trying the activity, students may find that if they make the hole too small, the sand will sit in a pile instead of running out. To make an accurate timer, students will have to decide on the right combination of hole size and amount of sand. To make the three different timers, students will need to adjust the hole size, the amount of sand, and the shape of the cone funnel. For cone shape, the steeper the slope, the faster the sand will run out.

Results:

In general, for a given amount of sand, the larger the hole and the steeper the cone, the less time it takes for the sand to run out. Conversely, the smaller the hole and the less steep the cone, the more time it takes for the sand to run out.

Unit 13
Measuring Time

The Big Clock in the Sky!

Ask students how days, weeks, months, and years can be measured by looking at the sun, moon, and stars. (They probably will not know how the stars can be used in this way.) To give students an idea of how the sun can be used to tell time, look at "Shifting Shadows!" in the Shadows unit. Students may know that the moon goes through a full cycle of phases from new moon to new moon in twenty-eight days.

Results:

Step 2: The sun rises in the east and sets in the west. If you are looking east, pictures 1 and 2 show the sun in the early morning and at mid- to late morning, respectively. If you are looking west, pictures 3 and 4 are late afternoon and dusk.

Step 3: There are thirteen phases of the moon shown that cover a 28-day period. That means that there is a little more than two days between each phase. So picture 1 would be about October 14, picture 2 would be about October 21, and picture 3 would be about October 25.

Step 5: If you observe the stars at the same time each night, all through the year, you will see the constellations drift steadily westward. When students draw the Orion constellation in the sky, suggest they include some landmarks—buildings or trees—and the compass direction, if possible. Encourage them to add the date and time to their drawing.

Once upon a Time. . .

For the example about Galileo, have students count the number of pulse beats in 30 seconds. Ask them what they could time with their "internal clock." (something slow)

NATIONAL SCIENCE EDUCATION STANDARDS

The activities in this unit can be used to support the teaching of the following standards:

✔ Unifying Concepts and Processes

Evidence, Models, and Explanation

Models are tentative schemes or structures that correspond to real objects, events, or classes of events, and that have explanatory power. *(All activities)*

Evidence for interactions and subsequent change and the formulation of scientific explanations are often clarified through quantitative distinctions—measurement.
It's Swing Time!

Form and Function

The form or shape of an object or system is frequently related to use, its operation, or function. *(All activities)*

✔ Science as Inquiry

Abilities Necessary to Do Scientific Inquiry

Design and conduct a scientific investigation. *(All activities)*

Think critically and logically to make the relationships between evidence and explanations. *(All activities)*

Review and summarize data, and form a logical argument about the cause-and-effect relationships in the experiment. *(All activities)*

✔ Physical Science

Motions and Forces

The motion of an object can be described by its position, direction of motion, and speed.
It's Swing Time!

✔ Earth and Space Science

Earth in the Solar System

Most objects in the solar system are in regular and predictable motion. Those motions explain such phenomena as the day, the year, phases of the moon, and eclipses.
The Big Clock in the Sky!

✔ Science and Technology

Abilities of Technological Design

Design a solution or product.
Water Clock: Set It and Wet It!
Secondhand Sand!

✔ Science in Personal and Social Perspectives

Science and Technology in Society

Science and technology have advanced through contributions of many different people, in different cultures, at different times in history.
Once upon a Time. . .

STUDENT ACTIVITY SHEET

NAME ______________________________ **DATE** __________

It's Swing Time!

Use the charts below to record your observations for the pendulum activities.

The length of the pendulum is 10 cm

Number of washers	Number of swings in 20 seconds
1	____
2	____
4	____

Does changing the number of washers change the number of swings the pendulum makes in 20 seconds?

The length of the pendulum is 40 cm

Number of washers	Number of swings in 20 seconds
2	____

Compare the 10 cm pendulum with two washers to the 40 cm pendulum with two washers. Is there a difference in the number of swings they make in 20 seconds? ____________________

Describe how the length of the pendulum affects the number of swings in an amount of time.

____

____

____

Time	Number of swings	Length of pendulum (centimeters)
20 seconds	20	Prediction: ______ Actual: ______

CHALLENGE!

How long would you make a pendulum if you wanted it to make 20 swings in 20 seconds? ____________________

STUDENT ACTIVITY SHEET

NAME ______________________________ **DATE** __________

Water Clock: Set It and Wet It!

Water Clock Challenge!

Describe the design of your 30-second clock

____
____
____
____

20-second clock

____
____
____
____

10-second clock

____
____
____
____

Secondhand Sand!

Sand Timer Challenge!

Describe the design of your: 30-second timer

____
____
____
____

10-second timer

____
____
____
____

Have you ever seen a clock with something swinging back and forth inside? The part that swings is called a **pendulum**. How do you think the pendulum helps the clock keep time? Let's see what we can find out.

It's Swing

1 Cut a piece of string about 12 centimeters (cm) long. Partly unbend a paper clip. Tie the paper clip to the string. Hook one washer on the paper clip to make a pendulum as in the drawing at right.

2 Tape or tie one end of the string to the top of a table or chair as shown so that 10 cm of the string hangs down. Let's see if you can use your pendulum to keep time. Make a chart like the one below or use the chart in the Student Activity Sheet to record your observations.

3 Pull your pendulum back a short distance and let it go to see how many swings it makes in 20 seconds. A "swing" is defined as the complete back and forth movement of the pendulum. Have your partner watch the clock while you count the swings. Record the number of swings on the chart.

Do you think the number of washers makes a difference in how many swings there will be in 20 seconds?

4 Now use two washers on your pendulum. Again, pull it back the same distance as before. Count the number of swings it makes in 20 seconds.

5 Now put all four washers on the pendulum. Pull it back to the same distance you just used and let it go. Count the number of swings in 20 seconds. Was it very different from what you got with one washer or was it pretty close to the same?

The length of the pendulum is __10 cm__

Number of washers	Number of swings in 20 seconds
1	———
2	———
4	———

150

Time!

How about the length of the string? Do you think that pendulums of different lengths will have different numbers of swings in 20 seconds? Let's see.

6 Cut a piece of string about 42 cm long. Tie a partly unbent paper clip to one end. Tape or tie the other end to the top of a table or chair so that 40 cm of string hangs down. Hang two washers on the paper clip.

7 Pull back the pendulum the same distance as before and count the number of swings it makes in 20 seconds. Record your results on the chart. Compare the number of swings to the 10 cm pendulum with 2 washers from step 4. Does it make more or fewer swings than the shorter pendulum?

The length of the pendulum is ____40 cm____

Number of washers	Number of swings in 20 seconds
2	_____

CHALLENGE!

8 Suppose you wanted a pendulum that would make 20 swings in 20 seconds. Use your charts to predict how long the string of the pendulum should be. Record your prediction on the chart at right.

9 Now build the pendulum and test your prediction. How did your prediction compare with your result? Adjust the length of the string until you get it right.

Time	Number of swings	Length of pendulum (centimeters)
20 seconds	20	Prediction: _____
		Actual: _____

Water Clock:
Set It and Wet It!

People in ancient China and Greece measured time using water clocks.

You can make a water clock too.

1 Use a pencil to poke a hole near the edge of the bottom of a small paper cup as shown.

2 Place a marble in the cup so that it is near or on the hole. This is your clock cup.

3 Fill a large cup about three-quarters full of water. Place your clock cup in the large cup as shown.

4 Time how long it takes for the clock cup to sink.

CHALLENGE!

5 You can change the time it takes the clock cup to sink. You could add marbles, make the hole bigger or smaller, or add more holes. Try these different ways to see if you can make clock cups that sink in 30 seconds, 20 seconds, and 10 seconds.

152

Secondhand Sand!

Have you ever seen an hourglass? It measures time by how long it takes sand to run from one container into another. Let's see if we can measure time by making a sand or salt timer.

YOU WILL NEED:

sand or salt (about 1/2 cup)

3 sheets of paper

small paper cup (3 oz)

tape

bowl

blunt-end scissors

clock or watch
(with second hand)

1 Cut a circle from a piece of paper. Fold the circle in half and then in half again. Open the cone as shown and tape the inside seam and the outside seam.

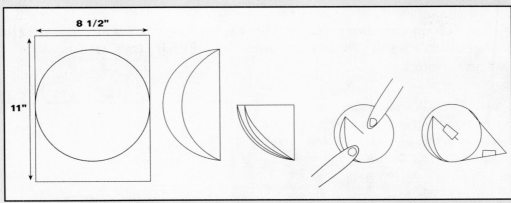

2 Use the scissors to snip off the point of the cone to make a small hole. Hold your finger over the hole while your partner pours about one-half cup of sand or salt into the cone.

3 Hold the cone over a bowl and remove your finger. Have your partner time how long it takes for all the sand or salt to flow from the cone.

CHALLENGE!

4 By changing the amount of sand or salt and the size of the hole, see if you can make a 30-second timer and a 10-second timer.

The Big Clock in the Sky!

Suppose you had no timekeeping devices. How could you measure the passage of time? Throughout the ages, people have measured time in days, weeks, months, and years by using astronomy.

1 What could you learn about time from where the sun is in the sky? (Remember, never look directly at the sun.) How could you use the sun to tell what time it is? Check out the sundial activity in the Shadows unit.

In that activity, the sun's changing position in the sky made the length and position of shadows change. These shadows were used to tell time. But the position of the sun itself, even without a shadow, can be used to tell time. Some people get so used to the position of the sun at different times of the day that they can tell what time it is just by noticing where the sun is in the sky.

2 Look at the four pictures at right. You know that the sun rises in the east and sets in the west. Assuming these pictures were taken in the summer, see if you can guess from the sun's position, at about what time of day each picture was taken.

| Looking East | Looking East | Looking West | Looking West |

3 How about using the moon to tell what date it is? To go from one new moon to the next takes about 28 days. The cycle of the phases of the moon is shown below. Look at the three photographs of the moon at right. Assume they were all taken in October. If the first was taken on October 13, what do you think the dates are for the other two?

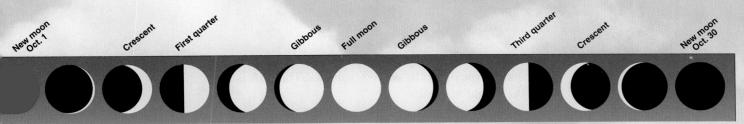

New moon Oct. 1   Crescent   First quarter   Gibbous   Full moon   Gibbous   Third quarter   Crescent   New moon Oct. 30

4 Now think about the stars. Do you know the constellation Orion, the hunter? Orion is easy to see by looking to the southern sky on a winter evening.

5 Suppose at midnight you find the middle star in Orion's belt. Record where you see the star. You might say, "next to the top of the big tree" or "near the top of the apartment building." One month later, observe and record the position of this star again. Wait another month, and observe again. What pattern do you see in your observations?

One year later, that star will be back in the same place at midnight. That's how to tell a year has passed. The Earth has gone once around the sun and the stars are back where they were before.

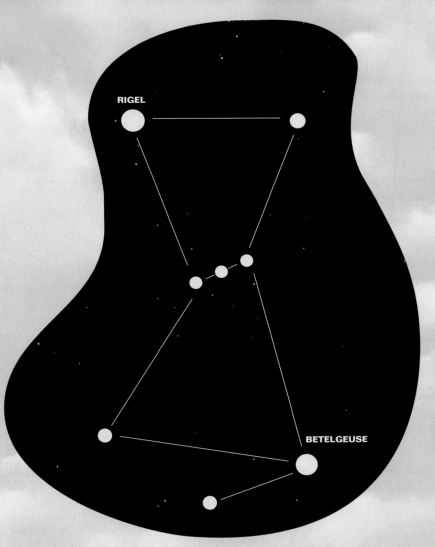

RIGEL

BETELGEUSE

155

Once upon a Time...

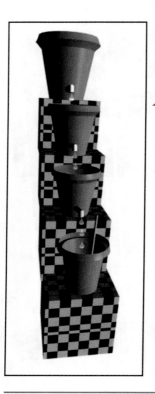

Remember how the water slowly filled the paper cups in the Water Clock activity? The ancient Chinese made a timepiece like this, only they let the water leak out, not in. The drawing shows a modern version of a Chinese water clock from the 1300s. Water drips down from one container to another until the water reaches the bottom vessel. The bottom container holds a float that moves up as the water level rises. The time is read from the height of the float.

This arrangement of stones is actually a timepiece! These stones weigh about 100 tons each. They were set up about 4,000 years ago in what is now England. The stones are arranged to predict the location of the sun at sunrise on the longest day of the year. Predictions like this helped farmers decide when to plant their crops.

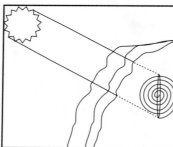

The Anasazi lived in the southwestern United States. They made large solar clocks on rocky cliffs near where they lived. In one of these clocks, the sunlight makes a dagger of light that moves right through the center of a spiral on the longest day of the year.

There is a story that the scientist Galileo used his body as a clock. He observed the swinging sanctuary lamp that hung down from the cathedral's high ceiling. Galileo was interested in pendulums. How could he time the pendulum? He used his pulse as a timer. Galileo observed the lamp as it swung and he counted his heartbeats. When he figured out the time for one swing, it was just what he had predicted.

ILLUSTRATIONS BY JIM WISNIEWSKI/STEVE EDSEY & SONS UNLESS OTHERWISE INDICATED

WONDERSCIENCE

Understanding Scale

The topic of scale is important because the systems we study in science occur on a variety of scales, from the subatomic scale to the human scale to the scale of the planets and stars. This unit explores the basic principles of scale by starting with a map of the eastern United States and providing successively closer views of smaller areas until a single ant is shown. In each picture, the scale is different so that greater detail of a smaller area can be shown. To do these activities effectively, each student or pair of students will need a photocopy of the map or picture to accompany a particular activity.

On the Trail of the Wonders of Scale

Ask students how they can use a map to find the distance between two places. If there is a large map in the room, ask students to pick two cities on the map and have another student show how to find the distance between the two points.

Results:

Step 1: From Louisville, KY, to Frankfort, KY, is 1 centimeter (cm) on the map. Since 1 cm represents 100 km, the cities are 100 km apart.

Step 2: From Greenville, MS, to Memphis, TN, is 2 cm on the map. Since 1 cm represents 100 km, the cities are 200 km apart.

Step 3: From Chicago, IL, to Gary, IN, is 5 millimeters (mm) or 0.5 cm. Since 1 cm represents 100 km, the cities are 50 km apart.

To introduce the next map, ask students how much Vermont would have to be blown up to almost fill an entire page. The answer is ten times. Now point out the scale on the full-page Vermont map. On this map, each centimeter represents 10 kilometers, ten times less than on the previous map.

Results:

Step 1: On the eastern U.S. map, Vermont's northern border is 1.4 cm long, which represents 1.4×100 km = 140 km.

Step 2: On the full-page Vermont map, the northern border is 14.2 cm long, which represents 14.2×10 km = 142 km. Notice that these answers are perfectly consistent.

Step 3: On the eastern U.S. map, Vermont's length north-to-south is 2.5 cm. On the full-page Vermont map, the length north-to-south is 24.4 cm (about ten times larger because the scale is ten times larger).

Step 4: On this map, 40 km is represented by 4 cm, so Waterbury is about 4 cm to the right of Burlington on Route 89.

Step 5: The distance on the map is 5 cm. Since the scale is 1 cm represents 10 km, the distance between the cities is 50 km. Time = distance/speed = 50 km/(25 km/hr) = 2 hours.

Design Your Own Scaled-Down Town!

Ask students how the scale will change in a map that shows only a town. Have them turn the page and note the scale. It might seem odd to students that as objects on the map are pictured larger and larger, the scale is actually getting smaller and smaller (1 cm is representing successively smaller distances). Ask students what features have disappeared from this map compared to the one before (the Canadian border, the Green Mountain National Forest) and what features are present that were not shown before (farm, lake, individual buildings).

Results:

Step 1: The farm dimensions on the map are 3 cm $\times$ 4 cm, which represents 300 m $\times$ 400 m.

Step 2: The school building is 0.8 cm $\times$ 0.4 cm, which represents 80 m $\times$ 40 m.

Step 3: On the map, this playground will be 1 cm $\times$ 0.5 cm.

Scale-a-School!

To introduce this picture, ask students to look at the scale. Ask students what features appear on this map that have not appeared on any of the previous ones (details of the ball field, trees, cars). Ask what features have disappeared that were on previous maps (river, lake, highway intersections). Ask students if it makes sense for objects to become larger and more detailed as the scale gets smaller. Have students pick out something familiar, such as a car, and measure it. Students can then convert the measurement to meters to see if the scale makes sense.

Results:

Step 1: The street is 1 cm wide, which represents 1×10 m = 10 m wide.

Step 2: On the map, a 40 m $\times$ 25 m addition will be represented in cm as 4 cm $\times$ 2.5 cm. It would fit best to the east of the school.

Unit 14
Understanding Scale

One-to-One and Your Scale Is Done!

To introduce this drawing, ask students what features have completely disappeared (buildings, except for the three bricks at the right) and what new details have appeared (grass). Point out the bricks of the school. Explain that 1 cm on the picture represents 1 cm in real life, so simply measuring the object in the picture gives the object's actual size. If the students want to find out how large a brick in the school is, they can measure one in the drawing. Point out the small ant in the square to the right, which will be in the next drawing.

Up Close and Personal!

Ask students what they would see if they looked at an ant through a magnifying glass. What details would the magnifier reveal that can't be seen with the naked eye (the ant's eyes, the bends in the legs, etc.)? This page shows such a magnified view.

Results:

Step 1: On the drawing, the ant is 5 cm long. Since 1 cm equals 1 mm, the ant is actually 5×1 mm or 5 mm long.

Step 2: The blades of grass taper, so the best we can do is to measure an average width, which is about 3 cm on the drawing. That represents 3 mm. The answer should be close to what you found on the previous map.

Zooming In on Scale

Ask students how this series of changing views is similar to looking through a zoom lens (as the lens zooms in, the view is more and more magnified, and the area you see—the field of view—becomes smaller and smaller). Ask the students to draw what they would see if the view continued zooming in, ten times closer with each new drawing (increasing detail on the ant; individual cells in the ant and the blade of grass; eventually, molecules and atoms). An excellent short film on the topic of scale change is *Power of Ten* by Charles Eames.

Results:

Lake: Eastern U.S. or full-page Vermont

Seed: Close-up of grass and ant

Amusement park: Town map

Mouse: Close-up of chipmunk

Hill: Town map

Swimming pool: School map

NATIONAL SCIENCE EDUCATION STANDARDS

The activities in this unit can be used to support the teaching of the following standards:

✔ **Unifying Concepts and Processes**

Constancy, Change, and Measurement
Scale includes understanding that different characteristics, properties, or relationships within a system might change as its dimensions are increased or decreased. (*All activities*)

✔ **Science as Inquiry**

Abilities Necessary to Do Scientific Inquiry
Use mathematics in all aspects of scientific inquiry. (*All activities*)

NOTES

Design Your Own Scaled-Down Town!

Use the drawing below and any of the area around it to draw in everything you think would make your town a great place to live in. Remember to draw everything to scale: 1 cm equals 100 m.

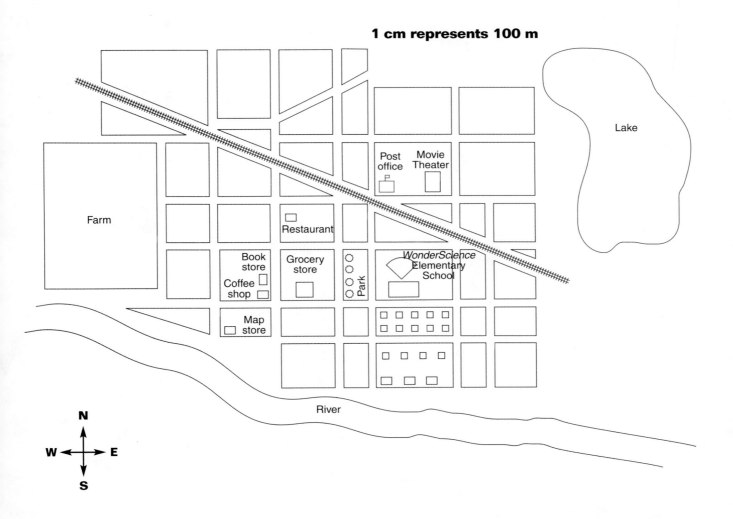

1 cm represents 100 m

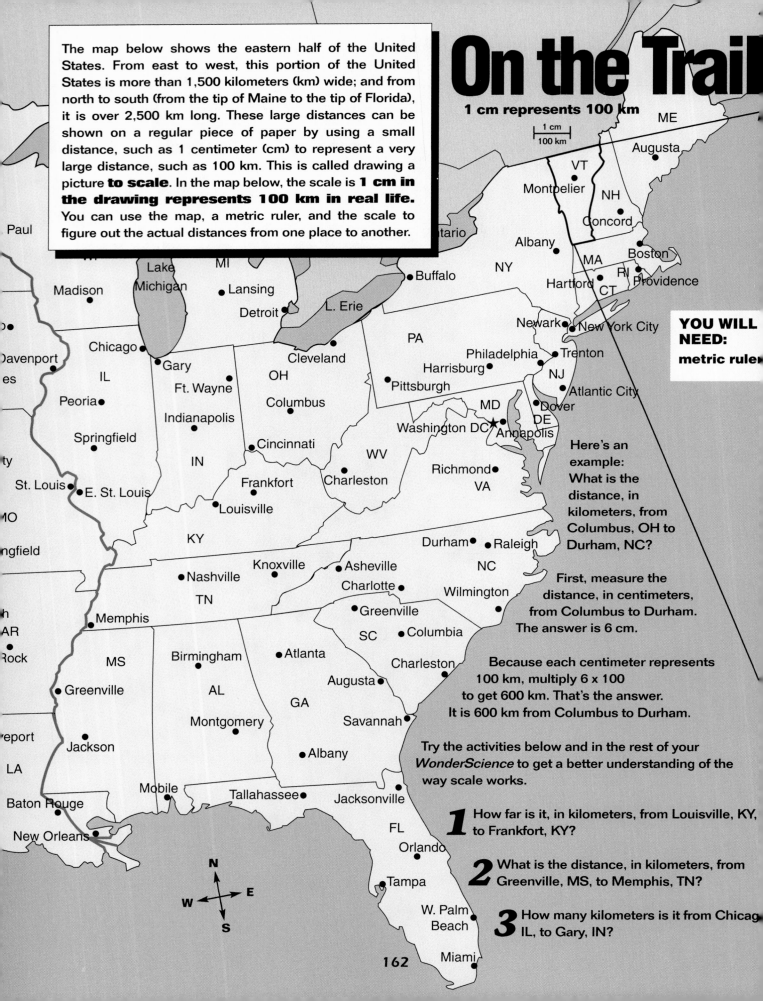

The map below shows the eastern half of the United States. From east to west, this portion of the United States is more than 1,500 kilometers (km) wide; and from north to south (from the tip of Maine to the tip of Florida), it is over 2,500 km long. These large distances can be shown on a regular piece of paper by using a small distance, such as 1 centimeter (cm) to represent a very large distance, such as 100 km. This is called drawing a picture **to scale**. In the map below, the scale is **1 cm in the drawing represents 100 km in real life.** You can use the map, a metric ruler, and the scale to figure out the actual distances from one place to another.

On the Trail

1 cm represents 100 km

1 cm
100 km

YOU WILL NEED:
metric ruler

Here's an example: What is the distance, in kilometers, from Columbus, OH to Durham, NC?

First, measure the distance, in centimeters, from Columbus to Durham. The answer is 6 cm.

Because each centimeter represents 100 km, multiply 6 x 100 to get 600 km. That's the answer. It is 600 km from Columbus to Durham.

Try the activities below and in the rest of your *WonderScience* to get a better understanding of the way scale works.

1 How far is it, in kilometers, from Louisville, KY to Frankfort, KY?

2 What is the distance, in kilometers, from Greenville, MS, to Memphis, TN?

3 How many kilometers is it from Chicago, IL, to Gary, IN?

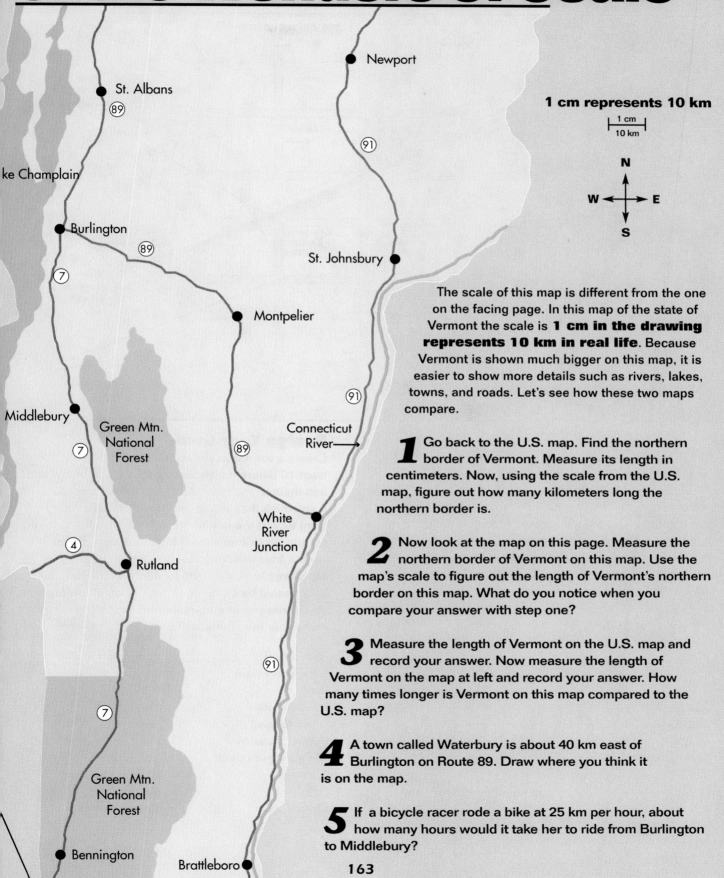

1 cm represents 10 km

1 cm
10 km

N
W ← → E
S

St. Albans
(89)

Newport

(91)

ke Champlain

Burlington
(89)

(7)

St. Johnsbury

Montpelier

(91)

Middlebury

Green Mtn.
National
Forest
(7)

Connecticut
River ⟶

(89)

(4)

Rutland

White
River
Junction

(91)

(7)

Green Mtn.
National
Forest

Bennington

Brattleboro

The scale of this map is different from the one on the facing page. In this map of the state of Vermont the scale is **1 cm in the drawing represents 10 km in real life**. Because Vermont is shown much bigger on this map, it is easier to show more details such as rivers, lakes, towns, and roads. Let's see how these two maps compare.

1 Go back to the U.S. map. Find the northern border of Vermont. Measure its length in centimeters. Now, using the scale from the U.S. map, figure out how many kilometers long the northern border is.

2 Now look at the map on this page. Measure the northern border of Vermont on this map. Use the map's scale to figure out the length of Vermont's northern border on this map. What do you notice when you compare your answer with step one?

3 Measure the length of Vermont on the U.S. map and record your answer. Now measure the length of Vermont on the map at left and record your answer. How many times longer is Vermont on this map compared to the U.S. map?

4 A town called Waterbury is about 40 km east of Burlington on Route 89. Draw where you think it is on the map.

5 If a bicycle racer rode a bike at 25 km per hour, about how many hours would it take her to ride from Burlington to Middlebury?

163

Design Your Own Scaled-Down Town

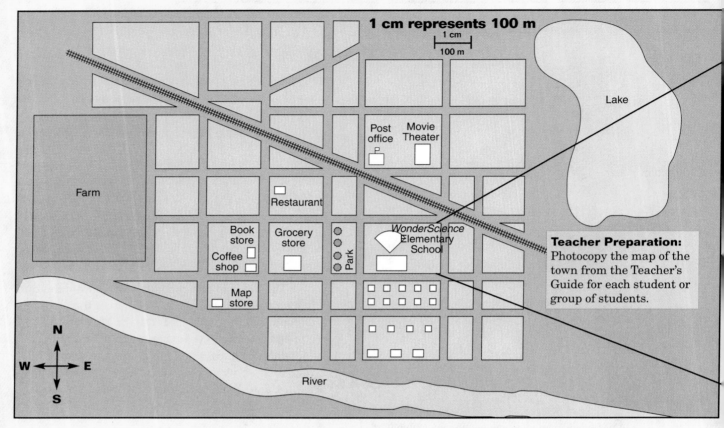

1 cm represents 100 m

1 cm
100 m

Lake

Post office

Movie Theater

Farm

Restaurant

Book store

Grocery store

Coffee shop

Park

WonderScience Elementary School

Map store

River

N
W — E
S

Teacher Preparation: Photocopy the map of the town from the Teacher's Guide for each student or group of students.

Here is a map of a pretend small town in Vermont. To draw the details of a small town such as houses, stores, and streets, the scale of the map needed to change again. Now the scale is **1 cm in the drawing represents 100 meters (m) in real life**. Your job is to fill in some more of the town's buildings and other details. To do this, you will need to measure in both centimeters and millimeters (mm). Because there are 10 mm in 1 cm, and each centimeter represents 100 meters, then each millimeter would represent 10 meters.

1 Find the farm on the west side of town. How wide is the farm, in meters, from east to west? How long is the farm, in meters, from north to south?

2 Find the *WonderScience* elementary school on the map. Measure the length of the elementary school in millimeters. Because each millimeter represents 10 m, how many meters long is the school? How many meters wide is it?

3 There needs to be a playground on the east side of the elementary school. It is 100 m long and 50 m wide. Draw it in.

Design Your Own Town!

Create a town that you would love to live in! Pick at least 10 different structures from the list below and add them to the town. Add other structures to the list if you think they would improve the town. You can even extend the boundaries of the town if you think certain structures should be farther from the town center. Measure very carefully and draw the structures to scale in the location where you think they should be on the map. Write down how big your structures are, in meters, on the list. Be creative and make your town unique! Then give it a great name!

High school	Apartment building
Department store	Amusement Park
Bank	Zoo
Hardware store	College
Office building	Hospital
Science museum	Fire station
Miniature golf course	Police station
Factory	Railroad station
Hotel	Boat house
City hall	Community pool

Scale-a-School!

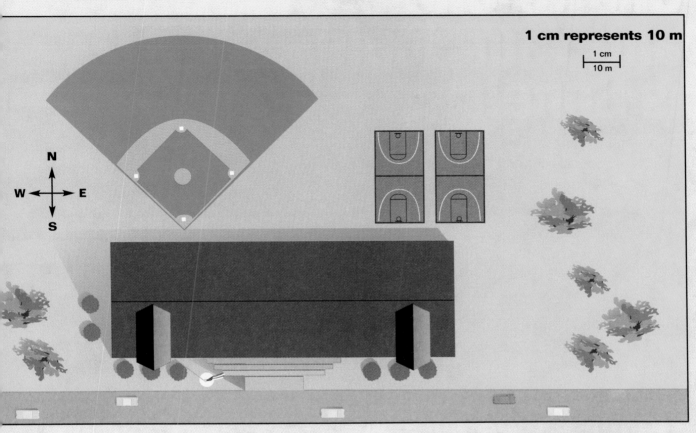

1 cm represents 10 m

1 cm
├──┤
10 m

N
W ← → E
S

Here is a picture of the elementary school from the map on the facing page. It's drawn much bigger in this picture because the scale of the drawing has changed again. The scale is now **1 cm in the drawing represents 10 m in real life**. You can see lots of detail that you could not see on the previous map. To do the following activities, you may have to measure in both centimeters and millimeters. Because there are 10 mm in 1 cm, and each centimeter represents 10 meters, then each millimeter would represent 1 meter.

1 How wide, in meters, is the street in front of the school?

2 The school needs a large addition for extra classrooms. The addition is to be 20 m x 25 m. Decide if it will be attached to either the east or west side of the school and draw it in.

Let's Take a Look at Your Own School:

Go outside with your teacher and measure the entire outside of your school building. Draw pictures and take good notes so you know the shape of the building and the measurements of all the lengths and widths. You could measure the inside of the school too, such as the gym, cafeteria, auditorium, hallways, and classrooms.

From your measurements and rough drawings, use the scale of 1 cm represents 10 m to make an accurate scale drawing of your school.

One-to-One and Your Scale is Done!

1 cm represents 1 cm

| 1 cm |
| 1 cm |

We took a small area from the corner of the school on the previous page and show it here on a different scale. This scale is **1 cm in the drawing represents 1 cm in real life**, or **actual size**. This means that the size of the objects in the picture are the same as they are in real life.

You can see some of the problems you run into when you try to show things of very different sizes on an actual-size scale. The only part of the school building you can see are the three bricks at the base. You can't even see the entire chipmunk when it is pictured at actual size because it is too big for the paper. In fact, everything in your *WonderScience* so far has been too large to show at actual size.

The eastern half of the United States is so huge compared to a piece of paper that it could only be pictured the way it was by using a scale where 1 cm on the paper represents 100 km of distance across the actual United States. The state

of Vermont isn't as big as the eastern half of the United States so it could be pictured on a standard size piece of paper by using a scale where 1 cm represents only 10 km. We made up a town in Vermont that was small enough that it could be pictured on a piece of paper using a scale where 1 cm represents 100 m. The elementary school is smaller still, so it could be shown using a scale in which 1 cm represents only 10 m.

But if you want to show some smaller objects on the school grounds such as the grass, sticks, and leaves, you can use a scale of actual size, where 1 cm represents 1 cm. These objects seem to be about the right size to be shown at actual size on a standard size piece of paper, but you don't get to see much else. Just as the building and the chipmunk are too large to be pictured at actual size, an ant is too small to be shown in much detail. To see how to deal with the problem of things being too small, just look at the next page!

Up Close and Personal!

1 cm represents 1 mm

|— 1 cm —|
1 mm

Just as very large objects or areas of land can be *shrunk* by drawing them to scale, very small objects can be made larger by drawing them to scale. When shrinking something large, 1 cm in the drawing always represents a much larger distance such as 100 km or 100 m. But when enlarging something, 1 centimeter in the drawing will represent a distance *less* than 1 cm such as 1 mm. That is the scale of the drawing above: **1 cm in the drawing represents 1 mm in real life.**

1 Measure the ant, in centimeters, in the drawing. Measure from the tip of the head to the tip of the rear section. If each centimeter in the drawing represents 1 mm in real life, how long is the actual ant?

2 Go back to the previous page and measure the length of the ant in millimeters. Since the scale of the drawing is actual size, the length you measured, in millimeters, should be the actual size of the ant. Your answer should agree with the length, in millimeters, that was calculated above. Does it?

3 If the picture is drawn to scale, you should also be able to figure out the actual width of a piece of grass. In the picture above, measure the width of one blade of grass, in centimeters. If each centimeter in the drawing represents 1 mm in real life, how wide is the actual blade of grass? You can check your answer by finding the same piece of grass on the previous page and measuring its actual size in millimeters. Was your answer pretty close?

Zooming In on Scale

This sequence of pictures from your *WonderScience* shows how changing the scale allows you to get a closer and closer look at something. By changing the scale from picture to picture, you have been able to go all the way from half a country down to a detailed view of an ant!

Look at the list below. Beside each item is its actual size. Based on the item's size, decide which of the six pages in your *WonderScience* has the right scale to show the listed items best. Look back at the actual *WonderScience* pages to make your decision and explain in each instance why you matched the item to a particular scale.

Lake (about 50 km long x 30 km wide)
Seed (about 3 mm x 2 mm)
Amusement park (about 2 km x 2 km)
Mouse (about 10 cm long)
Hill (about 500 m x 500 m at the base)
Swimming pool (25 m x 15 m)

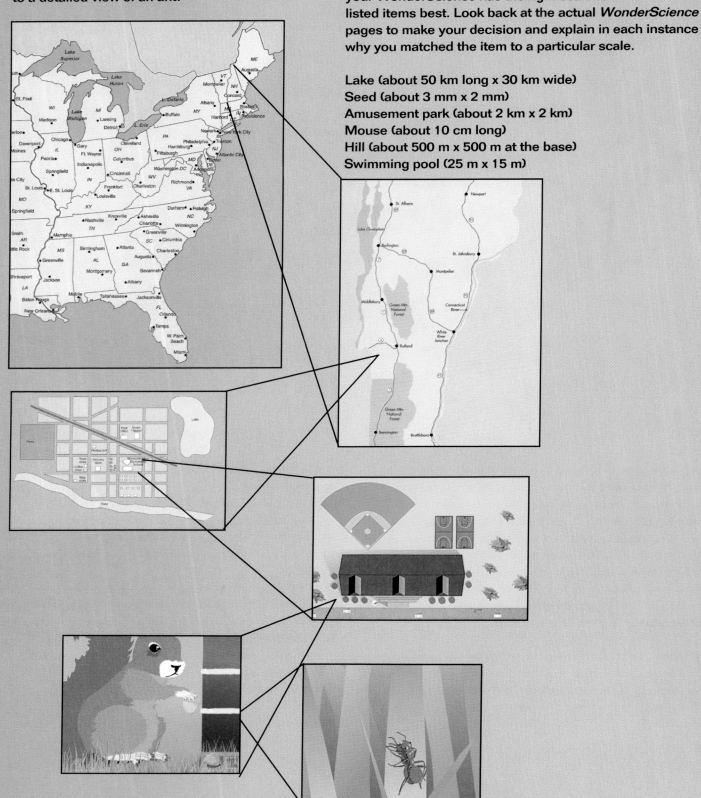

In this unit, students locate objects with a compass, practice navigation with maps and charts, and make a compass. They will learn that a compass is a magnet, and that the Earth is a magnet as well. They will tell direction by the traditional compass points and also by the angle made with the direction of north. In the final activity you can take the class outside to test their skills on a student-made orienteering course.

Your Direction Connection

To introduce the unit, ask students what they already know about the compass. Record their responses on the board or on chart paper. Then ask if any students have ever used the compass to find their way. Have them explain what they did. Then begin the activity. When they point in the direction of the colored end of the compass needle, everyone should be pointing in the same direction. If not, a compass may have lost its magnetization, and you may be able to remagnetize it by bringing it near a magnet. Or if not, a piece of iron or another magnet may be nearby. Also, if the students stand too close to each other, their compasses may attract each other, since both are magnets. Encourage students to rotate the compass so the "N" for north is directly under the colored end of the needle. Then they can read off the other directions accurately and easily.

Do Your Degrees Agree?

To introduce the activity, ask what would happen if a sea captain or airline pilot needed to go on a course between north and northeast. What would that course be called? You might also ask if students have heard commands like "Come right to 290°" in movies about airplanes or ships. You can also ask how a protractor works. To help students visualize the compass direction, draw an arrow pointing up on the board and label it with "north." Now draw various angles measured clockwise from the way this arrow points. Explain that angles are measured in degrees. You can have the students find the angles of north, east, south, and west (zero or 360°, 90°, 180°, and 270°) and points in between. In the illustration, the teacher's desk is at zero or 360°, the bookcase is at 90°, the window at 180°, and the door at 240°.

Earth—A Planet with Pull

Ask students what makes the compass needle turn toward north. The answer is that the Earth is a giant magnet, with a north and south magnetic pole. These poles do not line up exactly with the geographic poles. One is located in northern Canada, about 1,000 miles from geographic north. Over geological time, these magnetic poles wander about over the face of the Earth. In fact,

the poles have completely reversed many times in the history of the Earth. In relatively recent times, the reversals have come about every 1 million years and sometimes much more often than that. As for the naming of the magnetic north and south poles, this can cause some confusion. By definition, the colored end of the compass—the end that points north—is the north pole of the magnetic compass needle. That choice determines the poles of all other magnets, including the Earth. The Earth's magnetic pole that attracts the colored end of the compass is therefore a south magnetic pole.

Compass Making—Just Follow the Directions!

You can begin this activity by asking the students to tell if they have ever made a magnet and how they did it. In magnetizing the straightened clip, first rub one end of the magnet against one end of the clip. Be sure to turn the magnet around to rub the other end, because otherwise the magnetism will cancel out (for instance, if you rub both ends of the clip with the north pole of the magnet). Incidentally, the straightened clip is an ideal shape for a permanent magnet, because long, thin objects are easy to magnetize and retain the magnetization well. In addition to the Styrofoam mentioned in the activity, you can also tape the clip to a short piece of dowel about $\frac{1}{8}$ inch in diameter. You can ask the students to compare the motion of the compass they make with the compass they used in the first activity.

Land Ho! Where'd You Go?

To begin, ask students how the compass directions are shown on a map. If you have some maps in the classroom, have the students find the compass rose. The compass rose shows the orientation of north, south, east, and west on the map. Point out that north is usually toward the top of a map. When you have the students cut out the compass in the upper right hand corner of their map, they can then place that compass anywhere on the map to help find the direction to another spot. Navigators on boats have special instruments that roll over a map or chart to help them do the same thing.

Unit 15
Finding Your Way with the Amazing Compass

Make a Compass Course. . .of Course!

Explain to the students that they will make a course by using their compass and by measuring distances.

Another way to do the activity is for you to set up the course yourself, in advance. You can also write various sequences of the course on pieces of paper for the students to draw. They would then go outside and follow the course. If each sequence you write is different, the groups will probably be able to stay out of each other's way.

Assessment/Integration:

Have students write a story about a group of kids who get lost in the woods and find their way out with a compass.

Finding Your Way
with the Amazing Compass

NATIONAL SCIENCE EDUCATION STANDARDS

The activities in this unit can be used to support the teaching of the following standards:

✔ **Unifying Concepts and Processes**

Evidence, Models, and Explanation

Models are tentative schemes or structures that correspond to real objects, events, or classes of events and that have explanatory power.

Compass Making—Just Follow the Directions!

✔ **Science as Inquiry**

Abilities Necessary to Do Scientific Inquiry

Communicate scientific procedures and explanations.

Do Your Degrees Agree?

Land Ho! Where'd You Go?

Make a Compass Course. . .of Course!

LAND HO!
Where'd You Go?

YOU WILL NEED:

photocopy of this 2-page spread

scissors
ruler

Take a look at the map.

1 Imagine that you are on Big Rock Island and need to get to Danger Island. Carefully cut out the compass in the upper right-hand corner. Place it on the "X" on Big Rock Island so that 0 degrees and "N" are lined up straight up and down according to the N on the compass rose that's on the bottom of the map.

2 You can figure out the direction the captain needs to go by placing the edge of a ruler from the center of the compass to the "X" on Danger Island. The number on the compass that the ruler crosses is the angle or course the captain needs to take. According to our measurements, the course is 130 degrees. Did you get the same answer?

3 What is the course from Danger Island to Pelican Island?

4 Make a list of all five islands in the order you want the captain to visit them. Then give the compass course for each part of the voyage.

5 Make up an imaginary voyage including stops at all five islands. Write down the name of the island where you started. Measure and record the compass direction for each part of the trip. Do not write down the names of the islands. Give the paper to your partner. See if your partner can figure out the order in which you visited the islands.

Your Direction Connection

You have probably seen a compass before and maybe even turned one around to see where the needle pointed. But have you ever really tried to use one or to figure out how it works? After you do the activities in this unit of *WonderScience*, your knowledge of the compass will definitely be heading in the right direction!

1 Hold the compass level in your hand. The part that spins is called the compass needle. Stand up and hold the compass so you look straight down at it. Which way is the colored end of the compass needle pointing? Point your arm in this same direction. Look around the classroom. Which way are your classmates pointing?

2 Pick something in the room that the colored end of the needle is pointing to. Slowly turn around. As you turn, check to see if the needle still points to the same object. What do you notice?

3 Look at the letters around the outside of the compass. What letters are there? What do they stand for? Turn the compass so that the N is under the colored end of the needle. This is the first step in using a compass to tell directions. You always need to have the colored end of the needle over the N. Once your compass is set this way, you can tell the actual directions of north, south, east, and west.

4 Your compass also shows the in-between directions of northeast, northwest, southeast, and southwest. After turning your compass so that the colored end of the needle points toward the N, pick four objects in the room that you think are either north, south, east, west, or northeast, northwest, southeast, or southwest.

5 Write the four objects down and give the list and the compass to your partner. See if your partner can tell in which direction each object is located. Now switch around so your partner picks the objects and you try to figure out the direction.

YOU WILL NEED:

1 compass for each pair of students

Do Your Degrees Agree?

A compass can tell you more than the four major directions of north, south, east, and west and the in-between directions of northeast, northwest, southeast, and southwest. It can also give you even more detailed directions by using the degrees of a circle.

Look at the picture of the compass below. It is marked with the 360° of a circle. This type of compass can be used to tell the direction of something in degrees by seeing how many degrees away from north an object is.

Here's an example. If you have a compass set to north like the compass shown in the picture, you can see that the direction to the bookcase is 90° from north. Because the degrees are always measured from north, you can just say "90 degrees."

1 Use the compass in the drawing and give the directions for the teacher's desk, window, and door.

2 Imagine that you are standing where the compass is in the picture and you are facing the teacher's desk. If you turned to face the bookcase, through how many degrees would you turn? How about if you turned from the bookcase to the window? How about if you turned from the window to the door?

3 In your own classroom, pick four objects in different areas and write them down. Use your compass to figure out how many degrees from north each object is. (Remember to always start with the colored end of the needle at the N.) Write down the degrees next to the object.

4 Make a copy of your list of objects but without including the degrees. Hand your partner the compass and the list. Ask your partner to give the directions and see if they are the same as yours. Then switch around so your partner can pick the objects and you try to get the right directions.

175

EARTH— A Planet with Pull!

The needle of a compass is actually a small magnet. The reason why a magnetized compass needle works as a compass is because the Earth is a magnet too!

The Earth acts like a gigantic magnet. Like any other magnet, the Earth has its magnetic poles at opposite ends. A compass needle will always line up with the Earth's north and south magnetic poles.

But...
the Earth's magnetic poles are not exactly at the geographic North and South Poles...

...If you think that's strange, see if you can figure this one out:

OK, you know that the needle of a compass is really a magnet. And you know that the Earth is also a magnet. Now—magnets have a north and a south pole, right? That means that the compass needle and the Earth each have a north and a south pole.

Here's an important part that you may or may not know: In magnets, opposite poles point toward each other or attract; same poles point away from each other or repel. This means that north and south poles attract, but north and north, and south and south repel.

OK, we've got that settled. Now—the colored end of your compass needle is the north pole of a magnet. It should be attracted to the south pole of another magnet, like the Earth. Then why does the north pole of your compass needle point toward the north? What's going on with that?

Here's your answer: The Earth's *south* magnetic pole is actually up there in the *north,* and the Earth's north magnetic pole is in the south!! And we are not kidding.

A Little History:

When sailors went out on the ocean, out of sight of land, they had to find their way. The first sailors navigated with the sun and stars. But if the sky was cloudy, they couldn't see these objects in the sky. There needed to be some way to tell directions on a cloudy day. The compass was the answer!

Sailors from several countries began using the compass between 1100 and 1300 A.D. An early compass may have been a magnetized needle attached to a piece of wood. The needle and wood could float in a bowl of water, so the needle could turn freely.

To help the sailors read the compass direction, a card was added to the floating magnet. The card was usually labeled with the eight compass directions. The card also included 32 points, shown by arrows.

Compass Making—
JUST FOLLOW THE DIRECTIONS!

The needle of a compass is a thin lightweight magnet. Like any other magnet, the needle of a compass has a north pole at one end and a south pole at the other. The compass works because the magnetism from the Earth turns the needle so that it points toward the Earth's north and south poles. You can see how this works by making your own compass.

1 Hold one side or end of the magnet against one end of the straightened paper clip. Rub in one direction as shown. Now hold the *other* side or end of the magnet against the other end of the paper clip and rub in the other direction.

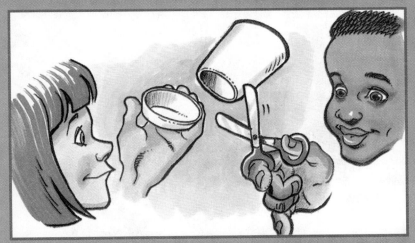

2 Use the scissors to cut out the bottom of a Styrofoam cup. Place the paper clip on the cup bottom as shown.

3 Add water to the bowl until it is about 3/4 full. Gently lower the cup bottom with the paper clip into the water. What happens?

4 Gently change the direction of your compass. What happens? Bring another compass over. Compare the way your water compass needle points with the way the needle in your regular compass points. But don't bring them too close together. Do you know why not?

LAND HO!
Where'd You Go?

YOU WILL NEED:

photocopy of this 2-page spread

scissors

ruler

Take a look at the map.

1 Imagine that you are on Big Rock Island and need to get to Danger Island. Carefully cut out the compass in the upper right-hand corner. Place it on the "X" on Big Rock Island so that 0 degrees and "N" are lined up straight up and down according to the N on the compass rose that's on the bottom of the map.

2 You can figure out the direction the captain needs to go by placing the edge of a ruler from the center of the compass to the "X" on Danger Island. The number on the compass that the ruler crosses is the angle or course the captain needs to take. According to our measurements, the course is 130 degrees. Did you get the same answer?

3 What is the course from Danger Island to Pelican Island?

4 Make a list of all five islands in the order you want the captain to visit them. Then give the compass course for each part of the voyage.

5 Make up an imaginary voyage including stops at all five islands. Write down the name of the island where you started. Measure and record the compass direction for each part of the trip. Do not write down the names of the islands. Give the paper to your partner. See if your partner can figure out the order in which you visited the islands.

178

Make a Compass Course...
of Course!

YOU WILL NEED:
(EACH GROUP)

5 markers such as sticks or dowels labeled 1–5 (each group should use a different color)

compass

string

meter stick

pencil

paper

Your compass skills can be tested by this activity in which different groups create different outdoor navigation courses. Your teacher will organize the groups and show you where to create your compass challenge!

1 Place stick 1 in the ground. From stick 1, set your compass needle to north, and pick a direction (such as 60° or 210°) where you want the direction of stick 2 to be. Mark down the direction and measure and record the distance you go and then place stick 2 in the ground.

2 Go back to stick 1 and see if you can use your own directions to get to stick 2. Repeat these steps to go from stick 2 to 3, from 3 to 4, and from 4 to 5. Do not use distances of more than 20 meters from one stick to the next.

3 When you are done, make sure your directions and distances from stick to stick are clearly written down. Check them by navigating through your whole course.

4 Put group names into a hat. Choose so that each group picks another group's course.

5 Work your way through the course you pick. Mark down the directions and distances as you move from stick 1 to stick 5. See how close your answers match those of the group that set up the course.

WONDER SCIENCE

Unit 16
Let's Graph It!

Graphing is an important tool for interpreting scientific data as well as information from many different sources. In this unit, students use graphs to explore situations in which changing one variable causes a change in a second variable. We hope that students will not only learn to plot points on a coordinate plane and interpret the graph in context, but also develop a strong foundation for two important mathematical concepts: variables and slope.

Graphing—It'll Grow On You!

Begin a discussion by asking students how they might design an experiment to see if the amount of water given a plant affects the height of the plant. Would they use more than one plant in their experiment? Would all the plants be the same kind? Should they all be in the same type of soil? What might they expect to happen if a plant received too little water? What might happen if a plant got too much water? In this activity, students should recognize that the amount of water given the plants is one variable and the height that the plant grows as a result is another variable.

Results:

Students should use metric rulers because these heights measured in inches will be very inconvenient decimals. The measurements in the table are in centimeters.

The graph would look like this:

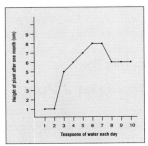

Interpreting the graph:

Teaspoons	1	2	3	4	5	6	7	8	9	10
Height (cm)	1	1	5	6	7	8	8	8	6	6

Giving the plant more water made the plant grow taller at first, but we can see that more than 6 teaspoons of water per day did not cause the plant to grow taller. We would guess that a plant

given $5\frac{1}{2}$ teaspoons of water per day would have been about $7\frac{1}{2}$ cm tall at the end of one month, and we can be reasonably confident that this is approximately correct.

Guesses about a plant given 12 teaspoons of water a day might vary from 0 (the plant died) to 6 cm. Any such guess is reasonable; we cannot be confident about any particular number in that range given the data we have. However, we are fairly confident that the correct answer is in the range from 0 to 6 cm.

The slope of this graph is upward from 2 teaspoons to 6 teaspoons; it is level from 1 to 2 teaspoons, and from 6 to 7 teaspoons, and again from 8 to 10 teaspoons. The slope of the graph is downward from 7 to 8 teaspoons.

Where the slope was upward (mathematicians call this a positive slope), adding one more teaspoon of water per day caused the plant to grow taller. Where the slope was level (mathematicians call this a zero slope), adding one more teaspoon of water per day caused no change in the height of the plant. Where the slope was downward (mathematicians call this a negative slope), adding one more teaspoon of water per day caused the plant's growth to slow so that the result was a shorter plant.

Plot-a-Shot!

In this activity, students will be launching little rolled-up balls of paper or masking tape from a flexible spoon. Be sure to warn students not to stand in the path of the ball. Also, be sure to show students the proper way of stabilizing the spoon with the nonshooting hand. Also, be sure that the zero on the ruler is properly lined up with the spoon.

Results:

Our results were as follows (but results will vary):

cm pulled back	1	2	3	4	5
Distance (cm)	52	204	340	460	495

Unit 16
Let's Graph it!

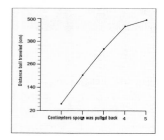

If the graph has an upward slope (reading from left to right) throughout, then that demonstrates that the farther the spoon is pulled back, the greater the horizontal distance the ball traveled. If the slope levels off or increases more steeply, then students should also be able to say something about the amount of increase in distance traveled per amount of increase in distance the spoon was pulled back. Discussion of these results can help your students (1) understand the concept of a relation between variables and (2) begin to understand the concept of slope.

Graphing—It's Gonna Be Big!

As you know, balloons can be very difficult to blow up. Be sure students stretch the balloons quite a bit to make inflating the balloons as easy as possible. Although results will vary depending on each student's ability to blow up a balloon, the general trend in the data should be the same for all students.

Results:

The circumference of the balloon will increase with each added breath of air. However, the amount of increase decreases; that is, the circumference increases faster at first than it does later on.

Here's what we got:

Breaths	1	2	3	4	5
Circumference (cm)	48	59	66	71	74

Graphs will vary, but should slope upward less and less steeply.

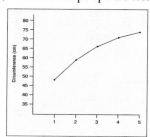

We see that the circumference of the balloon increases with each breath because the graph slopes upward everywhere. But

we also see that the amount of increase in the circumference is less and less with each breath by observing that the steepness of the slope is decreasing. The graph continues to slope upward, but less and less steeply.

Putting Time on the Line

In this activity, it is important to use a plastic, as opposed to a wooden, spool to be sure the spool slides smoothly down the thread. The spool can either have thread on it or not. If you or your students do not have enough stopwatches, inexpensive stopwatches (less than $10.00) can be purchased from American Science and Surplus, 1-847-982-0870.

Results

Our graph looked like this:

	1	2	3	4	5
Height (cm)	90	120	150	180	210
Time (seconds)	8.3	4.2	3.2	2.6	2.2

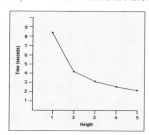

If students are able to time their spool's trip accurately, the graph of their data will have a downward (negative) slope throughout. This shows that the greater the height of the end of the string where the spool begins its trip, the less time it will take the spool to reach the floor.

Stretching to Make a Point

Results here will vary widely according to the attributes of the rubber bands your students use. It might be interesting to have two or three kinds of rubber bands, and give some groups of students one kind to test and other groups another.

Results:

Here's what we got:

Number of pennies	0	5	10	15	20	25	30	35	40	45	50
Length (cm)	15	15.5	16	16.5	17.3	18.1	18.8	19.8	20.7	21.6	22.9

(Continued on page 184)

NATIONAL SCIENCE EDUCATION STANDARDS

The activities in this unit can be used to support the teaching of the following standards:

✔ **Unifying Concepts and Processes**

Evidence, Models and Explanations

Using evidence to understand interactions allows individuals to predict changes in natural and designed systems.
> Plot-a-Shot!
> Graphing—It's Gonna Be Big!
> Putting Time on the Line
> Stretching to Make a Point
> Hot Plots!

Constancy, Change, and Measurement

Mathematics is essential for accurately measuring change. *(All activities)*
Rate involves comparing one measured quantity with another measured quantity. *(All activities)*

✔ **Science as Inquiry**

Abilities Necessary to Do Scientific Inquiry

Design and conduct a scientific investigation. *(All activities)*
Use appropriate tools and techniques, including mathematics, to gather, analyze, and interpret data. *(All activities)*
Use mathematics in all aspects of scientific inquiry. *(All activities)*

Unit 16
Let's Graph it!

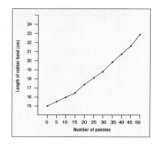

If the rubber band stretches the same amount each time five more pennies are added, the graph will be a straight line. This should be viewed as quite significant because what makes a graph a straight line is that its slope is constant.

If instead the rubber band stretches more than it did before, the graph will get steeper (the slope increases). If it stretches less than before, the graph becomes less steep (the slope decreases, even though it is still positive).

Hot Plots!

This activity requires a fair amount of coordination among students working in a group. After the yeast is added to the hydrogen peroxide, one student will swirl the cup and call out the temperature every 10 seconds. Another student needs to work the stopwatch and call out the time every 10 seconds. A third student needs to write down the temperature every 10 seconds.

Results:

Our graph looked like this:

Time (seconds)	0	10	20	30	40	50	60	70	80	90	100
Temperature (°F)	72	74	76	80	82	84	86	88	89	89	89

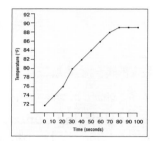

Where the temperature rose fastest, the slope of the graph is the steepest. This occurred from 20 to 30 seconds. Where the temperature rose more slowly, the slope of the graph begins to level off. This happened between 70 and 80 seconds. Where it hardly rose any more at all, the graph is nearly horizontal. This occurred between 80 and 120 seconds.

Assessment/Integration:

Have students write a newspaper article or advertisement that mentions a graph. Have them draw the graph and explain it in the article.

Graphing—

A graph is a way of showing information by using a special kind of picture. Graphs are very useful when doing scientific experiments. A graph can be used to show how changing something in the experiment causes a change in the results. Here's an example:

Let's say you were doing an experiment to find out the best amount of water to give to a certain type of plant so that it would grow the tallest. So the question is:

How does the amount of water a plant gets affect how tall the plant grows?

Let's say you and your partner together planted 10 seeds and gave each one a certain amount of water each day. Seed 1 gets 1 teaspoon, seed 2 gets 2 teaspoons, seed 3 gets 3 teaspoons, and so on. (In an experiment, the one thing that you change to see the effect it has is called the **variable**. In this experiment, the amount of water is the variable.) Let's also say that you take care of the even-numbered plants (2, 4, 6, 8, and 10). Your partner takes care of the odd-numbered plants (1, 3, 5, 7, and 9). After the seeds sprout and the plants begin to grow, you continue watering them in this way and then measure their height at the end of one month. Here is a chart for your data:

Teaspoons	1	2	3	4	5	6	7	8	9	10
Height (cm)										

1 First you need to collect your data. Draw a chart like the one above. Use your ruler to measure the height of each plant in the illustrations. Record the results in the chart.

LET'S GRAPH IT!

It'll Grow on You!

2 Make a graph like the one at right. The horizontal and vertical lines that make up a graph are each called an axis of the graph. In graphing, we usually put the variable that *we* change, such as the amount of water, on the horizontal axis. The two axes together would look like the drawing at right.

3 To graph the information in your chart, first look at 1 teaspoon on the chart. Put your pencil on the "1" on the teaspoon axis of your graph and then look at the height of the plant that got 1 teaspoon of water.

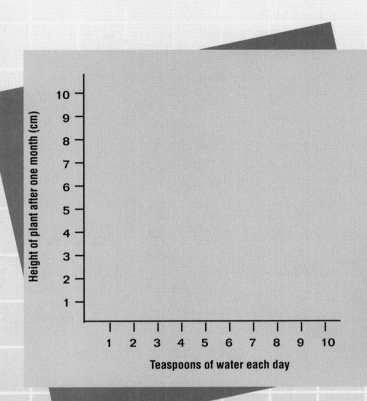

The height is 1 centimeter (cm) so move your pencil straight up until it is directly across from the "1" on the height axis. Put a dot right at that spot.

Now look at the height of the plant that got 2 teaspoons of water. Put your pencil on the "2" on the teaspoon line of your graph and then look at the height for 2 teaspoons. Move your pencil up until it is directly across from the height that you measured. Place a dot on that spot.

Continue drawing the dots for the rest of the teaspoons and their heights. Then draw a smooth line connecting the dots.

4 Let's use your graph to answer some questions about how different amounts of water affected the heights of the plants.

Does giving the plant more water make it grow taller?

In this experiment, no plant got 5 1/2 teaspoons of water each day. From looking at your graph, make a good guess about how tall a plant would get if given 5 1/2 teaspoons of water each day. How about one given 12 teaspoons of water each day? How sure can you be about these answers?

The **slope** of a graph is the way it goes up or down when looked at from left to right. The slope of your graph can give a lot of information about the experiment. Where does the slope of your graph go up? Where is it level? Where does it go down? What do you think these different slopes mean?

Plot-a-Shot!

You can graph lots of different experiments. How about if you were making a toy or game to throw a ball? You need to find out how far back to bend a plastic spoon to throw a little ball the right distance. So the question is:

How does the distance you pull back the spoon affect how far the ball goes?

YOU WILL NEED:

students at least three per group

masking tape

books

plastic spoon (flexible)

metric ruler (to place on books)

paper and pen

meter stick or measuring tape

1 Make a chart like the one below. With three pieces of masking tape, tape the spoon to the edge of a table as shown.

2 Place one or two books next to the spoon so that the books are about as high as the top of the spoon. Place a ruler on the book, and tape it down so that the front of the spoon is at the 0 centimeter mark.

3 Use a piece of tape to mark a spot on the floor right below the spoon. This is your **launch spot**.

4 Roll a piece of masking tape or small piece of paper into a ball about 1 cm in diameter and hold it in place on the spoon.

5 Use your thumb to hold the spoon firmly against the table; pull the spoon back 1 cm and let it go. Mark the spot where the ball hits the floor. Measure the distance from the launch spot to where the ball landed. Record this distance in your chart under 1 cm.

> **Do not stand directly in front of the spoon when the ball is launched.**

> **Be careful not to pull the spoon back so far that it breaks.**

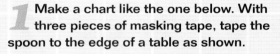

Cm pulled back	1	2	3	4	5
Distance (cm)					

6 Repeat step 5, pulling the spoon back 2 cm and then 3 cm and so on up to 5 cm. Record the distance the ball travels each time.

LET'S GRAPH IT!

Use the horizontal axis for the distance the spoon was pulled back. Use the vertical axis for the distance between the launch spot and where the ball landed. Make a copy of the graph below.

Use the data from your chart to make a graph of the results of your experiment. If you are not sure where to put the dots, go back and see what you did when you graphed the seed-watering experiment.

What does the slope of the graph tell you?

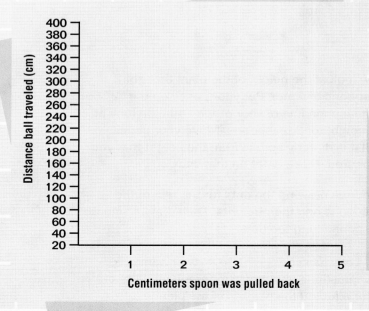

Graphing—It's Gonna Be Big!

Pretend your company has made a new balloon material that needs testing. So the question is:

How does each breath you blow into a balloon affect how big around the balloon gets?

YOU WILL NEED:

large round balloon
measuring tape or string and metric ruler
paper and pen

1 Make a chart like the one below.

Breaths	0	1	2	3	4	5
Circumference (cm)						

2 Stretch the balloon a few times so that it will be easier to blow up. Blow one breath into the balloon and then pinch the end closed. Have your partner measure around the balloon at its fattest part. This is the **circumference.**

3 Record the number of centimeters your balloon measured next to "circumference" under "breath 1" in the chart.

4 Use four more breaths the same size as the first, and measure the balloon each time. Try to measure the circumference around the same area of the balloon each time. Fill in the rest of the chart.

LET'S GRAPH IT!

Make a graph like the one at right. Use the data from your chart to make a graph of your experiment.

How does the circumference of the balloon change with each breath?

How does the slope of the graph show how the circumference changes?

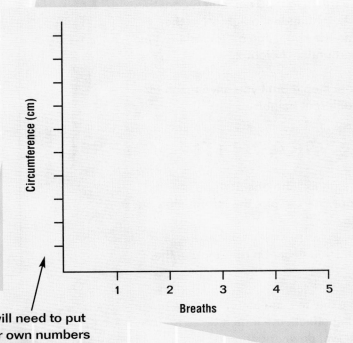

You will need to put in your own numbers based on the size of your balloon.

189

Putting Time on the Line

YOU WILL NEED:

plastic spool of thread

meter stick

stopwatch or clock
with second hand

paper and pen

Pretend you are making a ride for a playground or theme park that has a car that slides down a cable. You use a spool sliding down a string to be a model of the car. To make the spool slide, you raise one end of the string.

The question is: How does the height you hold one end of a string affect how long it takes the spool to slide all the way down the string?

1 Make a chart like the one below. Cut off a piece of thread about 5 meters long. Tape or tie one end of the thread to the bottom of a chair or desk leg. Push the other end of the thread through the center hole of the spool.

2 Pull the thread tight. Find the lowest height you can hold the string and still have the spool slide all the way to the bottom. Don't move the thread while the spool is sliding. Measure this height and record it in your chart under "height 1."

3 When your partner is ready to time the spool, say "GO" as you release the spool. Your partner should time the spool all the way to the bottom of the thread. Record the time in the chart under "height 1."

4 Raise the height 30 cm, and record this new height under "height 2" in the chart. Time the spool again. Record the time in the chart under "height 2."

5 Repeat step 4 until you have times for five different heights.

LET'S GRAPH IT!

Draw a graph like the one at right. Use the data in your chart to plot the information on the graph.

How would you describe the slope of the line?

What does this tell you about how the height of the string affects the time it takes for the spool to travel down the thread?

Height (cm)	1	2	3	4	5
Time (seconds)					

Each height should be 30 cm higher than the previous one.

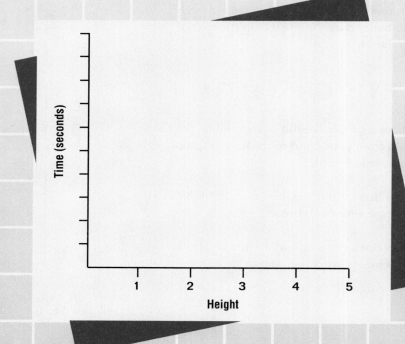

Stretching to Make a Point

If you worked in a rubber band factory and needed to understand the way a rubber band stretched, you could do a test to figure it out. Your question would be:

How does the amount of weight added to the rubber band change the distance the rubber band stretches?

YOU WILL NEED:

rubber band
metric ruler
scissors
paper clip
pennies (50 per group)
Dixie cup (3 oz)
string
masking tape

1 Make a chart like the one below. Carefully use your scissors to cut a rubber band. Unbend part of a paper clip and tie it securely to the end of the rubber band as shown.

2 Cut a piece of string and tape it to the top of the Dixie cup to make a little handle. Hook the handle onto the paper clip.

3 Place the end of the rubber band over the ruler and tape it around so that the rubber band is secure and the rim of the cup is at about the 15 cm mark. Under "0" for Number of pennies, record where the rim of the cup is on the ruler when no pennies are in the cup.

4 Place five pennies in the cup. Check where the rim of the cup is on the ruler and record that length under "5" for number of pennies.

5 Continue adding 5 pennies each time and recording the length on the ruler until you have added all 50 pennies.

LET'S GRAPH IT!

Use the data in your chart to plot the information on your graph.

Does the graph show you that every time you added 5 pennies, the rubber band stretched the same amount?

Is there any place on the graph that shows the rubber band stretching more or less than it did before? How does the slope of that part of the graph compare with the slope of the other part?

Number of pennies	0	5	10	15	20	25	30	35	40	45	50
Length (cm)											

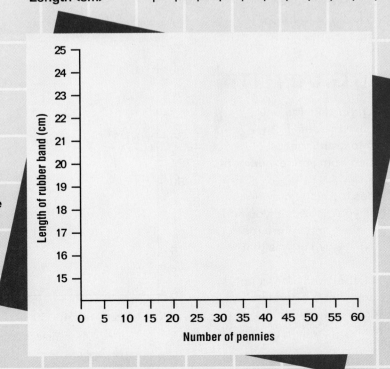

Length of rubber band (cm) vs. Number of pennies

Hot Plots!

YOU WILL NEED:

students at least three per group
dry yeast
hydrogen peroxide (3%)
thermometer
stopwatch or watch with second hand
plastic cup
paper and pen
measuring spoons

If you were working with a chemical reaction and needed to know how it heated up over a period of time, you could do an experiment and then graph it.

The question is: How does the amount of heat produced by a chemical reaction change during the reaction?

LOEL BARR

Students must wear goggles for this activity.

1 Make a chart like the one below. Pour 2 tablespoons of hydrogen peroxide into a cup. Place the thermometer into the cup. Hold the thermometer and the cup so they do not fall over.

2 Read the temperature and record it on the chart under "time 0." Have one partner watch the thermometer and another look at the second hand on the watch.

3 Measure 1 teaspoon of yeast and dump it into the cup. Gently swirl the cup while one partner calls out the time every 10 seconds. When each 10 seconds is called, another partner should call out the temperature. The third partner should record the temperature in the chart.

Time (seconds)	0	10	20	30	40	50	60	70	80	90	100
Temperature (°F)											

LET'S GRAPH IT!

Set up a graph like the one at right. Use the data from the chart to graph the information from your experiment.

What does the slope of your graph tell you? How can you find out when the temperature rose most quickly? When was that?

Where on the graph does the slope show that the temperature rose more slowly and then not much at all?

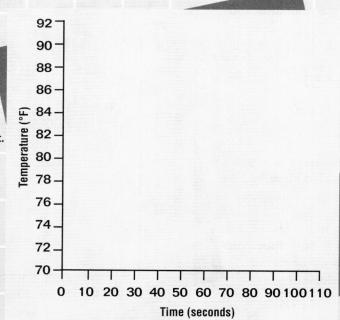

The concept of volume as a measure of three-dimensional space is not an easy one for students to grasp. Even if they understand how to measure length, width, and depth and multiply to get the volume, they often do not completely understand that the number they get is a measure of the space enclosed by these measurements. Reconciling this with volume as milliliters or liters poses still another problem. We have placed the activities in an order to first give students a sense of volume in general and then to show how volume is commonly used to measure liquid quantity.

Throughout this unit, students will be measuring with metric rulers and by other means. Be sure to advise students that some of their measurements and calculations may not come out as precisely as they might expect. Discuss the possible errors that would cause these differences, and student results will be more meaningful.

Make Room for Volume

The first activity introduces students to volume as the amount of space inside a container. When students put water in the small carton, they see that the water fills up the entire space or volume of the carton. Students observe that they can put two small cartons of water in the medium carton and four small cartons of water in the large carton. This means that the medium carton must be twice the volume of the small carton and that the large carton is four times the volume of the small carton.

Looks Can Be Deceiving

You could introduce this activity by placing equal volumes of colored water in a clear tall narrow container, such as a bud vase, and into a clear short wide container, such as a glass bowl. Ask students which container has a greater volume of liquid. There may be some difference of opinion. This can lead to a discussion about how the same volume of liquid can look different in different containers. Students may conclude that to compare the volume of the two liquids, they would need to use identical containers or a measuring cup or some other calibrated container.

The purpose of the activity is to help students realize that a one-carton volume of water takes up the same amount of space in the 1- and 2-liter bottles, but the space just looks different in the different bottles. In the 1-liter bottle, the one-carton volume is a taller, narrower cylinder of water, and in the 2-liter bottle, the one-carton volume is a shorter, wider cylinder of water. Although these shapes look different, they have the same volume, which is the same volume as the one small carton.

Down for the Count!

You could start the activity by asking students if anything happens to the level of water in a container when something like stone or brick sinks in the water or when a piece of wood is pushed down into the water. If students say that the water level goes up, you could ask them if they think the amount that the water goes up has anything to do with the shape, weight, or volume of the object pushed down or sunk in the water.

In this activity, students should see that the volume of water displaced (the volume of water that rises) is equal to the volume of the object pushed down into the water (the small carton).

Measuring Volume the Handy Way!

You could ask students if they wanted to measure the length of something very accurately, would it be better to use a ruler with a few marks wide apart or one with many marks closer together? After discussing their answers, you could ask students if the same reasoning would apply to measuring volume.

The activity is an extension of "Down for the Count!" and is a fun way to measure volume by displacement. It also provides a lesson in how to increase the accuracy of measurements.

After students have completed this activity, you might tell them how Archimedes, one of the best scientists ever, was asked to solve a problem for the king. A jeweler had been asked to make the king a crown out of gold, but when it was finished, the king was not certain that the jeweler had used only gold. He was suspicious that the jeweler might have mixed in too much of a less valuable metal. He asked Archimedes to determine whether the crown was made of the quality of gold he required. Archimedes knew how he could compare gold with other metals: Just compare the weights of like volumes. But how could he determine the volume of something shaped as irregularly as the king's crown? He pondered this question for quite some time before he got an idea. Ask if anyone in the class can think of a way to determine the volume of the king's crown. Since they have just worked on "Measuring Volume the Handy Way!," they are quite likely to think of doing exactly what Archimedes did! He put the crown into a measured volume of water and then measured the amount of water that was displaced!

Volume: Full of Surprises!

Archimedes had this remarkable insight while he was bathing. He noticed that his body displaced water in the tub and thought, "Aha!" He had been thinking about this problem for some time, so naturally he got quite excited when he realized he had the solution. It is said (but who knows?) that he leapt from the bath and ran through the streets shouting "Eureka!"

The Cubic Centimeter: A Measure of Success!

This activity shows students that you can take an object and measure it and calculate its volume in units called *cubic centimeters* (cm³). Once students calculate the volume of the small carton in cubic centimeters, ask them to predict the volume of the middle and largest cartons in cubic centimeters. (Try to get them to think of using their results about the relative amounts of water that could fit into each carton from "Make Room for Volume.") After students have made their predictions, have them make the actual measurements to see if their predictions were correct.

The second part of the activity tries to give students a more concrete feeling for the volume of a cubic centimeter. It is much easier to make the boxes out of construction paper than notebook paper, and they are also easier to handle. This activity also illustrates that a volume of space is usually larger and can accommodate more than people initially think it can. Students probably would not have thought that 245 little cubic centimeter boxes could fit into the small carton, but after working with them enough, they will see that it can be done.

Both parts of the activity are intended to help students develop their understanding of the three measurement concepts of length, area, and volume, and to provide enough familiarity with all three to provide a base for understanding in later work in their math classes.

Spill and Fill!

This final activity attempts to show students the relationship between a cubic centimeter and a milliliter—namely, that a milliliter of water has a volume of 1 cm³. Students know the volume of the smallest carton in cubic centimeters from measuring it with a metric ruler in "The Cubic Centimeter: A Measure of Success!" They then push the carton down into a container of water, allowing the displaced water to spill out. They know from "Down for the Count!" that the amount of displaced water should equal the volume of the carton. So now they know the volume of the displaced water in cubic centimeters. Now, all they have to do is figure out the volume of the water in milliliters. Students do this by pouring the displaced water into some kind of graduated container. They should see that the volume of the water displaced in milliliters equals the volume of the container in cubic centimeters.

This means that 1 cm³ is the same as 1 milliliter. You could explain to students that 1 milliliter of water would exactly fill a 1 cm³ box. Also, if you pushed a 1 cm³ box into the water, it would displace 1 milliliter of water. Actually, 1 cm³ and 1 milliliter are different ways of saying the same amount of volume.

Volume: Full of Surprises!

NATIONAL SCIENCE EDUCATION STANDARDS

The activities in this unit can be used to support the teaching of the following standards:

✔ **Unifying Concepts and Processes**
Constancy, Change, and Measurement
Changes in systems can be quantified. Mathematics is essential for accurately measuring change. *(All activities)*
Different systems of measurement are used for different purposes. *(All activities)*

✔ **Science as Inquiry**
Abilities Necessary to Do Scientific Inquiry
Students should develop general abilities, such as systematic observation, making accurate measurments, and identifying and controlling variables. *(All activities)*
Use appropriate tools and techniques to gather, analyze, and interpret data. *(All activities)*
Think critically and logically to make the relationships between evidence and explanations. *(All activities)*

NCTM PRINCIPLES AND STANDARDS FOR SCHOOL MATHEMATICS

✔ **Standard 2: Patterns, Functions and Algebra**
Use mathematical models and analyze change in both real and abstract contexts. Represent and investigate how a change in one variable relates to the change in a second variable.

✔ **Standard 3: Geometry and Spatial Sense**
Develop the idea of decomposing a three-dimensional shape into cubic units in order to measure its volume.

✔ **Standard 4: Measurement**
Apply a variety of techniques, tools, and formulas for determining measurements.
Measurement techniques are strategies used to determine a measurement.
Determine the perimeter, area, and volume of shapes and solids by counting segments, square units, or cubic units.

STUDENT ACTIVITY SHEET

NAME _____   **DATE** _____

Make Room for Volume

1. Use the chart at right to record your observations for steps 3 and 4.

	Small	Medium	Large
Number of small cartons of water			

2. The volume of the medium carton is how many times as big as the volume of the small carton? _____

3. The volume of the largest carton is how many times as big as the volume of the smallest carton? _____

4. The volume of the largest carton is how many times as big as the volume of the medium carton? _____

Looks Can Be Deceiving

1. Look at the distance between the marks on your two bottles. Is the distance between the marks on one bottle the same as the distance between the marks on the other bottle? _____

2. The distance between the marks is different. How can the amount of space taken up by one carton of water be the same in each bottle? Hint: Think about the shape of each bottle.

_____

_____

_____

3. If you had a bud vase that looked like this: and a glass bowl that looked like this:

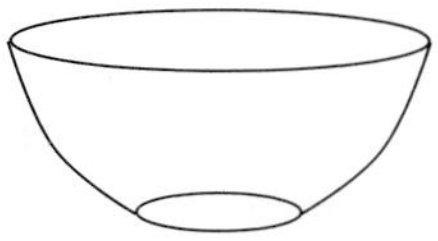

Draw where you think the water level would be in both containers if one cup of water were added to both.

Explain why you drew the water levels where you did for the two containers.

_____

_____

_____

STUDENT ACTIVITY SHEET

NAME _____   DATE _____

Down for the Count!

1. When you started pushing the carton down into the water, what happened to the water level?

_____

_____

2. When you pushed the carton down so that the top of the carton was even with the surface of the water, how much had the water level gone up?

_____

_____

3. If you had pushed a smaller carton (one with less volume) down into the water, do you think the water level would have gone up more, less, or about the same as it did using the original carton? Why?

_____

_____

4. If you had pushed a larger carton (one with more volume) down into the water, do you think the water level would have gone up more, less, or about the same as it did using the original carton? Why?

_____

_____

Measuring Volume the Handy Way!

1. After placing your hand in the water, how many one-carton volumes of water did the water level go up? _____

2. How many film canister volumes make up a 1-carton volume? _____

3. What is the volume of your hand in film canisters? _____

4. How many of your fingers does it take to equal the volume of one film canister? _____

The Cubic Centimeter: A Measure of Success!

Use the chart at right to record your measurements and to calculate the volume of the three cartons in cubic centimeters (cm^3).

	Width	Depth	Base area	Height	Volume (in cubic centimeters)
Carton 1				5 cm	
Carton 2				10 cm	
Carton 3				20 cm	

197

Make Room for Volume

The word **volume** is used in different ways in science. When talking about sound, volume means how loud the sound is. But for this *WonderScience*, we are dealing with a different meaning of the word volume. The volume that we are talking about is the amount of space that something takes up.

For example, a computer and an apple each take up their own amount of space. The amount of space each takes up is its volume:

Volume is also the amount of space in an empty container. For example, a drinking glass or a coffee pot each has a certain amount of space inside. That space is the volume inside the container:

YOU WILL NEED:

3 identical quart-sized milk cartons

metric ruler

pen

container of water
(about 8 cups)

scissors

Let's first look at the space inside three different cartons to learn something about volume. Because each carton has a different amount of space inside, each carton has its own volume.

1 Use a metric ruler to measure and mark the cartons at a height of 5 centimeters (cm), 10 cm, and 20 cm.

2 Use scissors to cut the tops off the cartons at the 5-, 10-, and 20-cm marks. You now have three containers, each with a different amount of space inside, or volume.

Make a chart like the one shown, or use the chart from the Student Activity Sheet.

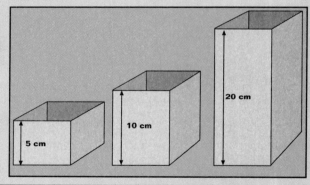

	Small	Medium	Large
Number of small cartons of water			

3 How many small cartons of water do you think it would take to fill the medium carton completely? Try it and see.

4 How many small cartons of water do you think it would take to fill the largest carton completely? Try it and see.

According to your observations, the volume of the medium carton is how many times bigger than the volume of the smallest carton? The volume of the largest carton is how many times bigger than the volume of the smallest carton? The volume of the largest carton is how many times bigger than the volume of the medium carton?

L👀ks Can Be Deceiving

The same volume of water can look different in different containers. Have you ever noticed that if you pour a glass of water into a tall skinny container, the water goes up pretty high in the container? But if you pour the same volume of water into a much wider container, the water level doesn't go up as high. When you first look at the two containers, you might think that there is a greater volume of water in the skinny container, but that would not be true. Let's prove this to ourselves in the following activity.

TEACHER PREPARATION:

Ask students to bring in empty clear plastic 1-liter and 2-liter soda bottles so that each group can have one of each bottle. The bottles should be clear all the way to the bottom with no opaque collar at the base. Carefully cut off the tops of the bottles right where the top begins to taper. This is easiest if you first punch a hole in the bottle with a nail and hammer. Starting at the hole, use scissors to cut the tops off. Place a piece of masking tape around the rim of each bottle to cover any pointy or sharp edges.

1 Stick a piece of masking tape along the side of each bottle as shown. Fill your small carton with water and pour the water into the 1-liter bottle. Use your pen to make a mark on the tape right at the water level.

2 Continue to add cartons of water to the bottle. Mark the water level on the tape each time you add a carton of water until you have added four cartons.

3 Repeat steps 1 and 2 using the 2-liter bottle until you have added four cartons of water and made four marks. Look at the space between the marks. The volume of one carton of water takes up how much space in each bottle?

A one-carton volume of water takes up exactly the same amount of space in both bottles. One space is tall and skinny, and the other one is shorter and wider, but the amount of space or volume the water takes up is equal.

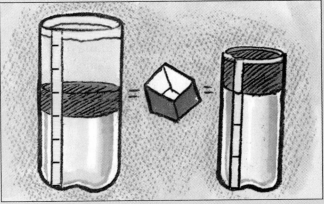

Down For the Count!

Here's another way to show that the space, or volume, between the lines on your bottles is equal to the space inside, or volume, of your small carton. You can do it by pushing the carton down into the water and seeing how much the water rises. Try it and see!

YOU WILL NEED:

2-liter bottle
small carton
water
plastic wrap
rubber band

1 Add small cartons of water, one at a time, to the 2-liter bottle until you have added six cartons and have six marks.

2 Dip your carton into the bottle, and take out a one-carton volume of water. How far down did the water level drop? Spill out that carton of water. Do not pour it back into your bottle.

What do you think would happen if, instead of putting a carton of water back into the bottle, you pushed the carton itself down into the water?

Let's try it and find out!

3 Place a piece of plastic wrap over the carton. Use a rubber band to hold the plastic wrap firmly to the carton as shown.

4 Start pushing the carton down into the water while observing the water level in the bottle. As you push the carton down, what happens to the level of the water? Push the carton down until the top of the carton is level with the surface of the water. Where does the water level end up?

The water level should have increased to the next mark. The water level increased by the same volume as the volume of the carton. In fact, since the water level increased by a one-carton volume, this tells you that the volume of the thing you put in the water must be equal to one carton.

You can use this method of placing an object in water to figure out the volume of the object.

Let's try it!

200

Measuring Volume
the Handy Way!

YOU WILL NEED:

2-liter bottle
film canister
water
paper towels

Let's see if you can measure the volume of your hands and fingers using the dunk-in-the-water method!

1 Make sure the water level in the bottle is at the 4-carton mark. Let's see if we can figure out the volume of your hand.

2 Place your hand into the water up to your wrist. How many one-carton volumes of water did the water level go up? Is it about 1/2-carton? More? Less? Try to estimate the fraction of a carton that the water rose in the bottle.

We can make our volume-finder bottle more accurate if we use smaller volumes to make the marks on the tape.

3 Be sure the water level is at the 4-carton mark. Add one film canister of water and mark the tape at the new water level. Continue to add film-canister volumes of water until you reach the 5-carton mark. How many film canister volumes make up a 1-carton volume?

4 Remove enough water so that the water level is again at the 4-carton mark. Now put your hand back in the water up to your wrist. What is the volume of your hand in film canister volumes?

5 How many of your fingers are equal in volume to the volume of one film canister of water? Check to see if your right hand and left hand have equal volumes. How much of your arm do you need to put in to make the water level rise by 1 carton?

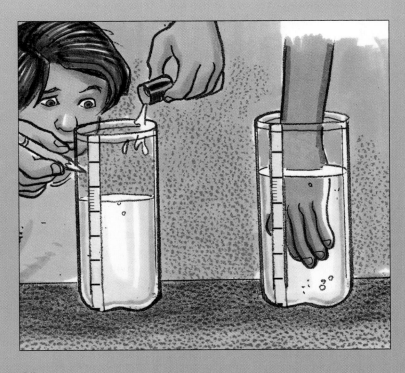

The Cubic Centimeter:

We have been measuring volume in cartons, canisters, or whatever else is around. If other people don't have the same containers, it is hard to explain to them what volume you found. Luckily, there is a way to measure volume so that everyone will know exactly what you are talking about. There is a standard unit of volume that you can measure using a metric ruler. Let's try it!

1 Make a chart like the one below, or use the chart in the Student Activity Sheet. On your small carton, use your ruler to first measure straight across the front of the carton. Measure it in centimeters. We will call this the **width** of the carton. Record your result in the chart under "width."

2 Now use your ruler to measure along the side of the carton to see how far back it goes. We will call this the **depth** of the carton. Record your result in the chart under "depth." We already know the **height** is 5 cm, so we wrote that in the chart under "height."

3 Pick up the small milk carton and look at the bottom, or its base. When you set the carton down on a tabletop, the space that the base takes up on the flat surface is called the **area** of the base. Finding the area of the base tells you how big the base is.

width X depth = base area

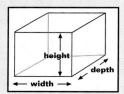

The base of our carton is 7 cm wide × 7 cm deep, so its area is 49 square cm. The base of our carton could be shown like the sample at right, to show that its area is 49 square cm.

Once you know the area of the base, all you need to do is multiply that area by the height of the carton to get the volume. Your answer will be in something called **cubic centimeters**. (More about those later.)

4 Now figure out the base area of your small carton. Multiply the base area times the height of the carton and get the volume of the carton in cubic centimeters. Record your answer in the chart.

base area X height = volume

5 Next, multiply the base area times the height of the other two cartons to get the volume of each carton. Record the volumes in the chart.

What do you notice about the volume in cubic centimeters for the largest carton compared with the medium and the smallest cartons? Does this make sense with how the volumes compared in the first activity?

	Width	Depth	Base area	Height	Volume (in cubic centimeters)
Carton 1				5 cm	
Carton 2				10 cm	
Carton 3				20 cm	

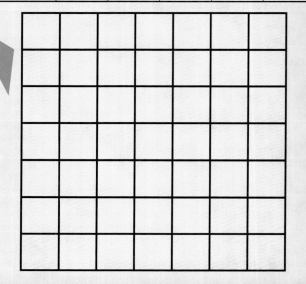

A Measure of Success!

Let's look at this thing called a cubic centimeter. What is this thing anyway? A cubic centimeter is a small volume that scientists use a lot when measuring the volumes of objects and substances. Let's make one so you can see how much space it takes up.

YOU WILL NEED:

cubic centimeter modeling strip
construction paper
tape
small carton
metric ruler
scissors
pencil

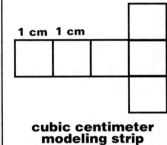

cubic centimeter
modeling strip

1 On a piece of construction paper, use your ruler and a pencil to make a cubic centimeter pattern like the one shown.

2 Fold the sides as shown to make a little box. Use small pieces of tape to hold the sides together and to close the top and bottom of the box. This little box has a volume of 1 cubic centimeter because it is 1 cm wide, 1 cm deep, and 1 cm high.

It now contains one cubic centimeter of air. If it could hold water, you could fill it with a volume of 1 cubic centimeter of water. If you filled it with clay or some other solid, it could hold 1 cubic centimeter of clay or other solid.

3 This little box takes up 1 cubic centimeter of space. Look back at how many cubic centimeters your smallest milk carton was. Our carton was 7 cm wide × 7 cm deep × 5 cm high = 245 cubic centimeters. That means that 245 of these little 1 cubic centimeter boxes could fit in our smallest milk carton. What about your carton?

4 Make two more cubic centimeter boxes so that everyone has made three. Now make a larger box that is 2 cm wide, 2 cm deep, and 2 cm high. How many of the little cubic centimeter boxes will fit in? First, figure out the area of the base. Then multiply the area of the base by the height to get the volume. This should be equal to the number of cubic centimeter boxes that will fit in. Put in the boxes to find out.

5 How about if you made a box that was 5 cm wide, 2 cm deep, and 3 cm high, how many cubic centimeter boxes would fit in? Try it with cubic centimeter boxes from the whole class.

6 Using cubic centimeter boxes from the whole class, fill up the bottom of the small carton with one layer of cubes. How many did you need? Imagine putting in enough layers to fill the carton all the way to the top. How many layers would it take? How many centimeter cubes would it take to fill the carton?

Spill and Fill!

YOU WILL NEED:

- **2-liter soda bottle**
- **small milk carton**
- **aluminum pie pan**
- **plastic wrap**
- **rubber band**
- **beaker, graduated cylinder,** or **measuring cup** with metric markings (at least 500 milliliters)
- **water**

In "A Cubic Centimeter: A Measure of Success!" you found the actual volume of the smallest carton, in cubic centimeters, by finding the area of the base and multiplying the area of the base by the height. But with the right equipment, you can find the actual volume in cubic centimeters without even using a ruler! Try this next activity to see what we mean!

1 Place the 2-liter soda bottle in the center of a clean, dry aluminum pie pan. Fill the bottle all the way to the very top with water.

2 Place a piece of plastic wrap over the smallest carton. Use a rubber band to hold the plastic wrap firmly to the carton as shown.

3 Start pushing the carton down into the water. As you push the carton down, the water should spill out of the bottle and land in the pie pan. Push the carton down until the top of the carton is level with the surface of the water.

4 Carefully remove the bottle from the pan. Now, carefully pour the water from the pan into a beaker, graduated cylinder, or measuring cup. What is the volume of water in milliliters? Record your answer.

5 Now check back to see what the volume of the carton was in cubic centimeters from when you measured it with a millimeter ruler. How does this number compare with the number of milliliters?

How about that! The volume of water in milliliters is equal to the volume of the container in cubic centimeters!

Wow! One cubic centimeter of water is the same as one milliliter of water!

Probability

Scientists use probabilities for reporting many of their observations about the natural world. We use both our knowledge and our intuition about probabilities to make decisions in our daily lives. Is there an 80% chance of rain? I'll take my umbrella along. Is there a 30% chance of rain? I don't expect to need my umbrella. If I buy a candy bar with the words, "Look inside to see if you are the winner of the big cash prize!" how likely is it that I am actually the winner? Considering the number of candy bars manufactured, I probably shouldn't get too excited about it.

In this unit, we have two objectives. One is to help students develop a basic understanding of what a mathematical probability means. The second is just as important: These activities can help students develop an understanding of fractions. A better "feel" for fractions helps students develop number sense, which is critical for children's understanding of mathematics. Lack of number sense is often a hidden cause of weakness in problem solving.

Give Probability a Chance

This activity introduces the notion of describing the probability of an event with a number. We open by telling students that the probability that they will find the eraser hidden under just one of a total of two cups is $\frac{1}{2}$. We go on to say that if there were an eraser hidden under just one of ten cups, the probability of finding it would be $\frac{1}{10}$. Discuss this idea with the students until they are comfortable with it. They may come to feel that it is "obvious" that the probability of finding the eraser in the two-cup situation is much greater than the probability of finding it in the ten-cup situation. If so, you can help them to use their belief about this situation to reinforce their understanding that the number $\frac{1}{2}$ is considerably bigger than the number $\frac{1}{10}$.

In Step 6, we introduce the concept that we can use the probability of finding the eraser to predict how many times we "expect" to find it in ten trials. This can be an elusive concept. We hope that this activity helps students to get some idea of what it means. Help them understand that in any particular set of 10 trials, any outcome is possible! It is possible that someone might never find the eraser in any of the ten trials, even though the probability of finding it is $\frac{1}{2}$. It is possible that someone else might find it in all ten tries! Or a person could find it once, or twice, or any number of times from zero to ten. But we hope students will begin to see that the more trials we do, the more we "expect" that the number of times the eraser is found will be about $\frac{1}{2}$ of the number of trials.

The chance of finding the eraser is the same as the chance of not finding the eraser in this activity. This is because just as one out of the two cups has the eraser hiding under it, there is also one out of the two cups that has nothing under it. Thus, there is a probability of $\frac{1}{2}$ that we will find the eraser and a probability of $\frac{1}{2}$ that we will not find the eraser.

Hide and Seek!

Following the pattern from the previous activity, students should set up an experiment with one eraser and three cups. If some of the children don't know how to set up this activity, it may mean that the basic concept of probability from "Give Probability a Chance" is not clear to them.

When students get to Step 4, they should realize that it is more likely that they will not find the eraser when they have three cups and just one eraser. In fact, there is a $\frac{2}{3}$ chance that they will not find it. They should know what the numbers in $\frac{2}{3}$ chance mean: the 2 is the number of cups that do not have an eraser hidden under them, and the 3 is the total number of cups.

Each student then compares the number of times that he or she found the eraser with the "expected outcome." If your students have experience with fractions, they can find the fraction of times that they found the eraser out of the total number of trials. Then they can compare that fraction with the "expected outcome." For example, if one student found the eraser six times, then the fraction would be $\frac{6}{12}$. This fraction could then be compared to the fraction $\frac{1}{3}$.

At the end of this activity, students are challenged to redesign this game to improve their chances of finding the eraser to $\frac{2}{3}$. Students can use two erasers and three cups. They can hide each of the erasers under a different cup leaving one cup with nothing hidden under it, giving 2 chances out of 3 that they will find it.

Probability: Give It a Whirl!

Encourage students to make "fair" spinners. That means that they must follow the instructions exactly so that each spinner will be equally likely to land on any one of its four wedges.

Step 5: The probability (chance) that the spinner will stop on the colored wedge is $\frac{1}{4}$.

Step 7: Since the probability that the spinner will stop on the colored wedge is $\frac{1}{4}$, we would "expect" it to stop on the colored wedge four times ($\frac{1}{4}$ of the sixteen trials). As before, have students discuss the idea that it is not really surprising that in any given set of sixteen trials we might not get exactly four stops on the colored wedge. When you collect data from the whole class, you might see that the average was closer to the expected number of 4.

Step 8: We "expect" eight stops on a colored wedge when $\frac{2}{4} = \frac{1}{2}$ of the wedges are colored. The fraction for this chance is $\frac{1}{2}$. We "expect" twelve stops on a colored wedge when three out of the four wedges are colored, since $\frac{3}{4} \times 16 = 12$. The fraction for this chance is $\frac{3}{4}$.

Be sure students realize that, of these spinners, the spinner with three colored wedges out of four gives them the best chance of landing on color. Point out that we can see this mathematically by comparing the probabilities: $\frac{3}{4} > \frac{1}{4}$ and $\frac{3}{4} > \frac{1}{2}$.

A Sure Thing!

This activity provides a physical model for certain and impossible events. Students will color one spinner completely, so that it always stops on a colored wedge. They will not color the other spinner at all, so that it never stops on a colored wedge. After students have done this activity, ask them to describe some events with probability 0. They could mention a few impossible things like "it will rain piglets this afternoon" or "after I squeeze all the toothpaste out of a tube, it will run back in." Someone might say, for instance, "There is 0 chance that

my parents will get me a dog for my birthday." This might give you an opportunity to clarify the difference between a probability of 0 and a very small probability. Probability of 0 means that an event is impossible.

Then ask them to describe some events that have a probability of 1. For example, when I drop a coin from somewhere in the air in my classroom, it will fall downward. Probability of 1 is reserved for events that are certain.

Discuss the idea that the probability of any event that is neither impossible nor certain is between 0 and 1. Help them relate that to the fractions they have been writing for probabilities:

$$\frac{\text{number of times the event "turns out right"}}{\text{total number of "trials"}}$$

The numerator of such a fraction could never be more than the denominator. Be sure students see why not.

What Are the Chances?

Your students can apply their learning about probability by choosing all sorts of events and making their best guesses about the probabilities. They can then place them on a number line making use of the "impossible, almost impossible, not very likely, as likely as not, pretty likely, almost certain, and certain" designations used above the number lines. Remember that the smallest probability value is 0 and the largest is 1. Try to get them to include a few events for which they actually know (or can figure out) the numerical probabilities. Discussion relating the fractions to the concepts "almost impossible," "not very likely," "as likely as not," "pretty likely," and "almost certain" can help students gain a better sense of the numbers that may help them in all of their work with fractions.

NATIONAL SCIENCE EDUCATION STANDARDS

The activities in this unit can be used to support the teaching of the following standards:

✓ Unifying Concepts and Processes

Systems, Order, and Organization
Prediction is the use of knowledge to identify and explain observations, or changes, in advance. The use of mathematics, especially probability, allows for greater or lesser certainty of predictions. *(All activities)*

Evidence, Models, and Explanation
Models help scientists and engineers understand how things work.
> *Give Probability a Chance*
> *Hide and Seek!*
> *Probability—Give It a Whirl!*
> *A Sure Thing!*

✓ Science as Inquiry

Abilities Necessary to Do Scientific Inquiry
Design and conduct a scientific investigation.
> *Give Probability a Chance*
> *Hide and Seek!*
> *Probability—Give it a Whirl!*

Use appropriate tools and techniques to gather, analyze, and interpret data. *(All activities)*
Think critically and logically to make the relationships between evidence and explanations. *(All activities)*

Understandings about Scientific Inquiry
Mathematics is important in all aspects of scientific inquiry. *(All activities)*

NCTM PRINCIPLES AND STANDARDS FOR SCHOOL MATHEMATICS

✓ Standard 1: Number and Operation

Understand numbers, ways of representing numbers, relationships among numbers, and number systems. Read and write fractions . . . and relate the notation to the meaning of these numbers. *(All activities)*
Develop strategies for judging the size of fractions and decimals and for comparing them using a variety of models and of benchmarks (such as 1/2 or 0.5). *(All activities)*

Number Concepts and Properties
By using parallel number lines . . . students can see fractions as numbers related to 1, and can see relationships among fractions.
What Are the Chances?

✓ Standard 5: Data Analysis, Statistics, and Probability

Pose questions and collect, organize, and represent data to answer those questions.
Design data investigations to address a question.
> *Hide and Seek!*   *A Sure Thing!*

Collect data using observations, measurement, surveys, or experiments.
> *Give Probability a Chance*
> *Hide and Seek!*   *Probability—Give It a Whirl!*

Develop and evaluate inferences, predictions, and arguments that are based on data.
Compare the data from one sample to other samples and consider why there is variability.
> *Give Probability a Chance*
> *Probability—Give It a Whirl!*

Understand and apply basic notions of chance and probability.
Discuss events as likely or unlikely and give descriptions of the degree of likelihood in informal terms (e.g., unlikely, very unlikely, certain, impossible).
> *What Are the Chances?*

Estimate, describe, and test probabilities of outcomes by associating the degree of certainty with a value ranging from 0 to 1 (e.g., in simple experiments involving spinners with different fractions shaded).
> *Give Probability a Chance*   *Hide and Seek!*
> *Probability—Give It a Whirl!*

Understand what it means for events to be equally likely and for a game or process to be fair.
> *Give Probability a Chance*
> *Probability—Give It a Whirl!*

Compute simple probabilities using appropriate methods . . . *(All activities)*

✓ Standard 10: Representations

Create and use representations to organize, record, and communicate mathematical ideas.
Such representations [drawing pictures, doing simulations] help to portray, clarify, or extend a mathematical idea by focusing on certain essential features.
> *Give Probability a Chance*   *Hide and Seek!*
> *Probability – Give It a Whirl!*   *A Sure Thing!*

Science and mathematics are closely connected in that it is natural for content within one area to emerge as investigations in the other area are underway. *(All activities)*

STUDENT ACTIVITY SHEET

NAME _____   **DATE** _____

Give Probability a Chance

1. Use this chart to record whether or not you found the eraser in each of your trials.

Trial	Found Eraser!	No Eraser
1		
2		
3		
4		
5		
6		
7		
8		
9		
10		
Total =		

2. Why is your chance of finding the eraser the same as your chance of not finding the eraser?

_____

_____

_____

_____

_____

Hide and Seek!

1. Use this chart to record whether or not you found the eraser in each of your trials.

Trial	Found Eraser!	No Eraser
1		
2		
3		
4		
5		
6		
7		
8		
9		
10		
Total =		

2. Redesign your experiment so that there is a $\frac{2}{3}$ chance of finding the eraser. How many cups and how many erasers would you use?

_____

_____

_____

_____

NAME _____   **DATE** _____

Probability: Give It a Whirl!

1. Record the results of your trials with each spinner in these charts.

1/4 Spinner		
Trial	Colored	Plain
1		
2		
3		
4		
5		
6		
7		
8		
9		
10		
11		
12		
13		
14		
15		
16		
Total =		

1/2 Spinner		
Trial	Colored	Plain
1		
2		
3		
4		
5		
6		
7		
8		
9		
10		
11		
12		
13		
14		
15		
16		
Total =		

3/4 Spinner		
Trial	Colored	Plain
1		
2		
3		
4		
5		
6		
7		
8		
9		
10		
11		
12		
13		
14		
15		
16		
Total =		

Give Probability

What are the chances that you will find an eraser that is hiding under one of two cups? Because there is only one eraser and two cups, your chance is 1 out of 2. You could write that chance as $\frac{1}{2}$. The number for your chance is $\frac{1}{2}$ because the eraser is under 1 out of a total of 2 cups. If there were 1 eraser and 10 cups, your chance of finding it would be 1 out of 10 or $\frac{1}{10}$. (That's a much smaller chance!) Using math to figure out the chance that something will happen is called **probability**. Let's try it!

Fractions, like $\frac{1}{2}$ or $\frac{1}{10}$, are a great way to write down probability because they can give a lot of information in a small space.

1 Draw a chart like the one shown, or use the chart from the Student Activity Sheet. Working with a partner, decide who will hide the eraser and who will try to find it.

2 Hider's Job: Turn both cups upside down on your desk. Place the eraser under one cup. Your partner is not allowed to look while you mix up the cups. Let your partner know when it is time to choose a cup.

3 Finder's Job: Don't peek when your partner is mixing up the cups. When it is time to choose a cup, lift the cup that you think might have the eraser under it. Then put a mark in the chart to show whether you did or did not find the eraser.

YOU WILL NEED:

2 opaque cups
1 small eraser
1 chart per person
pen or pencil

Trial	Found Eraser!	No Eraser
1		
2		
3		
4		
5		
6		
7		
8		
9		
10		
Total =		

a Chance

4 Repeat steps 2 and 3 for a total of 10 trials. Count the number of times you found the eraser and write it in your chart.

5 Trade jobs with your partner, and do 10 more trials.

6 Remember when we said your chance of finding the eraser was $\frac{1}{2}$. This means that you could expect to find the eraser about half the time. Out of 10 trials did you find the eraser about 5 times? Compare your results with your partner's.

You may not have found the eraser exactly 5 times. It does not mean that you made a mistake. It does not mean that the math is wrong either. When you average together the results of many people though, the average is likely to be very close to 5.

TEACHER:
To get a larger sample of results, record the number of times that each student found the eraser and have the students find the average. Are your class's results very close to 5?

Why are your chances of finding the eraser the same as your chances of not finding the eraser?

Hide and Seek!

YOU WILL NEED:

opaque plastic cups

erasers

chart (from Student Activity Sheet)

(Students should determine the number of cups and erasers needed.)

In "Give Probability a Chance," did everyone in your class get the same results when they tried to find the eraser? Probability tells you what to expect in the long run, but it doesn't predict what will happen each time you try something! Still the numbers are very useful. This time, you design the experiment!

1 Set up cups and an eraser so that a person has a probability of $\frac{1}{3}$ (a 1 out of 3 chance) of finding the eraser.

2 With a partner as the hider and you as the finder, run your experiment for 12 trials. Record your results in a chart like the one you used for the first cup-and-eraser activity.

3 Switch jobs so that you are the hider, and your partner is the finder and run the experiment for 12 more trials.

4 Look at your chart and your partner's chart. What is more likely, finding the eraser or not finding the eraser? How many times did you actually find the eraser during your trials? Was it exactly $\frac{1}{3}$ of the time?

There is a probability of $\frac{2}{3}$ (a 2 out of 3 chance) that a person will *not* find the eraser during one trial. Where did the numbers "2" and "3" in $\frac{2}{3}$ probability come from?

In the experiments you and your partner did, what fraction of the trials was the eraser *not* found? How close is it to $\frac{2}{3}$?

5 Redesign the experiment so that there is a $\frac{2}{3}$ chance of *finding* the eraser. How is this arrangement different from your experiment in step 1?

Trial	Found Eraser!	No Eraser
1		
2		
3		
4		
5		
6		
7		
8		
9		
10		
11		
12		
Total =		

PROBABILITY
Give It a Whirl!

Here is another chance to experiment with probability. Let's take a spin!

YOU WILL NEED:

construction **paper** (any light color)

scissors

markers

pencil

3 charts per person (from the Student Activity Sheet)

cup (for the tracing option)

TEACHER PREPARATION: Have students trace a circular object with a diameter of about 10–15 cm onto construction paper. All circles should be identical and each student will need three circles.

1 Cut out three disks. Fold one in half and open it.

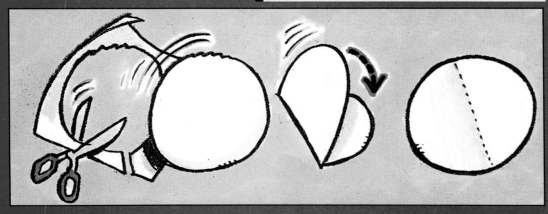

2 Make a perpendicular fold by matching up the creases from the first fold. Now open up your circle. You should notice that all folds bend the same way and that there is a little point at the center of your circle. Do the same for the other two circles.

3 Color one wedge of one disk. Color two wedges on another disk. Color three wedges on your last disk.

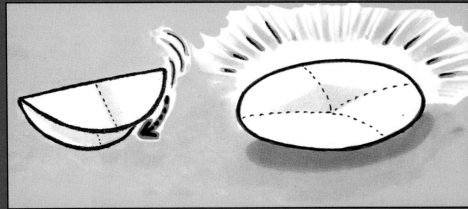

Continued on next page

4 Practice spinning one of your disks by putting your hand on it and twisting it as shown. The spinner should turn pretty quickly. As soon as you let go of your spinner, place your index finger flat on your desk so that it points at the spinner. Make sure that you don't touch the spinner or move your finger while it is spinning.

5 Begin with the spinner that has only one wedge colored. Spin it and point your finger like you did in practice. Did it stop with your finger pointing to a colored part? Because there is a total of four wedges and only one wedge is colored, there is a 1 in 4 chance that it will land on a colored part. How would you write this chance as a fraction?

6 Now it is time to begin your trials! Spin the $\frac{1}{4}$ colored spinner. When the spinner stops, put an "x" in the chart to show whether it stopped with your finger on a colored wedge or an uncolored wedge. Repeat this step until you have a total of 16 trials recorded in your chart for this spinner.

7 Count up the total number of times your spinner stopped on the colored part and write it in the chart. Remember that the chance of landing on a colored wedge is $\frac{1}{4}$. This means that you could expect the spinner to stop on the colored part about one-quarter of the time. How many times did your spinner stop on a colored wedge? Is this what you would expect?

8 How many times do you think that the spinner with *two* colored wedges will stop on a colored wedge out of 16 trials? How many times do you think that the spinner with *three* colored wedges will stop on a colored wedge out of 16 trials? How would you write each of these chances as a fraction?

9 Repeat steps 4 and 5 with your $\frac{1}{2}$ colored spinner and then with your $\frac{3}{4}$ colored spinner. Record your results for each spinner in its own chart. Are your results what you expected?

TEACHER: Collect data from the whole class for each spinner and see how close the class average is to the expected results.

If your goal is to land on a colored part and you only get one spin, which spinner would you use? Why would that one be a good choice?

WHICH SPINNER?

TRIAL	COLORED	PLAIN
1		
2		
3		
4		
5		
6		
7		
8		
9		
10		
11		
12		
13		
14		
15		
16		

A Sure Thing!

YOU WILL NEED:

construction paper
(any light color)

markers

scissors

pencil

cup (for the tracing option)

There is one special probability that tells you when something **definitely will happen** and one that tells you when something **definitely won't happen.** While you are doing this activity, think of some real life situations where you could use these probabilities.

TEACHER PREPARATION:
Either photocopy two circles onto construction paper or have students trace objects with diameters of at least 10 cm.

1 Cut out two circles. Fold each into fourths the way you did for the previous activity. Be sure that the folds all bend the same way and that there is a little point at the center of each spinner.

2 Take one spinner and color every single wedge so that your spinner is completely colored. Spin it and point your finger like you did in practice. Did your spinner stop on a colored wedge? Will it always stop on a colored wedge? When an event is certain to happen, like this one, we say that it has a probability of 1.

3 This step is a bit tricky! Color your other spinner so that whenever you spin it, it will never land on a colored wedge. How many wedges did you color? When an event is completely impossible like this one, we say that it has a probability of 0.

What Are the Chances?

You probably have had a lot of experience guessing how likely it is that something will happen. For example, how likely is it that you will get a day off school tomorrow due to bad weather? Thinking about probability can be fun!

Fractions that show chance can be arranged on a number line. Remember the meanings for zero and one. What is the smallest probability that could ever be written? What is the largest probability that ever could be written? Mark your guess on each number line showing how likely it is that each event will happen.

Event	Impossible	Almost impossible	Not very likely	As likely as not	Pretty likely	Almost certain	Certain

When you toss a penny into the air, it comes back down.
0 ——————————— $\frac{1}{2}$ ——————————— 1

When the tossed penny lands, it comes down heads.
0 ——————————— $\frac{1}{2}$ ——————————— 1

When the tossed penny lands, it comes down tails.
0 ——————————— $\frac{1}{2}$ ——————————— 1

You will take a trip to Africa.
0 ——————————— $\frac{1}{2}$ ——————————— 1

Any giraffe you see on a trip to Africa will have a long neck.
0 ——————————— $\frac{1}{2}$ ——————————— 1

The sun will rise tomorrow.
0 ——————————— $\frac{1}{2}$ ——————————— 1

You will walk on Mars tonight.
0 ——————————— $\frac{1}{2}$ ——————————— 1

You will ride a bicycle to school tomorrow.
0 ——————————— $\frac{1}{2}$ ——————————— 1

You will eat a banana some time during the next week.
0 ——————————— $\frac{1}{2}$ ——————————— 1

When you spin the 1/4 spinner, it lands on a colored wedge
0 ——————————— $\frac{1}{2}$ ——————————— 1

When you spin the 1/4 spinner, it does not land on the colored wedge.
0 ——————————— $\frac{1}{2}$ ——————————— 1

Make up some of your own events. Decide how likely they are to happen and place them on this number line.

0    $\frac{1}{10}$ $\frac{1}{4}$ $\frac{1}{3}$ $\frac{1}{2}$ $\frac{2}{3}$ $\frac{3}{4}$ $\frac{9}{10}$ 1

In this unit, students investigate a type of symmetry called *reflection* or *mirror* symmetry. In an object with *reflection* or *mirror* symmetry, such as the external human body, for every part on the left, there is a corresponding part on the right at the same position and distance from the line of symmetry. Many designed objects, such as chairs and barbells, have this kind of symmetry, too. Since these objects must be balanced to perform correctly, their parts are the same on each side. Reflection symmetry also is an important property of many objects in geometry, such as an equilateral triangle, a circle, and a star. When students learn the elementary ideas of symmetry, it helps to prepare them for future studies of related ideas in mathematics and science.

Symmetry—Two Sides to the Story

Ask students if they have heard the word *symmetry*. Perhaps they will be able to point out some objects in the classroom that are symmetrical. If not, show them some symmetrical objects, such as a pencil or roll of masking tape. Maybe have a student come to the front of the class and show how the student, at least on the outside, is symmetrical.

For reflection or mirror symmetry activities, the best type of mirror is one in which the reflecting surface is right on the front of the mirror. Some plastic mirrors are thick and have the silver coating far behind the front surface of the mirror. This is not good for symmetry activities because a "ghost" image distorts the view of the reflection.

Results:

Step 1: Students will see a complete letter E. Make sure students understand that they are looking at a combination of what is on the paper and what is in the mirror. If an object has mirror symmetry, this combination should look like the actual object. Encourage students to talk about their observations.

Step 2: When the mirror is placed somewhere other than on the dashed line, we no longer see an E. Help students realize that their observations are valuable and need to be written down, so that they can fully explore the concept of symmetry.

Step 3:

Letter	E	H	V	O	S	R
No. of lines of symmetry	1	2	1	many	0	0

Step 4: O has the most, with an infinite number of lines of symmetry. Note that this O is a perfect circle. Most Os are slightly elongated and would have only 2 lines of symmetry. The letter S does have "point symmetry" or "rotational symmetry" but not mirror symmetry.

Step 5: These letters have only one line of symmetry. Students could include letters that have more than one line of symmetry when they do this step.

A C D E M T U V W Y

Step 6: These letters have two lines of symmetry:

H I X

Step 7: These letters have no line of symmetry:

B F G J K L N P Q Z

Step 8: Possible comments:

If a letter has a line of symmetry, then it has two halves that look just alike. One part of it is exactly the mirror image of the other part. When you put a mirror on the line of symmetry, the combination of what's on the paper and what's in the mirror looks just like the letter.

Fold and Behold!

Students will need to cut out the shapes from the Student Activity Sheet and find and draw a line of symmetry.

Results:

Three out of the four shapes have at least one line of symmetry. When students fold their shapes along the line of symmetry, the opposite halves should coincide exactly.

When the shapes are unfolded, the matching holes are exactly the same distance from the fold line, in corresponding positions on the two sides of the figure.

The objective is to get students to notice that the distance from a point on one side of the line of symmetry is the same as the distance from the "matching" point on the other side.

Reflect, Connect, Inspect!

To introduce this activity, ask the students what they learned from the last activity (matching points are the same distance

Unit 19
Symmetry: Two Sides to the Story

from the line of symmetry). Tell them that they will now measure the position of the reflection by holding a ruler right in front of the mirror. This activity will help students recognize that the reflection is at a particular distance *behind* the mirror. Many students believe the reflection is *in* the mirror. Observing the reflection of the ruler at a distance behind the mirror may help them get beyond this preconception—looking at the reflection of the ruler actually permits them to measure this distance!

If at all possible, give students rulers that start at zero for this activity. Many rulers have the zero indented from the end, which will make this activity difficult or inaccurate. Be sure students have the zero end of their ruler flat against the mirror, so that the distance they measure is a perpendicular distance.

Results:

Step 3: The reflection of the ruler measures the distance of the reflection of the dot from the mirror's surface. So, the measurement students get for step 2 is also their answer for step 3.

Step 4: The line joining the two dots should meet the dashed line of symmetry at right angles. The two dots should be the same distance from the line of symmetry.

Step 5: Students should realize that they would need to measure the rectangle and reproduce it exactly on the other side of the dashed line to make a symmetrical shape.

A New Angle on Symmetry

If at all possible, give students protractors that have 0° right on the baseline of the protractor. That way, when the protractor is pushed up against the mirror, the angles can be measured accurately from the edge of the mirror.

Make sure the protractor's straight side is flat against the mirror. If the 0° mark is not right on the baseline of the protractor, students can lift the mirror up and slide the edge of the protractor underneath. The vertex point on the protractor needs to be right at the vertex of the angle they are measuring.

Results:

Step 3: If students lay the protractor on the angle they drew, as if to measure it, they can see the measure of the reflected angle, too. The reflected angle has the same measure as the original angle, but it opens in the opposite direction.

Step 4: Students should use the mirror line as one side of the second angle, and they should start from the same vertex. They should use the same measurement as their original angle and draw it in the direction it appeared in the mirror. The equal angles will be symmetrical.

Step 5: Here is one way to do this: with the mirror on the dashed line, students can mark a dot on the paper just beyond the reflection of the line at the top of the mirror. A ruler can then be used to draw a line from that dot to the vertex of the angle. The angles should be equal and symmetrical. (Remind students to try to hold the mirror perpendicular to the paper to increase the accuracy of their measurements and drawings.)

The Art of Symmetry

Students can be very creative here! When they explain how they make a symmetrical drawing, hopefully, students will tell you that they made a shape with two matching sides. Perhaps they will even say that each point on one side of its line of symmetry has a point on the other side that is the same distance from the symmetry line.

Imagine Your Image!

If you have physically handicapped students in your class, pair them with students who are likely to be sensitive to their limitation. Then, instruct them to have the student with the handicap be the leading partner in the first round.

Watch all the pairs. If they are not reflecting each others' movements, they can step in front of the mirror and watch the action, to see how an actual mirror image would look.

Asymmetrical Spectacle!

1. The bird would have a much harder time keeping its direction if the length or shape of its wings were not symmetrical.

2. An asymmetrical pitchfork would pick up less hay on one side than the other.

3. An asymmetrical chair would be uncomfortable for a symmetrical human being. It would be hard to balance if its legs were asymmetrical.

Outside, students might find symmetrical leaves or symmetrical flowers; some buildings are symmetrical, as are cars, trucks, bulldozers, bridges, and much more.

For assessment:

Give the students a ruler, a protractor, and colored pencils or markers. Tell them to make a design with zero lines of symmetry, a design with one line of symmetry, and a design with two lines of symmetry. Ask them to explain how they determined the number of lines of symmetry of each design. Then, give students a mirror and ask them to make reflections to show the symmetry of each design.

Symmetry: Two Sides to the Story

NATIONAL SCIENCE EDUCATION STANDARDS

The activities in this unit can be used to support the teaching of the following standards:

✔ **Unifying Concepts and Processes**

Evidence, Models, and Explanations

Evidence consists of observations and data on which to base scientific explanations.
Symmetry—Two Sides to the Story
Fold and Behold!
Reflect, Connect, Inspect!
A New Angle on Symmetry

✔ **Form and Function**

The form or shape of an object or system is frequently related to its use, operation, or function.
Asymmetrical Spectacle!

✔ **Science as Inquiry**

Abilities Necessary to Do Scientific Inquiry

Develop descriptions, explanations, predictions, and models using evidence.
(All activities)

NCTM PRINCIPLES AND STANDARDS FOR SCHOOL MATHEMATICS

✔ **Standard 12: Geometry**

. . . so that students can explore transformations of geometric figures; understand and apply geometric properties and relationships; develop an appreciation of geometry as a means of describing the physical world.

✔ **Standard 13: Measurement**

. . . so that students can extend their understanding of the process of measurement; estimate, make, and use measurements to describe and compare phenomena.

✔ **Standard 2: Mathematics as Communication**

. . . so that students reflect on and clarify their own thinking about mathematical ideas and situations.

STUDENT ACTIVITY SHEET

NAME _____   **DATE** _____

Symmetry—Two Sides to the Story

Look at the letters below. For each letter, use your mirror to see if the letter has one or more lines of symmetry. Record the number of lines of symmetry in the chart.

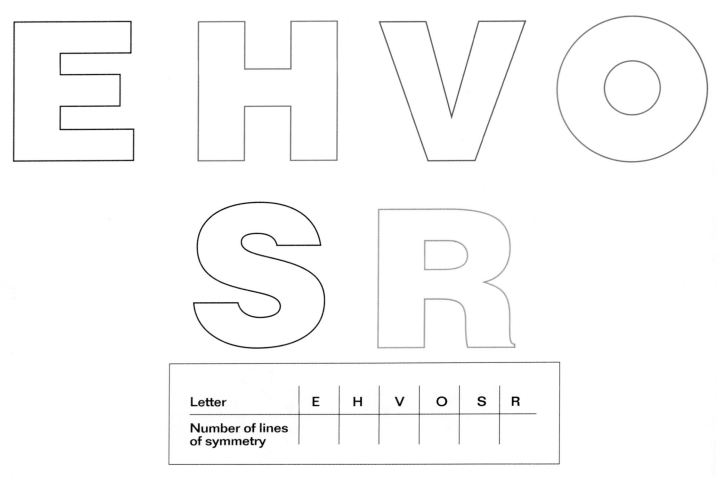

Letter	E	H	V	O	S	R
Number of lines of symmetry						

Go through the alphabet and record the letters that have 0, 1, 2, or more lines of symmetry.

Lines of symmetry	
0	
1	
2	
more than 2	

NAME _____   DATE _____

Fold and Behold!

Using your mirror, check each picture to find whether it has one or more lines of symmetry.
Cut out the symmetrical drawings and fold each one along a line of symmetry.
Place the folded drawing on a piece of cardboard and poke a hole anywhere through it with a pencil.
Unfold the drawing.

What do you notice about the position of the holes on each half of the drawing?   _____

Measure the distance from each hole to the line of symmetry. What do you notice?

_____

_____

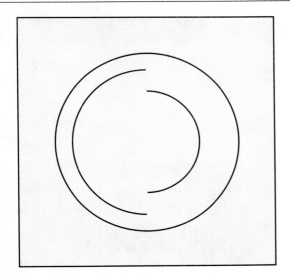

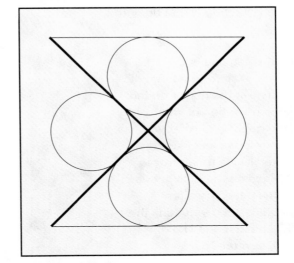

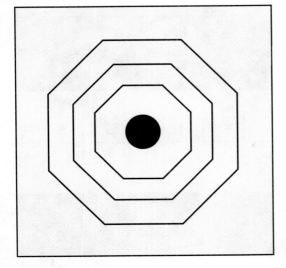

YOU WILL NEED:

small mirror with a straight edge
Student Activity sheet

What do a ball, a cube, an arrow and a human skeleton all have in common? They are all symmetrical. You may have heard the words "symmetry" or "symmetrical" before. These words describe something about the shape of an object. Let's explore some objects to see what symmetry is about!

1 Look at the letter "E" on the handout. Hold the mirror on the dashed line, as in the drawing, and look at the reflection. What do you see?

2 The dashed line is the **line of symmetry** for the letter "E." When you have the mirror on this line, the combination of what you see on the paper and what you see in the mirror looks just like the whole letter. Move the mirror to another place on the E. What do you see this time? Try a few different places. Do you think the letter "E" has just one line of symmetry, or more?

3 Use your mirror to discover any lines of symmetry on the capital letters on the Student Activity sheet. When you find a line of symmetry, make a dashed line on the drawing. Record your results in a table like this. Some letters can have more than one line of symmetry. See if you can find those!

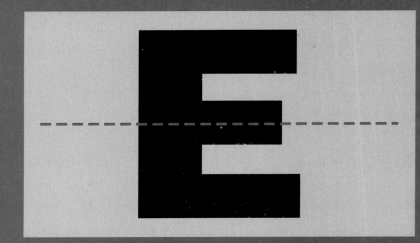

Letter	E	H	V	O	S	R
Number of lines of symmetry						

Two Sides to the Story

E H

V O

S R

4 Which letters had the most lines of symmetry? Which letters had none? Which had only one?

5 See if you can find other capital letters with symmetry. Name two other capital letters that you think have only **one** line of symmetry. For each letter, draw the letter, check it with your mirror, and then draw the line of symmetry.

6 Name two other capital letters with two lines of symmetry. For each letter, draw the lines of symmetry.

7 Name two other capital letters with no lines of symmetry.

8 Write a few sentences to summarize what you have learned about the symmetry of letters. What characteristics of a letter make it symmetrical?

Fold and Behold!

YOU WILL NEED:

small mirror with a straight edge

scissors

Student Activity sheet

ruler

small piece of corrugated cardboard

sharp pencil

In the last activity, you learned about mirror symmetry of letters. What other kinds of objects have this symmetry? Let's find out more!

1 Cut out each shape from the Student Activity sheet.

2 For each shape, predict where you think a line of symmetry might be. Use a mirror to check your prediction. When you find one, draw a dashed line to show the line of symmetry.

3 Using the shapes that have a line of symmetry, fold each shape along its dashed line. What can you say about how the opposite sides of the object match up?

4 Place the cardboard under the folded shape. **Carefully** push your pencil anywhere through the folded shape. If you unfold these shapes now, what do you notice about the holes?

5 Unfold the shapes and measure the distance from each hole to the line of symmetry. What do you notice?

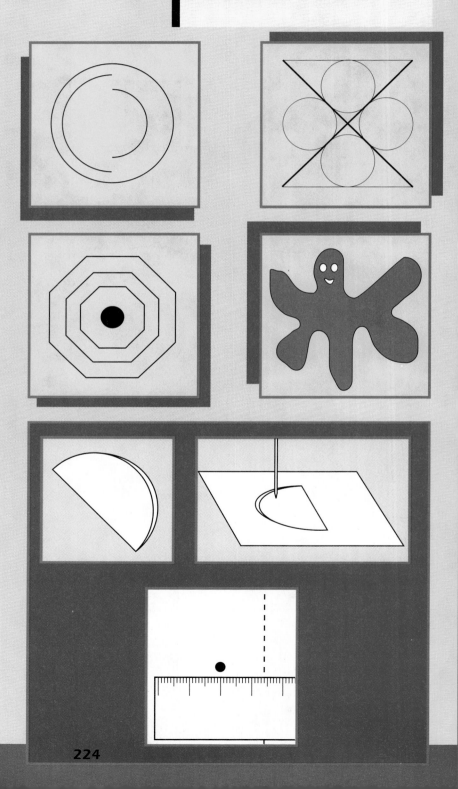

Reflect, Connect, Inspect!

YOU WILL NEED:

small mirror with a straight edge

piece of paper

pencil

ruler

In the previous activities, you used a mirror to help you figure out which letters and objects are symmetrical. Let's see if you can use a mirror to make your own symmetrical drawing.

1 Make a dashed line on a piece of paper. Put the mirror on this line, as before.

2 Place the ruler on the paper with one end against the mirror, as shown. Make a dot on the paper anywhere along the ruler. Measure the distance from the dot to the mirror. Leave your ruler in place.

3 Now look at the reflection of the dot in the mirror. How far from the mirror's edge does the reflection appear to be? Hint: Look at the reflection of the ruler.

4 Remove the mirror, measure the distance on the other side of the line where the reflection of the dot appeared, and place an actual dot there. Connect the two dots with a straight line. You have created a very simple symmetrical drawing with its line of symmetry right on the dotted line.

5 Look at the rectangle at right. How could you use your ruler to make a rectangle on the other side of the line so that the big rectangle that results would be symmetrical? When you are done, use your mirror to check if it looks symmetrical.

A New Angle on Symmetry

In "Reflect, Connect, *Inspect!*" you found out that the distance from a dot to a mirror is the same as the distance from the mirror to the reflection of the dot. You also learned how to use that fact to make a symmetrical shape. Let's see if angles work the same way.

1 Make a dashed line on your paper. You will place the mirror on the line, but do not put it there yet.

2 Use a protractor and a ruler to draw an angle from the dashed line. Mark the angle with the number of degrees.

3 Place the mirror on the dashed line as before. Is it possible to use the **reflection** of the protractor to measure the **reflection** of the angle? Try it. What do you notice? Write a sentence that describes how the reflection of the angle looks compared to the actual angle on the paper.

4 Use your protractor and ruler to make another angle on the other side of the mirror line that equals the first angle. Do the angles look symmetrical? Use your mirror to find out!

5 Make another dashed line and another angle. Using only a mirror and ruler, see if you can make a symmetrical angle on the other side of the line. How would you do it?

The Art of Symmetry:

Take a sheet of paper and make a dashed line on it as before. See if you can make a new drawing or design that is symmetrical, with the mirror line as the line of symmetry. You may use any combination of ruler, protractor, mirror, or paper folding. Explain how you made your drawing symmetrical. Hint: Think about the dots you made in "Reflect, Connect, *Inspect!*"

Imagine Your Image!

You have seen that an object and its reflection are symmetrical with each other using the mirror as the line of symmetry. Let's see if you and your partner can be symmetrical across an imaginary mirror as your line of symmetry.

1 Stand one or two meters from your partner and face each other. At first, you are the object and your partner is the reflection.

2 Raise your hands over your head. Your partner should do what your reflection would do if you were looking in a mirror. What does your partner do?

3 Now reach out your right hand as if you were going to shake hands. What does your partner do? If you have a mirror, compare what your partner did to what your reflection actually does.

4 Walk toward your partner. Now walk backwards. How does your partner move? In what way are your and your partner's movements like the drawings you made in the previous activities?

5 Trade roles with your partner and repeat the activity. Try to be perfect reflecting partners.

Asymmetrical
SPECTACLE!

Being symmetrical is very important to objects and animals. Here are three examples of objects that are normally symmetrical. We made them **asymmetrical**, which means not symmetrical. For each object or animal, explain the problems that would be caused by being asymmetrical, and explain why being symmetrical is so important.

On your way home from school today, look for other symmetrical objects. Try to figure out why they were designed that way.

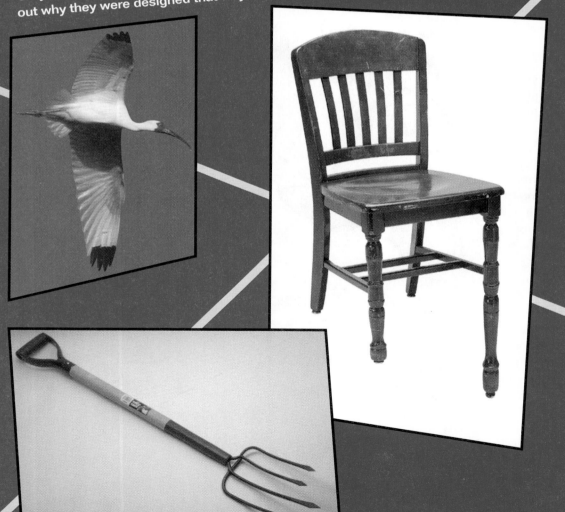

ILLUSTRATIONS BY JIM WISNIEWSKI/STEVE EDSEY & SONS UNLESS OTHERWISE INDICATED

WONDERSCIENCE

Unit 20
The Force of Friction!

Friction is a force that affects our lives all the time. It keeps us from sliding out of our chair. It allows the tires on a car or bus to grip the road. It slows us down when we swim or run, but without it we couldn't move at all. Friction affects objects that rub against other objects. It also affects objects that move through liquids and gases. Students will investigate all three situations. They will study the variables that determine the amount of friction on a sliding object. They will also investigate how size and shape affect the friction on an object moving through fluids. They will see that sometimes friction works against us, but at other times we can't do without it.

Friction: More Than Just Scratching the Surface

To introduce the unit, ask students what they know about friction. Write their responses on the board or on chart paper. Probably one of those responses can lead right into the first activity. Note that the students can get a direct, tactile sense of the force of friction by gently pushing the lid from the side and feeling how much force they need. There are two kinds of friction: static friction and sliding friction. Static friction is a resistance to the beginning of motion. It happens when two objects touch and are at rest. Moving friction is a resistance to motion that already exists. In general, static friction is greater than sliding friction. It may be necessary to give the lid a gentle tap to get it going, and then it will slide along at a slow, constant speed. As an extension activity, have the students fasten some other surface to the bottom of the lid and find out how the friction changes.

Friction: Just Weight and See!

In this activity, students explore how sliding friction increases with downward force. Pressing a hand down on a tabletop, and then trying to slide the hand along the table, is an excellent example. The more you press down, the harder it is to slide your hand. The graph in Step 4 should show a regular increase in the number of washers pulling the lid as more washers are added to the lid. To help the students answer Step 6, suggest that they imagine where the line of the graph is heading after six washers. They can extend it with a dashed line and estimate what the graph would read for eight washers.

So What's the Rub?

To understand sliding friction, a scientist must first understand the nature of the surfaces that are sliding together. Are they smooth? Certainly sandpaper is not. You can imagine how the grains of sandpaper can dig into a soft surface like wood and increase the friction. And when sandpaper rubs sandpaper, the grains can catch each other and practically lock up. Even a polished metal surface is full of pits and irregularities when seen under sufficient magnification. That's why maintaining a layer of oil between moving metal parts is so important.

Go with the Flow!

For this activity, you need either a single container as wide as a 64-oz juice bottle or two identical smaller containers. If you have two containers, the students can drop one clay shape in each container (at the same time). The clay pancake will fall much more slowly in water than the clay ball. There are two reasons for this difference. First, since friction happens at the surface of an object, the larger the surface area, the more friction. A flattened pancake has much more surface area than a ball, and more flattening makes the surface area even larger. This larger surface increases the friction. Second, the pancake usually stays horizontal as it falls, so it must push the water under it out of the way as it moves. This slows down the pancake even more.

Unit 20
The Force of Friction!

Air Brakes

Folding the paper to make the airplane has several effects. First, it reduces the amount of surface of paper that moves through the air. Second, and more important, the shape of the paper airplane keeps it pointed straight as it falls, so it cuts through the air cleanly. The motion of the unfolded sheet is complex, a series of dips, lifts, and curls. When the paper falls in a relatively horizontal position, it must push air out of the way, just as the pancake-shaped piece of clay did in the previous activity. Blowing up the balloons in the second activity has the opposite effect of folding the paper into an airplane. First, the blown-up balloon has far more surface area than the uninflated one. And second, in order to fall, the inflated balloon must push a very large volume of air out of the way.

Friction: Friend or Foe?

Wheel bearings and brakes offer excellent examples of "bad" and "good" friction. In the most simple bearing on a vehicle, the axle turns in a hole made in the frame. The metal of the axle rubs against the metal of the frame. Oil can reduce the friction, but metal is still sliding against metal. This much friction is unacceptable, so engineers have designed various kinds of bearings. Typically cylinders or ball bearings turn with the axle, so there is no sliding friction at all. But for the braking system, sliding friction is essential. The brake pads in a bicycle squeeze against the outer rim. Without friction, there would be no braking.

Assessment/Integration:

Challenge students to write a short story in which something about friction puts the characters in a dangerous situation, and something about friction helps save them.

The Force of Friction!

NATIONAL SCIENCE EDUCATION STANDARDS

The activities in this unit can be used to support the teaching of the following standards:

✔ **Unifying Concepts and Processes**

Evidence, Models, and Explanation
Evidence consists of observations and data on which to base scientific explanations. *(All activities)*

Form and Function
Form and function are complementary aspects of objects, organisms, and systems in the natural and designed world. The form or shape of an object or system is frequently related to its use, operation, or function. *(All activities)*

✔ **Science as Inquiry**

Abilities Necessary to Do Scientific inquiry
Design and conduct a scientific investigation. *(All activities)*
Use appropriate tools and techniques to gather, analyze and interpret data.
   Friction: Just Weight and See!
Think critically and logically to make the relationships between evidence and explanations. *(All activities)*

✔ **Physical Science**

Motions and Forces
If more than one force acts on an object along a straight line, then the forces will reinforce or cancel one another, depending on their direction and magnitude. *(All activities)*

Friction: More Than Just Scratching the Surface

1. With one washer on the lid, how many washers did it take to make the lid slide across the table?

   _____

2. Did you need to give the lid a little push, or did it begin to slide on its own?

   _____

3. With the lid sitting on sandpaper and one washer on the lid, how many washers did you need to hang on the paper clip to get the lid moving?

   _____

4. Cut out a round piece of sandpaper the same size as the lid and tape it to the bottom of the lid. With one washer on the lid, how many washers did you need to hang on the paper clip to make the lid move?

   _____

Friction: Just Weight and See!

1. Use the following chart to fill in the number of washers it took to make the lid slide with two, four, and six washers on the lid.

Number of washers on lid	2	4	6	8
Number of washers on clip				

2. Make a graph of the data you collected.

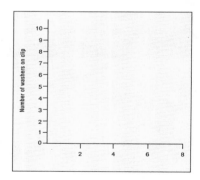

3. What does the graph show you about the way weight affects friction?

   _____

   _____

4. Judging from your graph, how many washers do you think it would it take to move the lid if eight washers were stacked in the middle of the lid? _____ Now try it to see how close your prediction was.

NAME _____   **DATE** _____

Friction: Friend or Foe?

Look at the following pictures. Each object deals with friction in a different way. In some cases, friction helps the object work better, but in others, the object is shaped to reduce friction.

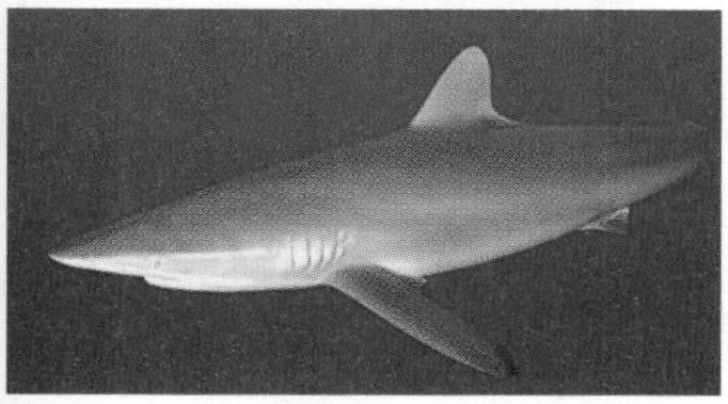

1. In what way do the wide fins and tail of the shark use friction to the shark's advantage?

_____

_____

2. Does the overall shape of the shark produce a lot of friction or a little? _____

3. In what way do people take advantage of friction to move in the water? And how do we reduce friction to move through the water better?

_____

_____

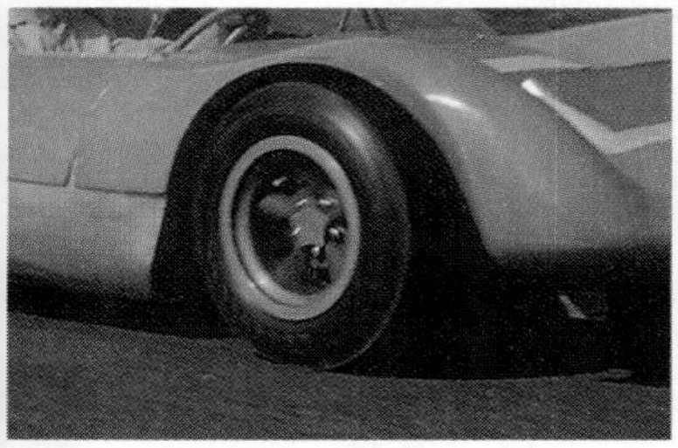

1. Does the race car tire need to have a lot of friction with the road or a little?

_____

Why?

_____

2. What is it about the tire that helps create friction with the road?

_____

3. How is the rest of the car shaped to reduce friction?

_____

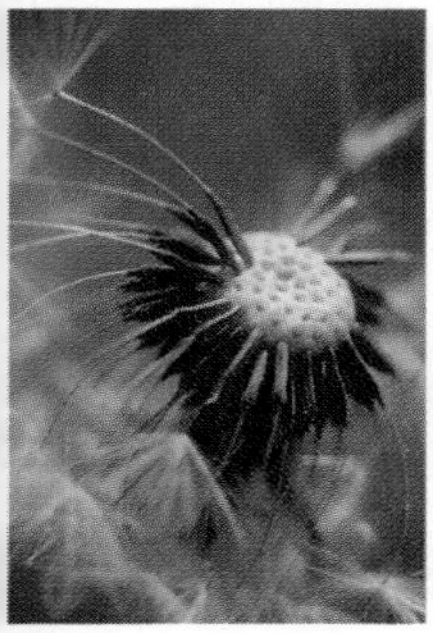

1. Does the dandelion seed need a lot of friction with the air or a little? _____

Why? _____

_____

2. What is it about the shape of the seed that creates friction with the air?

_____

_____

3. What human-made device works in a similar way? Explain how it works.

_____

_____

Friction:
More Than Just Scratching the Surface

Push down on a table. While you are pushing, move your hand back and forth. Can you feel the force that tries to keep your hand from moving? That force is called friction. Let's investigate how friction works!

1 Using a paper punch, carefully make a hole near the edge of the plastic container lid. Tie one end of the thread to this hole.

2 Unbend part of a paper clip and tie it to the other end of the thread. Put the lid on the table and hang the paper clip over the end of the table. Put one washer on the lid.

3 Gently push the lid from the side. How hard was it to move the lid? Hang one washer on the paper clip. Did the lid slide along the table? Add washers, one at a time, to see how many washers it takes for the lid to slowly slide along the table. Record your result. Keep this result for the next activity.

4 Tape a piece of sandpaper to the table and repeat Step 3 above, with the lid sitting right on the sandpaper. Again, record your results.

5 Which has more friction, the tabletop or the sandpaper? Explain your answer.

6 Suppose you taped a piece of sandpaper to the bottom of the lid. Then you would have sandpaper sliding over sandpaper. Predict what you think would happen. Repeat Step 3 above to see if you are right.

Friction: Just Weight and See!

YOU WILL NEED:

lid from plastic container

thread, 40 cm

10 washers (the same size)

paper clip

paper

pen

1 Set up your friction experiment, just as in the last activity (without sandpaper). This time, place two washers on the lid.

2 Gently push the lid from the side. How hard was it to move the lid? Find out how many washers you must hang on the paper clip so the lid will slowly slide along the table. Record your result in a table like the one below.

3 Now place two more washers on the lid, for a total of four. Repeat what you did in Step 2. You may have to work with another group to have enough washers for this step. Also try a total of six washers on the lid. Record all your results.

4 Draw a graph of your results. Set up your graph on axes like the ones shown or use the chart and graph in the Student Activity Sheet.

5 Write a sentence to tell what the graph shows. In general, as you add weight to the lid, what happens to the friction?

6 Suppose you put eight washers on the lid? From your graph, estimate how many washers you would need to move the lid. After you have recorded your estimate, try the experiment. Compare the result with your estimate.

Number of washers on lid	2	4	6	8
Number of washers on clip				

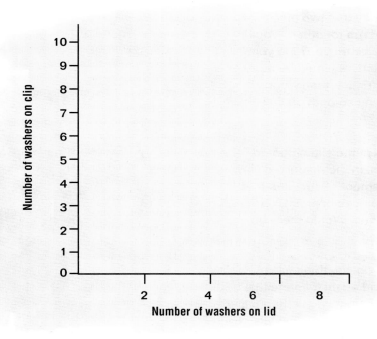

235

So What's the Rub?

There are two kinds of friction—**static friction** and **sliding friction**. If two objects are touching but not moving, they have static friction. When they move and rub against each other, they have sliding friction. In general, static friction is greater than sliding friction. In the previous activity, you may have needed to give the lid a little push to get it moving. If you did this, and the lid then slid on its own, the static friction was greater than the sliding friction.

What causes friction? Let's take a look at these photos and see what we can find out. They show magnified views of different materials.

Look at the pictures. Which do you think would have more friction: sandpaper rubbing sandpaper, or sandpaper rubbing wood? Explain how you used the photos to come up with your answer.

Imagine that two pieces of wood rub together. Would there be friction? Do you think there would be more or less friction than wood rubbing smooth metal? Why?

Look at the sliding board metal. In the magnified view, is it smooth? Imagine that two pieces of metal rub together. Would there be friction?

Why do you think oil is spread on metal parts that rub against each other in a wagon or bicycle wheels or in a car engine?

Go with the Flow!

YOU WILL NEED:

64-oz juice bottle with wide mouth, or see-thru tennis ball can

a small piece of clay

water

metric ruler

Friction happens whenever one object rubs against something else. The "something else" can be a solid or a liquid or a gas. You have already investigated what happens when an object rubs against a solid. Now let's investigate friction when an object moves through a liquid!

1 Add water to the container so it is almost full.

2 Roll the clay into two little balls, each about a half-centimeter across.

3 You are going to have a friction race. You will drop one ball just as it is. That ball is smooth and round. Take the other ball and flatten it into a pancake.

4 When you are ready, hold both pieces of clay close to the surface of the water. Drop both at the same time. What do you observe?

5 Do you think friction had anything to do with the different speeds of the clay? Explain.

6 Why do you think speedboats and fish have such smooth shapes?

237

Air Brakes

YOU WILL NEED:

2 pieces of paper
3 balloons
ruler

You have investigated friction in solids and liquids. Now let's investigate friction when an object moves through the gases in air!

1 With one piece of paper, make a simple paper airplane.

2 Hold the other piece of paper level, as high as you can. Have your partner hold the paper airplane by the tail so its nose is at the same height as the sheet of paper.

3 Now drop the airplane and the sheet of paper at the same time. What happens? Repeat it to make sure. Write a sentence or two to describe what you observed. In what way do the different speeds have anything to do with friction?

Streamlined is the word that describes the smooth shape of airplanes, fish, and cars. Tell why you think it's important to choose a streamlined shape to reduce friction.

4 Now put aside the paper and pick up the balloons. Blow one up all the way. Blow up another so its diameter is about half the diameter of the first. Use a ruler to check on the diameters. Do not blow up the third balloon.

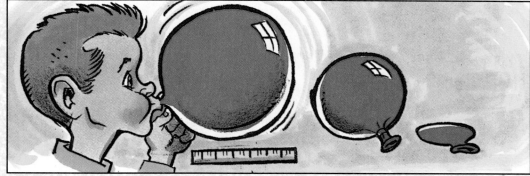

5 Hold the uninflated and small balloon at the same height. Before dropping the balloons, predict which will land first. Drop them at the same time. Record which one lands first in a chart like the one below.

6 Now hold the uninflated and large balloon at the same height. Before dropping the balloons, predict which will land first. Now drop them and record which one lands first. Repeat, using the large and small balloons.

7 Do your results make sense? Can you explain your results based on the friction between the balloons and the air? How are your results similar or different from what you found in the activity "Go with the Flow!"?

UNINFLATED WITH SMALL	UNINFLATED WITH LARGE	LARGE WITH SMALL

Friction—Friend or Foe?

Often we have to work against friction. If you ride your bike on a flat road, the bike slows down when you stop peddling. There is friction between the wheels and the road, between the wheels and the bike frame, and between the air and the rider. All of this friction acts to slow the bike down. And when you use the brakes, it is friction that brings the bike to a stop.

But sometimes friction can help us do things. You need friction to do something as simple as walking across a room. If there were no friction, you would slip each time you tried to take a step. It would be like trying to walk on slick ice—you would fall right over. Even writing your name with a pencil would be impossible. Without friction, the pencil would shoot right out of your hand.

For the three photos shown, answer these questions:

1. Does the form or shape of the object produce a lot of friction or only a little?

2. How does the object's shape affect whether there is a lot of friction or a little?

3. How does this friction help the object work better?

WONDER SCIENCE

This unit provides students with activities that explore what levers can do and how they work. A lever is one kind of simple machine. The others include the wheel, the inclined plane, the pulley system, and the gear. Simple machines can increase your force. This increase is called *mechanical advantage*.

Suppose you need to dig up a large rock, but the rock is too heavy to lift directly. You can slide the end of a crowbar under the rock. By pushing on the other end of the crowbar, you may be able to pry the rock loose. The crowbar acts as a force amplifier. It pushes harder on the rock than you push on the crowbar. You can move the rock, but only a short distance. And to move it that short distance, your hands had to move the end of the crowbar a long distance. You're trading distance for force—that's the story of the lever and of all simple machines.

Never Say Never When It Comes to a Lever!

A seesaw is a lever. The hinge right in the middle of the seesaw is the fulcrum—the pivot for the lever's turning motion. The weight of the children and their distance from the fulcrum are the two variables in balancing the lever. If one child weighs twice as much as the other, to balance the seesaw, the smaller child must be twice as far away from the fulcrum as the larger child.

The activity should show students that as fewer pennies are used, they can still balance the three-penny load if they are moved further from the fulcrum. The exact mathematical relationship between number of pennies and distance from the fulcrum is complicated by the fact that not all pennies have the same weight.

Hark: A Knock at the Lever!

A door is like a big lever but with nothing on the other side of the fulcrum. The fulcrum of a door is the hinge—that's what the door pivots around. Instead of lifting something on the other end like with a seesaw, you simply have to move the weight of the door and overcome the friction of the hinges. Just as with other levers, the farther from the fulcrum you push, the more force you produce and the easier it is to move the door.

Can a Lever Do It?—Yes, It Can!

In this activity, students should feel that it is easier to puncture the can if their fingers are farther away from the fulcrum. This is a classic case of increased "leverage" as you move further toward the end of the lever. Another example is using a wrench on a tight nut. The longer the wrench and the further from the nut you apply the force, the easier it is to loosen.

Something for Nothing?

Have you ever driven up a road that wound around and around a mountain? It was a long distance to drive, but because the incline wasn't very steep, it was a lot easier than going the shorter distance right up the mountain. The lever works in a similar way. Rather than lifting a heavy object straight up using lots of force, you can use a lever and make a hard job easier by applying less force but for a longer distance. In the activity, students should notice that it seems much easier to lift the five-penny load when pushing at the far end of the lever, but that they needed to push over a longer distance.

Living Lever-Limbs!

Throughout the unit, students have learned that when a force is applied farther from the fulcrum, it is easier to lift a load. As far as the position of the load is concerned, the closer the load is to the fulcrum, the easier it is to lift the load. Look at the drawings of the three students lifting buckets. As the load is moved closer and closer to the shoulder (the fulcrum of their lever arm), it should be easier and easier to lift. Students should also notice that although the load is easier to lift, it is lifted through a shorter and shorter distance.

ACTIVITY ANSWERS AND EXTENDERS

Never Say Never When It Comes to a Lever!

With one stack of three pennies at the 11 cm mark on the left, the other stack of three will balance somewhere near the 19 cm

The Clever Lever

mark on the right (each stack about 4 cm from the fulcrum). As it turns out, not all pennies have the same weight, so you may get a range of results. Feel free to use washers instead. But the important outcome should be clear anyway: the fewer the pennies on the right, the farther out from the fulcrum those pennies must be to balance.

You can do a math extension by having the students measure the distances from the washers to the fulcrum. Then they can multiply the number of washers times the distance to the pivot and see whether these products are the same on both sides of the fulcrum. Also, they can plot a graph of the different ways they balanced the stack of three washers on the left with a stack of washers on the right. They can plot the number of washers in the stack on the right versus the distance of the stack from the fulcrum.

Hark: A Knock at the Lever!

Indeed, less force is needed to push open the door as you move away from the pivot—away from the hinges and toward the knob. It takes a much stronger push to open the door when you push near the hinges. This result is similar to that of the first activity: one penny could lift three, if the one was much farther from the fulcrum than were the three.

Can a Lever Do It?—Yes, It Can!

The can opener has two long handles and a pivot where the handles meet. This pivot is the fulcrum. Each of the two long handles, which you squeeze to puncture the can, is a lever. To puncture the can, you place your fingers at the *ends* of the handles, so the force of your hands is applied as far as possible from the fulcrum. This gives you the greatest amount of leverage!

Something for Nothing?

Steps 5 and 6 provide students with a tactile awareness of how a lever increases the force applied. Students can feel that they are applying more force when their finger is close to the fulcrum than when their finger is near the end. The "price" of this increase in force is the extra distance the force must be applied. The students observe this increased distance in steps 7–9.

The Clever Lever

NATIONAL SCIENCE EDUCATION STANDARDS

The activities in this unit can be used to support the teaching of the following standards:

✔ **Unifying Concepts and Processes**

Evidence, Models, and Explanation

Evidence consists of observations and data on which to base scientific explanations. (All activities)

Constancy, Change, and Measurement

Evidence for interactions and subsequent change and the formulation of scientific explanations are often clarified through quantitative distinctions—measurement.

Never Say Never When It Comes to a Lever!

Something for Nothing?

✔ **Science as Inquiry**

Abilities Necessary to Do Scientific Inquiry

Design and conduct a scientific investigation. (All activities)

Develop descriptions, explanations, predictions, and models using evidence. (All activities)

Think critically and logically to make the relationships between evidence and explanations. (All activities)

✔ **Physical Science**

Position and Motion of Objects

If one or more forces act on an object along a straight line, then the forces will reinforce or cancel one another, depending on their direction and magnitude. (All activities)

NAME _____   DATE _____

Never Say Never When It Comes To a Lever!

Fill out the table to record your data to show where you placed your pennies on the right side of the ruler to balance the three-penny load on the left side.

<table>
<tr><td colspan="2" align="center">Left Side</td><td colspan="2" align="center">Right Side</td></tr>
<tr><td>Number
of pennies</td><td>Position
on ruler</td><td>Number
of pennies</td><td>Position
on ruler</td></tr>
<tr><td align="center">3</td><td>11 cm</td><td align="center">3</td><td></td></tr>
<tr><td align="center">3</td><td>11 cm</td><td align="center">2</td><td></td></tr>
<tr><td align="center">3</td><td>11 cm</td><td align="center">1</td><td></td></tr>
</table>

Describe in words what the numbers in the table show.

_____

_____

_____

Use your data from the preceding table to draw where your pennies balanced the three-penny load.

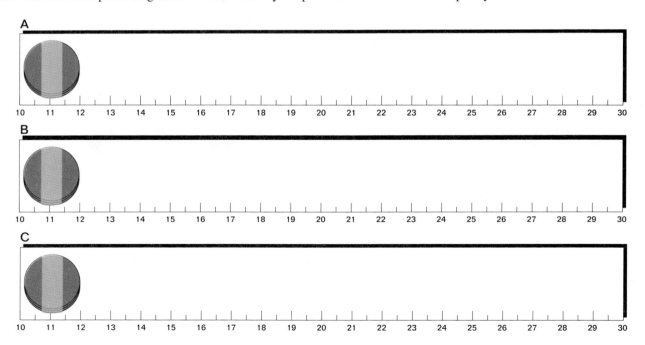

STUDENT ACTIVITY SHEET

NAME _____   DATE _____

Something for Nothing?

To help you record your results in "Something for Nothing?," fill out this table.

Left Side   Right Side

Distance from fulcrum to weight (stays the same)	Distance weight moves up	Distance from fulcrum to finger	Distance finger moves down

1. Suppose you changed the position of the weight. If you moved it all the way to the end of the straw, would it be easier or harder to lift? Try it and see. What did you find out?

_____

_____

2. How about if you moved the weight very close to the fulcrum? Is it easier or harder to lift?

_____

_____

3. Is there a difference in how high the weight goes if it is closer to or farther from the fulcrum? Explain.

_____

_____

4. What would happen if you went out on the playground and tried this same experiment on a seesaw? If you pushed down on the seat of a seesaw and the person on the other side was sitting near the fulcrum, would it be easier or harder to lift the person than if he or she were sitting on the seat? _____ Would the person go up as high? _____

Never Say Never When

A simple lever looks kind of like a seesaw you use on the playground. Did you ever notice that a small child can lift a much larger child if they sit at different distances along the seesaw? A lever works the same way!

Look at the pictures below:

As the small children move closer to the end of the seesaw, fewer and fewer of them are needed to balance the larger child. This is one of the great things about levers: the farther out you go from the fulcrum (the support on which the lever moves), the more force you can get out of your lever. Try this activity, and you'll never say never when it comes to levers!

1 Make a chart like the one at right or use the chart from the student worksheet.

2 Place the ruler down on the pencil as shown. Move the ruler on the pencil until the ruler is balanced. The pencil is the fulcrum. The ruler should balance somewhere near the 15-centimeter (cm) mark.

3 Tape 3 pennies together and place the taped pennies on the 11-cm mark on the ruler. This taped stack of pennies represents the large child. Place another stack of 3 pennies (untaped) on the other side of the ruler. This represents the 3 smaller children.

4 Move the untaped stack to the spot on the ruler where it just lifts the taped 3-penny load on the other side. In your chart, next to the number 3, record the place where the untaped stack was on your ruler.

		Where on the ruler the untaped pennies balanced the taped 3-penny load
Number of pennies in untaped stack	3	
	2	
	1	

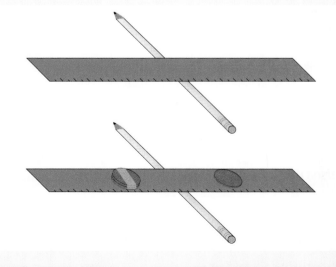

246

It Comes to a LEVER!

5 Keep your taped 3-penny load on the 11-cm mark. Remove the untaped 3 pennies and use 2 pennies to see where on the ruler your 2-penny stack just lifts the taped 3-penny load. In your chart, next to the number 2, record the place where the 2 pennies were on your ruler.

6 Now use 1 penny to see if you can find a place on the ruler where it can lift the taped 3-penny load on the other side. Record your results. When you used fewer pennies to lift the 3-penny load, did you move them closer to or further away from the fulcrum?

7 Look at the three rulers below. Draw a line across each ruler showing where your pencil balanced the ruler from step 2 (it should be near the 15 cm mark).

8 Look back at your chart from the page before. Draw a circle on ruler A where your 3 untaped pennies balanced the taped 3-penny load. Write a "3" on the circle. Next, draw a circle on ruler B where your 2 untaped pennies balanced the taped 3-penny load. Write a "2" on the circle. Finally, draw a circle on ruler C where your 1 penny balanced the taped 3-penny load. Write a "1" on the circle.
Are these rulers like the children on the seesaws? In what way?

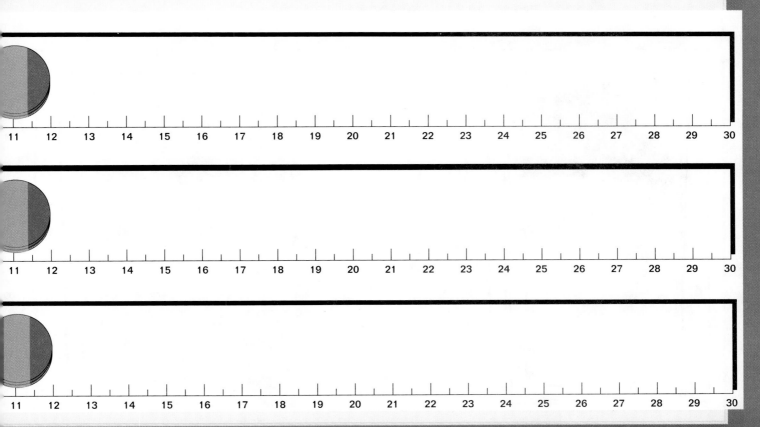

Hark:
A Knock at the Lever!

YOU WILL NEED:
door

You can find levers in a lot of places where you might not expect them. Look at a door. It may not look like one, but a door is a type of lever. The door has a fulcrum like the seesaw, but the door's fulcrum is harder to see; the door's fulcrum is its hinges.

In the last activity, you were able to lift a heavy weight on one side of a lever with less weight on the other side as long as you moved the lighter weight further from the fulcrum. You could say that you were able to lift the same weight with less force. A door works in a similar way. If you look at a door as a lever, a little bit of force far from the fulcrum should move the door better than the same amount of force near the fulcrum. Let's try it!

1 Stand on the side of the door where you can open the door by pushing on it. Put your index finger near the edge of the door that has the handle.

2 Slowly push to see if a gentle push will open the door.

3 Now place your index finger on the edge of the door near the pivot (hinges). Slowly push on the door to open it. What did you notice? Does this make sense based on what you have learned about levers so far? Does it seem like less force is needed as you move further from the pivot?

Be careful not to pinch your finger in the door.

CAN a Lever Do It? —Yes It CAN!

By now, you know that a lot of levers are out there in the world. Here's another one—a can opener! Let's see if it follows the same rules as the levers we've seen so far.

Do not put your hand into the can. Be careful of any sharp edges.

1 Look at a can opener. How is a can opener like a lever? How is it like a seesaw or a door?

2 If you wanted to open a can, would you place your fingers on the can opener **here** .... or **here**?

Why?

Let's try it to see which way works best?

3 Take a can opener and place it on a can as if you were about to open it— do not squeeze the can opener yet.

4 Place your thumb and index finger about halfway down the handle of the can opener as shown. Squeeze the handle together to try to puncture the can. What did you notice?

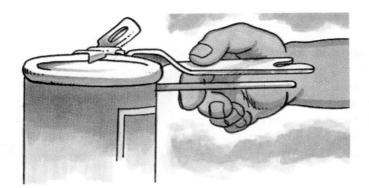

5 Now move your fingers to the end of the handle and try squeezing the handle together to puncture the can. Was it easier or harder than before? Is this what you expected? Why?

Something for Nothing?

YOU WILL NEED:

straws
tape
paper clip
5 pennies
string
index card
pencil
metric ruler

Aren't levers great? The further you go from the fulcrum, the less and less force you need to use to do the same job! But wait a second. That's too good to be true. To get a bigger force, don't you need to do something extra? Let's see if we can find out!

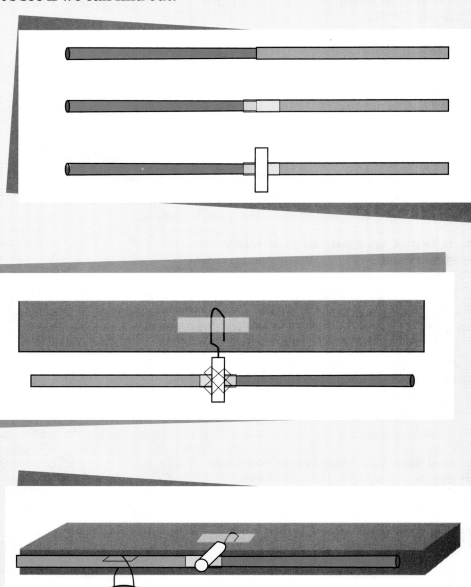

1 Squeeze the end of one straw and push it about 2 cm into another straw. The length of the two straws together should be about 38 cm. Use a piece of tape to hold the straws firmly together.

2 Cut a 2-cm piece of straw from another straw. Tape this straw across the middle of your long straw. (Use two pieces of tape so that it is secure.)

3 Unbend one side of a paper clip and tape it to the table as shown. Slip the short piece of straw over the paper clip so that the straw pivots freely on the paper clip. The paper clip is your fulcrum. The whole thing is your lever.

4 Tape 5 pennies together into a stack. Cut a short piece of string, and tape it to the penny stack to make a little handle. While holding the right side of the lever, place the stack of 5 pennies about 3/4 of the way toward the fulcrum on the left side and tape it to the straw.

5 Use your index finger to push gently down on the right side of the lever near the fulcrum. Push down hard enough to lift the weight a bit. Now move your finger further toward the end of the lever and push down again. Did it seem easier or harder to lift the weight?

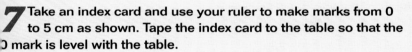

6 Now move your finger to the very end. Push down again. Was it easier or harder? Try pushing down near the fulcrum again and once more at the very end. Can you feel the difference?

7 Take an index card and use your ruler to make marks from 0 to 5 cm as shown. Tape the index card to the table so that the 0 mark is level with the table.

8 Have your partner hold the ruler upside down where you pushed down on the lever near the fulcrum. The 0 mark on the ruler should be level with the table. Push down so that the weight moves up 2 cm on your index card. How many centimeters did your finger have to move down to lift the weight up 2 cm?

9 Now have your partner hold the ruler near the end of the lever. Push down so that the weight again moves up by 2 cm. How many centimeters did your finger have to move down to lift the weight 2 cm this time?

Although it is easier to lift as you move further from the fulcrum, you have to push through a longer distance. Therefore, you don't get the extra force for nothing. You have to "pay" for it by pushing for a greater distance.

251

Living Lever-Limbs!

YOU WILL NEED:

small plastic bucket
with handle

belt

books

Remember the big child from the activity, "Never Say Never When It Comes To A LEVER"?

He was sitting on the seesaw pretty close to the pivot, and the smaller child sitting all the way at the other end was able to lift him. If the larger child was sitting all the way at the end of his side, the small child never could have lifted him. The closer a load is to the fulcrum, the easier it is to lift!

Let's test this out with your own body's levers—your arms and legs!

1 Slip the belt through the handle of a bucket. Put a few books in the bucket until the bucket is a little heavy to lift.

2 Hold your arm out straight and put the belt on your wrist as shown. Use your shoulder as the fulcrum and lift the bucket without bending your arm.

3 Move the belt to your elbow. Lift the bucket again with a straight arm. Was it harder or easier than before?

4 Move the belt close to your shoulder. Again lift the bucket with a straight arm. Is it getting easier or harder to lift as you move the bucket toward the fulcrum? What do you notice about the height the bucket rises each time it is moved closer to the fulcrum?

5 Sit in a chair and try the same activity using a straight leg and your hip joint as the fulcrum. Does moving the weight toward the fulcrum on your lever leg cause the same result as moving the weight toward the fulcrum on your lever arm?

The activities in this unit are designed to explore the relationship between an object's overall structure and how that form enables the object to perform its essential functions. This is an important concept because the relationship between structure and function occurs everywhere in both the natural and designed world.

Before starting the WonderScience activities, bring a common object, such as a hammer, into the classroom. Ask students what it is about the structure of the hammer that relates to its function. Consider the length of the handle. What if it were only one fourth as long? How about if it were 2 meters long? What if the heavy part were placed in the middle instead of at the end? Encourage students to consider the relationship between structure and function of other common objects, such as a spoon or tennis racket.

Structure & Function Come in Handy!

To begin this activity, ask students to consider their own hand and to suggest which structural features of the hand make it well-suited for its function. Structural features might include number of fingers, number and location of joints, and the position of the thumb and its ability to move across the hand. Make sure that when students tape each other's hands, the tape is not so tight that it hurts or cuts off circulation.

Results:

With the thumb taped to the hand, students should be able to easily pick up the pencil, marble, and toothpicks. Students may find that the penny is much more difficult to pick up. The thumb is useful in picking up objects because of its position on the hand. The thumb is opposite from the fingers, enabling the tip of your thumb and the tips of your fingers to meet and grasp objects.

With the fingers taped together and the thumb free, students should be able to pick up all objects. You might want to ask students what kinds of activities would be more difficult with only one giant bendable finger. Some answers might include typing, playing the piano, catching a baseball, and performing surgery.

With a Popsicle stick taped to the thumb and each finger, it was very difficult to pick up any items. Students may be able to pick up the items, but with much more difficulty than with the other hand structures. Simple hand motions such as a pat on the back or waving are no problem, but any function requiring dexterity is not easy.

The FUN in Structure and FUNction

This activity involves designing a simple device to lift a marble out of a cup. Since this is an activity in which students are asked to design a device, the amount of direction you, as a teacher give, will depend on the abilities of your students. Either give them the materials as well as the suggestions given in the activity, or decide to simply give them the materials and the challenge.

Results:

Two possible straw and pipe cleaner designs for picking up one marble are given. One possible design for picking up two marbles is to bend the bottom of the pipe cleaner into an "S" shape as shown.

Encourage students to come up with other designs.
One possible design for the "Form and Function Flinger," which uses only the pipe cleaner, is to bend the pipe cleaner in half and then to make a loop at one end. Hold it against the side of a table as shown. Place the Styrofoam ball on the loop and pull back and release. Students should be able to create several different designs.

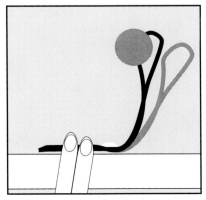

Unit 22
Structure and Function

Structure with Some Stretch!

When introducing this activity, point out to students that the principle of structure relating to function operates on many different levels. Just as an object's external structure influences its function, so does its internal structure. In this activity, students consider how the arrangement of the polymers in plastic helps determine certain observable properties of the plastic.

Results:

The plastic stretches in all directions. Students should relate this flexibility to the intertwined nature of the long polymer chains in the plastic. The flexibility of the polymer chains also accounts for the tight seal the plastic forms around the pencil, inhibiting water leaks.

Structured for Strength

In this activity, students investigate an ordinary material, corrugated cardboard, and discover some of its extraordinary characteristics. Close observation of the structure of corrugated cardboard may help heighten student awareness that simple design features can have a profound impact on function.

Results:

Students will find that the individual peeled-away layers of the corrugated cardboard will crush very easily, but that the combined layers are very difficult to crush. The strength of the corrugated cardboard becomes more evident as students stack books on the cardboard rings. The rings are so strong, in fact, that they will even support a student's weight.

Structure & Function in Nature: We Imitate What's Great!

This page could be used to round out a discussion of the relationship between structure and function. Give students the example from nature and challenge them to think of a human-made object that imitates the natural structure to perform a similar function.

Structure and Function

NATIONAL SCIENCE EDUCATION STANDARDS

The activities in this unit can be used to support the teaching of the following standards:

✔ **Unifying Concepts and Processes**

Form and Function

Form and function are complementary aspects of objects, organisms, and systems in the natural and designed world. The form or shape of an object or system is frequently related to its use, operation, or function. *(All activities)*

✔ **Science as Inquiry**

Abilities Necessary to Do Scientific Inquiry

Think critically and logically to make the relationships between evidence and explanations.

Structure with Some Stretch!

Structured for Strength

Structure & Function in Nature: We Imitate What's Great!

✔ **Physical Science**

Properties and Changes of Properties in Matter

A substance has characteristic properties . . . all of which are independent of the amount of the sample.

Structure with Some Stretch!

✔ **Life Science**

Structure and Function in Living Systems

Living systems at all levels of organization demonstrate the complementary nature of structure and function.

Structure & Function Come in Handy!

Sturcture & Function in Nature: We Imitate What's Great!

✔ **Science and Technology**

Abilities of Technological Design

Design a solution or product.

The FUN in Structure and FUNction

NAME _____   **DATE** _____

Structure and Function Come in Handy!

Answer the following questions regarding how each of the different structures of your hand functioned:

Four bendable fingers but no thumb:

1. Which items were you able to pick up easily?

_____

2. Which items were more difficult to pick up? Why?

_____

_____

_____

3. Describe which fingers you used and how you used them to pick up objects.

_____

_____

_____

4. Do you think that you could grip a hammer, a baseball bat, or a tennis racket well without the use of your thumb? Why or why not?

_____

_____

_____

A thumb and one big bendable finger:

1. Which items were you able to pick up easily?

_____

_____

_____

2. Which items were more difficult to pick up? Why?

_____

_____

_____

3. Describe how you used your one big bendable finger and thumb to pick up objects.

_____

_____

_____

STUDENT ACTIVITY SHEET

NAME _____   DATE _____

4. Although you might be able to grip objects fairly well with one big bendable finger and a thumb, what sorts of activities would be hard to do with hands like this?

_____
_____
_____
_____

Individual fingers and a thumb but not bendable:

1. Which items were you able to pick up easily?

_____
_____
_____

2. Which items were more difficult to pick up? Why?

_____
_____
_____

3. Describe how you used your nonbendable fingers and thumb to pick up objects.

_____
_____
_____

4. Although picking up items is difficult with nonbendable fingers and thumb, what sorts of activities could you do with hands like this?

_____
_____
_____

Structure & Function

Have you ever thought about how certain objects
are so perfectly designed for what they need to do?
Some examples are tools, such as hammers, pliers, and screwdrivers.

A different kind of example is the human hand.

With four fingers, a thumb that moves
all the way across the hand, and all those joints,
a hand is able to do many useful things.

Let's see what it would be like to have a hand that was built differently.

Four bendable fingers but no thumb:

YOU WILL NEED:

2 pieces of adhesive tape
pennies
toothpicks
marbles
pencils

1 Wrap two pieces of adhesive tape around one of your hands to tape your thumb securely to your hand as shown. Don't wrap the tape so tightly that it hurts.

2 Try picking up pennies, toothpicks, marbles, and pencils. What do you notice about picking things up without using your thumb? What makes your thumb so useful in picking up objects?

Come in Handy!

A thumb and one big bendable finger:

> **YOU WILL NEED:**
> 2 pieces of adhesive tape
> pennies
> toothpicks
> marbles
> pencils

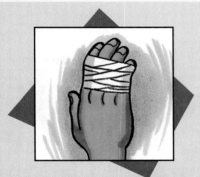

How about if you had the use of your thumb but instead of having four separate fingers with joints, you had one giant finger with joints?

1 Wrap two pieces of adhesive tape around the fingers of one hand to tape your four fingers securely together as shown.

2 Try picking up pennies, toothpicks, marbles, and pencils. What do you notice about picking things up with one giant finger and a thumb? What seems more useful, having the use of your thumb with one big finger or having individual fingers but no thumb?

Individual fingers and a thumb but not bendable:

> **YOU WILL NEED:**
> 10 pieces of adhesive tape
> 5 popsicle sticks
> pennies
> toothpicks
> marbles
> pencils

1 Have your partner place a popsicle stick on the back of your finger and wrap two pieces of adhesive tape around the stick and your finger as shown.

2 Repeat step 1 for each of your fingers and your thumb. When you are finished, you should be unable to bend the joints in your fingers and thumb.

3 Try picking up pennies, toothpicks, marbles, and pencils. What do you notice about picking things up without joints? Is there anything that you can do just as well without joints as with them?

The FUN in
Structure & FUNction

Throughout history people have used the materials in their environment to make devices to perform different functions. The structure of the device is always related, in some way, to its function. When prehistoric people made knives or arrowheads from stone, they made the edges sharp and the tip pointy to serve the function of piercing or cutting through material like animal hides or plant stems. Today, when we manufacture scissors, the structure of the two blades moving past each other serves the function of cutting paper or cloth. Try the activity below to see how the structure of a simple device is related to its function.

Challenge!

Using a straw and a pipe cleaner, can you design a device to lift a marble out of a cup without touching the marble with your fingers? (We'll give you a few hints.)

You could simply bend the straw at the flexible end and pick up a marble in the bend and drag it up the side of the cup as shown.

Or

You could make a little circle bend in the end of the pipe cleaner and reach down and lift the marble out as shown.

Or

You could improve your device by putting the pipe cleaner through the straw to give your device some extra support as shown.

Now try this!

How could you change your device to pick up two marbles at the same time?

Create a Form and Function Flinger!

Try using the pipe cleaner and the straw to make a device that will fling a small Styrofoam ball the farthest.

260

Structure with Some Stretch!

The way that structure relates to function can even be seen down on the molecular level. The structure of the molecules that make up a material is closely related to how the material behaves. A good example of this is the plastic from a clear plastic bag. The molecules that make up plastic are hooked together in chains that are very long. These long chains are called polymers.

In a plastic bag, these chains are loosely coiled and intertwined with each other, making the plastic flexible and stretchy.

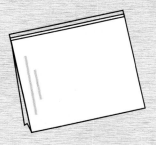

Below is an illustration of a model of what the long polymers in a sheet of plastic wrap might look like.

Lets investigate a piece of plastic wrap to see how its molecular structure is related to how it functions.

1 Cut the sandwich bag in half so that you have two pieces about the same size.

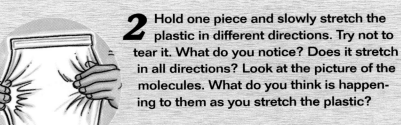

2 Hold one piece and slowly stretch the plastic in different directions. Try not to tear it. What do you notice? Does it stretch in all directions? Look at the picture of the molecules. What do you think is happening to them as you stretch the plastic?

3 Fill your cup about 3/4 full of water. Place your other piece of plastic over the cup and put a rubber band around the rim to hold the plastic firmly in place. Carefully turn the cup upside down to make sure that it does not leak. Turn it upright again.

4 Take a pencil and slowly push it through the plastic. Carefully turn the cup over again leaving the pencil stuck in the wrap. Does the water leak around the pencil? How do you think the structure of the plastic molecules helps to prevent leaking?

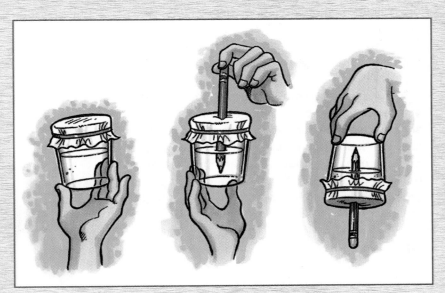

Structured for

The cardboard boxes you find at the grocery store and many other businesses are made from a material called corrugated cardboard. The boxes have to be very resistant to being crushed because many boxes are piled one on top of another. The structure of the corrugated cardboard serves this anti-crush function very well. If you look closely at the edge of a piece of corrugated cardboard, you'll see that it is made from two thin flat pieces of paper with a wavy piece of paper "sandwiched" in between. This wavy-paper sandwich structure gives corrugated cardboard a surprising amount of strength. Let's see how strong it is!

YOU WILL NEED:

- corrugated cardboard box
- masking tape
- cafeteria tray or cardboard pieces about tray size

TEACHER PREPARATION:

Because cardboard is difficult for students to cut, prepare a supply of cardboard strips in advance. Each pair of students should have three strips. The strips should be cut across the corrugation, not along it. Each strip should be about 3 centimeters (cm) wide and 30 cm long—approximately the dimensions of a standard ruler.

1 Pick up one of your pieces of cardboard. Try peeling away some of the two flat outside paper strips to get a better look at the wavy paper inside. What do you think is used to connect the flat papers to the wavy paper?

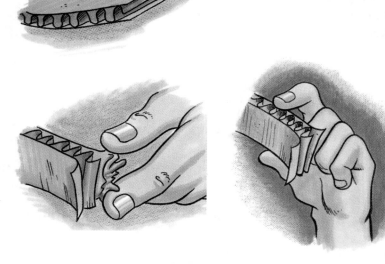

2 Use your thumb and index finger to see how hard it is to crush the individual flat or wavy strips that you peeled away. Now use your thumb and index finger to see if you can crush the "sandwich" cardboard that you did not peel. What do you notice?

3 Take your two remaining cardboard strips and curve each one into a circle as shown. Use masking tape to keep the circles closed. Place them on the floor and set a tray or piece of flat cardboard on top. Place a large book on the tray. Did the cardboard rings get crushed? Now add another book. Are the rings crushed yet?

4 Take the books off and carefully stand in the middle of the tray. Do the rings support your weight?

Strength

Because the cardboard rings can support a lot of weight, maybe you can use them to design a pair of shoes with a little lift!

TEACHER PREPARATION:
Each student will probably want to make a pair of shoes. This will require two rectangular pieces of cardboard per student that are 20 cm long and 10 cm wide. Each student will also need four strips of cardboard of the same dimension that you used before (30 cm x 3 cm). The basic design is as follows, but students should be encouraged to come up with designs they believe would be better.

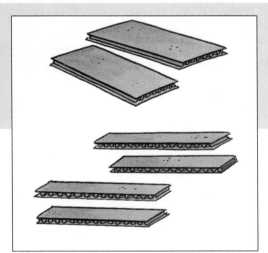

1 Bend each strip into a ring and use masking tape to hold each ring together.

2 Attach the rings to the bottom of each rectangle as shown.

3 Wrap the tape around your regular shoe and your new cardboard shoe as shown. Try walking on your shoes. Do the cardboard rings get crushed? Can you think of a design that would give you the same amount of lift but be better in another way? Try it and see!

263

Structure & Function in Nature:
We Imitate What's Great!

Living organisms have structures that perform certain functions to help the organisms survive. Over the years, people have created similar structures for objects that we want to have similar functions. Look at the pictures below to see what we mean.

The overall structures of birds and airplanes are pretty similar to help serve the function of flight.

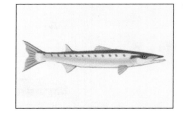 

A fish and a boat are both streamlined which helps them move through the water.

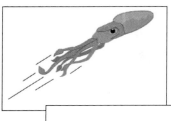

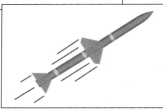

A squid has a structure that shoots water out in one direction, making its body move in the other direction. This jet propulsion idea is used to make rockets go.

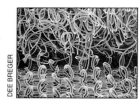

DEE BREGER

The tiny hooks on these seed burrs enable them to attach to hair on animals just like the tiny hooks of Velcro enable it to attach to fuzzy material.

DISCOVERING SCUBA

A seal has big flippers that help it swim through the water. Rubber flippers help divers move through the water in a similar way.

WONDERSCIENCE

The Essence of Speed

Many students first encounter the concept of speed from speedometer readings on vehicles or from speed measurements in sports, such as a baseball pitch or a tennis serve. Any student who has run a timed race has experienced the basic measurements necessary to determine speed: the *time* taken to go a known *distance,* from a start to a finish line. With a simple additional step—dividing the distance by the time—the students can calculate the speed.

Content Background

Suppose a car on a freeway travels 180 kilometers (about 108 miles) in two hours. What is its average speed? We divide the distance traveled by the time taken to travel that distance.

speed = distance ÷ time = 180 kilometers ÷ 2 hours

speed = 90 kilometers per hour (about 54 miles per hour)

Students may want to say "The speed is 90." Ninety what? We must give the speed units to specify the speed. Ninety kilometers per hour is a lot different from 90 centimeters per second. In cars and buses, the speed units of miles/hour or kilometers/hour are printed right on the speedometer.

Take the Lead—with Speed

The activity defines speed as the distance traveled divided by the time taken to travel that distance. In the example given, notice how the units divide just like the numbers do.

$$speed = \frac{10 \text{ meters}}{5 \text{ seconds}} = 2 \text{ meters/second}$$

We read the fraction "meters/second" as "meters per second." To calculate speed using actual measurements, students measure a distance and then time a partner moving over that distance. Students then calculate speed by dividing distance by time. Be sure students include the units of meters and seconds in their final speed answers. Also, make sure students move in such a way that there is a clear difference between their slow, medium, and fast speeds.

The Zip Line

The zip line allows students to use a more controlled experiment to calculate speed. Students change the tilt of the zip line by holding the upper end of the string at three different heights. At each height, students calculate the spool's speed three times for a more accurate measurement of speed. As students observe the spool moving, they may be able to observe it speeding up as it descends. But more often the spool will move with nearly a constant speed. This is because the spool speeds up until the force of friction, from the spool rubbing on the string, just balances the force of gravity that is pulling the spool along the string.

Speed Sinking!

It is easy to tape the ruler to a 2-liter bottle because a centimeter/inches ruler that is 12 inches long is the same height as the bottle. It helps if the zero mark of the ruler is right at the water surface. That way, when the student lets go of the peanut, it's right at the starting line. In this activity, the most important variable is the size of the falling peanut fragment. The key observation is that large fragments fall faster than small fragments. However, the whole peanut may fall more slowly than the half. This may be due to air trapped between the halves, or it might have to do with the surface area/weight ratio of the whole peanut. In fact, the whole peanut may float. If it does, go right to the half-peanut. But once you get past the whole peanut, the "larger-faster" rule holds.

Graphing to Go!

In this activity, students interpret a graph and describe the changes in speed of a car over a ten-second trip. This particular car undergoes a lot of speed changes over a short period of time, as a car might if it were entering a highway and soon got into a traffic jam and had to come to a stop. When interpreting the graph, students should notice that an upward slope of the line indicates an increase in speed, a downward slope indicates a decrease in speed, and a flat line indicates a constant speed.

And You Thought You Were Fast!

The maximum possible speed for any moving object is the speed of light. Scientists have made tiny subatomic particles go almost as fast. We can use a different speed—the speed of sound—to estimate the distance to a lightning strike by counting the number of seconds between when we see the lightning and when we hear the thunder. A five-second delay means the strike is about 1,600 meters, or about 1 mile, away. For a strike about 1,600 meters away, the sound takes about five seconds to reach you, but the light takes only about five millionths of a second!

Teacher Answer Key

Take the Lead—with Speed!

The data entered in the table will be different for each student. Encourage students to include units, such as meters, seconds, and meters per second, in their tabulated data. A measurement without units is incomplete.

The Zip Line

2. The spool can move in various ways, depending mostly on the height of the starting point and the tension of the string. If the string is tight, the spool usually speeds up as it descends and then reaches a constant speed. It may reach a constant speed earlier, later, or not at all, depending on the height and the tension of the string.

3. Lowering the end of the thread should reduce the speed of the spool. In fact, if the thread is lowered far enough, the spool may not slide at all. If the student lets the thread get slack, so the thread curves, then the spool will probably slow down as it descends and may stop before reaching the end of the thread.

7. When measurements are repeated, the results are often different. If the computed speeds are different, then to understand these differences, we must examine the distances and times that were used to compute the speed. The distance is relatively easy to measure. But the time is very difficult to measure accurately every time. It is hard to start timing when the spool is released and especially hard to stop timing when the spool reaches the end of the thread.

Speed Sinking!

Smaller pieces of peanut take longer to fall than larger pieces. The reason is complicated. The two forces on the peanut are gravity, which pulls the peanut down, and friction with the water, which reduces the peanut's speed. Friction occurs as the peanut's surface rubs on the water. This rubbing happens all over the peanut's surface. As the peanut bit gets smaller, both the weight and the amount of surface get smaller. But they don't get smaller in the same way. Progressively cutting the peanut in half reduces the weight more than the surface area. The result is that friction becomes more important as the peanut bit gets smaller, so the smaller bits fall more slowly than the larger bits. A tiny piece might fall 30 centimeters in 8 seconds, so its speed would be

30 centimeters ÷ 8 seconds = $3\frac{3}{4}$ centimeters per second or 3.75 centimeters per second.

Graphing to Go!

1. How fast was the car going at the end of the 1st second? 10 kilometers per hour

   How about at the end of the 2nd second? 20 kilometers per hour

   3rd second? 30 kilometers per hour

   4th second? 40 kilometers per hour

2. From 4 seconds to 6 seconds, did the car's speed increase, decrease, or stay the same? It stayed the same.

3. From 6 seconds to 7 seconds, how many kilometers per hour did the car's speed decrease? 20 kilometers per hour (40 km/hr – 20 km/hr)

4. From 7 seconds, how many seconds did it take the car to come to a stop? 3 seconds

5. Graph of answers to "Graphing to Go!"

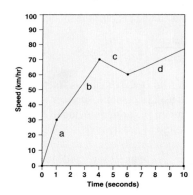

Extensions

Art

Invite students to make collages of images that express speed. The images could be from newspaper or magazine advertisements and photographs.

History of Technology

Take the students to a library so they can research the history of transportation. Have the students work in groups. Each group selects a different form of transportation—for instance, automobiles, boats, railroads, airplanes, and bicycles. Have each group make a time line to show how the speed of each form increases. Challenge the groups to provide an explanation for each increase in speed that they show on their time lines.

The Essence of Speed

NATIONAL SCIENCE EDUCATION STANDARDS

The activities in this unit can be used to support the teaching of the following standards:

✔ **Unifying Concepts and Processes**

Evidence, Models, and Explanation

Evidence consists of observations and data on which to base scientific explanations.
Take the Lead—with Speed

Using evidence to understand interactions allows individuals to predict changes in natural and designed systems.
The Zip Line
Speed Sinking!

✔ **Science as Inquiry**

Abilities Necessary to Do Scientific Inquiry

Design and conduct a scientific investigation. *(All activities)*
Use appropriate tools and techniques to gather, analyze, and interpret data. *(All activities)*

✔ **Understandings about Scientific Inquiry**

Mathematics is important in all aspects of scientific inquiry. *(All activities)*

✔ **Physical Science**

Motions and Forces

Motion can be measured and represented on a graph. *(All activities)*

STUDENT ACTIVITY SHEET

NAME _____   **DATE** _____

Take the Lead—With Speed!

Use the following charts to record the distance, time, and speed for you and your partner. Use one chart for each student.

Student's Name _____

	Slow	Medium	Fast
Distance	10 meters	10 meters	10 meters
Time			
Speed			

Student's Name _____

	Slow	Medium	Fast
Distance	10 meters	10 meters	10 meters
Time			
Speed			

The Zip Line

Use the following chart to record the distance, time, and speed for each of the three tries at each of the three heights.

	Height I _____			Height II _____			Height III _____		
	1st try	2nd try	3rd try	1st try	2nd try	3rd try	1st try	2nd try	3rd try
Distance spool traveled									
Time									
Speed									

NAME _____   **DATE** _____

Speed Sinking!

Use the following chart to record the distance, time, and speed for each peanut part.

Peanut Part	Distance	Time	Speed
Whole			
Half			
Quarter			
Tiny Piece			

Graphing to Go!

Use the following graph to produce a graph of the following changes in a car's speed.

a. During the first second, the car went from 0 to 30 kilometers per hour.

b. During the next 3 seconds, the speed climbed steadily to 70 kilometers per hour.

c. During the next 2 seconds, the speed dropped by 10 kilometers per hour.

d. From 7 to 10 seconds, the speed steadily climbed to 80 kilometers per hour.

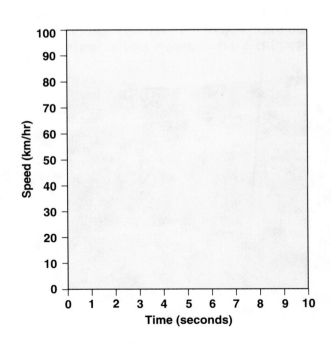

TAKE THE LEAD—

Speed tells how fast something moves. In a race, the runners all line up on the starting line, and the first one to the finish line is the winner. All the runners go the same distance, but the runner who gets to the finish line in the shortest time is the winner. The speed of the runners has to do with both distance and time.

When we talk about speed, we often use words like "really fast" or "kind of slow." But scientists need to be able to measure the actual speed of a moving object—they need to figure out the speed using real numbers for distance and time.

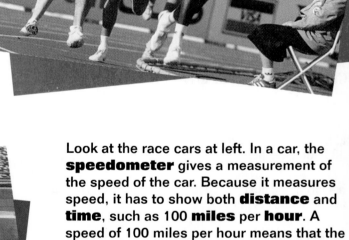

Here's how it works: Let's say that the distance of the race at right is 100 meters. Let's also say that the runner in the lead finishes the race in exactly 10 seconds. He won the race because his speed was the fastest, but what was it?

The trick to figuring out speed is in this formula:

SPEED = DISTANCE ÷ TIME

This means that you divide the distance the runner traveled by the time it took him to go that distance.

So for the race at the right:
SPEED = 100 meters ÷ 10 seconds
So the speed of the winning runner is:
SPEED = 10 meters per second

Look at the race cars at left. In a car, the **speedometer** gives a measurement of the speed of the car. Because it measures speed, it has to show both **distance** and **time**, such as 100 **miles** per **hour**. A speed of 100 miles per hour means that the car would travel a distance of 100 miles in a time of one hour.

Remember when figuring out speed, you always need to write down the distance such as "meters" or "miles," and the time such as "seconds" or "hours." These distance and time words are called **units**. You always need to write down the units. Now let's see how you can measure your own speed!

WITH SPEED

YOU WILL NEED:
metric ruler or meter-stick

clock or watch with sweep second hand

calculator

You and your partner can measure each other's speeds in the activity below. From slow to medium to fast, measuring speed is a blast!

1 You can do this activity outside or in the hallway. Pick a starting line and finish line that are 10 meters apart. Have your partner move from start to finish while you time how long it takes.

2 Ask your partner to go slowly the first time, faster the second time, and fastest the third time. After measuring the time for each one, record it in the chart and figure out the speed.

Suppose your partner traveled 10 meters in 5 seconds. What would be your partner's speed? You need to divide the distance your partner went by the time it took to go that distance. Here's how to do it:

Distance your partner traveled: 10 meters

Time to go this distance: 5 seconds

Speed = 10 meters ÷ by 5 seconds = 2 meters per second

3 Now **you** move from start to finish while your partner does the timing. Your partner should figure out your speed.

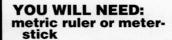

	Slow	Medium	Fast
Distance	10 meters	10 meters	10 meters
Time			
Speed			

The Zip Line

In "Take the Lead—With Speed," you and your partner timed each other's motion, but the motion was different each time. Now you will set up a kind of motion you can repeat. Repeating the motion will let you measure the speed more accurately.

1 Cut a piece of thread that is about 5 meters long. Tape or tie one end to the bottom of a chair or table leg. Slip the thread through the hole in the center of the spool, so the spool can easily slide on the thread. Now back away from the chair and pull the thread tight.

2 Have your partner slide the spool up the thread to you. Release the spool and observe how it moves. Does it seem to change speed as it slides? Describe its motion as it moves along the string.

3 Try lowering your end of the thread. How does this change the speed of the spool? Try pulling the thread less tightly, so it curves a little. How does the spool move?

272

Let's take some speed measurements!

4 Find the **lowest** height you can hold the string and still have the spool slide all the way down the string. Use your meter stick to measure this height and record it in the chart, Height I. To measure the distance the spool will travel, slide the spool all the way up the string. Then measure the distance from the front of the spool to where the spool hits the chair leg. Record this distance in your chart.

5 When your partner is ready to time the spool, say "GO" as you release the spool. Your partner should time it all the way to the end. Record the distance the spool traveled and the time the spool traveled in the chart under Height I, 1st try.

6 Now use the calculator to find the speed of the spool. You must divide the distance the spool traveled by the time for the spool to go this distance. Record the speed you found.

Speed of spool = distance the spool traveled ÷ time for spool to go this distance

7 Repeat step 5, and record your results under Height I, 2nd try. The distance will be the same as in your 1st try. Repeat one more time and record under Height I, 3rd try. If the speeds for your 1st, 2nd, and 3rd tries are different, why do you think that is?

8 Pick two more heights for the string: one that will make the spool go a bit faster and one that will make it go the fastest. Repeat steps 5, 6, and 7 for each of the two heights.

	Height I ____			Height II ____			Height III ____		
	1st try	2nd try	3rd try	1st try	2nd try	3rd try	1st try	2nd try	3rd try
Distance spool traveled									
Time									
Speed									

Speed Sinking!

YOU WILL NEED:

2-liter soda bottle (colorless)

metric ruler

tape

watch with second hand

peanuts

paper

pencil

In the last activity you investigated how the spool slid down the thread. Now you can investigate another kind of downward motion—how objects fall in water.

Peanut Part	Distance	Time	Speed
Whole			
Half			
Quarter			
Tiny Piece			

1 Remove the label from a 2-liter soda bottle. Tape a ruler to the outside so you can look into the bottle and read the ruler at the same time. Fill the bottle to the top with water.

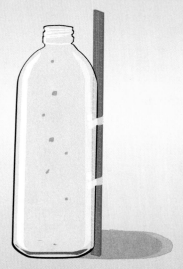

2 Hold the peanut at the surface of the water and let it go. Time the peanut as it falls. Record the distance and time and calculate the speed.

3 Break the peanut in half. Place the half peanut at the surface of the water and let it go. Time the half-peanut. Record the distance and time. Calculate the speed and record it.

4 Now break the half in half again to make a quarter peanut. Hold the peanut at the surface of the water and let it go. Time the quarter-peanut. Record the distance and time. Calculate the speed and record it.

5 Have an adult help you crush a quarter peanut to make many tiny pieces. Drop one of these pieces into the water and describe how it falls.

6 Now time one of these tiny pieces as it falls in the water. Record the distance and time. Calculate the speed and record it.

7 Pretend all the tiny bits are having a race to the bottom. Predict which bits will get to the bottom first and which bits will get there last. Write down your prediction and give a reason for it. Now pick up a lot of the bits and drop them all in at once. What do you observe? Was your prediction right? Which bits had the greatest speed?

274

Graphing to Go!

YOU WILL NEED:

paper and pencil

A car can have large changes of speed over short periods of time. Some cars can go from 0 kilometers per hour to 100 kilometers per hour in a few seconds. The graph below shows the changes in speed of a car on a busy road over a period of 10 seconds. Take a look at the graph and see if you can answer the following questions:

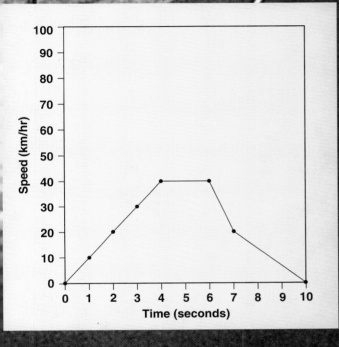

5 On a separate sheet of paper, make a graph like the one at left but without the points or connecting lines. See if you can use the information about a car's speed in a)–d) below to create a graph of the speed.

a) During the first second, the car went from 0 to 30 kilometers per hour.

b) During the next 3 seconds, the speed climbed steadily to 70 kilometers per hour.

c) During the next 2 seconds, the speed dropped by 10 kilometers per hour.

d) From 6 to 10 seconds, the speed steadily climbed to 80 kilometers per hour.

1 How fast was the car going at the end of the 1st second? _____. How about at the end of the 2nd second _____, 3rd second _____, and 4th second _____?

2 From 4 seconds to 6 seconds, did the car's speed increase, decrease, or stay the same?

_____

3 From 6 seconds to 7 seconds, how many kilometers per hour did the car's speed decrease?

_____

4 From 7 seconds, how many seconds did it take the car to come to a stop? _____

The next time you are in a car, watch the speedometer and notice how the speed changes. If you took a watch with a second hand into the car, could you graph the changes in speed? Try it and see!

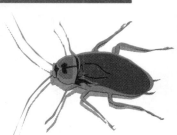

And You Thought You Were Fast!

Here are some speeds of living things and nonliving things. They may surprise you!

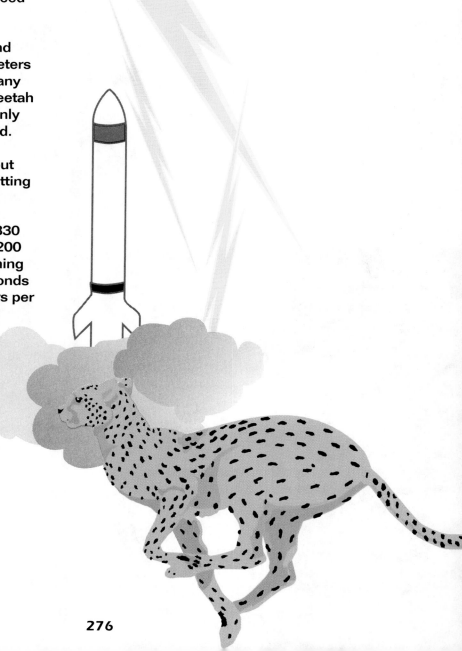

The fastest crawling insect is the cockroach! The cockroach's top speed is about 1.5 meters per second.

The cheetah, the world's fastest land animal, can run at about 100 kilometers per hour! That's about as fast as many cars go on the freeway! But the cheetah can't do this all day. It can run for only about 20 seconds at this high speed.

The fastest land vehicle can go about 1000 kilometers per hour. That's getting pretty close to the speed of sound.

The speed of sound in air is about 330 meters per second. That's about 1,200 kilometers per hour. Suppose lightning strikes and you hear thunder 5 seconds later. The sound traveled 330 meters per second for 5 seconds, for a total of 1,650 meters. This means the lightning was about 1,650 meters away.

The fastest rocket reached a speed of about 48,000 kilometers per hour as it left the Earth.

The world speed record holder is LIGHT! The speed of light is about 310,000 kilometers per second! At that speed, if light could travel in a curved path, it could travel around the entire Earth about 8 times in one second!

WONDERSCIENCE

States of Matter

The three main states of matter investigated in this issue are solids, liquids, and gases. Whether a substance is considered a solid, a liquid, or a gas is determined by the way in which the atoms and molecules that make up the substance interact. The activities in this issue deal with the more easily observable properties of solids, liquids, and gases and how a substance changes from one state to another.

What's the Matter Anyway?

This activity is designed for students to investigate the phenomenon of a gas changing to a liquid as a result of *condensation*. It is a two-part experiment in which students first observe the liquid forming on the cup and then try to determine where the liquid came from. The activity works best if it is done during the time of the year when the air is somewhat humid.

A Change in State Really Matters!

This is a fact sheet on the major differences among solids, liquids, and gases on the atomic level. Students in the elementary grades normally have difficulty conceptualizing the nature of the atom and the interactions occurring on the atomic level. The information presented is intended to help students begin to recognize that there is a relationship between the outward characteristics of a substance as a solid, liquid, or gas and the tiny things that compose it. You might want to have students actually act out the example of students representing the atoms of a solid, liquid, and gas.

Lose Some Mass—It's a Gas!

This activity allows students to observe the effects of a liquid turning to a gas, or *evaporation*. The activity shows that different substances have different rates of evaporation under the same conditions.

Salt and Water—No Easy Freeze

Students see that adding one substance to another can result in a change of state. The solid ice with the salt on it should melt to liquid water more rapidly than the ice with no salt. Students should see the ice actually melting or they should see more water on the paper towel under the ice with the salt, indicating more rapid melting.

A WonderScience State Debate!

The activity is intended to show that the characterization of a particular substance as a solid, liquid, or gas may not be so simple. Substances such as thick gels or waxes and products such as cream cheese or butter may seem like solids or liquids depending on the conditions and who you ask. Have students give their opinions as well as their reasoning.

States of Matter Hall of Fame!

This page highlights a few more or less common substances that are unusual in terms of their state. Mercury is the only metal that is a liquid at room temperature. Nitrogen and carbon dioxide, gases at room temperature, take on very different states at lower temperatures. Students are also introduced to *plasma*, as a fourth state of matter.

Activity Answers and Extenders

What's the Matter Anyway?

The activity allows students to think about the very common phenomenon of liquid beading up on the outside of a cold glass. We may not normally think of this process as a change in state, but it is. Water vapor (a gas) is condensing on the outside of the cup to become a liquid. In this case, condensation occurs when the molecules of water vapor are cooled near the surface of a cold cup. Cooling the molecules slows them down to the point where they get near each other and begin to interact as a liquid on the surface of the cup. Students should notice that the colder the cup, the more moisture it has on the outside. Where did this moisture on the outside of the cup come from? This question can be answered in the second part of the activity.

Unit 24
States of Matter

Lose Some Mass—It's a Gas!

After placing the paper towel strips in water and alcohol and balancing the ruler, students should notice the ruler tilting very gradually, with the water end going down and the alcohol end going up. This occurs because molecules of liquid alcohol are becoming a gas at a faster rate than molecules of liquid water are becoming a gas. A simpler way of stating this phenomenon is that the rate of evaporation of alcohol is greater than that of water. Evaporation occurs when the molecules of a substance have enough energy to change from a liquid to a gas. Different substances have different rates of evaporation.

Salt and Water—No Easy Freeze

In the first part of the activity, salt is added to ice. Students should see that the ice appears to melt more quickly with salt than without it. The reason for this is a bit complicated. On the surface of an ice cube, ice is melting to liquid water, but some of this water is refreezing. When salt is added, the liquid water that mixes with the salt creates a solution that needs a lower temperature to refreeze. Because less liquid refreezes, the ice with salt appears to melt faster.

In the second part of the activity, different amounts of salt are added to cups of water, which are then placed in the freezer. The water with the most salt requires the lowest temperature to freeze. Therefore, the cup with the most salt will be the least frozen and the cup with the least salt will be the most frozen.

A WonderScience State Debate!

Shaving cream that is contained in a pressurized can usually contains water, a soap base for cleaning and lubricating, some kind of emulsifier to improve the lather, one or more gases as a propellant, and a fragrance. One good answer for the state of shaving cream would be a combination of liquid and gas. When the shaving cream is exposed to the air for a day or two, much of the liquid evaporates, which also causes the gas in the liquid bubbles to escape. This leaves a very light solid soap material.

States of Matter Hall of Fame!

The only metal that is a liquid at room temperature is mercury. Solid carbon dioxide, or "dry ice", changes directly from a solid to a gas at room temperature. Changing directly from a solid to a gas is called *sublimation.* *Plasma* is sometimes referred to as another state of matter. The material in the center of the sun may be considered a plasma. Plasma is the result of a gas being at such a high temperature that the atomic collisions in the gas knock electrons off the atoms, resulting in a state in which free electrons and atomic nuclei exist.

States of Matter

NATIONAL SCIENCE EDUCATION STANDARDS

The activities in this unit can be used to support the teaching of the following standards:

✔ **Unifying Concepts, and Processes**

Evidence, Models, and Explanation

Evidence consists of observations and data on which to base scientific explanations. *(All activities)*

Models are tentative schemes or structures that correspond to real objects, events, or classes of events and that have explanatory power. *(All activities)*

✔ **Science as Inquiry**

Abilities Necessary to Do Scientific Inquiry

Design and conduct a scientific investigation. *(All activities)*

Think critically and logically to make the relationship between evidence and explanations. *(All activities)*

✔ **Physical Science**

Properties and Changes of Properties in Matter

A substance has characteristic properties… all of which are independent of the amount of the sample. *(All activities)*

What's the Matter Anyway?

1. After watching your three cups for about 5 minutes, describe the differences in the amount of moisture on the outside of the cups.

   _____

2. How does the temperature of the cup seem to affect the amount of moisture on the outside of the cup?

   _____

   _____

3. When you observed a cup of ice inside a bag and a cup of ice not inside a bag, which cup got more moisture on it?

   _____

4. Because these cups were about the same temperature, why do you think one got more moisture on it than the other?

   _____

   _____

CHALLENGE:

If you had an experiment set up like the one shown above, which cup do you think would have more moisture on the outside? Why?

_____

_____

_____

_____

_____

A WonderScience State Debate!

1. Look closely at the blob of shaving cream. Would you call it a solid, a liquid, or a gas? Why?

_____

_____

2. Gently slide your paper towel with the blob on it back and forth. Does the blob stay together or fall apart?

_____

Look around you at some objects that you would call solids. Solids keep their shape without being in a container. Does this mean your blob is more like a solid than a liquid or a gas? Why?

_____

3. Very gently place a penny on top of your shaving cream blob. Describe what happens.

_____

Does this make you change your opinion about whether your blob is a solid, a liquid, or a gas? Explain.

_____

_____

_____

4. A material like Styrofoam acts like a solid, but it has lots of gas in it. Although it has lots of gas, do you think most people would call Styrofoam a solid? Why or why not?

_____

_____

After looking closely at your blob, you know it has lots of gas in it, too. Does this change your opinion about whether it is a solid, a liquid, or a gas? Explain.

_____

_____

5. After leaving your blob out overnight, would you say that its state has changed? If so, how would you describe this change?

_____

_____

_____

_____

What's the Matter Anyway?

Matter is another word for the material that makes up all the stuff in the whole world. Matter is made up of tiny little particles called atoms and molecules. The three forms, or states, of matter are: solids, liquids, and gases.

One very useful thing about matter is the way it can change between solid, liquid, and gas. Try the activity below, and see if you can follow matter from state to state!

YOU WILL NEED:

ice

3 clear plastic cups

plastic zip-closing freezer bag

water

measuring cup

masking tape

ballpoint pen

paper towels

1 Use your masking tape and pen to label your cups **A**, **B**, and **C**.

2 Carefully place 1/2 cup of cold water in each of the cups. Wipe the cups with paper towels to be sure the outside is dry.

3 Do not add any ice to cup A. Carefully add one ice cube to cup B. Carefully add ice cubes to cup C until it is filled almost to the top with ice.

4 Allow the cups to sit for about 5 minutes. look at the outside of the cups. Describe what you observe. Use your finger to test for any liquid on the outside of the cups. What do you think the liquid is? Where do you think it came from? Does one glass seem to have more liquid on the outside than another? Why do you think it does?

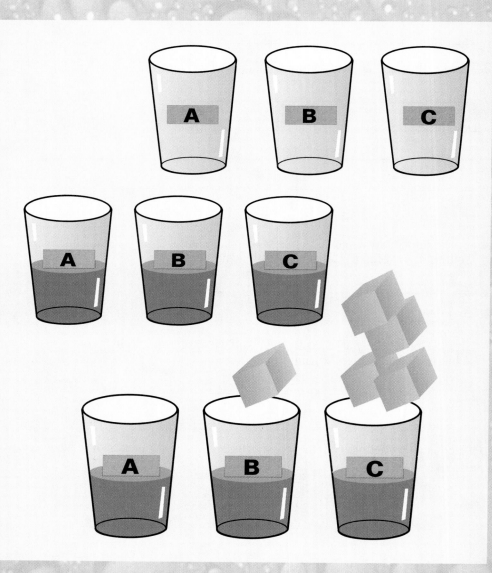

282

SO WHERE DOES THE LIQUID COME FROM?

A simple experiment can give you some idea about where the liquid on the outside of the cup comes from.

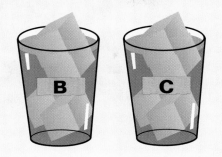

5 Empty two of your cups. Fill each cup 1/2 full of water and then add ice to fill it the rest of the way.

6 Place 1 cup in a zip-closing plastic bag. Get as much air out of the bag as possible and then seal the bag tightly. Place the other cup on the table near the cup in the bag.

7 Observe the cups. After about 5 minutes, what do you notice about the two cups? Does one have more liquid on the outside than the other? Which one has more? How does the bag change the way air can get to the cup? Based on your observations, where do you think the liquid comes from? Why?

A Change in State Really Matters!

All matter, whether a solid, liquid, or gas, is made up of extremely tiny particles called **atoms**. These particles are always moving. This is true even in solids, where the particles move back and forth over very small distances. When you look at a rock or a table, or any other solid, it is hard to imagine the little atoms they are made of. It may be even harder to imagine that these tiny little things are moving, even if it is just a very little bit. In a solid, the forces that hold the particles near to one another are pretty strong. This is why the particles don't move much and why solids don't fall apart easily.

In liquids, the particles move much more freely than in solids. The particles in a liquid bump into each other and move past each other all the time. In a liquid, the forces that hold the particles near to one another are not as strong as in a solid. This is why the particles in a liquid can move around so much and why liquids are so easy to splash around into different shapes and droplets.

In a gas, the particles are free to move all over the place, and they are very far apart. They zoom all around, bumping into each other and then bouncing off to zoom away in another direction. Compared with the forces in solids and liquids that keep their particles near one another, these forces have almost no effect in a gas. This is why the particles in a gas move around so much, so far, and so fast.

One way to think about the differences between solids, liquids, and gases is to imagine that you and your classmates are atoms. If you were all wiggling back and forth in chairs arranged close together, your class would be like a solid. Like the particles in a solid, you would be shifting in your seat, but your seat would stay in the same place. To be a liquid, you and your classmates would still be close together but would walk next to and between each other, gently brushing against and bumping into each other and changing directions all the time. To be like a gas, you and your classmates would need to run around in a big space like the gym, only rarely bumping into each other and changing direction.

The forces between the particles in solids, liquids, and gases affect how matter can change from one state to another. Water is a good example. In liquid water, some of the water molecules are moving fast enough to leave the liquid water and to go up into the air as a gas—water vapor. This is called **evaporation**. If the liquid water is heated, the molecules move faster and the evaporation speeds up. If the water vapor is cooled, the molecules will slow down and turn to liquid water again. This is called **condensation**. If the water is cooled enough, the particles will slow down further and **freeze** to become solid ice. And if the ice is heated, the particles will move faster and the ice will **melt** to become liquid water again.

Try the rest of the activities in this *WonderScience* unit to see that a change of state really matters!

Lose Some Mass— It's a Gas!

A liquid can change its state to a gas through **evaporation**. Different liquids have different rates of evaporation. You can set up an experiment to see the different rates of evaporation between water and alcohol.

YOU WILL NEED:

water (2 tablespoons)
alcohol (2 tablespoons, isopropol)
paper towel
scissors
pencil
ruler
2 paper or plastic cups (16 oz)
2 small paper or plastic cups
tape

1 Place the two large cups upside down on a flat surface. Place the pencil across the cups and tape the pencil down as shown.

2 Place a ruler on the pencil so that the ruler is balanced. Cut two strips of paper towel each 20 centimeters (cm) long and 4 cm wide. Write "W" on one strip and "A" on the other.

3 Pour 2 tablespoons of water into one small cup and 2 tablespoons of alcohol into another.

4 Dip the paper towel strip with the W into the water so that it gets completely wet. Your partner should dip the strip with the A into the alcohol until it is completely wet.

5 Work together to place the wet strips at opposite ends of the ruler. When both strips are on the ruler, move the ruler on the pencil so that the ruler is again balanced.

6 Observe the ruler as the water and alcohol evaporate. Which do you think will evaporate first? How does your experiment show you which liquid changes to a gas the fastest?

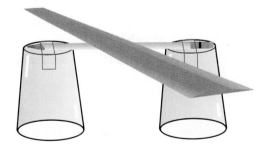

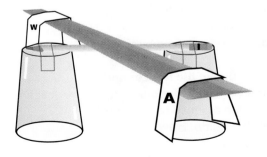

Salt and Water— No Easy Freeze

As you saw in "What's the Matter Anyway," water vapor (a gas) in the air can change to a liquid when it is cooled enough. You also know that ice will change its state from a solid to a liquid if it is warmed enough. But there is something else you can do to ice to help it change its state. Check it out!

1 Place each of your two ice cubes on a separate paper towel.

2 Sprinkle a pinch of salt over the surface of one of the cubes. Observe both cubes very closely. Does one cube seem to be melting faster than the other? If so, which cube is melting faster?

If salt seems to help ice melt, do you think saltwater is harder to freeze than fresh water? Maybe the saltier the water, the harder it is to freeze? To find out, let's do an experiment!

1 Use your masking tape and pen to label your cups A, B, and C. Place 1/2 cup of warm water into each of the three cups.

2 Do not add anything to cup A. Add 1 teaspoon of salt to cup B. Add 1 tablespoon of salt to cup C. Stir cups B and C until as much salt dissolves as possible.

3 Place all three cups in the freezer and keep them there overnight. Look at the cups the next day. Use a pencil to poke and scrape the ice on the inside. How does the hardness of the different samples compare? Did the liquid change to solid in the same way in each sample? What do you think caused the differences?

A *WonderScience* State Debate!

Although the three states of matter are solid, liquid, and gas, not all substances seem to fit perfectly into one of these three groups.

Take a look at the substance below, and see if you can decide whether it should be called a solid, liquid, or a gas.

TEACHER PREPARATION:
Place a mound of shaving cream about the size of a tennis ball on a paper towel for each group.

1 Look at your blob of shaving cream. Would you call it a solid, liquid, or a gas? Why? Gently slide the paper towel back and forth and watch the blob. Does the blob stay together or fall apart? Does that make it more like a solid, liquid, or gas? Why?

2 Look around you at some objects you would call solids. One characteristic of a solid is that it keeps its shape without being in a container. Does this mean that the shaving cream blob is a solid? Why or why not?

3 Very gently place a penny on top of your shaving cream blob. What do you observe? Does this mean the blob is a solid? Why or why not?

4 Shaving cream is very light. Another material that is very light is Styrofoam. Styrofoam is a solid. What makes it so light? What do you think makes shaving cream so light?

5 Put a tiny bit of shaving cream from the blob on your finger. Look at it very closely. Use a magnifying glass, if you have one. What does it look like shaving cream is made of? Does that mean shaving cream is a gas? Why or why not?

6 Rub the tiny bit of shaving cream between your index finger and thumb. Does it feel like soap? Some soaps are solid, and some are liquid. What do you think shaving cream is? Why?

7 Leave your shaving cream blob out over night. Look at it very closely the next day. How has it changed? Has it changed its state? Why or why not? Leave it for a few more days. What do you think it is now?

287

States of Matter Hall of Fame!

Most metals are solid at room temperature. In fact, there is only one metal that is a liquid at room temperature? Can you name it?

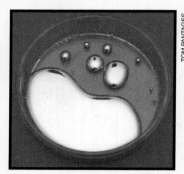

TOM PANTAGES

NEAL CLODFELTER

Banana being frozen in liquid nitrogen

Nitrogen is a gas at room temperature. To change it to a liquid, it must be cooled quite a bit. In fact, it needs to be cooled to almost −200 °C! At this temperature, some interesting things happen to common objects when they are dipped into liquid nitrogen.

After a few minutes in liquid nitrogen, the banana was frozen so solid it was used to hammer a nail into a board!

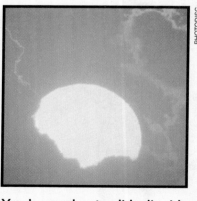

PHOTODISC

Some substances change directly from a solid to a gas. One of these substances is sometimes used to keep ice cream cold while it is being shipped. Can you name it?

GORDON MILLER

You know about solids, liquids, and gases, but have you heard of another state of matter called **plasma**? Plasma has characteristics that are different from the other three states of matter. The inside of the sun is made up of plasma. It's pretty hot. About 15,000,000 °C!

In this unit, a few main features of gases are explored. Students observe that gases must be made of something (that a gas is not nothingness or empty space), that a gas expands when heated and contracts when cooled, and that gas pressure can be used to do work. In keeping with the National Science Education Standards, the issue does not discuss gases on the molecular level, but allows students to investigate the observable properties of gases.

Air—It's Really There!

Before students do this activity, it is a good idea to demonstrate it first using clear plastic cups and an aquarium. Students may need to move up close to see well because the air, water, cups, and aquarium are all clear and colorless. As you begin the demonstration, ask the students what is in each cup that you put into the water. (One contains water; the other contains air.) Then, when you allow the air to flow from the lower cup into the water-filled upper cup, ask students to try to explain what is happening. (The air is moving all the way into the water-filled cup and pushing the water out). Students can see that air really is something because it takes up space and prevents the water from coming in.

After observing the demonstration, it will be much easier for students to understand the setup and to appreciate what they are seeing, as they do the activity themselves. Although they have seen it already, it still is a fun feeling to "pour" the air upward into the other cup.

A Gas Bubble-ometer

You could ask students if they have ever seen the lid of a pot tapping up and down when water is boiling in the pot. Ask students why they think the lid does this. As the steam is heated in the pot, it expands and pushes the lid up. After the steam escapes, the lid falls back down and the process repeats.

In this activity, the warmth from student hands will cause the air inside the bottle to expand, making the soap film over the opening of the bottle form a bubble. The plastic bottles that students are using are flexible, so be sure students do not squeeze the bottles, as this will alter the results. The soap bubble should get even bigger when the bottle is placed in hot tap water. When the bottle is placed in cold water, the gas in the bottle will contract, and the bubble will get smaller. The bubble may actually invert so that it goes inside the bottle.

When a gas is heated, the molecules increase in energy, which causes them to move faster. As the molecules of a gas move faster, they tend to spread out or expand. The reverse is true when the molecules are cooled and the gas contracts. Although this explanation may be useful for teacher understanding, students should focus on the observable characteristics of the heated and cooled gas, rather than seeking an explanation of the phenomena on the molecular level.

Gas Pressure: It's in the Bag!

You might start the activity by asking students if they can think of any way that air or another gas is used under pressure in a product they are familiar with. Bicycle tires are a good example. Ask students about the difference between tires with low pressure and those with normal or high pressure. Which are better for riding? Why? Ask how you go about increasing or decreasing the pressure in a bicycle tire. Students should understand that adding more gas to a closed container, such as a bicycle tire, increases the pressure and that removing gas decreases the pressure.

In this activity, students will see that the pressure they can create inside the plastic bag can lift a surprising amount of weight. Part of the reason why the bag can lift so much is that the pressure created by the gas is exerted over a large surface area. In fact, each unit of pressure per square inch is multiplied by the number of square inches in the surface area of the bag. So if the actual pressure was 1 pound per square inch, the overall effective pressure can lift 80 pounds because the bag has a surface area of 8" $\times$ 10" = 80 square inches.

Air Bags—Strong under Pressure!

Ask students if they have ever been on a "moon bounce" at a fair or carnival. Ask if the moon bounce works better when it is fully inflated or when it is partially full and why. Ask if students have ever seen a picture of an inflated air bag and whether they think the air bag works better when it is fully inflated or partially inflated and why.

The activity allows students to make a model of an air bag and to see why more air produces more pressure and better protection for the driver. You should stress that although air bags are useful, the safety belt is more important and should always be worn.

Heat Up and Head Up!

Some students believe that hot air balloons are filled with helium or some other light gas the way blimps are. The short article explains that the balloon is filled with air and that a burner heats the air, which makes the air expand. As air expands, it becomes less dense than the cooler air around it. Because the air inside the balloon is less dense than the air around it, the balloon floats. Students can see that heated air expands in the activity "A Gas Bubble-ometer."

NATIONAL SCIENCE EDUCATION STANDARDS

The activities in this unit can be used to support the teaching of the following standards:

✔ **Unifying Concepts and Processes**

Evidence, Models, and Explanation

Evidence consists of observations and data on which to base scientific explanations. *(All activities)*

Models are tentative schemes or structures that correspond to real objects, events, or classes of events and that have explanatory power.
 Air Bags—Strong under Pressure!

✔ **Science as Inquiry**

Abilities Necessary to Do Scientific Inquiry

Design and conduct a scientific investigation. *(All activities)*

Develop descriptions, explanations, predictions, and models using evidence. *(All activities)*

Think critically and logically to make the relationships between evidence and explanations. *(All activities)*

✔ **Physical Science**

Properties and Changes of Properties in Matter

A substance has characteristic properties . . . all of which are independent of the amount of the sample. *(All activities)*

NAME _____   **DATE** _____

Air—It's Really There!

1. When you turned the cup upside down and pushed it down into the water, describe how it felt.

   _____

   _____

   _____

2. When the cup was upside down and under water, would you say it was empty or full of something?

   _____

   _____

   _____

3. Describe what happened when you tilted the lower air-filled cup up toward the higher water-filled cup.

   _____

   _____

   _____

4. As air moved into the higher water-filled cup, where do you think the water went?

   _____

   _____

   _____

5. Describe what happened when you pushed the cup, with the paper towel in it, into the water.

   _____

   _____

   _____

6. Why do you think the paper towel can stay dry when the cup is turned upside-down in all that water?

   _____

   _____

   _____

7. There have been discoveries of natural gas underneath the ocean floor. Gas companies drill down into the ocean bottom to get the gas. Work with a partner and design (on paper) a system that could drill into the ocean floor, capture the gas without allowing much to escape, and then transport the gas to your company in a state on the coast.

A Gas Bubble-ometer

1. After dipping the opening of the bottle into the bubble solution, describe what the soap film looks like over the mouth of the bottle.

_____

_____

2. Describe what happened to the soap film when you put your hands gently around the bottle.

_____

_____

_____

3. What do you think your hands did to the gas inside the bottle that made the soap film do this?

_____

_____

_____

4. Describe what happened when you placed the bottle into hot water.

_____

_____

5. When a gas is warmed, does it expand or contract? _____

How does this experiment help you answer this question?

_____

_____

6. What happened to the soap film when you placed the bottle into ice water?

_____

_____

7. What do you think happened to the gas inside the bottle when you placed the bottle in the ice water?

_____

_____

Air

Gases are all around us, but we can't see them. Air is actually a mixture of different gases. Does air take up space? Let's find out.

1 Turn one cup upside down over the water. Slowly push the cup under water as shown.

2 Look carefully at the cup when it is underwater. What is inside the cup? Would you say the cup is empty, or is it full of something?

3 Keep the cup under water. Now take a second cup and lower it into the water so that it fills up with water. Now turn this cup upside-down.

4 You should now have one upside-down cup filled with air and one upside-down cup filled with water.

5 Hold the air-filled cup below the water-filled cup as shown.

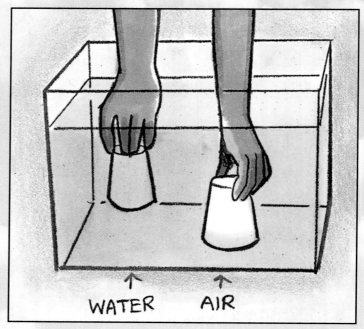

WATER   AIR

294

It's Really There!

6 Tilt the lower cup so that bubbles flow up into the higher cup that contains the water. What do you see? You have just "poured" air from one cup into the other. Try to pour it back and forth, from one cup to the other.

7 Now take both cups out of the water. Take a dry cup and wad up a paper towel and stuff it into the bottom of the dry cup, as shown.

8 Turn this cup upside down and lower it into the water. What do you observe? Pull the cup straight up so that it comes out of the water. Look at the towel. Is it wet or dry? What kept the water from reaching the towel?

Gases Galore!

Gases are all around us. When you take a breath, your lungs fill with air, which is a mixture of gases. The air takes up space inside you, and your chest swells up. When you breathe out, you push the gases out, and your chest gets smaller. Even though you can't see most gases, they do take up space in your lungs, in balloons, in open containers that look empty, in buildings, outdoors, and everywhere around us!

In "Air—It's Really There!" you poured gases from the lower cup filled with air to the higher cup filled with water. The air from the lower cup went up into the cup filled with water. The air went all the way up to the bottom of the cup and pushed the water out. When you put the paper towel in the bottom of the cup and then pushed the cup into the water, the space inside the cup was full of air, so very little water could enter the cup.

Gases, just like most solids or liquids, take up *more* space, or **expand**, when they are heated. The opposite is also true. Most solids, liquids, and gases take up *less* space, or **contract**, when they are cooled. But the difference is that gases expand a lot more than liquids or solids when heated and contract a lot more when cooled. You'll do an activity showing how heating makes a gas expand and how cooling makes it contract in "A Gas Bubble-ometer."

Another important characteristic of gases is gas **pressure**. The pressure of a gas can be increased by adding more gas to a container such as the plastic bag in "Gas Pressure: It's in the Bag." As you blow more air into the bag, the pressure increases and the amount of push on the books increases. In a similar way, the more air there is in a car's air bag, the more pressure there is. It is harder for the air bag to be pushed down, which gives the passengers more protection.

A Gas Bubble-ometer

In the first activity, you showed that air takes up space. What do you think you could do to air to make it take up *more* space? Or *less* space? Let's try changing its temperature.

1 Mix 1 teaspoon of liquid detergent with about 2 teaspoons of water to make a bubble solution in the cup. Lower the open mouth of the bottle into the bubble solution as shown.

2 Carefully tilt and lift the bottle out so that a film of bubble solution covers the opening of the bottle.

3 Gently hold your hands around the bottle, as shown, but make sure you do not squeeze the bottle. What happens? What do you think your hands have done to the gas inside the bottle?

4 Place some hot tap water in a bowl. If the soap film has popped, redip the bottle into the detergent solution. Place the bottom of the bottle in the water. What happens?

5 Put some ice and water in another bowl. Now place the bottom of the bottle into the ice water. What happens? How do you think the ice water changed the gas inside the bottle?

Gas Pressure:
It's in the Bag!

You have probably heard people talk about the **pressure** of a gas. One way to increase the pressure of a gas is to add more and more gas to a closed container. As the pressure increases, the gas pushes harder and harder against the inside of the container. The more gas, the more pressure, and the more push. Let's see if we can use this push to lift something with air pressure!

YOU WILL NEED:
gallon-sized zip-closing plastic freezer bag
flexible plastic straw
book

1 Place the plastic bag near the edge of the table. Close the bag except for a small spot in one corner.

2 Slip a straw into the bag with the flexible end sticking out. Bend the end of the straw up as shown. Use your fingers to press down on both sides of the straw to keep air from leaking out of the bag. Blow into the bag.

3 When the bag looks like a little pillow, take the straw out and seal the bag. Push on the bag. What do you feel? As you push down on the bag, the air pressure is pushing up on your hand.

Let's see if we can put this pressure to work.

4 Let all the air out of the bag, and put the straw back in the bag, as before. Place a book on top of the bag on your desk, as shown.

5 Blow air into the bag. Use your fingers to press down on both sides of the straw to keep air from leaking out of the bag. What happens to the book? Try lifting two books. How many books do you think you can lift with the power of air pressure? Try it and see!

298

Air Bags
Strong under Pressure!

YOU WILL NEED:

gallon-sized zip-closing plastic
   freezer bag

flexible plastic straw

tape

Have you ever seen a picture of an inflated air bag in a car? The way they work has a lot to do with the pressure of a gas.

If a car is in a head-on crash, a lot of gas blows up the air bag very quickly. The gas gives the bag enough pressure so that even though a passenger may push against the bag with a lot of force, the bag pushes back and protects the person from injury.

Let's do a short activity to see how the air bag works.

1 Seal the bag closed except for a small part in one corner. Tape the bag down so that it hangs in front of a solid surface. The solid surface is a **model** of the steering wheel or windshield inside the car.

2 Slip a straw into the bag, and blow some air in, so that the bag looks like a flat pillow. The bag is a model of an airbag. Take the straw out and completely seal the bag.

3 Your fist or fingertips can serve as a model of a driver in a car accident. Gently punch or poke the "air bag" to see if there is enough pressure to keep the "driver" from hitting the "steering wheel."

4 Now, blow enough air into the bag so that when you punch or poke the bag, your passenger does not hit the steering wheel even on a fairly hard impact.

You have just made a model of how the pressure of a gas is used in an air bag to protect passengers in a car accident.

Air bags give extra protection in a car crash. But remember, the safety belts are far more important. Always wear your safety belt! Also, kids should sit in the back seat, away from the air bag.

Heat Up and Head Up!

Look at the hot-air balloon. Check out the burner at the bottom of the balloon. To make the balloon rise, the burners are turned on. The burner flame heats the air inside the balloon. The heated air expands. It takes up more space. It is like floating in water. When you take a deep breath, your lungs expand and you float better. When the air expands in the balloon, the balloon floats in the air better.

The higher the balloon rises, the cooler the air becomes outside the balloon which, in turn, cools the air inside the balloon. If the air inside the balloon cools too much, the balloon will shrink and begin to sink. To keep the balloon from sinking, the burner must heat the air again. For a long flight, balloonists need a lot of fuel.

Because we are surrounded by the atmosphere and use it all day long, usually without thinking about it, the Earth's atmosphere might easily be taken for granted. But, of course, it is a precious resource that affects every aspect of our lives. So many issues are related to the atmosphere, such as the composition of the atmosphere, its characteristics at different altitudes, atmospheric pressure, weather, pollution, and the relationship between the atmoshere and living things. This unit concentrates on two main concepts: that the atmosphere is made of something (it is not emptiness) and that you can do experiments to learn about the gases that make up the atmosphere.

The Atmosphere: The Air We Share

This activity uses student-made parachutes to suggest that the air, or the atmosphere, is made of something and that this "stuff" that composes the air has an effect on things.

Learn Not to Err When It Comes to Air!

This page gives some basic information about the four main components of the atmosphere: nitrogen, oxygen, argon, and carbon dioxide. A pie chart and a bar graph are used to illustrate the relative amounts of each gas in the atmosphere.

The No-Zone in the Ozone

The activity allows students to chart the relative concentration of ozone during the spring in eight successive years. Students use their own color-coded pictures to interpret the changes in the ozone layer during this time. A slightly larger version with places for student answers is included in the first Student Activity Sheet.

Don't Be Blue—Use CO_2!

Students generate CO_2 and then learn to use an indicator to detect the presence of CO_2. Adding CO_2 to the indicator solution makes the solution more acidic, and the color change of the indicator is caused by this increased acidity. Because the added CO_2 caused the increased acidity and the increased acidity caused the color change in the indicator, this color change is an indirect measure of the increased CO_2.

Students may find it strange to tip the bottle to let only gas flow out, but that is what should be done. No liquid should leave the bottle. The activity works best with the freshly made indicator that the students have just prepared.

A WonderScience Air Compare!

The previous activity showed that CO_2 could be detected by using an indicator. This activity shows that the indicator can also show relative amounts of CO_2. In both activities, students should be reminded of the necessity of having the control cup to which the other cups can be compared.

A Water Uprising

This activity shows that the process of rusting removes a gas from the atmosphere. When steel wool rusts, oxygen from the air and water combine chemically with the iron in the steel to form iron oxide or rust. As oxygen is removed from inside the jar, the water should move up.

Activity Answers and Extenders

The Atmosphere: The Air We Share

Students should be familiar with the concept of a parachute slowing down a fall through the air. They will have seen parachutes on television or even in person. But students may not realize the critical role of the air itself in the way a parachute works. As the parachute falls, the molecules that make up the atmosphere offer resistance ("air resistance") to the parachute, slowing its fall. If the atmosphere were empty space (a vacuum), the parachute would fall unimpeded, as fast as the force of gravity would allow. Students should also see that increasing the area of the parachute, without an appreciable increase in weight, should cause it to fall through the air more slowly as more molecules beneath it offer resistance.

Learn Not to Err When It Comes to Air!

The pie chart and the bar graph give a rough idea of the relative amounts of the four main gases in the atmosphere. You could have students use a piece of graph paper or make one themselves that is 10 squares × 10 squares for 100 total squares. Students could make a color key for the four main gases and then fill in the appropriate number of squares for each.

Unit 26
The Atmosphere

The No-Zone in the Ozone

The normal oxygen in the air is O_2, which is a molecule made up of two oxygen atoms. Ozone is O_3, or a molecule made of three oxygen atoms. One confusing aspect of the ozone problem is that there are two ozone issues. There is ground-level ozone, which is a pollutant that we don't want; and there is the naturally occuring ozone in the stratosphere that we do want, which protects us from the sun's ultraviolet rays. As a result of the activity, students should be able to see a pattern of depletion in the ozone layer from 1985 to 1992. For more information on ozone depletion, write to the Environmental Protection Agency (EPA) and ask for the booklet *Stratospheric Ozone Depletion: A Focus on EPA's Research* (EPA 640/K-95/004 March 1995) from EPA Office of Research and Development, Washington, DC 20460.

Don't Be Blue—Use CO₂!

Students may be familiar with testing a liquid (or a solid dissolved in a liquid) by using litmus paper or some other indicator to detect an acid or a base. This may be the first time students have tested a gas in a similar way. The carbon dioxide gas (CO_2), produced by the vinegar and baking soda reaction, will pour out of the bottle when the bottle is tilted. It will lie on top of the indicator until the indicator is stirred. The CO_2 should then mix with the indicator and a color change should occur. Just to be sure that the stirring itself did not cause the color change, students are asked to stir the other cup of indicator also. The third cup is the control.

A WonderScience Air Compare!

One variable that is not controlled in this activity is the amount of gas that is bubbled through the three indicators. For the purpose of this activity, the comparison between the concentration of CO_2 in the different gases is qualitative. The challenge on the second Student Activity Sheet deals with this issue. One way to standardize the volume of gas used might be to blow up a balloon on the bottle with the vinegar and baking soda, to blow up a balloon using exhaled breath, and to blow up a balloon using a bicycle pump. The diameter of the balloons could be measured and all made the same. The entire contents of each balloon could be bubbled into the liquid.

One interesting extension of this activity might be to bubble a large volume of a student's breath into one of the indicators and then to see how little of the CO_2 from the balloon could be bubbled into another indicator to cause the same color change. This is a more direct illustration that the concentration of CO_2 in the balloon must be higher, since less of it was used to cause the same color change.

A Water Uprising

This activity takes two to three days to see results. As oxygen is used in the process of rusting, it is removed from the atmosphere inside the jar. Because the air pressure inside the jar decreases, a partial vacuum is created inside the jar, and the water moves up into the jar to fill it.

The Atmosphere

NATIONAL SCIENCE EDUCATION STANDARDS

The activities in this unit can be used to support the teaching of the following standards:

✔ **Unifying Concepts and Processes**

Evidence, Models, and Explanation

Evidence consists of observations and data on which to base scientific explanations.

The Atmosphere—The Air We Share
Don't Be Blue—Use CO_2
A WonderScience Air Compare!
A Water Uprising

✔ **Science as Inquiry**

Abilities Necessary to Do Scientific Inquiry

Design and conduct a scientific investigation.

The Atmosphere: The Air We Share
Don't Be Blue—Use CO_2
A WonderScience Air Compare!
A Water Uprising

Use appropriate tools and techniques to gather, analyze, and interpret data.

Learn Not to Err When It Comes to Air
The No-Zone in the Ozone

Think critically and logically to make the relationships between evidence and explanations. (All activities)

✔ **Physical Science**

Properties and Changes of Properties in Matter

A substance has characteristic properties . . . all of which are independent of the amount of the sample.

The Atmosphere: The Air We Share
A WonderScience Air Compare!

Substances react chemically in characteristic ways with other substances to form new substances (compounds) with different characteristic properties.

Don't Be Blue—Use CO_2
A Water Uprising

✔ **Earth and Space Science**

Structure of the Earth System

The atmosphere is a mixture of nitrogen, oxygen, and trace gases that include water vapor. The atmosphere has different properties at different elevations.

Learn Not to Err When It Comes to Air
The No-Zone in the Ozone

✔ **Science in Personal and Social Perspectives**

Risks and Benefits

The No-Zone in the Ozone

STUDENT ACTIVITY SHEET

The No-Zone in the Ozone

Carefully color in each area that has a letter according to the Ozone Concentration Key: Red (R) is high, Yellow (Y) is moderate, and Green (G) is low.

1. Which month of which year appeared to have the highest concentration of ozone?

   _____
   _____

2. Which month of which year appeared to have the lowest concentration of ozone?

   _____
   _____

3. How does the concentration of ozone change from April to June in any single year?

   _____
   _____

4. How does the concentration of ozone seem to change from year to year?

   _____
   _____
   _____

5. Does the area at the North Pole seem to be gaining or losing ozone over the years? Is this good or bad? Why?

   _____
   _____

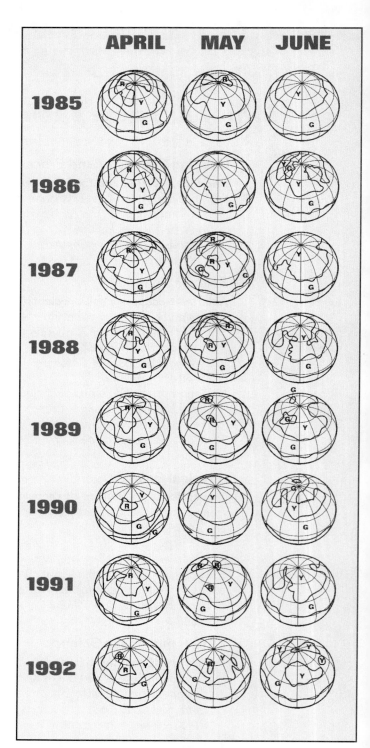

A WonderScience Air Compare!

1. After preparing your four cups of indicator and placing the cups on a white sheet of paper, look closely at the indicator. Describe the color.

_____

2. After you squeezed the plastic bag with air into the indicator, did you notice any color change in the indicator?

_____

If cabbage juice is a pretty good indicator for carbon dioxide, does this mean that the concentration of carbon dioxide in the air is pretty high or pretty low?

_____

3. After you blew through the straw into the indicator, did you notice any color change in the indicator? If so, describe it.

_____

_____

4. Does this mean that the air you exhale has more or less carbon dioxide than the air around you? Explain.

_____

_____

5. When you used the balloon with the gas in it from the vinegar and baking soda reaction, did you observe a change in the color of the indicator? If so, describe the color and whether it changed more than the others, faster than the others, or both.

_____

_____

CHALLENGE:

One problem with this experiment is that it is hard to control the amount of gas bubbled into the three cups of indicator. Explain what equipment you would use and how you would set up an experiment to be sure that the amount of air used from the room, the amount from your breath, and the amount from the vinegar and baking soda reaction were all the same.

_____

_____

_____

The Atmosphere: The Air We Share

What's all around you? What's every-where you look, but you can't see it (usually)?

It's the **atmosphere!** You know—AIR! If you can't see it, how do you know it's there? Try the activity below and see that there is definitely something in the air!

Air is not emptiness. A good example to show that air is really "stuff" is the way a parachute works. After doing this activity, think about the way a parachute would work if the air really was nothingness.

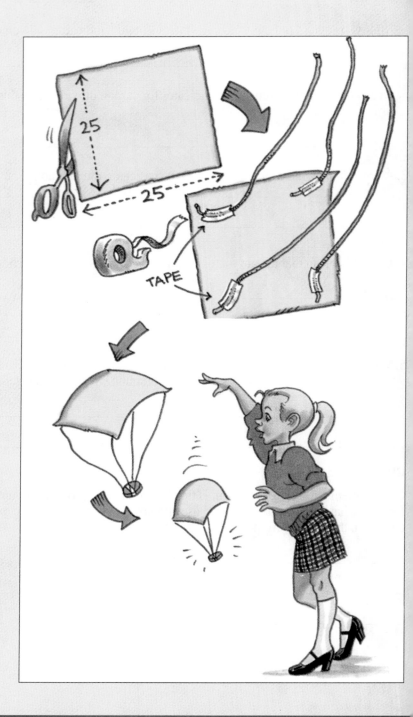

1 Work with your partner to cut out a square from one of your plastic bags. The square should be about 25 cm × 25 cm.

2 Cut 4 pieces of string so that each piece goes from one corner of the square to about 5 cm past the center of the square as shown. Tape each piece down at the corner.

3 Bring the free ends of the strings together and use a piece of tape to attach a penny to the four strings. Your piece of bag, strings, and penny should look like a little parachute.

4 Hold the parachute at the top and drop it from high above your head. Describe how it falls. Why doesn't it fall really fast like a stone? What keeps it from falling really quickly?

5 With the help of your partner, use the rest of your first bag and another bag to make two more parachutes. Make one about 15 cm × 15 cm. Make the other about 35 cm × 35 cm. Use one penny on each, as you did with your first parachute.

6 Which parachute do you think will take the most time to fall? Which do you think will take the least? Why? You and your partner can hold the parachutes at the same height and drop them at the same time to see how long each takes to fall.

Look at the picture below. If air was made out of tiny little particles, how could you use this picture to explain why the different parachutes take different times to reach the ground?

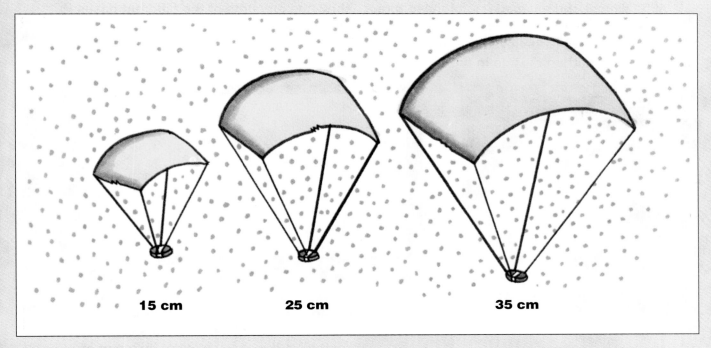

15 cm   25 cm   35 cm

Which person is more likely to have a safe landing? Why? What do you think air is made of that can support a parachute?

Learn Not to Err When It Comes to Air!

The atmosphere, or air, is made up of about 12 different gases. But three make up almost all the air: nitrogen, oxygen, and argon. There is about 78% nitrogen, 21% oxygen, and a little less than 1% argon. If you add these numbers up, you come up with just under 100%. That means that the air is almost entirely made up of these three gases. You might be wondering about carbon dioxide. Well, believe it or not, the amount of carbon dioxide in the air is only about 04%! There is also water vapor in the air, but the amount depends on the weather where the air is being tested. All together, the other gases in the atmosphere make up less than .004%—not much.

You can use a pie chart or a graph to show the amounts of the different gases in the atmosphere:

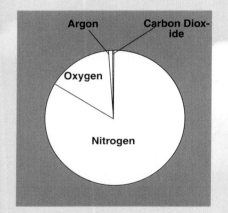

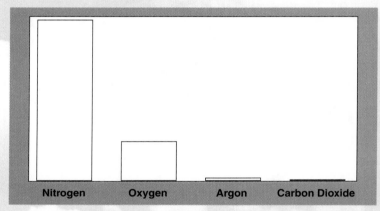

THE BIG FOUR

Nitrogen: Nitrogen is part of the DNA and proteins that make up the bodies of plants and animals. But plants can't get nitrogen directly from the atmosphere and neither can animals. Most of the nitrogen that plants get from the soil comes from animal waste and from decayed plants and animals. Animals get their nitrogen from eating plants and from eating animals that eat plants.

Oxygen: Oxygen is used directly from the atmosphere by animals to breathe. The oxygen we breathe is used in chemical reactions by the cells in our bodies to provide energy to move, grow, and function. People and other animals breathe out carbon dioxide.

Argon: Argon is a gas that has no known use for the life of organisms. Argon does have an important use in the manufacture of lightbulbs. It is the gas in the bulb part of lightbulbs!

Carbon dioxide: Carbon dioxide is used by plants for the process of photosynthesis. Photosynthesis takes place in the leaves of plants where it combines carbon dioxide, water, and sunlight to produce sugars for the food the plant needs to survive. The process of photosynthesis also releases oxygen into the atmosphere.

As you do the rest of the activities in your *WonderScience*, think some more about air, if you dare, because if you care about the air that we share, the more about air you should be aware!

The No-Zone in the OZone

In the atmosphere, about 25 kilometers above the earth, is an area that contains a chemical called ozone. You may have heard of this area as the "ozone layer." This ozone layer is important because it helps block out the sun's damaging ultraviolet rays.

During the course of a year, the amount of ozone increases and decreases in a cycle. The most severe decrease is usually in the spring. A problem occurs when the amount of ozone decreases too much. Certain chemicals, when released into the atmosphere, cause ozone to break apart. This can cause an extra decrease in the amount of ozone in the ozone layer. The use of these chemicals has been reduced very much, and some have been banned completely.

Teacher Preparation: Photocopy the globes shown. You may want to increase the size somewhat. Each student or group of students should have a red, yellow, and green pencil.

1 Look at the pictures of the Earth and at the color key. Carefully color in each area with red, yellow, or green, according to the key.

2 Which month of what year appeared to have the highest concentration of ozone? Which month of what year appeared to have the least?

3 How does the amount of ozone in April 1985 seem to compare with the amount in April 1992? How about May and June 1985 compared with May and June 1992?

4 Does the area at the North Pole seem to be gaining ozone over the years or losing it? Is this good or bad? Why?

5 In what year was there the greatest loss in ozone from April to June?

Beginning in 1996, there was a total ban on the gases that are most dangerous to the ozone layer. If all countries follow the ban, the ozone layer should slowly start to heal after the year 2000 and be back to normal in about 100 years.

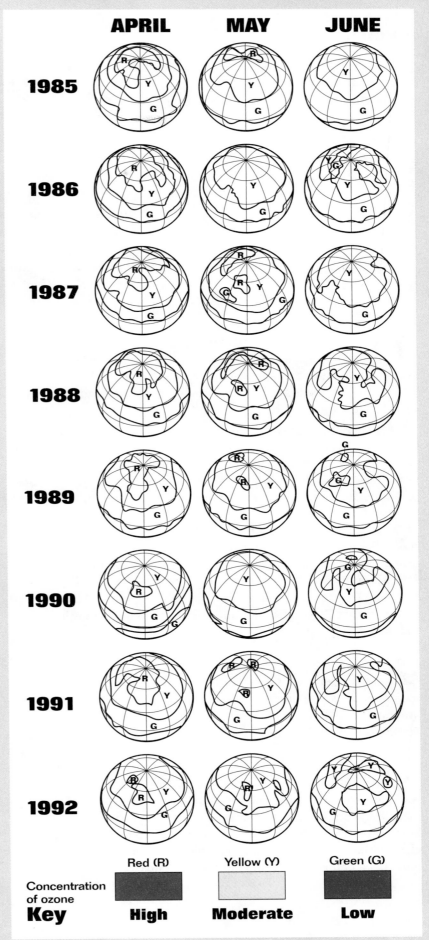

YOU WILL NEED:

red cabbage leaves
3/4 cup water
zip-closing plastic bag
3 clear plastic cups
white sheet of paper
baking soda
plastic soda bottle
(20 oz)
vinegar
straw
tablespoon
measuring cup

Don't be Blue— Use CO$_2$

Carbon dioxide (CO$_2$) is essential for life on Earth. Scientists are very interested in knowing how much CO$_2$ is in the air and use different ways of testing the air for CO$_2$. In the activity below, you can do your own test for CO$_2$!

1 Tear up two leaves of red cabbage and place them in a zip-closing plastic bag. Add about 3/4 cup of warm water. Let most of the air out of the bag and seal the bag tightly. Squish the leaves in the water until the water turns a light to medium blue color.

This is your indicator solution; it will change color when certain substances are added to it.

2 Place 3 cups on a white sheet of paper. Divide the indicator solution evenly among the 3 cups.

3 Use a paper funnel to place about 3 tablespoons of baking soda into an empty soda bottle. Add about 1/4 cup of vinegar. Place your hand gently over the top of the bottle. Gently swirl the bottle to get as much mixing and bubbling as possible. You will feel gases escaping; but that's OK, because CO$_2$ is heavier than air, much of it will stay in the bottle.

4 Also because CO$_2$ is heavier than air, you should be able to pour the CO$_2$ gas from the bottle into the indicator. Slowly tilt the bottle as if you are pouring the gas into one of the cups of indicator. Be sure that none of the liquid from the bottle drips into the cup. Do not do anything to the other cups.

5 Use a straw to mix the indicator solution with the CO$_2$ gas. What did you observe? Now use another straw to mix the indicator in your other cup. What did you observe? Don't do anything to the third cup. It is used to compare any change that may have occurred in the other two cups. What must have caused the change in the first cup?

A *WonderScience* Air Compare!

You used an indicator in the last activity to show there was CO_2 in the bottle. You can also use an indicator to compare the amount of CO_2 in the air with the gases we exhale and with the gases from a chemical reaction.

YOU WILL NEED:

red cabbage leaves
3/4 cup water
zip-closing plastic bag
4 clear plastic cups
large round balloon
plastic soda bottle
baking soda
vinegar
straws
measuring cup
funnel

1 Prepare the indicator solution as you did in the previous activity. This time, divide the indicator solution evenly among 4 cups. Place the cups on a white sheet of paper.

2 Inflate and deflate the balloon two or three times so that it is very flexible. Use a funnel to place about 1/4 cup of baking soda into an empty soda bottle. You and your partner should carefully fill the round part of the balloon with about 1/4 cup of vinegar. Place the end of the balloon over the top of the bottle as shown.

3 Lift the bottom of the balloon so that the vinegar pours into the bottle. As the vinegar and baking soda bubble, gently swirl the bottle to get as much mixing and bubbling as possible without splashing up into the balloon.

4 After the balloon has inflated as much as possible, twist it so that none of the gas inside will escape and then remove the balloon from the bottle. You now have some CO_2 gas in the balloon. Keep the balloon closed until step 7.

5 Open a zip-closing plastic bag, get some surrounding air in it and then seal the bag tightly. Open a corner of the bag just wide enough to insert a straw. Put the straw into the bag, and then bubble the air from the bag, through the straw and into one of the indicator cups.

6 Put a clean straw in your mouth and blow into the next indicator cup. What did you observe?

7 With your partner's help, insert a straw into the balloon and let the gas from the balloon bubble into the third cup. Do not do anything to the fourth cup. It is used to compare any change that may have occurred in the other three cups. Which gas caused the greatest change in the color of the indicator? Which gas do you think had the most CO_2?

A Water Uprising

You know that oxygen is a very important gas in the atmosphere. But did you know that the chemical reaction that causes rusting uses up some of the oxygen in the air? Try the activities below to see what happens when you take some oxygen out of the air.

1 Fill a bowl with water to a height of about 5 cm. Turn a clear plastic cup upside down and place it directly down into the water.

2 You should notice that the water does not move up into the cup. That's because the air in the cup is blocking it. If you tilt the cup a little and let some air out, some water will be able to get in. Try it and see.

Losing air and gaining water is the basis for the main activity that follows. You have learned that the air is made up of about 21% oxygen. If you could turn a container over in water and then somehow take out or use up some of the oxygen, the water should move up into the container. Right?

The chemical reaction that causes rusting uses up oxygen. Try the activity below, and if you are patient, you may see the effects of oxygen from the air being used up in a chemical reaction!

Do this activity on a Friday so that you can observe the results on Monday.

YOU WILL NEED:
tall narrow jar
(such as an olive jar)
steel wool
(not treated, no soap)
plate
water
pennies

1 Place about 2 cm of water in the plate. Place two pennies in the plate. Wet some steel wool and stuff it into the bottom 1/4 of the container. Turn the container upside down with its open end on the pennies as shown.

2 Allow the container to sit there for about 48 hours. If the steel wool rusts, and rust uses up oxygen, what do you think might happen to the water in the container?

WONDER SCIENCE

Erosion! Go with the Flow

Erosion is a basic process that shapes the land. There are several different types of erosion. The Mississippi Delta and the Grand Canyon demonstrate how moving water can be a powerful agent of erosion. Wind is also a significant source of erosion. Wind blows away topsoil, especially after drought has dried out the soil and allowed it to break into small particles. Drought and wind created the dust bowl of the 1930s, with its devastating effect on American agriculture. A third source of erosion is the moving ice of an advancing or receding glacier. The ice drags boulders over the land and scrapes out valleys as the ice moves between mountains. Of these sources of erosion, moving water is the one most familiar to students and is fairly easy to model, so this unit focuses on erosion by water.

Erosion: Going with the Flow

To introduce this activity, ask students if they have ever seen moving water change the ground during a rainstorm. Have they ever noticed that the color of a pond or stream sometimes changes after a rain? What might be causing this change?

Step 2: Note that only a very thin layer of soil is required, since the amount of moving water is also small.

Step 3: Premoistening is important, because without it, the running water may simply be absorbed by the dry loose soil, so very little erosion will occur.

Results:

Steps 5 through 7: Students can probably observe moving soil particles. They may be able to see particles dropping out of the moving water. Since sand particles are relatively dense, they fall out quickly and are not transported far. Fine clays, on the other hand, may remain in the water that ends up in the low end of the tray. Encourage students to observe how the soil was worn away. They may notice that, for the sand–potting soil mixture, the soil at the high end seems more sandy than before, since the eroded potting soil stays in the water for a much longer distance than the sand.

You can begin by asking students to imagine rocks rolling down hills of different steepness. Ask which rocks would do the most damage if they hit something along the way (the ones rolling down the steepest hill; they move the fastest and have the most energy). Similarly, the water flowing down the steepest slope speeds up the most and can cause the most erosion.

Results:

Steps 3 through 5: The students can probably observe the effect of the different slopes. If deltas are formed, the one at the bottom of the steepest slope should be the largest. The water at the bottom of the steepest slope should contain the most soil.

From Mountains to Molehills

Erosion works in similar ways on both very large and very small scales. The main difference is that at the large scale, geological time is required to make changes in the Earth. Geological time is usually measured in hundreds of thousands or in millions of years.

Ask students if they have observed the three processes described on this page. Perhaps you can show the students a smooth rock and discuss how its surface was formed. The description of the Great Salt Lake states that streams flow in, bringing dissolved salt with them, but nothing flows out. Of course, the water does escape by evaporation, but the salt remains behind. In a similar way, rivers flow into all the oceans of the Earth, and nothing flows out. As in the Great Salt Lake, water escapes from oceans by evaporation, but the salt stays behind.

Let's Settle the Matter

To introduce the activity, have students review their observations of the movement of different kinds of soil in the previous erosion experiments. Ask specifically about sand (it probably moved only a short distance) and potting soil or clay (these probably moved farther). Then tell the students that they will place a mixture of sand and potting soil in a jar, shake it well, and then observe what happens. You can ask for predictions, with reasons, if you like.

Results:

Steps 3 and 4: The sand drops out almost immediately. Through the magnifier, the students can see a "rain" of smaller soil particles. Eventually this ceases, and the water simply looks cloudy.

Step 5: The next day, the water will be much more clear. Evidently, the cloudiness observed the day before was due to particles that settled out overnight.

Caves: The "Hole" Story

You can begin by asking students how they think caves are formed. Then suggest that moving water might somehow create the space inside the cave. Naturally, the sugar cube cave is an extremely simple model. The chemistry of dissolving away minerals in rock is complex, but students can still get the idea that the moving water scoured out the inside of the cave through some process like dissolving. Whether or not a model of a cave results will depend on the tilt of the tray, the arrangement of the sugar cubes, and the degree to which the water contacts the cubes.

Waving Sand Goodbye

Ask students to think back to any examples of erosion they have seen outside and to tell whether there were plants covering the ground. (Root systems provide tremendous resistance to the removal of soil. Grass, with its extensive root system, is very good at holding the soil in place. This is what the activity models.) If you buy three-stranded cotton string, encourage the students to unwind the strands in each piece, so that there are as many pieces as possible. The more pieces, the more resistance to erosion.

Results:

Step 5: The strands of the string can hold the soil in place, much like the plant roots. Roots are actually much better than the string, since all are attached to the plant and typically surround the soil and prevent it from moving away.

Erosion Spectacular!

Students can speculate about how water may have produced some of the unusual land formations pictured. They should consider different rock and soil types having different rates of erosion as well as the speed of the moving water. One concept not brought out in this unit is the effect of the freeze/thaw cycle that water has on erosion. Some areas go through hundreds of such cycles per year, resulting in significant breaking away of rock and soil.

Assessment:

Write a short story that describes a downpour from the point of view of a piece of soil that was picked up by moving water and deposited somewhere else.

NATIONAL SCIENCE EDUCATION STANDARDS

The activities in this unit can be used to support the teaching of the following standards:

✔ **Unifying Concepts and Processes**

Evidence, Models, and Explanation

Use evidence to help understand interactions and predict changes in natural and designed systems. (All activities)

Models are tentative schemes or structures that correspond to real objects, events, or classes of events, and that have explanatory power. (All activities)

Evolution and Equilibrium

Evolution is a series of changes, some gradual and some sporadic, that accounts for the present form and function of . . . natural . . . systems.

> From Mountains to Molehills
> Caves: The "Hole" Story
> Erosion Spectacular!

✔ **Science as Inquiry**

Abilities Necessary to Do Scientific Inquiry

Design and conduct a scientific investigation.

> Erosion: Going with the Flow
> Caves: The "Hole" Story
> Waving Sand Goodbye

Think critically and logically to make the relationships between evidence and explanations. (All activities)

✔ **Physical Science**

Properties and Changes of Properties in Matter

A substance has characteristic properties, such as . . . solubility, all of which are independent of the amount of the sample.

> Let's Settle the Matter
> Caves: The "Hole" Story

✔ **Earth and Space Science**

Structure of the Earth System

Land forms are the result of a combination of constructive and destructive forces . . . destructive forces include weathering and erosion. (All activities)

Soils are often found in layers, with each having a different chemical composition and texture.

> Erosion: Going with the Flow

Water is a solvent. As it passes through the water cycle, it dissolves minerals and gases and carries them to the oceans.

> Caves: The "Hole" Story

Erosion: Going with the Flow

Does the type of soil affect the rate of erosion?
Please write your observations of each area in the boxes provided.

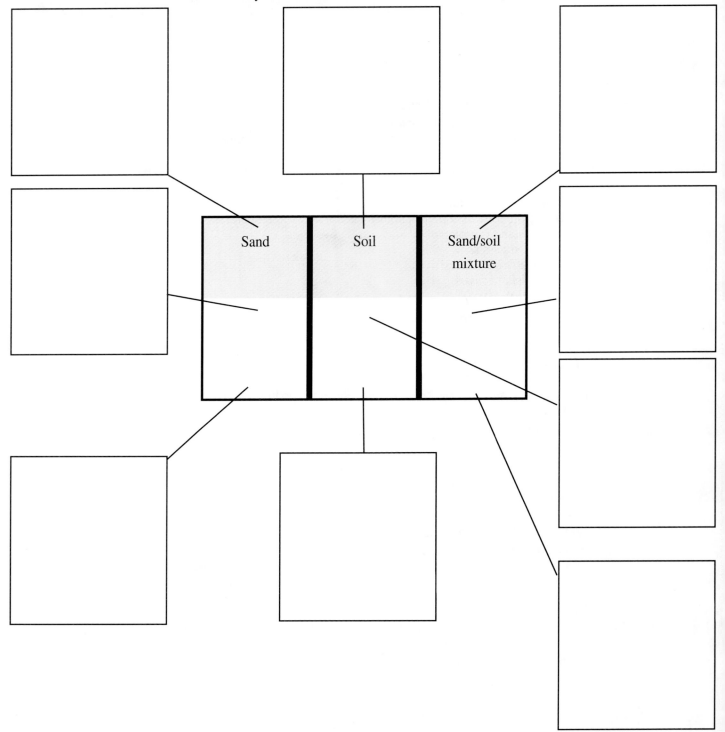

NAME _____   DATE _____

Erosion: Going with the Flow

Does the speed of the water affect the rate of erosion?
Please write your observations of each area in the boxes provided.

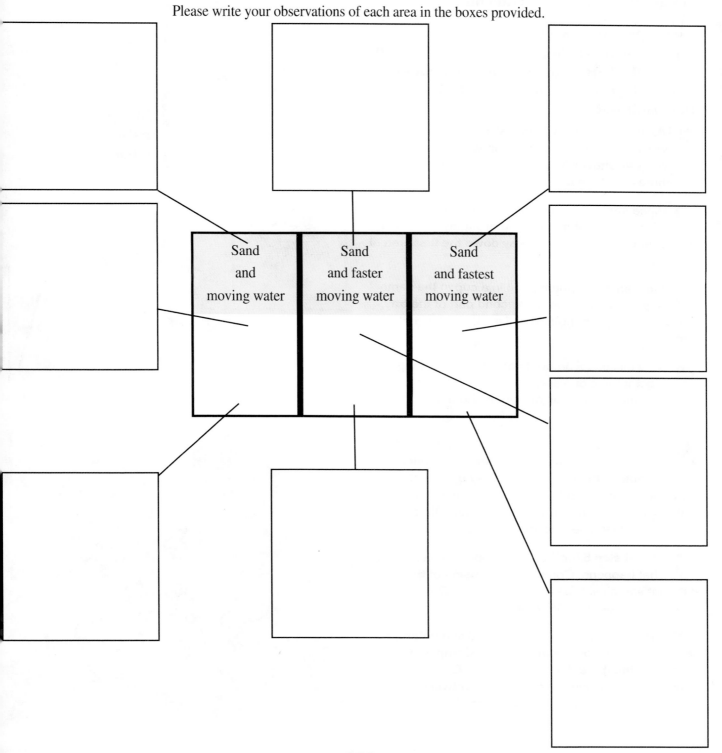

We can see the effects of erosion in many different places. Erosion works on ant hills and the Grand Canyon and almost everything in between. Although erosion can be caused by wind, water, and other forces, your *WonderScience* deals only with erosion caused by water. Let's see what happens when water runs across land. How does the water change the land? Does the type of land the water runs over make a difference? Let's find out!

Erosion:

YOU WILL NEED:

flat-bottomed pan or tray

modeling clay

paper cups

ballpoint pen

3 books (about 2–3 centimeters thick)

fine sand

potting soil

magnifier

TEACHER PREPARATION:
Use the tip of a ballpoint pen to poke a small hole in the bottom of enough paper cups so that each group gets one. Poke the hole from the inside out.

1 Make two long thin "snakes" of clay. Press these two pieces down onto the pan to form two low clay walls as shown. Your pan should now be divided into three equal areas.

2 Place some sand in a cup. Moisten the sand with a little water and stir thoroughly. Spread a thin layer of sand about halfway down the first area of the tray.

3 Moisten some potting soil in a cup in the same way as the sand. In the second part of the tray, make a thin layer of potting soil as you did with the sand.

4 Now mix equal amounts of sand and potting soil together in a cup and moisten. Make a layer of the sand and potting soil mixture in the third part of the tray.

5 Place a book under one side of the pan to lift that end a few centimeters. Place your finger over the hole in the cup and add 1/4 cup of water. Hold the cup close to the high end of the sand sample. Let the water run out of the cup. Observe the sand with a magnifier. Record what you observe.

6 Repeat step 5 for the potting soil sample. Record what happens. Compare the erosion of the two different samples. Was there a difference? What do you think caused the difference?

7 Again, repeat step 5 for the sand and potting soil mixture. Record what happens. Compare the erosion of the three different samples. Can you think of any way to explain the differences between the samples? Share your results with the class.

Going with the Flow

Does the *speed* of the moving water make a difference in erosion? Let's find out!

1 Use the same pan as on page 318 or divide another pan into three sections in the same way. Moisten some sand and spread a thin layer of sand about halfway down each area of the tray

2 Place a book under one side of the pan to lift that side a few centimeters. Measure the height of the end you lifted. Record the height.

3 As you did in the last activity, allow 1/4 cup of water to run onto the sand in the first area. Observe and record what happens.

4 Now add another book under the pan so that the high end of the pan is higher than before. The extra height should make the water move faster. Measure and record the height. Repeat step 3 for the second part of the tray. Record what happens. Compare the erosion of the two samples.

5 Add the third book to make the high side even higher. Measure and record the height. Repeat step 3 for the third area of sand. Record what happens. Compare the erosion of the three different samples. Did the speed of the water seem to have an effect on the erosion of the sand? Share your results with the class.

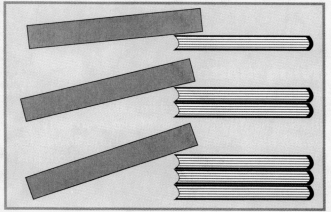

From Mountains to Molehills

In the first activity, you saw how water can pick up different kinds of soil and move them from one place to another. How does water really do this on a small scale, like in the park after a rain, and on a huge scale like widening a river or digging a canyon? See if the pictures below can give you some ideas!

Moving soil:

Moving water picks up particles of soil and carries them along. After a while, the soil settles out. The heavier particles settle first and the smaller particles travel further and settle later. These small particles can travel a long distance. That's how this gully was formed in a playground. That's also how the huge Mississippi Delta was made—all by erosion caused by moving water!

Moving rocks:

Flowing water can move sand, pebbles, and even boulders. As these rocks roll along, their sharp edges grind against other rocks and the stream bed. As a result, the rocks get smoother and the depth and shape of the stream change.

Dissolving matter:

Water can also *dissolve* some of the material it runs over. Water can dissolve a rock called limestone to create caves and caverns. The Great Salt Lake is so salty because water dissolves salt in the soil and flows into the lake. Water does not flow out of the lake, so it has become extremely salty.

SALT LAKE CONVENTION & VISITORS BUREAU

Let's Settle the Matter

You've seen what happens when water moves different kinds of soils. Now let's find out what happens to the different types of soil when they stop moving.

TEACHER PREPARATION: Mix equal amounts of sand and soil so that each group of students will get 1/2 cup of mixture.

1 Carefully pour the soil sample into the jar. Then add water until the jar is about 3/4 full.

2 Screw the cap on tightly and shake well. Then put the jar down and observe. Do not touch the jar. Shine a flashlight into the jar and use a magnifying glass to get a better view. What part of the mixture falls to the bottom of the jar first? What part seems to take longer to settle?

3 Repeat step 2 to get another look at the way the soil mixture settles in water. Did it settle like it did the first time? Record the time and draw and explain what you see.

4 After five or ten minutes has gone by, record the time and make another drawing of what you see. The process you are watching is called settling. Write a few sentences to describe what you see. Do not shake the jar again.

5 The next day, make your last drawing to show how the jar looks. Write a few sentences to tell what happened overnight.

Go back and review what happened in the experiments in "Erosion: Going with the Flow." Compare those results with what happened in the settling activity.

YOU WILL NEED:

clear plastic juice jar
with cap

spoon

sand

potting soil

water

flashlight

magnifier

Caves: The "Hole" Story

Water can dissolve certain material in rock and soil. Over millions of years, enough rock has been dissolved in certain areas to create huge underground caves. You can make a model of a cave in the activity below!

1 Place a book under one end of the tray as before. Place 12 sugar cubes close together to form a rectangle in the tray, as shown.

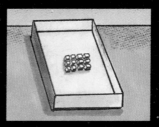

2 Take a piece of clay and form it into a pancake that can cover the sugar cubes. Place the clay over the cubes and press the outer edge down so that it attaches to the tray. Leave openings in the front and back as shown.

The sugar cubes represent rock that dissolves. The clay represents rock that does not dissolve easily in water.

3 Slowly pour about 1/2 cup of water in a stream that runs into the sugar cubes. After a few minutes, look to see if a cave has begun to form. Use the flashlight and explore inside.

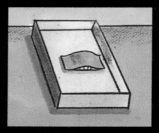

4 After a few more minutes, check the cave again. Is there any evidence of where the water ran through the cave?

EXTENSION: This time, place pieces of clay of different sizes among the sugar cubes. This model represents an area where some rock dissolves faster than others. Pour the water and use the flashlight to explore your *WonderScience* cave!

YOU WILL NEED:

12 sugar cubes
modeling clay
book (2–3 cm thick)
cup of water
tray (flat-bottomed)
flashlight

Waving Sand Goodbye

YOU WILL NEED:

pan or tray (flat-bottomed)
book (2–3 cm thick)
1 cup fine sand
string (1 meter)
2 cups or bowls
plastic teaspoons
scissors
water

Erosion from waves can shrink gigantic piles of sand called sand dunes. The roots of grasses and other plants growing in the sand dunes can help keep the dune in place. You can make a model of a dune without plant roots and one with plant roots to see which dune the waves will doom.

1 Place 1/2 cup of sand in each of your two cups. Add two or three teaspoons of water to each and mix until the sand is moist.

2 Cut the string into about ten 10-centimeter pieces. If you can, untwist each piece of string into its separate strands. Add the strands to the sand in one of the cups and stir until they are well mixed with the sand.

3 Place a book under the tray as before. Place one pile of sand without string on one side of the tray. Place another pile of sand *with* string on the other side of the tray.

4 Add water to the bottom of the tray. To make waves, *gently* lift and then lower the front of the tray so that water flows and hits the sand piles and then returns to the front of the tray. Do this about 10 or 15 times, as if waves were hitting sand dunes.

5 What do you notice when you compare the size of the sand piles? How are the strands of string like the roots of plants in a sand dune?

Erosion Spectacular!

Look at the places below.

What do you think caused these strange land formations?

Think about different rocks eroding at different rates and about water moving slowly or quickly. Although some areas may look like desert now, there may have been lakes, rivers, or even oceans at some point in time!

NATIONAL PARK SERVICE

ILLUSTRATIONS BY JIM WISNIEWSKI/STEVE EDSEY & SONS UNLESS OTHERWISE INDICATED

Soil forms a thin layer at the surface of much of the Earth's land mass. Soil provides essential nutrients for plant growth and development. Soil contains air, water, ground-up minerals and rocks, microorganisms, and the decomposed remains of plants and animals. Students learn that to support plant life, a soil must strike the right balance between holding water and letting water drain through. An important factor affecting water drainage is soil particle size. To investigate this property of soil, students test the rate of water drainage through soil samples with different-sized particles. They also discover the natural variation in soil particle size through a soil-settling experiment. Students will also do some small-scale composting to follow the process through which microorganisms in the soil transform dead plant material into humus, an important source of soil nutrients.

Get the Dirt on Soil!

Much of topsoil consists of ground-up rocks and minerals. Students may see tiny pebbles and also shiny flakes as they examine their soil sample. When comparing soil with sand, students should begin to develop a familiarity with the variety of soil particle sizes. Students may also find an assortment of living things in the soil sample. The rolling and smearing of soil are actually tests that soil scientists do to help determine the soil's composition. After handling soil, students should wash their hands.

Rain and Drain!

To support plant life, a soil must strike the right balance between holding water and letting it drain through. The soil must hold water well enough so plants have plenty to absorb between rains, yet let water drain fast enough so pools of water do not stand for long periods of time. Students compare a sample of soil with a sample consisting of soil and sand. The more sand in the soil, the faster the water should drain.

From Grass to Soil—Let Microbes Toil!

Composting is the process through which microorganisms in the soil transform dead plant and animal material into humus, an important source of soil nutrients. Gardeners create compost piles by placing layers of kitchen scraps and dead plant material between layers of garden soil. The garden soil provides the microbes to decompose the plant matter. Earthworms contribute to this process as well by helping to digest organic material.

Soil Sizes—Some Surprises!

We've designated this activity for take-home use to encourage parental involvement. Feel free, however, to use it in the classroom if you choose. Soil scientists perform the settling test to investigate the particle size and the soil parts present in a sample of soil. The large soil particles settle out first, and the

smallest particles can remain suspended in the water for days. Silt, a soil part made of relatively fine particles, settles slowly and can be carried great distances by moving water. The particles of clay are even finer than those of silt.

Soak It Up!

Plants get their water from rain that percolates down through the soil. After a heavy rain, water can drain down even below a plant's roots. Water can move up through soil in the same way that it seeps up in a paper towel partially sitting in water. The attractive forces between the water molecules and the soil particles, together with the attractive forces between the water molecules themselves, contribute to water's upward movement through the soil.

Activity Answers and Extenders

Get the Dirt on Soil!

Make sure students wash hands thoroughly after handling the soil.

Student responses will depend on the soil sample they examine. If possible, use fresh garden soil, which should have living things for the students to find. Step 2: Small, shiny flakes are small fragments of minerals. In general, about half of soil is ground-up rocks and minerals. Step 4: If your soil contains clay, the variety of particle sizes may be misleading, because the tiny clay particles stick together readily and form large clumps as they dry. Steps 5 and 7: Soil scientists rub the soil between their fingers and smear wet soil on paper to help determine its composition.

Rain and Drain!

Sand, with its relatively large particle size, drains rapidly but dries out easily. Clay drains poorly but dries out slowly. Garden soil balances absorbing and draining to hold enough water for most vegetables and flowers. Soil contains air, and when it rains, water can fill these air spaces. Step 6: In the soil with the larger particle size, water will drain through more rapidly. Step 7: If the soil is dry, less water will come through than went in, because some water is absorbed into the soil. Ask the students to feel the soil to try to find out where the water went. Step 8: If more water is added, it may drain through or remain on top, depending on the size of the soil particles.

From Grass to Soil—Let Microbes Toil!

Grass decomposes rapidly because the blades are narrow, thin, and free of any waxy material. You may have already felt the heat in a bag of freshly mown grass—it starts decomposing immediately! Having the right amount of water in the compost bag is crucial: too little and the microbes cannot live and eat the grass; too much and there is no room for air, which the microbes need as well. The contents should feel slightly moist.

Soil Sizes—Some Surprises!

Different soil parts settle at different rates, depending on the particle size. Sand settles almost immediately. Silt and clay take much longer and can make well-defined layers. Clay may take several days to settle completely. When the soil contains humus, some of the humus floats while the rest settles. Eventually some of the floating humus becomes waterlogged, and it settles, too.

Soak It Up!

The upward pull on the water comes from the forces between the water molecules and the soil particles as well as from evaporation occurring at the soil surface. The water rises more readily in the sand than in the soil. The narrow passageways formed by the sand particles provide channels for the upward movement of water.

Soil Science

NATIONAL SCIENCE EDUCATION STANDARDS

The activities in this unit can be used to support the teaching of the following standards:

✔ **Unifying Concepts and Processes**

Evidence, Models, and Explanation

Evidence consists of observations and data on which to base scientific explanations.
  Get the Dirt on Soil!

Models are tentative schemes or structures that correspond to real objects, events, or classes of events and that have explanatory power.
  Rain and Drain!
  Soil Sizes—Some Surprises!
  From Grass to Soil—Let Microbes Toil!
  Soak It Up!

Constancy, Change, and Measurement

Changes occur in the properties of materials. Energy can be transferred, and matter can be changed.
  From Grass to Soil—Let Microbes Toil!

✔ **Science as Inquiry**

Abilities Necessary to Do Scientific Inquiry

Design and conduct a scientific investigation. *(All activities)*
Use appropriate tools and techniques to gather, analyze, and interpret data.
  Get the Dirt on Soil!
Develop descriptions, explanations, predictions, and models using evidence. *(All activities)*
Think critically and logically to make the relationships between evidence and explanations. *(All activities)*

✔ **Life Science**

Populations and Ecosystems

Decomposers, primarily bacteria and fungi, are consumers that use waste materials and dead organisms for food.
  From Grass to Soil—Let Microbes Toil!

✔ **Earth and Space Science**

Structure of the Earth System

Soil consists of weathered rocks and decomposed organic material from dead plants, animals, and bacteria. Soils are often found in layers, with each having a different chemical composition and texture. *(All activities)*

NAME _____   **DATE** _____

Get the Dirt on Soil!

Use this chart to record your observations for steps 2–7 for both the soil and the sand.

Observation for	Soil	Sand
Step 2		
Step 3		
Step 4		
Step 5		
Step 6		
Step 7		

STUDENT ACTIVITY SHEET

NAME _____   **DATE** _____

Rain and Drain!

1. When you and your partner pour water into each sample, do you think more water will flow through one than the other? _____
Why? _____
_____
_____
_____

2. After allowing the water to drain through
   your samples, use a pencil to draw in the
   level of the water in the bottom of each cup.

3. Did the soil or the sand + soil allow more water to drain through? _____

4. Why do you think a sandy soil lets water drain better? _____
_____
_____

5. If drainage is important for plants, why don't farmers grow plants in sand or a soil mixture with a lot of sand? _____
_____
_____

6. If less water came through each sample than went in, where do you think the extra water gets trapped in the sample? _____
_____
_____

7. Do you think the amount of water trapped in the sample has anything to do with the size of the soil or sand particles? Explain. _____
_____
_____

8. How much water do you think will go through each sample when you add the second amount of water? Why?
_____
_____
_____

9. Use a pencil to draw
   in the new level of the
   water in the bottom of each cup.

10. Why do you think the second amount of water drained through the way it did? _____
_____
_____

Get the DIRT

Do you ever look at soil? Soil scientists do. Why do you think they are so interested in soil? You can begin to find out more about the characteristics of soil by taking a very close look at some and by getting your hands a little bit dirty. Let's try it!

YOU WILL NEED:

1/4 cup of potting soil
1/4 cup of sand
tablespoon
Popsicle® stick
magnifying glass
paper and pencil
water in a plastic cup
straw

1 Draw 2 large circles on your paper. Label one **soil** and the other **sand**. Place a tablespoon of soil in its circle and a tablespoon of sand in its circle. Use a whole piece of paper to draw a chart like the one below, or use the chart in the Student Activity Sheet.

For steps 2–7, observe both the soil sample and the sand sample. Make your observations and descriptions as detailed as you can, and record them in the chart.

TEACHER NOTE:
Students should wash hands thoroughly after handling soil.

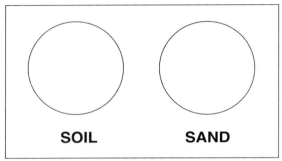

SOIL   SAND

2 Spread the sample around with a Popsicle stick. Does it all look brown or black, or are there some other colors? Is there anything you recognize as a piece of plant or insect? Is there anything shiny? Describe what you see in the sample in as much detail as you can.

3 Use a magnifying glass to take an even closer look. Use your Popsicle stick to move the sample around and to scrape and smash some pieces if you can. Describe what you see that's different from what you saw before.

4 Look at the size of the soil particles. Are they different sizes, or are most particles about the same size? Are the bits of soil clumped together, or are they mostly separate from each other?

Observation for	Soil	Sand
Step 2		
Step 3		
Step 4		
Step 5		
Step 6		
Step 7		

on Soil!

5 Pick up some of the sample, and gently move it around between your thumb and index finger. Does it crumble or smear? Does the way the sample feels between your fingers tell you anything about the size of the particles?

6 While observing closely with the magnifying glass, place a few drops of water on the sample. What do you notice? Does the water seem to be absorbed into the sample or not? Does the water seem to break any of the sample apart?

7 Now that the sample is a little bit wet, use your index finger to smear a little of the sample on the paper. Does the sample make a mark? Why do you think one smears more than the other?

8 Look at your recorded observations in your chart. Were your two samples mostly the same or mostly different? What were the major similarities and differences?

JIM WISNIEWSKI

SOIL SAND

Soil is a precious resource for life on Earth. Soil allows plants to produce nutrients that people and other animals need to live. For plants to grow well, the soil must have certain qualities. In the rest of this *WonderScience* unit, you'll learn more about soil and how it helps plants grow.

RAIN and DRAIN!

YOU WILL NEED:

- 4 plastic cups
- 3/4 cup of potting soil
- 1/4 cup of sand
- container for mixing
- spoon
- 2 paper towels
- 2 rubber bands
- 1/4 cup of water
- masking tape
- pen
- metric ruler
- measuring cup

One of the most important characteristics of soil is how well it holds water. Some plants grow best if their soil stays moist most of the time. Others grow well if the soil drains more and doesn't hold water for too long. In the following activity, you can test two different types of soil for how well they absorb water and how well water drains through them.

1 Use the masking tape and pen to label one empty cup **soil** and the other empty cup **soil + sand**. Label your other two empty cups **water**.

2 Place a piece of tape on the side of each cup as shown. Use a ruler to mark lines for 1, 2, and 3 cm measured from the bottom of the cup.

3 Lay a paper towel over the top of the **soil** and the **soil + sand** cup, and push the towels about halfway in. Fasten each paper towel in place with a rubber band as shown.

4 Gently pour about 1/2 cup of the soil sample into the paper towel in the **soil** cup.

5 In your mixing container, add 1/4 cup sand to 1/4 cup soil and mix thoroughly with a spoon. Pour this mixture into the paper towel in the **soil + sand** cup.

6 Pour water up to the 2-cm mark in each **water** cup. What do you think will happen when you and your partner pour the water into each soil sample at the same time? Do you think there will be any difference between the way the water moves through the two soil samples? Why?

7 Now add the water to the soil in each paper towel. Be sure to add the water to each cup at the same time. Watch to see how much water drips into each cup. Is there any difference between how much water or how fast the water drips into each cup? Compare how much water comes through the soil with how much went in. What do you notice?

8 Now predict what will happen if you add the same amount of water again to each cup of soil. Give a reason for your prediction. Repeat step 7. What do you notice?

EXTENSION:

After no more water drips from the paper towels, carefully remove the paper towels from the cups. Lay them out flat and be sure to label which is soil and which is soil + sand. Which do you think will dry out first? Why?

Yum. This soil sure is tasty!

JIM WISNIEWSKI

Soil Sizes—*Some Surprises!*

The size of the particles is a very important characteristic of soil. The smaller the particles, the harder it is for water to move through the soil. A good soil for a garden must have particles small enough to store water for the plants. At the same time, the particles must be big enough for water to drain through, so no mud puddles will be left behind after a rain.

By just looking at soil, you might be able to see some of the different particle sizes, but it's very hard to tell the approximate amount of each particle size in the soil. Here is a simple test you can do to get an idea of the amount of each particle size in a sample of soil.

1 Use your masking tape and pen to label one bottle **soil** and the other bottle **soil + sand**. Place about 1 cup of soil in a cup.

2 Fill the soil bottle about 3/4 full of water. Very slowly pour the soil into the water. What do you notice about the way the soil particles sink in the water? Do the different sizes seem to sink at different speeds?

3 After all the soil is in the water, fill the rest of the bottle with water if the water is not to the top already. Put the lid tightly on the bottle. Shake the bottle back and forth several times. Place the bottle on a flat surface where it will not be disturbed.

4 Take your remaining 1/2 cup of soil and add 1/2 cup of sand to the soil. Mix thoroughly with your spoon.

5 Repeat steps 2 and 3 with the soil + sand bottle and the soil and sand mixture. Wash hands after handling soil. Allow both bottles to stand overnight. Observe the bottles the next day. Look at the bottles from the side.

Do you notice any layers in the bottles? How would you describe the particles that make up these layers? Are some layers thicker than others? Do you think this is a good way of finding out the amount of different size particles in soil? Why or why not?

YOU WILL NEED:

potting soil (1 1/2 cups)

sand (1/2 cup)

2 juice bottles with wide mouths (with tops)

paper or plastic cup

masking tape

pen

metal teaspoon

water

JIM WISNIEWSKI

From Grass to Soil— Let Microbes Toil!

What do you think happens to grass clippings after they are cut and fall onto the ground? Let's see what we can find out!

1 Place one handful of grass clippings in each of two plastic bags.

2 In one bag, add a cup of fresh potting soil and mix well. In the other, leave the clippings as they are. Seal both bags.

3 With a pencil, carefully poke 5–10 air holes in each side of the plastic bags. Be careful not to poke yourself.

4 Place the bags in a dark place. Once each week, open the bags and add a teaspoon of water. After one week open the bags and look inside. Look closely at the grass. Aside from being dirty in the soil bag, does the grass in either bag look like it has changed from when you put it in?

Think about what happens out in the woods. What happens to all the leaves that fall year after year? Do the leaves on the ground just keep getting deeper and deeper?

5 After another week, look closely again at the grass in the two bags. What has happened to the grass that was in the soil? What happened to the grass without soil? Describe what you see. Continue observing for the next few weeks. Explain what you think is happening to the grass.

Have you heard of a compost pile? You have just made some compost. In a compost pile, dead plant material and soil are combined and kept moist. Tiny organisms (*microorganisms*) in the soil begin to eat the plant material, causing it to break down or *decompose*. The decomposed plant material and the wastes the microorganisms give off all add nutrients to the soil. In fact, gardeners often use compost as a natural fertilizer for growing plants.

YOU WILL NEED:

2 handfuls of grass clippings
1 cup of potting soil
2 zip-closing plastic bags
a sharp pencil
teaspoon

JIM WISNIEWSKI

Soak It Up!

In a well-draining soil, water can sometimes flow so far down that the water gets below the roots of the plants. Do you think the water can then travel **up** through the soil to meet the roots? Let's see if it can!

YOU WILL NEED:

- 2 plastic Dixie® cups (3 oz.)
- 2 clear plastic cups (9 oz.)
- zip-closing plastic bag
- 1/2 cup of dry potting soil
- 1/2 cup of dry sand
- metal spoon
- pushpin
- water
- paper towel
- 2 pennies
- tablespoon

TEACHER PREPARATION:
Turn the Dixie cups upside down on a table. Use a pushpin to poke 15 holes in the bottom of each cup. Each group of students will need two cups.

1 Put the soil in a zip-closing plastic bag and crush it up as much as you can.

2 Place the soil in one Dixie® cup until it is 3/4 filled. Put sand in the other Dixie® cup until it is 3/4 filled.

3 Tear or cut two small squares of paper towel (about 3 cm x 3 cm). Place a square of paper towel in the center of the top of each cup. Place a penny in the center of each paper towel and press down a little. (The paper towel will show you when water reaches the surface.)

4 Place 2 tablespoons of water in the larger plastic cups. At the same time, place the two small cups in the water. Watch the top of the sand and soil. What do you notice?

5 If the top of the sand and soil never seem to get wet, take a pencil and scrape the very top of the soil and sand. Was there water close to the surface? Did the water seem to rise near the top of one faster than the other? Is this what you expected? Why?

JIM WISNIEWSKI

Children—and adults for that matter—are fascinated by the power, beauty, and science of volcanoes. The processes that create volcanic eruptions occur on such a vast scale that it is difficult to model them in the classroom. With the combination of interacting factors, such as extreme heat and pressure, changes of state, convection, expanding gas, and changes in density and viscosity, it is hard to imagine a model that could accurately and safely depict the processes of a volcanic eruption. Rather than attempting to recreate a small-scale eruption, we have chosen to divide these major processes and to model them *outside the context of the volcano*. After understanding each principle, students can then apply the principles when thinking about how volcanoes work.

Our Earth—From the Inside Out

You could begin with a simple demonstration to suggest to students the scale of the main layers of the Earth. One interesting model is an apple. You could tell students that the Earth's crust is between 10 and 50 miles thick. But if you use an apple as a model of the Earth, the crust would be thinner than the apple's skin.

The main point of "Our Earth—From the Inside Out" is to introduce students to the four main layers of the Earth and to get them thinking about how to accurately represent something as huge as the Earth by making a model. Students should understand that to make a model "to scale," the dimensions of all of the Earth's layers need to be reduced by the same amount. Working with very large numbers, such as 100,000 centimeters in a kilometer, may be challenging for students, but it can also be a fun concept to play with. You could have students look at something small and imagine what it would look like if it were 100,000 times bigger. Depending on your students, they could measure a small object and make the actual calculations. The Earth is so huge that students will need to think in terms of not only 100,000, but also 100,000,000!

You might want to ask some questions so that students can better understand the illustrations in "Our Earth—From the Inside Out." Ask what each picture represents. The first picture shows a slice taken out of the Earth to reveal a more three-dimensional-looking interior. The second is a cross-section through the Earth, giving, a more two-dimensional look. Asking questions about shape, relative size, and distance from one layer to another can help students become familiar with the two ways of representing the major Earth layers.

Convection: A Moving Experience

The key concept of convection is that warming a material makes it less dense and causes it to rise, but when that same material cools, it will become more dense and sink. A familiar example is a hot air balloon. The heated air in the balloon is less dense than the air around it. Therefore, the balloon floats. If the balloon's burner is shut off, the air in the balloon cools and becomes more dense, and the balloon sinks. What is true for air is also true for liquids and solids. The hotter, less dense material in the asthenosphere moves up, displacing the cooler, denser material, which drops down. Although the asthenosphere is mostly solid material, it still undergoes these convection current movements.

When doing the activity, it helps if there is not too much hot water in the outer cup. You want just enough to warm the water in the lower part of the inner cup. Students should see the food coloring rise and then curve down toward the bottom of the cup. Unfortunately, the color disperses in the water so students will only see one cycle of convection.

Expanding Possibilities

Some of the most explosive volcanic eruptions involve super-heated gas and ash bursting from a volcano, sometimes with no lava flow at all. While still under the ground, magma contains a large amount of trapped gas. The gas cannot expand and escape because of the tremendous pressure on it deep inside the Earth. But once the magma gets near the Earth's surface, the gas will rapidly expand and sometimes, as in the Mount St. Helens eruption, blow off huge portions of the volcano.

The activity titled "Expanding Possibilities" is only intended to show students that gas does expand when heated. You will have to explain that under the enormous pressures beneath the Earth, this expansion would not be possible. Where "Expanding Possibilities" deals mostly with the influence of heat on gas expansion, the next activity, "Magma—Gassed Up to Go!," deals more with the influence of pressure on gas expansion.

Magma—Gassed Up to Go!

Students may not be familiar with the concept of a gas being *dissolved* in a liquid. It is analogous to the more familiar situation of a solid dissolved in a liquid. Molecules of one or more gases enter the magma and are thoroughly mixed with the

Unit 29
Volcanoes: What a Blast!

liquid, just as the molecules of a dissolved solid are thoroughly mixed throughout a liquid. In the first part of the activity, students feel the outside of a full, unopened bottle of soda. They should notice that the bottle feels very hard. This is because gas has been added and dissolved into the liquid at high pressure. When the pressure is released by opening the bottle, students should see gas bubbles coming out of the liquid. This is because the lower pressure gives the gas a chance to expand. This is similar to the way the gas in magma expands when it is finally under less pressure near the surface of the Earth.

The second part of the activity is an attempt to combine the two factors of heat and pressure to model the expansion of gas in magma as it reaches the Earth's surface. Students should see more bubbling when they release the pressure from the bottle in hot water.

NATIONAL SCIENCE EDUCATION STANDARDS

The activities in this unit can be used to support the teaching of the following standards:

✔ Unifying Concepts and Processes

Evidence, Models, and Explanation

Using evidence to understand interactions allows individuals to predict changes in natural and designed systems.

> *Convection: A Moving Experience*
> *Expanding Possibilities*
> *Magma—Gassed Up To Go!*

Models are tentative schemes or structures that correspond to real objects, events, or classes of events, and that have explanatory power.

> *Convection: A Moving Experience*
> *Expanding Possibilities*
> *Magma—Gassed Up To Go!*

Evolution and Equilibrium

Evolution is a series of changes, some gradual and some sporadic, that accounts for the present form and function of…natural…systems.

> *What on Earth Is a Volcano, Anyway?*

✔ Science as Inquiry

Abilities Necessary to do Scientific Inquiry

Design and conduct a scientific investigation.

> *Convection: A Moving Experience*
> *Expanding Possibilities*
> *Magma—Gassed Up To Go!*

Think critically and logically to make the relationships between evidence and explanations.

> *Convection: A Moving Experience*
> *Expanding Possibilities*
> *Magma—Gassed Up To Go!*

✔ Earth and Space Science

The solid earth is layered with a lithosphere; hot, convecting mantle; and a dense metallic core.

> *What on Earth Is a Volcano, Anyway?*

Major geological events, such as…volcanic eruptions…result from these [lithospheric] plate motions.

> *What on Earth Is a Volcano, Anyway?*

NAME _____   **DATE** _____

Our Earth—From the Inside Out

Look at the scale drawing of the main layers of the Earth. The picture shown is called a "cross-section." It is an illustration of what you would see if the entire Earth were cut in half right through the center, and one half was lifted off, and you were looking down at the remaining half.

1. If you wanted to make a scale drawing of a cross-section of the Earth similar to this one, but *half* as big, what would be the measurements of the four main layers?

   Inner core _____

   Outer core _____

   Mantle _____

   Crust _____

2. On a separate sheet of paper, use a metric ruler and a compass to draw a cross-section of the Earth based on these measurements. Label the four main layers.

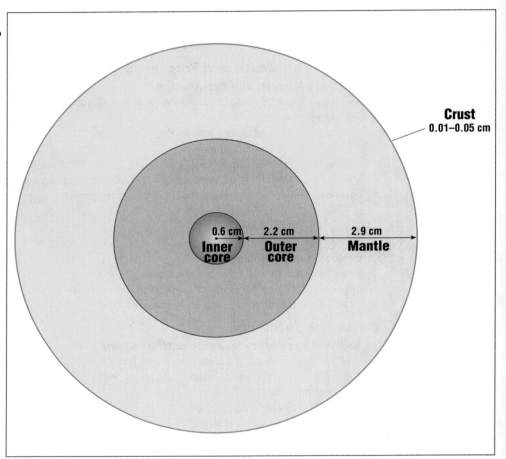

3. If you wanted to make a scale drawing of a cross-section of the Earth similar to the original one shown on this page, but *twice* as big, what would be the measurements of the four main layers?

   Inner core _____

   Outer core _____

   Mantle _____

   Crust _____

4. On a separate sheet of paper, use a metric ruler and a compass to draw a cross-section of the Earth based on these new measurements. Label the four main layers.

NAME _____   **DATE** _____

Magma—Gassed Up to Go!

Most magma has lots of gas dissolved in it. A more common example of a gas dissolved in liquid is the carbon dioxide gas that is dissolved in soda pop. Let's see what we can learn about the way temperature and pressure affect the way gas dissolved in soda pop behaves.

1.   Look at a full, unopened bottle of soda pop. Do you see any gas bubbles? _____

2.   You know there is gas in the soda, so where do you think it is?

_____

_____

3.   Press the outside of the bottle. Does it feel hard or soft? _____

4.   Why do you think the bottle feels the way it does?

_____

_____

5.   When you slowly release the bottle top, what do you see in the soda pop?

_____

_____

6.   What do you think caused the difference between what you saw in the unopened bottle and the opened bottle?

_____

_____

7.   When you slowly unscrewed the caps from the bottles of soda in hot and cold water, what difference did you notice?

_____

_____

8.   What do you think caused the difference?

_____

_____

Our Earth

Volcanoes are formed from hot melted rock coming up through cracks in the earth. When this hot liquid rock is still in the earth, it is called **magma**. When it comes out during a volcanic eruption, it is called **lava**. But where in the earth is this supply of hot melted rock anyway?

To get an idea of where this magma is inside earth, let's look at a drawing of what scientists believe the structure of the earth looks like:

Crust
10–50 km

Inner core
600 km

Outer core
2,200 km

Mantle
2,900 km

Inner core—a radius of about 600 kilometers (km) (about 360 miles). This would be about the same as a ball whose diameter is about 1/3 the distance across the United States.

Outer core—about 2,200 km thick (about 1,320 miles). The Empire State Building, one of the tallest skyscrapers in the world, is about 1/4 of a mile high. The outer core is more than 5,000 skyscrapers thick!

Mantle—about 2,900 km thick (about 1,740 miles). The mantle is almost 7,000 skyscrapers thick!

Crust—varies between about 10–50 km thick (about 6–30 miles).

From the Inside Out

You could make a scale model of the earth, but to do this, we need to reduce the size of all the different parts of the earth by the same amount:

First, let's shrink everything from kilometers to centimeters. Since there are 100,000 centimeters (cm) in a kilometer, a centimeter is 100,000 times smaller than a kilometer. If we reduced all of the kilometers to centimeters, the model would be 100,000 times smaller than the earth.

So now we have:
Inner core—about 600 cm
Outer core—about 2,200 cm
Mantle—about 2,900 cm
Crust—varies between about 10–50 cm

But 600 centimeters are equal to 6 meters (m)—that's way too big for our model, and that would just be the radius of the core! If we made the core this big, the whole model would end up being over 100 meters in diameter. That's a big ball! The diameter would be bigger than a football field!

We can shrink the model down another 1000 times by dividing each measurement by 1000. This would make the model 1000 times smaller **again**. Here's what we get:

Inner core—about 0.6 cm (or 6 mm)
Outer core—about 2.2 cm
Mantle—about 2.9 cm
Crust—varies between about 0.01 and 0.05 cm
          (1/10th millimeter–1/2 millimeter)

We now have a model that is about 100 million times smaller than the earth. That works out pretty well since the inner core is about the size of a marble, and the whole model is about the size of a softball.

Using the measurements above, here is a scale drawing of the size of each part of the earth.
Scale: 1 cm represents 1,000 km

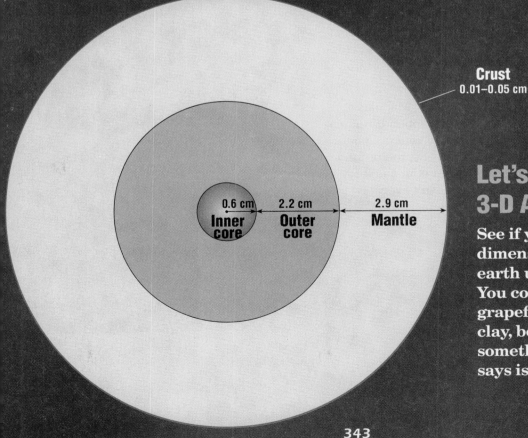

Crust
0.01–0.05 cm

0.6 cm   2.2 cm   2.9 cm
Inner   Outer   Mantle
core   core

Let's try a 3-D Activity!

See if you can make a three-dimensional model of the earth using this same scale. You could use a cantaloupe, grapefruit, papier mâché, clay, bowl of Jell-O®, or something else your teacher says is OK. Good Luck!

What on Earth Is a Volcano, Anyway?

What exactly is a volcano anyway? Where does the lava come from? Why do volcanoes erupt? What comes out when they do erupt?

The part of a volcano that we can see is made from the lava, ash, and rock that has come out of the volcano during past eruptions. This material builds up over time and forms the outside above-ground part of the volcano. Volcanoes look different depending mostly on the type of material that comes out during an eruption.

In "Our Earth—From the Inside Out," you saw that the mantle surrounds the outer core of the earth. The mantle itself is made up of two huge layers of rock material. The layer closest to the outer core is called the **asthenosphere**. The layer on top of the asthenosphere is called the **lithosphere**. The material that makes up the asthenosphere is under tremendous heat and pressure. As material in the asthenosphere is heated, it becomes less dense than the material around it, so it rises very slowly toward the lithosphere. As this material gets closer to the lithosphere, it begins to cool and to fall back down toward the outer core. This slow movement of the asthenosphere can push and pull on the lithosphere, causing earthquakes and volcanic eruptions.

Some material in the asthenosphere melts so much that it becomes even more fluid and less dense than the material around it. This hot liquid material works its way through the asthenosphere and may collect in a pool near the lithosphere. This material is the magma that comes out as lava during a volcanic eruption.

Sometimes, so much magma builds up that it pushes on the rock above it, so that the rock finally gives way, and an eruption takes place. Other times, movement of the asthenosphere causes cracking of the lithosphere, and magma finds its way into the crack. Since magma is less dense than the material around it, it will continue to move toward the surface. The heat from the magma itself can melt rock in the lithosphere, making the crack even bigger and allowing more magma to move up. As the magma moves closer to the surface, it expands very rapidly and can burst through the surface in an explosive volcanic eruption.

Volcanoes can have different kinds of eruptions. Magmas that are thick tend to create more explosive eruptions. Thinner magmas often flow smoothly from the volcano with little or no explosiveness. If the magma contains lots of gas, the eruption may be more explosive than with magma that contains less gas. In some volcanic eruptions, magma doesn't even come out. What does come out is an enormous quantity of hot gas and ash. Sometimes, these are the most dangerous and deadly eruptions.

Lithosph

Magma

Asthenosphere

Convection:
A Moving Experience

The material in the asthenosphere moves up and down in very slow moving patterns called **convection currents**. A convection current occurs when material is heated and becomes less dense than the material around it. The warm material moves up until it cools off and becomes denser. It then begins to sink again to the warmer area. Again, it heats up and begins to rise again.

You can make a simple model of convection currents in the activity below:

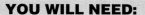

YOU WILL NEED:

food coloring

small cup

eye dropper

2 clear plastic cups
(one about 8 oz and another wider punch cup that the 8-oz. cup can fit in)

water (room temperature and hot from tap)

1 Place two or three drops of food coloring into a small cup.

2 Fill the 8-oz. cup about 3/4 full of room-temperature water.

3 Use a dropper to pick up two or three drops of food coloring from the small cup.

4 Push the dropper through the water in the 8-oz. cup, all the way to the bottom. Very gently, squeeze the dropper to put the food coloring on the bottom of the cup. (This may take a couple of tries.)

5 Place two or three tablespoons of hot water in the wider punch cup. Carefully pick up the cup with the water and food coloring, and place it in the wider cup with the hot water.

Observe the food coloring. Describe how it moves.

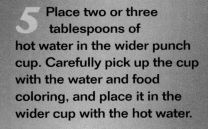

Expanding Possibilities

When a gas is heated, it normally expands. But the gases in magma are under such extreme pressure beneath the earth that they cannot expand much until they get very near the earth's surface. It is easy to show how heat makes a gas expand under the normal pressure on earth's surface. Remember, deep within the earth, gases are not able to expand, but when they get to the surface, watch out!

1 Place the straw in the bottle so that the flexible end is sticking out. Squeeze the clay tightly around the straw and the mouth of the bottle to make an airtight seal.

2 Fill a cup about 3/4 full of water. Bend the flexible end of the straw, so that you can place the end of the straw in the water while holding the bottle over the tray or bucket, tilted downward as shown below.

3 Hold the bottle near the top end while your partner pours hot tap water over the bottom end of the bottle.

4 Watch the end of the straw in the water. What do you notice? If you see bubbling, what do you think caused it?

In magma, hot gas is ready to expand and escape like you just saw, but it can't escape under the intense pressures beneath the earth. In the next activity, let's see what happens when that pressure *is* released!

346

Magma—
Gassed Up To Go!

YOU WILL NEED:

club soda (unopened, 1 or 2 liter)

2 plastic bottles with lids (from bottled water, empty, 1/2 liter)

ice and hot water

2 bowls

clock or timer

As you have read, the gases in magma are under extreme pressure beneath the earth's surface. When magma gets close to the earth's surface, the gas expands to such an extent that it can blow a hole in the volcano!

In the activity below, you can see how releasing pressure allows gas to expand and come out of a liquid.

1 Look at the soda in the bottle. Can you see any gas bubbles in the soda? Do you think there is gas in the soda?

2 Feel the outside of the bottle. Does it feel hard or soft? If it feels hard, it is because the soda has been packed in the bottle under a lot of pressure.

3 Open the bottle very slowly and observe the soda. As you opened the bottle, you released the pressure on the soda. Did you see any bubbles form while opening the bottle?

As magma moves up toward the surface of the earth where there is less pressure, the gases in magma also expand and come out of the liquid.

Do more gas bubbles form when pressure is released from hot liquid than from cold liquid? Try the following activity to find out.

1 Carefully pour the club soda into each of your smaller bottles until they are about half full. Put the lids on securely. Place one bottle in hot tap water and the other in ice water. Let the bottles sit for about three minutes.

2 Slowly unscrew the cap from the bottle in ice water. Listen for any gas escaping and watch to see any new bubbles form.

3 Now, slowly unscrew the cap from the bottle in the hot water. Again, listen to the gas escaping, and watch for any new bubbles forming.

How did the amounts of gas coming out of the two bottles compare? Did one seem to have more gas escaping than the other?

The release of pressure can allow a lot of gas to come out of a hot liquid. That goes for soda, as well as for the earth's magma.

Mount Saint Helens—
A Blast from the Past

▲Mount St. Helens is a volcano in southwestern Washington state. Before the eruption in May of 1980, it was about 3,000 meters high.

◀In March 1980, a bulge of rock began developing on one side of the volcano. It continued to grow as magma inside the volcano pushed on the rock from the inside. Measurements showed that it was growing at about 1.5 meters (about 5 feet) per day. By the middle of May, the bulge had been pushed upward and outward by 135 meters (over 450 feet).

◀ On May 18, 1980, an earthquake shook Mount St. Helens, causing the bulge and the rock surrounding it to tumble down the volcano in a gigantic rockslide. This relieved the pressure over the bulge area, allowing hot gas and ash to blast out of the side of the volcano.

◀ The following three illustrations show the landslide (green) and the gas and ash (red) blasting from the volcano.

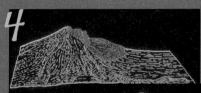

◀After the May 18 eruption, Mount St. Helens had lost almost 500 meters in height and was left with a giant crater about 1.5 kilometers wide (about 1 mile).

◀Plumes of steam, gas, and ash often occur years after the 1980 eruption. Magma is still coming out of the area of the blast and slowly filling it in. A lava dome is forming that, by 1990, was about 282 meters (925 feet) tall.

Having suitable drinking water is a primary health concern for people everywhere. Balanced ecosystems can clean water quite efficiently. However, large groups of people can pollute the water faster than nature can clean it. In the late 1800s, some very serious illnesses were linked to contaminated water, so water treatment plants were developed to clean water. By using cleaner treated water, people would not be taking a health risk every time they drank or used water. The activities in this issue investigate water quality issues for people and wildlife.

Clump and Clean!

In this activity, students compare the settling of dirt mixed in water in two different containers. One container will be treated with alum, and the other will be a control. Alum is a chemical used in the initial stage of cleaning at some water treatment plants. It causes dirt particles to stick together. These large particle clumps become heavy so they sink to the bottom, leaving the water clear. Students will notice that the container treated with alum settles much more quickly and, after settling overnight, is remarkably clearer than the untreated water.

You may want to call your local water treatment plant to learn their procedure for cleaning the water, since it varies due to local environmental conditions.

The Secchi disk that students will make is a very small model of ones used to test water in rivers, streams, lakes, and ponds. Its purpose is to measure how far down into the water light can penetrate. This measurement is important to water treatment plants because it provides information that will help determine the quantity of chemicals needed to clear the water. Secchi disks are also used to monitor the health of an ecosystem. Sunlight is important in underwater ecosystems for the same reasons that it is important on land: It provides warmth and light. Without sunlight, plants, including underwater plants, cannot undergo photosynthesis. This affects the whole ecosystem because underwater plants produce some of the dissolved oxygen that fish and other animals with gills breathe. The oxygen problem becomes worse as the plants die. Certain bacteria use oxygen to decompose the dead plants. Therefore, if sunlight is blocked, there is danger of widespread suffocation.

Filters—Particularly Purifying

Be sure to discuss with students the idea that clear colorless water is not necessarily fit to drink. There may be microscopic organisms or other substances in the water that make it unhealthy. In this activity, students will compare the ability of two different amounts of sand to clean water. They should notice that more sand cleans water better. Don't expect the water to look completely clear. However, you and your students should notice a big improvement when the water is filtered through sand as compared to the control cup.

Slow the Flow

In this activity, students compare different materials for their abilities to filter water. The rate at which the water flows through the media and the clarity of the water are related. Students should notice that the slower flow produces cleaner water. Generally, the tighter the spaces in the media, the slower the flow of water. These small spaces cause tiny dirt particles to be held in the filter so that the flowing water becomes cleaner. It is interesting to look and to dig if necessary, to see the dirt trapped in the filtering medium.

Our coffee filter paper cleaned the water better than the cotton balls or the sand.

Testing the Waters

Testing the pH of water is one test done when monitoring rivers, streams, lakes, and ponds. It is also done during the process of cleaning water at the water treatment plant. Water in freshwater ecosystems is naturally slightly acidic. The pH of pure water is neutral. The water that you receive from your faucet has been treated with chemicals to be very slightly alkaline.

In this activity, students place vinegar, an acid, and laundry detergent, a base, into cups of red cabbage juice to see a distinct color change. They are asked to neutralize a solution of cabbage juice and vinegar with laundry detergent. Students add small amounts of detergent and swirl until the color changes back to blue. If they add too much detergent, they can add a little vinegar and try again. Neutralizing the solution will give students an idea of how pH can be adjusted at the water treatment plant.

Up, Up, and Away!

When a cup of carbonated water is placed in a bowl of cold water, some gas bubbles rise to the surface while many bubbles collect on the bottom and sides of the cup. When a cup of carbonated water is placed in a bowl of hot water, gas bubbles

Unit 30
Water: Clearly Wonderful

rise to the surface much more quickly and pop. Your students may need help realizing that these popping bubbles are actually gas being removed from the water and released into the air. After a while, few bubbles can be seen inside the cup that is sitting in the hot water.

This helps to explain why people keep opened bottles of soda pop refrigerated. The lower temperature keeps the dissolved gas in the soda for a longer period of time.

Hard Water Woes

The difference between hard water and soft water is that hard water contains the minerals calcium, magnesium, and iron, whereas soft water does not. Hard water can be a problem because the minerals chemically bond with your soap and cause a solid, or precipitate, to form. This is a problem for two reasons. One is that your soap is no longer free to do its job.

The other is that the precipitate left behind, soap scum, is difficult to remove. Soft water causes other problems. People sometimes complain that they don't feel clean when they bathe with soft water because it is more difficult to rinse off all the soap.

When your students blow bubbles in each of the three soapy waters, they will notice a difference. The hard water will not produce many bubbles because much of the soap has bonded with the minerals. The soft water will bubble up nicely. Your class is left to theorize about the local tap water.

Water: Clearly Wonderful

NATIONAL SCIENCE EDUCATION STANDARDS

The activities in this unit can be used to support the teaching of the following standards:

✔ Unifying Concepts and Processes

Evidence, Models, and Explanation

Using evidence to understand interactions allows individuals to predict changes in natural and designed systems.

Testing the Waters, Up, Up and Away!, Hard Water Woes

Models are tentative schemes or structures that correspond to real objects, events, or classes of events, and that have explanatory power.

Clump and Clean!, Filters—Particularly Purifying, Slow the Flow

✔ Science as Inquiry

Abilities Necessary to Do Scientific Inquiry

Design and conduct a scientific investigation. *(All activities)*

Develop descriptions, explanations, predictions and models using evidence. *(All activities)*

Think critically and logically to make the relationships between evidence and explanations. *(All activities)*

✔ Physical Science

Properties and Changes of Properties in Matter

Substances react chemically in characteristic ways with other substances (compounds) with different characteristic properties.

Clump and Clean!, Testing the Waters, Hard Water Woes

✔ Life Science

Populations and Ecosystems

For ecosystems, the major source of energy is sunlight. Energy entering the ecosystem as sunlight is transferred by producers into chemical energy through photosynthesis.

Clump and Clean!

The number of organisms an ecosystem can support depends on the resources available and abiotic factors, such as quantity of light and water, range of temperatures, and soil composition.

Clump and Clean!, Testing the Waters, Up, Up and Away

✔ Science and Technology

Understandings about Science and Technology

Technology is essential to science, because it provides instruments and techniques that enable observations of objects and phenomena that are otherwise unobservable. . . .

Clump and Clean!, Testing the Waters

NAME _____   **DATE** _____

Clump and Clean!

1. Use this chart to record the depth at which the Secchi disk disappears.

Depth, in centimeters, at which the disk disappeared

Test #	Alum	Control
1 (10 min.)		
2 (20 min.)		
3 (30 min.)		

2. At the end of the third test, which container of water, alum or control, became the clearest?

_____

_____

3. Each time you tested the water, the depth at which the Secchi disk disappeared was farther from the surface of the water.

Describe what the water in a container would look like if the Secchi disk disappeared 18 cm below the surface.

_____

_____

_____

_____

Describe what the water in a container would look like if the Secchi disk disappeared 3 cm below the surface.

_____

_____

_____

_____

4. If you were responsible for testing how far down the sunlight goes into the water in a lake, you would probably use a big Secchi disk with measurements on the cord. Why do you think people measure how far the disk is from the surface of the water and not how far away the disk is from the bottom of the lake?

_____

_____

_____

_____

NAME _____   **DATE** _____

Up, Up, and Away!

1. Since you used a carbonated beverage, the bubbles in this experiment are carbon dioxide gas. When they rise to the top, what happens to them?

    _____

    _____

2. Where does the carbon dioxide go?

    _____

    _____

3. Which temperature of water (hot or cold) releases more gas bubbles? _____

4. Which temperature of water (hot or cold) keeps the gas inside the best? _____

5. Power plants that make electricity often use water from nearby rivers. Explain why they cool the water before returning it to the river.

    _____

    _____

    _____

    _____

6. Why is the temperature of the water very important for fish and other animals with gills that breathe underwater oxygen gas?

    _____

    _____

7. If you want to keep your newly opened bottle of soda fizzy for a long time, would you keep it in the refrigerator or out on the counter?

    _____

    Why? _____

    _____

Clump

We like the water that comes from our faucets to be clean and clear. To help make water clear, water treatment plants add a chemical that makes small dirt particles stick to each other so that they sink. See what happens when one of these chemicals, **alum**, is mixed with very dirty water! You'll also make a special tester called a **Secchi** (set-chee) **disk** to see how clear the water becomes!

YOU WILL NEED:

- **small opaque plastic cup** (white on the inside, about 8-oz. size)
- **scissors**
- **scrap paper**
- **pencil**
- **metric ruler**
- **50 cm of string**
- **pushpin**
- **5 pennies or washers**
- **masking tape**
- **black permanent marker**
- **dirt**
- **water**
- **tablespoon**
- **2 empty clear tennis ball containers**
- **alum** (found in the spice section at grocery stores)
- **chart**

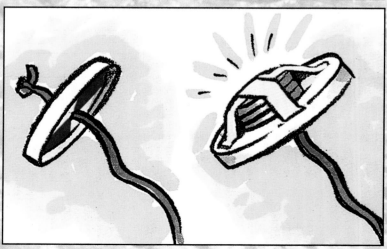

1 Carefully poke a hole through the center of the cup bottom with the pushpin and move it around to make the hole a little bigger. Push the tip of your pencil through that hole to make it big enough to thread a piece of string through.

2 Now cut along the bottom of the cup to make a disc with a very small raised edge. Use your permanent marker to divide the cup bottom into four equal wedges, and color two wedges as shown.

3 Tie a knot at the end of the string and thread it through the bottom of the cup, as shown below.

4 Lay a stack of five pennies or washers on top of the knot at the center of the disk. Tape them down so that the pennies are securely attached. Two pieces of masking tape should do it. Now your Secchi disk is ready!

5 Label one tennis ball container **control** and the other one **alum**. Fill each tennis ball container with water, to about 4 cm from the top. Add four tablespoons of dirt to each container and stir well with the spoon.

and Clean!

6 Add 1/4 teaspoon of alum to the container labeled **alum**. Stir both containers.

7 Slowly dip your Secchi disk into the container labeled **alum** until you can't see the disk anymore. Now lift it slightly until you can see it. Dip and lift until you've found the exact point where the disk disappears. Hold it steady right there.

8 Have your partner measure the depth of the disk, as shown. Record this depth in your chart. After measuring, carefully raise the Secchi disk out of the water so that you do not stir up the water.

9 Follow steps 7 and 8 for the container labeled **control**.

10 Let the dirty water in each container settle for 10 minutes. Then, every 10 minutes, repeat steps 7 and 8 for each container until you have tested each one a total of three times. What do you notice about the depth of the disk in each container? How can using a Secchi disk give you better information than just looking at the two water samples?

Let both containers settle overnight. You will notice a big difference!

Depth, in centimeters, at which the disk disappeared		
Test #	Alum	Control
1 (10 min.)		
2 (20 min.)		
3 (30 min.)		

Filters—*Particularly Purifying*

Filtering is an important step in cleaning water. The filters at the water treatment plant where you live are designed to handle the types of dirt, microscopic organisms, and small pieces of dissolved rocks that are in your area. Most treatment plants use sand as a part of their filters to trap unwanted particles. Let's see how the amount of sand affects how well the filter works.

YOU WILL NEED:

potting soil
1 toilet paper tube
1 piece of cloth handkerchief
water
wide clear tape
3 small cups
3 clear plastic cups
masking tape
pen
1/4 cup measure
1 cup of sand
spoon for stirring

TEACHER PREPARATION:
Cut the handkerchief or similar cloth into 10 cm by 10 cm pieces (one per filter). Pour 1/4 cup of water into each of four small paper cups. Put 1/2 teaspoon of potting soil into each of these cups and stir.

1 Completely cover the outside of your toilet paper tube with wide tape. Secure the handkerchief piece to one end of the tube with the masking tape. This is your filter.

2 Label your three clear plastic cups **control**, **1/4 cup sand**, and **3/4 cup sand**. Stir each of your cups of dirty water.

3 Hold your filter over the plastic cup labeled **control** and pour a paper cup of dirty water through the filter.

4 Add 1/4 cup of sand to your filter and hold it over the cup labeled **1/4 cup sand**. Pour a paper cup of dirty water through this filter. Let the water drain completely. What differences do you notice between the two cups of water?

5 Add two more 1/4 cups of sand into your filter, so that it now has 3/4 cup of sand. Hold the filter over the cup labeled **3/4 cups sand**. Pour the last paper cup of dirty water through this filter. Compare the dirtiness of each water. Why do you think sand is often used to filter water?

Slow the Flow

In the last activity, you saw that a sand filter can make a big improvement in cleaning dirty water. In this activity, you will compare the way filters made from different materials clean dirty water.

TEACHER PREPARATION:
Follow the same preparation directions for the previous activity.

1 Make a filter using a toilet paper tube and cloth the way you did in the previous activity.

2 Label your cups **control**, **cotton balls**, **sand**, and **coffee filter**. Stir each little cup of dirty water. Pour one of the cups of dirty water through the filter into the cup labeled **control**.

3 Lay the coffee filter over the open end of your filter and push it in slightly. Hold it over the cup labeled **coffee filter**. Pour the paper cup of dirty water directly into the filter in small amounts until all the water is emptied. What difference do you see between the filtered water and the control. Remove the coffee filter.

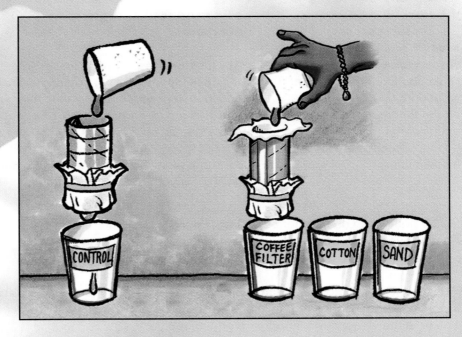

4 Stuff your filter with the cotton balls. Pour a paper cup of dirty water through the filter. When all the water has drained, pull out the cotton balls. Compare this filtered water to the control.

5 Add 3/4 cup of sand to your filter and hold it over its cup. Pour the dirty water through the filter. Which is the fastest filtering material, coffee filter, cotton balls, or sand? Which filtering material produces clearest water?

How does the water that went through the coffee filter compare with the water from the sand and the cotton? Think about the spaces in each material that allow the water to go through. Think about the size of the dirt particles. Which material do you think is the best filter? Why do you think that this filter works the best?

Testing the Waters

YOU WILL NEED:

safety goggles
red cabbage
   leaves (about 1/2 bag full)
water
scissors
3 small cups
   (paper or plastic)

zip-closing
   plastic bag
   (sandwich size)
5 plastic cups
3 droppers
laundry
   detergent
vinegar

When water treatment plants are cleaning water, they need to add certain chemicals that make the water more acidic. This helps in the water cleaning process. Other chemicals are then added to make the water slightly basic. This helps prevent the water from making holes in the underground pipes it flows through. You can see how to make a solution acidic, basic, or neutral in the activity below!

TEACHER PREPARATION: Label three plastic cups for each group **vinegar**, **tap water**, and **laundry detergent solution**. Make the laundry detergent solution by adding 1 teaspoon detergent to 1 tablespoon water. Place 1 tablespoon of each liquid in its labeled cup.

1 Put on your safety goggles. Label each of your five cups **control**, **vinegar**, **tap water**, **laundry detergent**, and **vinegar & detergent**.

2 Cut 1 or 2 red cabbage leaves into small pieces with your scissors and place them in a zip-closing plastic bag. Add about 1/2 cup of warm tap water. Let out as much of the air as you can and carefully zip the bag closed. Mash the leaves in the water until the water turns medium to dark blue. This is your indicator solution

3 Carefully open one corner of the bag. Pour the cabbage juice evenly into the five empty labeled cups while keeping the cabbage pieces in the bag. Throw away the bag and cabbage.

4 Using separate droppers, add two or three drops of vinegar, laundry detergent, and water to the indicator in its labeled cup. Do not add anything to the indicator in the vinegar and laundry detergent cup yet.

5 Swirl each cup gently, and notice if there is any change in color. Record this color in the chart from the Student Activity Sheet. With red cabbage juice, a change to pink shows that the solution tested is an acid. A change to a greenish-blue shows that the solution is a base. If the juice stays blue, then the solution is neutral.

6 In your cup labeled **vinegar & detergent**, add a small amount of vinegar and swirl. Then add a little laundry detergent solution and swirl. Continue adding a little detergent solution to the cup and swirling the solution until you get the color to return to blue or neutral again.

Up, Up, and Away!

Water has different gases in it. Usually, you can't see them, but if you have ever seen bubbles in water, you have seen some gas! Oxygen gas is produced by underwater plants during photosynthesis. Oxygen also travels into water from the air above. Oxygen also *leaves* water and goes into the air. Find out whether oxygen and other gases leave water faster when the temperature is cold or when it is hot!

YOU WILL NEED:

carbonated water
(Any fizzy soda will do.)

2 bowls

2 clear plastic cups

cold water

hot tap water

Water from the tap can be quite hot.
Be careful when using it.

1 Pour about 1/2 cup of carbonated water into the two clear plastic cups.

2 Half fill one bowl with hot water and the other with cold water. Make sure that the water doesn't spill out when a cup is placed in the bowl.

3 Place each cup of soda upright into each of the bowls and watch both at the same time. What do you notice about the bubbles in each? How are they different?

Since you used a carbonated beverage, the bubbles in this experiment are carbon dioxide gas. When they rise to the top, what happens to them? Where does the carbon dioxide go? Which temperature of water (hot or cold) releases more gas bubbles? Which temperature of water (hot or cold) keeps the gas inside the best? Why do you think that fish sometimes gulp air at the surface of the water in the summer? Why is the temperature of the water very important for fish and other animals with gills that breathe under water? If you want to keep your newly opened bottle of soda fizzy for a long time, would you keep it in the refrigerator or out on the counter?

Hard Water Woes

Sometimes water runs over minerals in the ground like calcium, magnesium, or iron. If enough of these minerals get dissolved in the water, then it is called **hard water**. **Soft water** does not have these minerals dissolved in it. Even though you can't see a difference between hard water and soft water just by looking, if you do the activity below, you should definitely see a difference!

TEACHER PREPARATION:
Soak a bar of Ivory soap overnight in a bowl of water. Pour some soap solution into a cup for each group.

1 Label three cups **hard water**, **tap water**, and **soft water**.

2 Pour 1/2 cup of distilled water into the cup labeled **soft water**. Pour 1/2 cup of tap water into each of the other two cups. To make **hard water**, pour 1/2 teaspoon of Epsom salt into the **hard water** cup and stir until dissolved. Place a straw in each cup.

3 Add 1/2 teaspoon of the very soapy water to one of the cups. Gently stir with a straw to mix the soap and water. Watch the cup closely! What happened to the soap? Repeat for the other two cups.

4 Blow bubbles into each cup of water with its straw. Be sure not to suck the water up the straw. Which type of water makes the most bubbles? Which type of water makes the fewest bubbles? If you wanted to blow giant bubbles, which type of water would you use to make the soap solution? Why is this a good choice? Why do you think hard water is blamed for leaving behind a lot of soap scum?

ILLUSTRATIONS BY JIM WISNIEWSKI/STEVE EDSEY & SONS UNLESS OTHERWISE INDICATED

WONDER SCIENCE

Looking at the Moon

This unit offers students the opportunity to make long-term observations of the moon, to find patterns in these observations, and to use models to interpret these patterns.

The moon is an object of scientific interest and also of great beauty. It plays a major part in folklore and mythology of cultures all over the world. Much of its importance stems from the regular pattern of phases, from new moon through full moon and then back to new moon again.

What's New in the Moon?

Have your students start observing the moon's phases as soon as possible, because this activity extends over two months. The period (time to go through one cycle) of the moon's orbit around the Earth is about 28 days. If the moon is full on a particular day, it will be full again about 28 days later. When students observe this pattern, they then can use it to make predictions for the following month. Early calendars were based on the phases of the moon.

Gaze-a-Phase!

The diagram shows sunlight hitting the Earth from the left, so the sun is far, far away to the left. Notice how the sun lights up the half of the Earth and moon that face the sun. Sunlight can't reach the other half, so it's in shadow. As the Earth rotates daily on its axis, most places on the Earth move through both sunlight and shadow (day and night) every 24 hours.

Simulating the phases of the moon with the ball-and-lamp model can be a challenge. Be sure to see the tips given in "Activity Answers and Extenders" for this unit.

The Moon on the Move!

We observe the sun moving across the sky from east to west each day. In fact, the moon moves across the sky in the same way. But this motion of the sun and the moon is only apparent. It occurs because we, the observers, are turning, along with the surface of the Earth. As the Earth rotates, the sun and moon appear to sweep by from east to west. Check your newspaper for times that the sun and moon rise and set each day.

Craters—The Hole Story

Craters are formed when objects from space hit the moon. These objects range in size from about 250 km (about 150 mi) down to microscopic size. Because the moon has no atmosphere, there is no weathering from moving air or water to remove craters once they are formed. The surface of the moon is covered with about 5 cm of fine powder (remember that famous photo of the astronaut's footprint?). The impacts of thousands of microscopic objects have ground up the surface into this powder.

What's New in the Moon?

As students accumulate data, ask them to give a summary of what patterns they have identified. They might say that the moon goes from a crescent to full and then back to a crescent again, changing a little bit each night. Have students look back at their moon drawings to notice that the two crescents and the two quarter moons are opposites of each other. This is because the sunlight strikes a different part of the moon as the moon goes around the Earth. Because the moon goes through a complete cycle in 28 days, four weeks make up a complete cycle.

Gaze-a-Phase!

This is a challenging model. If the room is not very dark, it may be hard to distinguish the lit and unlit portions of the ball. You may want to have students work near the lamp in small groups in a dark part of the room.

If you cannot get this model to work, here is another idea: Take a white ball and paint half of it black. In this model, the white half represents the portion of the moon that is facing the sun. The black half represents the part of the moon that is not facing the sun. The student holding the ball is the Earth. The white side of the ball must always face in the same direction—as if it is facing the sun. The diagram of the boy holding the ball will give you a good idea of how this model can represent the portions of the moon that are lit and not lit in different positions around the Earth.

The student representing the Earth describes the shape of the "lit" portion in each position. In the diagram, position 1 is a new moon (not visible). Positions 2 and 4 are the first and third quarters (the moon is half-lit). Position 3 is a full moon.

Students may ask about eclipses. In an eclipse of the moon, the Earth blocks sunlight from hitting the moon. Students may expect an eclipse of the moon to occur every month. But the moon's orbit is slightly tilted compared with the Earth's orbit around the sun, so eclipses happen only infrequently.

Unit 31
Looking at the Moon

The Moon on the Move!

As an extension activity, have students model the Earth and the moon. Have the "Earth" student turn completely around in about 11 seconds. The "moon" moves around the "Earth" once every 5 minutes. Have the "Earth" student look straight ahead and report how the moon's position changes as the "Earth" turns. This model should make it clearer that the apparent movement of the moon across the sky in a single night has more to do with the rotation of Earth than it does with the actual movement of the moon.

If you and your students are very patient, add a third student to model the sun. Then the "Earth" and "moon" will rotate together around the "sun" about once every hour. This model shows that the Earth–moon system (the moon revolving around the Earth) itself rotates around the sun as part of the solar system.

Craters—The Hole Story

Craters are caused when objects from space crash onto the surface of a planet or a moon. Most planets (including Earth, but excluding the gas giants Jupiter and Saturn) show evidence of craters. When we look at craters on the moon, we see the shadows cast by the crater walls. These shadows depend on the direction of the sunlight as it hits the surface of the moon. If the sunlight comes straight down, there are hardly any shadows, and it's not easy to see the craters. But if the sunlight strikes the surface at a glancing angle, the shadows are long and much easier to see. If you look at a quarter moon with binoculars, you will see that the shadows are much more distinct at the edge of the lighted part than in the areas that face the sun more directly.

A Moon Myth: Don't Let It Phase You!

Encourage students to go to the library and find other myths about the moon. Challenge them to create a skit based on one of these myths.

Looking at the Moon

NATIONAL SCIENCE EDUCATION STANDARDS

The activities in this unit can be used to support the teaching of the following standards:

✔ Unifying Concepts and Processes

Evidence, Models, and Explanation

Evidence consists of observations and data on which to base scientific explanations. (All activities)

Using evidence to understand interactions allows individuals to predict changes in natural and designed systems.

  What's New in the Moon?
  Gaze-a-Phase

Models are tentative schemes or structures that correspond to real objects, events, or classes of events, and that have explanatory power.

  Gaze-a-Phase!

Constancy, Change, and Measurement

Changes might occur, for example, in . . . position of objects, [and] motion. Interactions within and among systems result in change.

  The Moon on the Move!

✔ Science as Inquiry

Abilities Necessary to Do Scientific Inquiry

Design and conduct a scientific investigation. (All activities)

Develop descriptions, explanations, predictions, and models using evidence.

  What's New in the Moon?
  Craters—The Hole Story

Think critically and logically to make the relationships between evidence and explanations. (All activities)

✔ Earth and Space Science

Earth in the Solar System

Most objects in the solar system are in regular and predictable motion. Those motions explain such phenomena as the day, the year, phases of the moon, and eclipses.

  What's New in the Moon?
  Gaze-a-Phase!

STUDENT ACTIVITY SHEET

NAME _____   **DATE** _____

What's New in the Moon?

Use the following calendar to record your moon observations during the month.

Month_____						
S	**M**	**T**	**W**	**T**	**F**	**S**

364

Gaze-a-Phase!

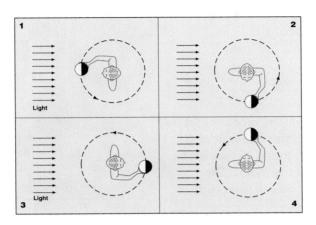

New moon   Crescent   First quarter   Gibbous   Full moon   Gibbous   Third quarter   Crescent

1. When you look at the ball as in picture 1, what phase of the moon does the ball look like?

_____

2. When you look at the ball as in picture 2, what phase of the moon does the ball look like?

_____

3. Describe where the ball would need to be to get a crescent moon like the one after the new moon.

_____

_____

4. When you look at the ball as in picture 3, what phase of the moon does the ball look like?

_____

5. When you look at the ball as in picture 4, what phase of the moon does the ball look like?

_____

6. Describe where the ball would need to be to get a gibbous moon like the one after the full moon.

_____

What's New in the Moon?

The moon has fascinated people throughout history and in every culture. People have learned a lot about the moon just by watching it. In the following activity, you can investigate why the moon's surface looks the way it does and why the moon appears to move and change its shape.

YOU WILL NEED:

pencil

photocopy of calendar for the next month

two photocopies of calendar for the month after next

8 index cards

1 Go outside and find the moon. The moon might be visable in the morning, the afternoon, or at night. Find the space in the calendar for today. In that space, draw what you see as you look at the moon. The drawing at right shows how your calendar record might start.

S	M	T	W	T	F	S
		1 ◯	2	3	4	5
6	7	8	9	10	11	12
13	14	15	16	17	18	19
20	21	22	23	24	25	26
27	28	29	30	31		

2 Day by day, keep a record of what you see when you look at the moon. Don't worry if it's cloudy. Just skip that day and continue your observations when it's clear. Keep going for at least five weeks.

. . . five weeks pass . . .

New moon   Crescent   First quarter   Gibbous   Full moon   Gibbous   Third quarter   Crescent

3 Now look at the drawings shown above. Each drawing shows a different phase of the moon. Each phase is a different way the moon can look. Go back and label each of your calendar drawings with its phase. First check the example at right:

4 As you look at your calendar, what patterns do you see in the phases of the moon?

Full moon

5 Let's use these patterns to predict what you will observe in the next month. Take one of the calendars for that month and write "Predictions" in big letters at the top. Now draw in the moon you expect to see during each day of the next month. Explain how you made your predictions.

6 Use your other copy of the next month's calendar to continue making and recording observations of the moon's phases. Write "Observations" in big letters on the top of this calendar. Keep the records in the same way you did last month.

. . . a month passes . . .

7 Now compare your predictions with your observations. Describe how well they match.

8 Now that you have recorded two months of observations, how could you make better predictions for the next month?

The phases of the moon go through a cycle. A cycle is a pattern that repeats. That's what you have been observing with the moon. Ancient civilizations used this cycle to make calendars. Does the modern calendar seem to be based on the phases of the moon?

9 Let's put our records of the moon onto index cards. On each card, make a drawing of one phase of the moon that you observed. Be sure to include one completely dark card for the new moon.

10 Now shuffle the cards and challenge a friend to lay them out in the right order.

Gaze-a-Phase!

The sun is a hot ball of gas. It gives off its own light and heat. The moon is made of rock. By itself, it does not give off either light or heat. Light from the sun travels through space and shines on the moon just as it shines on the Earth. When you see the moon, you are looking at sunlight lighting up the surface of the moon. That's how we are able to see the moon. So moonlight is really sunlight!

Distances in space are so big that it's hard to think about what's going on with this light. Let's make simple models of the sun, Earth, and moon to see what happens. A model can help us learn about something big and complicated.

YOU WILL NEED:

lamp without lampshade
white ball

1 Take a look at the drawing below. It shows how sunlight lights up half of the moon—and half the Earth too! But wait a minute, if the sun lights up half the moon, what causes the moon to look different all the time?

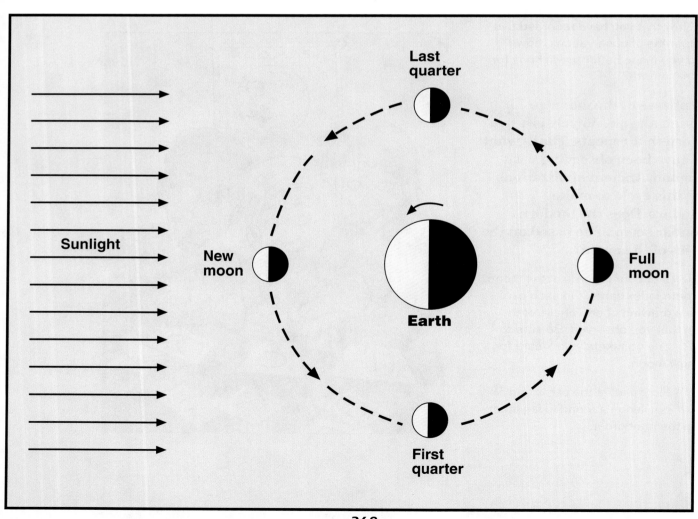

This model will help you understand why the look of the moon changes. Your head will model the Earth. A ball will model the moon. A light from a lightbulb will model the sun. The moon revolves around the Earth in about one month, so in our model, you will slowly move the ball around your head in a circle. Your head will also need to turn, like the Earth does, in order to see the moon

2 Look at the four drawings below. Each drawing shows the moon model in a different place in its path around your head. Turn off all the lights to make the room as dark as you can. Hold the ball at arm's length a little higher than the top of your head. Point the ball directly at the light as in picture no. 1.

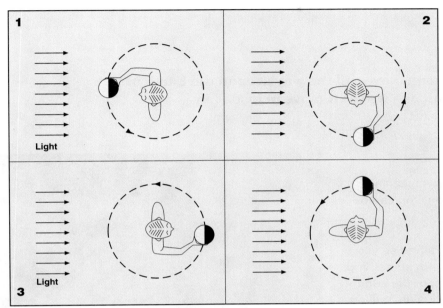

3 Describe what you see as you look at the ball. Look at the set of drawings below; these are some of the main phases of the moon. As you hold the ball as in picture no. 1, what phase does it look like?

New moon   Crescent   First quarter   Gibbous   Full moon   Gibbous   Third quarter   Crescent

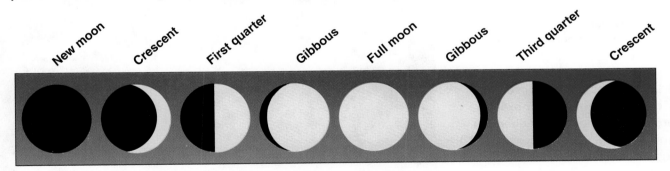

4 Very slowly begin to move the ball around you in the direction of the arrow. Remember, the ball models the moon. As you look at the ball, you model what someone on Earth sees while looking at the moon. Describe what you see.

5 Look at the pictures of the phases again. After moving the ball a short distance from its spot in picture no. 1, which phase does the ball look like?

6 Continue moving the ball around you very slowly. When the ball is in the position shown in picture no. 2, describe what you see. What phase does it look like?

7 See if you can find the right position for a full moon. How would you describe this position? Which of the four pictures is it most like?

8 Where does the moon need to be to look like the third quarter? Which of the four pictures is this most like?

The phases of the moon shown here happen over 28 days as the moon goes around the Earth. How can you use the model above to understand how the moon can appear in these different ways over this period of time?

The Moon on the Move!

We know that the moon moves all the way around the Earth in about one month, but can we see it move in just a few minutes? Let's find out!

1 Find a place where you can sit and watch the moon. You can be inside or outside.

2 If you are outside, stand so you line up the moon with something, like the branch of a tree, or the edge of a building. If you are inside, pull up a chair. Line up the moon with part of the window. As you watch the moon, keep your body and head very still.

3 After a couple of minutes, what do you notice about the position of the moon?

4 Line the moon up again as you did before. Remember exactly where you are and in what direction you are looking. Go away for about 10 minutes. Come back to the exact same spot, looking in the exact same direction. What has happened to the moon's position?

5 Now predict where the moon will be in an hour. Explain how you made your prediction.

6 Come back in an hour and observe the moon's position again. How does your prediction compare with your observation?

What do you think is causing the moon to appear to move so much in such a short time?

Craters—
The Hole Story

Take a good look at the surface of the moon with your "naked" eye. Your eye sees mainly areas of light and dark but not much detail. About 350 years ago, a scientist named Galileo was the first person to use a telescope to look at the night sky. From then on we have been able to see the moon and other objects in space with a lot of detail.

Here is a telescopic look at an area of the moon. You can see lots of craters dotting the moon's surface. You can also see shadows cast by the walls of the craters. Just as on Earth, the shadow cast by an object on the moon depends on where the sunlight is coming from.

In the activity below, you can make a model of the moon and the sun and see if you can create shadows on your craters just like the picture you see here! If you get the shadows just right, you can get an idea of where the sun was compared to the moon when the picture was taken!

1 Flatten a ball of clay into a pancake that is about 15 centimeters in diameter. Wrap the clay pancake around a tennis ball until the entire ball is covered.

2 Use the eraser end of a pencil to make three or four holes that you can shape into craters like those in the picture.

3 Use your thumb and index finger to build up the rim of the craters. Notice how some craters appear to be deeper than others and how the depth affects the shadows. See if you can make your craters at different depths like the ones in the picture.

4 Darken the room and use a flashlight to represent the sun. Shine the flashlight on your moon at different angles until you get shadows like the ones in the picture. You may have to change your craters a bit.

When you get the shadows just right, you will have an idea of where the sun was when the moon photograph was taken! Based on your model, where do you think the sun was when the picture was taken?

You can now make some more craters and mountains and other features until your moon is completely covered!

NASA/NATIONAL GEOGRAPHIC IMAGE SALES

A Moon Myth

Don't let it phase you!

The moon is important in myths from many lands. Here is part of a folktale from the Aleuts, an Indian tribe in the northwest part of North America.

A girl fell in love with the man in the moon. She looked at the moon all night long. She had to turn several times and face a different way so she could look directly at the moon all night. Finally the moon selected her to be his wife.

Although she was happy as the wife of the moon, she thought some of his habits were strange. He slept most of the day and usually worked at night. Sometimes he worked throughout the night. Sometimes he went to work in the afternoon and returned late at night. All he would say was that he did hard, important work, and he had to do it alone.

One night the young wife went for a walk. She came upon a small house that her husband, the moon, had forbidden her to enter. But she could not resist. When she stepped inside, she saw a full moon, a half moon, a moon that was a crescent, and one was almost full. They were beautiful, and she wondered how one would look on her. She put on the moon that was almost full. But she became frightened when it would not come off.

When her husband returned, he said, "Now you can join me in my work. I will be the full moon, and after that I will rest. You can finish the month until I have to return to work." Since then they have happily shared the job of being the moon that we see.

Students will measure and model shadows to get a better understanding of why they occur. Quantifying certain shadow phenomena is stressed throughout the unit. Students measure and graph object length versus shadow length. They also graph shadow length versus the distance an object is from a light source. Students also make a sundial and then model one using a flashlight to reproduce the relative length and position of shadows as they would appear at different times of day. These activities will heighten student awareness of the factors at play in causing shadows to appear and move the way they do.

Now Appearing: A Cast of Shadows!

Students graph the relationship between the length of objects and the length of their shadows. The relationship or ratio of object length to shadow length should be constant. For instance, if the shadow of the shortest stick is 1.5 times the height of the stick, then the shadow of the longest stick should be 1.5 times its height. In fact, the shadow of any object measured at that time should be 1.5 times its height. This results in a straight-line graph that can be used to find the height of an object if the shadow length is known.

Shifting Shadows!

We've designated this activity for take-home use to encourage parental involvement. Feel free, however, to use it in the classroom if you choose. Be sure your paper is wide enough to mark the shadows in the beginning and end of the day. The length you need depends on what time of day and year you do the activity and how tall your stick is. As the day wears on, the sun moves in the sky and the angle of the sun with respect to objects on Earth changes. This changes the length of the shadows. When the sun is low in the sky, the shadows are long. As the sun becomes higher in the sky, the shadows get shorter. As the sun moves from east to west, the shadows move from west to east. Students should be able to create an indoor model of these changes in shadow length and position by using a flashlight and pencil.

Sizing Up Shadows!

In "Now Appearing: A Cast of Shadows!," the shadows were cast by sunlight, whose rays are virtually parallel. But in "Sizing Up Shadows!," the shadows are cast by light spreading out from a bulb. Students see how the shadow size becomes larger as the object gets close to the bulb. Students graph shadow length versus the object's distance from the bulb. Students should try to explain why the shadows grow the way they do.

Meet Some Shady Characters!

Some of the information gained from "Sizing Up Shadows!" can be applied to this activity. As students bring the drawing on the transparency up to the light, the lines on the drawing block the light and make shadows or images on the wall. This is like the pencil in the last activity. As the drawing is brought closer to the light, all the shadows on the wall become bigger. The activity also serves to make students aware that overheads, film, and slides are special uses of shadows.

Super-Size Shadows!

A lunar eclipse occurs when the Earth gets between the sun and the moon. This causes a shadow of the Earth to be cast on the moon. This is the dark area that moves across the moon during a lunar eclipse. In a solar eclipse, the moon gets between the sun and the Earth. This causes a shadow to be cast on the Earth. That's why it can get pretty dark, even on a sunny day, during a full solar eclipse. This shadow of the moon is less than 300 kilometers in diameter, so only a small portion of the Earth is in darkness at any one time.

Activity Answers and Extenders

Now Appearing: A Cast of Shadows!

Step 4: Whether the stick or the shadow of the stick is longer is determined by the height of the sun in the sky. If the sun is less than 45 degrees above the horizon, the shadow will be longer than the stick. In step 7, the graph should be close to a straight line through the origin (0, 0). The end of step 8 introduces the concept of a ratio. If the sun has not moved significantly, the ratio of object length to shadow length is essentially the same for all three objects.

Shifting Shadows!

Step 3: Because the sun moves from east to west in the sky, the shadow of the stick moves in the opposite direction—from west

Unit 32
Shadows

to east. Step 5: The shadow is longest at the earliest and latest time of day, when the sun is the lowest in the sky. The shadow is shortest at the time of day nearest to noon (standard time), when the sun is most directly overhead. Also, if you live at the edge of a time zone, the shortest shadow will be as much as several minutes before or after noon. Step 8: The highest position of the flashlight—modeling the sun at noon—makes the shadow the shortest. The lowest positions of the flashlight—modeling the sun early or late in the day—make the shadow the longest.

Sizing Up Shadows!

Step 4: As the pencil moves farther from the flashlight, the shadow gets smaller. When the pencil is close to the flashlight, the shadow is large. Step 6: The graph shows that each 10 cm change in distance makes a much bigger change in the shadow size when the pencil is close to the light. When the pencil is very close, it blocks a lot of the light from the bulb, so the shadow is large.

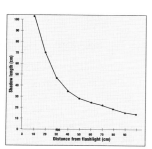

Distance from flashlight (cm)	10	20	30	40	50	60	70	80	90	100
Shadow length (cm)	110	70	47	35	28	24	21	19	15	14

The following diagram shows why the shadow size changes when the pencil is at different distances from the flashlight bulb.

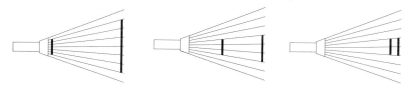

Meet Some Shady Characters!

Step 2: The dark areas you see on the wall block the light from the bulb, so they are shadows of what you drew on the transparency. When the drawing is close to the bulb, the shadow becomes very large.

Super-Size Shadows!

Students may ask why there is not a lunar and a solar eclipse every month, since the moon goes all the way around the Earth every 28 days. If the Earth, moon, and sun all moved in the same plane, there would be a solar and lunar eclipse every month. But the orbit of the moon around the Earth is tilted compared with the orbit of the Earth around the sun. Because the moon and the Earth are orbiting in different planes, there are only two points where the planes intersect, and it is rare for the moon and Earth to be at one of these points at exactly the same time.

NATIONAL SCIENCE EDUCATION STANDARDS

The activities in this unit can be used to support the teaching of the following standards:

✔ Unifying Concepts and Processes

Evidence, Models, and Explanation

Evidence consists of observations and data on which to base scientific explanations. *(All activities)*

Models are tentative schemes or structures that correspond to real objects, events, or classes of events, and that have explanatory power.

   Shifting Shadows!

Constancy, Change, and Measurement

Most things are in the process of becoming different–changing. Changes vary in rate, scale, and pattern, including trends and cycles.

   Now Appearing: A Cast of Shadows!

   Shifting Shadows!

Mathematics is essential for accurately measuring change.

   Now Apperaring: A Cast of Shadows!

   Sizing Up Shadows!

✔ Science as Inquiry

Abilities Necessary to Do Scientific Inquiry

Design and conduct a scientific investigation. *(All activities)*

Use appropriate tools and techniques to gather, analyze, and interpret data.

   Now Appearing: A Cast of Shadows!

   Shifting Shadows!

   Sizing Up Shadows!

Develop descriptions, explanations, predictions, and models using evidence.

   Now Appearing: A Cast of Shadows!

   Shifting Shadows!

   Sizing Up Shadows!

Think critically and logically to make the relationships between evidence and explanations. *(All activities)*

✔ Physical Science

Transfer of Energy

Light interacts with matter by transmission (including refraction), absorption, or scattering (including reflection). *(All activities)*

✔ Earth and Space Science

Earth in the Solar System

Most objects in the solar system are in regular and predictable motion. Those motions explain such phenomena as . . . eclipses.

   Super-Size Shadows!

NAME _____   **DATE** _____

Now Appearing: A Cast of Shadows!

Use the following chart and graph to record and graph your measurements for object and shadow length.

Object	Length of object (in cm)	Length of shadow (in cm)
Meter stick	100 cm	_____
2 meter sticks	200 cm	_____
Your body	_____ cm	_____

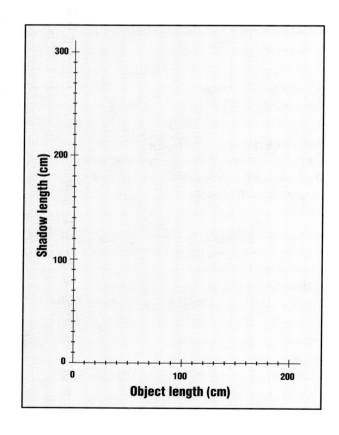

NAME _____   **DATE** _____

Sizing Up Shadows!

Use the following chart and graph to record and graph your measurements for the distance from the flashlight and the shadow length.

Distance from flashlight (cm)	10	20	30	40	50	60	70	80	90	100
Shadow length (cm)										

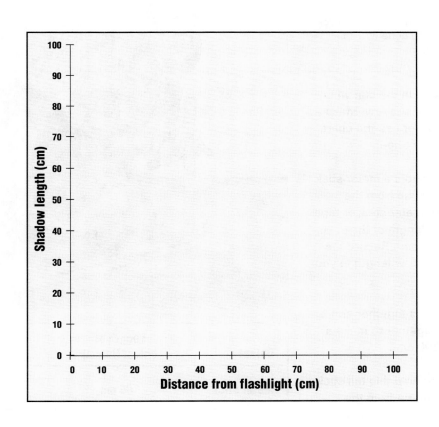

NOW APPEARING:

YOU WILL NEED:

two meter sticks

metric tape measure or another meter stick

tape

a sunny day

a pen or pencil

TEACHER NOTE:
To compare shadows accurately, the three measurements should be done within a 10-minute time period.

1 Find a place outside in the sun where you can make a nice shadow. Make a chart like the one below or use the chart from the Student Activity Sheet.

2 Have your partner hold a meter stick so it points straight up from the ground. Using another meter stick or tape measure, measure the length of the shadow in centimeters (cm). Record the stick length and the shadow length in your chart.

3 Place 2 meter sticks together end-to-end. Tape them together to make a stick 2 meters long (200 cm).

4 Have your partner hold this tall stick so it points straight up from the ground. Mark both ends of the shadow and measure its length. Record the stick length and the shadow length in your chart. Which is longer, the stick or the *shadow* of the stick? Is the answer the same for the shorter stick too?

Can you figure out the height of something by measuring its shadow? In the activity below, you can use measurements of shadows to figure out the height of your partner. Try it and be convinced beyond a shadow of a doubt!

Object	Length of object (in cm)	Length of shadow (in cm)
Meter stick	100 cm	_____
2 meter sticks	200 cm	_____
Your body	_____ cm	_____

A Cast of Shadows!

5 Let's work with the shadow of something else. How about you? Measure the length of your shadow. Now measure your own height, and record the results in your chart. Be sure to use the same *units* (centimeters) that you used when you worked with the sticks.

6 Now plot your results on a graph. Set up the graph like the one below, or use the graph on the Student Activity Sheet.

7 Remember that each pair of numbers in your table (**object length** and **shadow length**) will become one point on the graph. Plot the three points. Draw a line to connect them. How can you describe this line? Is it curved, crooked, straight, wiggly, or something else?

Suppose you measured the length of your partner's shadow. How could you use this measurement and your graph to find the height of your partner? Lets try it!

8 Measure your partner's shadow. Now find this length on the axis marked **shadow length**. Now move across the graph until you hit the line you drew. From this point on the line, move straight down to the axis marked **object length**. This should be your partner's height. Now measure your partner's height and compare. How close did you get?

Just for fun, let's do a little calculating. Divide the length of your shadow into your height. Do the same division for the lengths of the sticks and their shadows. What do you notice about your results?

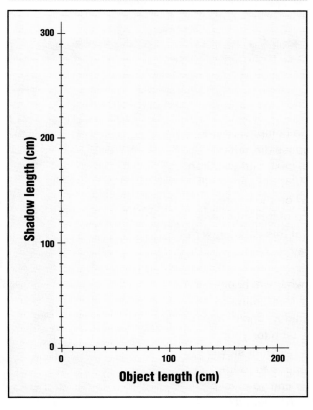

SHIFTING SHADOWS!

You may have noticed that the shadow of an object changes throughout the day. It changes its length and location all day long. By observing these changes and making a model based on them, you can figure out why these changes happen!

YOU WILL NEED:

a sunny spot

a stick (about 30 cm)

paper (2 sheets taped end-to-end)

a pen or pencil

tape

ruler

some stones

compass

flashlight

1 Find a place in the sun where you can lay the paper flat on the ground. Push the stick into the ground so its shadow falls within the paper. Lay some stones on the corners of the paper to keep it in place.

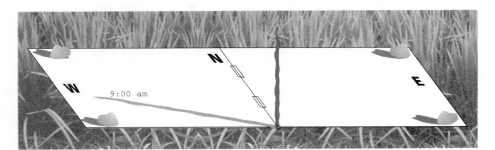

This activity is best started before 10:00 in the morning!

2 Using the compass, mark the compass directions (north, south, east, and west) on your paper. With the pencil, fill in the shadow on the paper to make a record of its length and position. Label this drawing with the time of day.

3 Predict what will happen if you wait 1 or 2 minutes and look at the shadow again. If you can, give a reason for your prediction. Now count slowly to 100. What happened to the shadow? How can you make sense of what happened?

380

…an hour later…

4 Make a new observation of your stick and its shadow. Do this every hour throughout the school day. Fill in the shadow on your paper and label it each time to keep a good record of what happens.

5 At what time of day was the shadow the longest? At what time was it the shortest? How are these different lengths related to where the sun is in the sky? Hint: At what time is the sun the highest in the sky? Would that cause long or short shadows?

Could you use your shadow record to tell time? On the next sunny day, go outside with a compass. Set up your shadow record and stick exactly the way you did before. Observe the shadow and predict the time. Then look at a clock and see if you are right!

JIM WISNIEWSKI

…back in the classroom…

In the picture at right, we marked the length and position of a shadow every hour from 9:00 in the morning until 5:00 at night on April 15 in Los Angeles, California. Let's see if you can use a flashlight to make a model of the way the sun produces changing shadows.

MIKE ROSEN

6 Using the compass, mark the compass directions on another piece of paper. Tape a pencil to the edge of a desk so that it stands straight up at the edge of the paper.

7 Look at the record of the shadows in the picture. How did those shadows change throughout the day? Shine a flashlight down on the pencil. Try moving a flashlight around the pencil to make the same changes.

8 What position of the flashlight makes the shadow the shortest? What time of day is the sun in this position? What position makes the shadow the longest? What time of day is the sun in this position?

JIM WISNIEWSKI

Sizing Up Shadows!

Can you change the size of a shadow? Let's try.

YOU WILL NEED:

flashlight (with reflector covered)
pencil
paper
2 meter sticks
tape

TEACHER NOTE:
The activity will work best if the reflective concave mirror can be removed from behind the flashlight bulb. If it cannot be removed, you can cover the mirror with black tape or with pieces of masking tape and then color the tape black with a marker. This activity requires groups of at least three students working together.

1 Make a chart like the one below or use the chart in the Student Activity Sheet. Use a meter stick to measure 1 meter from the wall. One partner should hold the flashlight and aim it at the wall from this 1-meter distance.

2 Darken the room as much as possible. Another partner should hold a pencil 10 centimeters from the flashlight as shown. Turn on the flashlight and observe the shadow.

3 A third partner should measure the length of the pencil's shadow and record the length in the chart under **10 cm**.

4 Move the pencil to 20 cm away from the flashlight. Measure the shadow and record the length under **20 cm.** Continue to move the pencil 10 cm farther from the flashlight, and measure and record the length of the shadow each time. What did you notice?

5 Now let's plot our results on a graph. Set up the graph like the one to the right, or use the graph in the Student Activity Sheet.

6 Remember that each pair of numbers in your table (**distance from flashlight and shadow length**) will become one point on the graph. Plot your points on the graph. Draw a smooth line to connect them.

What is interesting about the shape of this line? What happens to the size of the shadow as the stick is closer to the flashlight bulb? How about when it is farther away? How can you explain this?

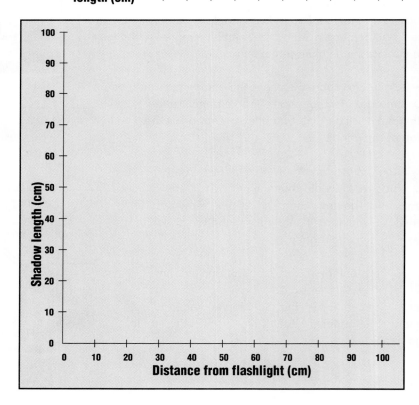

JIM WISNIEWSKI

Distance from flashlight (cm)	10	20	30	40	50	60	70	80	90	100
Shadow length (cm)										

382

Meet Some Shady Characters!

Shadows come in very handy for many different uses. One way we use shadows is to project a word or a picture on a screen. The images we see when light passes through movie film or the transparency on an overhead projector are actually shadows. Try the activity below to see what we mean!

TEACHER PREPARATION:
Cut a transparency in half and then in half again to make 4 equal-size pieces.

YOU WILL NEED:

overhead transparencies

flashlight (with reflector removed or covered)

black transparency marker

large piece of white paper (or several sheets taped together)

crayons or colored markers

tape

1 Use a black marker to draw a person, animal, or other object on your piece of transparency.

2 Darken the room as much as possible. Turn on a flashlight and aim it at a light-colored wall or screen. Hold the transparency in front of the light. Can you see the image of your drawing on the wall? How can you change the size of the image? Try to explain why this image is actually a shadow.

3 Try slowly moving the flashlight or the transparency from side to side or up and down to make your shadow move.

If you had more than one transparency, you could make different characters get bigger and smaller and move in different directions and interact with each other. You could project a shadow play on the wall!

4 Draw a scene on a large piece of paper for the background scenery of your play. The scenery can be a city street, the beach, a park, another planet, or some other setting.

5 Think about the characters and plot of your play. Draw your characters on the transparencies, practice your lines, and then use your transparencies in front of the light to present your play to the class!

JIM WISNIEWSKI

Super-Size Shadows!

Have you ever seen an eclipse?
Eclipses are really shadows!

In an eclipse of the sun, the moon gets between the sun and the Earth. The moon blocks out some of the sun's light, causing a shadow to fall on Earth. When it becomes darker during one of these solar eclipses, it is because a shadow is cast on the Earth. The shadow does not fall on a very large part of the Earth. In fact, the shadow from a solar eclipse is less than 300 kilometers in diameter.

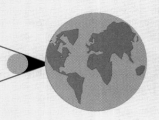

In an eclipse of the moon, it's the Earth that gets between the sun and the moon. The Earth blocks some of the sun's light, causing a shadow to fall on the moon. This is why the moon gets darker during a lunar eclipse.

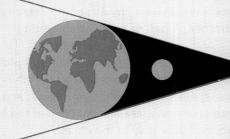

APPENDIX:
Safety in the Elementry (K-6) Science Classroom*

Introduction

Science is safe as long as teachers and students are aware of potential hazards and take necessary and appropriate precautions and safety measures. If students can take the responsibility of being safety conscious, they will be better prepared for safely dealing with materials in their everyday lives as well as in future science courses.

Objectives

1. To make teachers aware of the potential hazards that exist in an elementary science classroom

2. To help teachers organize their classes so that injuries can be prevented

3. To help teachers evaluate safety aspects of an experiment or science activity and become aware of hazards that may exist

4. To make students aware of the importance of safety in the classroom

Safety through Organization

Many potential hazards can be eliminated if the teacher has an organized approach to the activity. To do this, the teacher needs first to perform the experiment prior to assigning it to the students. Then, as a result of the prior performance, the teacher will be familiar with the activity, will have the materials ready to distribute to the students, will be ready to supervise the activities of the students, will have a plan for collecting materials after the activity, and will be able to instruct the students in what is expected of them.

Helpful suggestions can be found in several resources. The teacher's edition of the textbook being used should have safety information on the activities. The state department of education should have publications available to assist with matters of safety and disposal. Many science supply houses, such as Flinn Scientific, have safety and disposal publications available. Experts are available through organizations such as the American Chemical Society, the Institute for Chemical Education, the Laboratory Safety Workshop, the National Association of Biology Teachers, and the National Science Teachers Association. If a college or university is nearby, members of the science faculty are usually willing to assist in safety matters. (Addresses and telephone numbers of the organizations listed here are given at the end of this section.)

Eye and Personal Protection

1. Teachers and students should always wear chemical-splashproof safety goggles when working with chemicals. Child-sized goggles are available from science materials suppliers.

2. Safety goggles should also be worn by the teacher and students when there is a possibility of flying objects or projectiles, such as when working with rubber bands.

*Adapted from *Safety in the Elementary (K-6) Science Classroom*, published by the Committee on Chemical Safety, American Chemical Society, 1155 Sixteenth Street NW, Washington, DC 20036. Photoduplication of this appendix is encouraged. Please give proper credit to the American Chemical Society.

3. Safety goggles used by more than one person should be sterilized between uses. One possible method of sterilization is to immerse the goggles in diluted laundry bleach followed by thorough rinsing and drying.

4. Proper precautions must be taken when using sharp objects such as knives, scalpels, compasses with sharp points, needles, and pins.

5. Students should not clean up broken glass. Teachers should use a broom and dustpan without touching the broken glass. Broken glass must be disposed of in a manner to prevent cuts or injury to the teacher, students, and custodial staff.

6. The teacher may decide to wear a laboratory apron or smock to prevent soiling or damage to clothing; if so, students should be similarly attired.

7. When working with hot materials, noxious plants, or live animals, appropriate hand protection should be worn.

8. The teacher and students should wash their hands upon completion of any experimental activity or at the end of the instructional session.

Fire and Heating Safety

1. Teachers should never leave the room while a flame is lighted or any other heat source is in use.

2. Never heat flammable liquids. Heat only water or water solutions.

3. Use only glassware made from borosilicate glass (Kimax or Pyrex) for heating.

4. When working around a heat source, tie back long hair and secure loose clothing.

5. The area surrounding a heat source should be clean and have no combustible materials nearby.

6. When using a hot plate, locate it so that a child cannot pull it off the worktop or trip over the power cord.

7. Never leave the room while the hot plate is plugged in, whether or not it is in use; never allow students near an in-use hot plate if the teacher is not immediately beside the students.

8. Be certain hot plates have been unplugged and are cool before handling. Check for residual heat by placing a few drops of water on the hot plate surface.

9. Never use alcohol burners.

10. Students should use candles only under the strict supervision of the teacher. Candles should be placed in a "drip pan" such as an aluminum pie plate large enough to contain the candle if it is knocked over.

11. The teacher should know the location of a fire extinguisher nearest the activity area and be trained in its use.

12. The teacher should know what to do in case of fire. If a school policy does not exist, check with local fire officials for information.

Dangerous Materials and Procedures

1. Use only safety matches. Even safety matches should be used only with direct teacher supervision.

2. Use only nonmercury thermometers. Mercury from broken thermometers is difficult to clean up, and the vapors from spilled mercury are dangerous. Remember that thermometers are fragile; supervise their handling to prevent occurrences such as a thermometer being used as a stirring rod or placed so it could roll off the edge of a table.

3. Store batteries with at least one terminal covered with tape. Batteries exhibiting any corrosion should be discarded. Because the contents of batteries are potentially hazardous, batteries should not be cut open or taken apart. Check to see if batteries can be recycled in your area.

4. Never tell, encourage, or allow students to place any materials in or near their mouth, nose, or eyes.

5. Make sure that all materials used in your science activities are approved by your school or district safety guidelines. Materials to be used may include household chemicals. Before using household chemicals or other materials, study the label carefully to learn the hazards and precautions associated with such materials. Similarly, study the labels of chemicals purchased from a scientific supply house. The commercial suppliers of laboratory chemicals will furnish Material Safety Data Sheets (MSDSs), which describe the hazards and precautions for such materials in detail. These MSDSs must be on file in the school district office, and copies must be available in the classroom.

6. Do not touch "dry ice" (solid carbon dioxide) with the bare skin. Always wear cotton or insulated gloves when handling dry ice. Do not store or place dry ice in a sealed container.

7. Liquid spills may be slippery. Clean up any spill immediately and properly as soon as it occurs. Follow the cleanup instructions given on the label or the MSDS for the substance.

8. Do not mix or use chemicals in any manner other than as stated in the approved procedure. At no time should a teacher undertake a new procedure without prior and full investigation of the chemical and physical properties of the materials to be used, and of the outcomes of the proposed procedures. When planning to undertake a new procedure, it is a good practice to consult with a professional who is familiar with the potential problems of the new procedure.

Safety with Plants

1. Wash hands after working with seeds and plants. Many store-bought seeds have been coated with insecticides and/or fertilizers.

2. Never put seeds or plants in the mouth.

3. Do not handle seeds or plants if there are cuts or sores on the hands.

4. Some 700 species of plants are known to cause death or illness. Be aware of plants in the local area that are harmful. For more information, contact the local county agricultural agent.

5. Be aware of the signs of plant poisoning and act quickly if a student exhibits such signs after a lesson. Symptoms may include one or more of the following: headache, nausea, dizziness, vomiting, skin eruption, itching or other skin irritation.

6. Be particularly alert to plant safety on field trips.

Safety with Animals

1. All handling of animals by students must be done voluntarily and only under immediate teacher supervision.

2. Students should not be allowed to mishandle or mistreat animals.

3. A safety lesson should be given to teach the students how to care for and treat the animal. This safety lesson should be given before the animal is brought into the classroom.

4. Animals caught in the wild should not be brought into the classroom. For example, turtles are carriers of salmonella, and many wild animals are subject to rabies.

5. On field trips or other outdoor activities with potential exposure to wild animals, be aware of the danger of rabies exposure. Also be aware of potential hazards of insect bites such as bee stings of allergic individuals or diseases spread by ticks or fleas.

6. At no time should dissection be done on an animal corpse unless it was specifically purchased for that purpose from a reliable supplier.

7. Any animal species that has been preserved in formaldehyde should not be used.

Emergency Procedures

1. Establish emergency procedures for at least the following: emergency first aid, electric shock, chemical spills, poisoning, burns, fire, evacuations, and animal bites.

2. Evaluate each experimental procedure in advance of classroom use so that plans may be made in advance to handle possible emergencies.

3. Be sure that equipment and supplies needed for foreseen emergencies are available in or near the classroom.

4. Establish procedures for the notification of appropriate authorities and response agencies in the event of an emergency.

Disposal

Except for the disposal procedures described in the textbook in use, it is not likely that any of the wastes generated in elementary science activities will be harmful to the environment. If the teacher has any questions concerning waste disposal, the science supervisor for the school or school district should be consulted.

Safety Awareness of Students

Safety instructions should begin at the earliest possible age. Students can begin to learn the importance of safety in the classroom, laboratory, and life in general at the elementary school level. The teacher must set the rules, but the teacher should explain to the students why the rules are necessary. The students must also realize that any student who does not follow the rules will lose the privilege of taking part in the fun, hands-on activities.

To reinforce the rules, you may encourage the students to discuss them. One activity could be a poster contest. The winning posters could be displayed in the room and used throughout the year to stress safety and enforce the safety rules.

General Safety Rules for Students

Always review with the students the general safety rules prior to the beginning of an activity.

1. Never do any experiment without the approval and direct supervision of your teacher.

2. Always wear your safety goggles when your teacher tells you to do so. Never remove your goggles during an activity.

3. Know the location of all safety equipment in or near your classroom. Never play with the safety equipment.

4. Tell your teacher immediately if an accident occurs.

5. Tell your teacher immediately if a spill occurs.

6. Tell your teacher immediately about any broken, chipped, or scratched glassware so that it may be properly cleaned up and disposed of.

7. Tie back long hair and secure loose clothing when working around flames.

8. If instructed to do so, wear your laboratory apron or smock to protect your clothing.

9. Never assume that anything that has been heated is cool. Hot glassware looks just like cool glassware.

10. Never taste anything during a laboratory activity. If an investigation involves tasting, it will be done in the cafeteria.

11. Clean up your work area upon completion of your activity.

12. Wash your hands with soap and water upon completion of an activity.

Resources

American Chemical Society
Chemical Health and Safety
   Referral Service
1155 Sixteenth Street NW
Washington, DC 20036
(800) 227-5558

Institute for Chemical Education
University of Wisconsin
Department of Chemistry
1101 University Avenue
Madison, WI 53706
(608) 262-3033

Laboratory Safety Workshop
101 Oak Street
Wellesley, MA 02186
(617) 237-1335

National Association of Biology Teachers
1150 Roger Bacon Drive, No. 19
Reston, VA 22090-5202
(703) 471-1134

National Science Teachers Association
1840 Wilson Boulevard
Arlington, VA 22201
(703) 243-7100

Disclaimer

The materials contained in this appendix have been compiled by recognized authorities from sources believed to be reliable and to represent the best opinions on the subject. This appendix is intended to serve only as a starting point for good practices and does not purport to specify minimal legal standards or to represent the policy of the American Chemical Society or Wadsworth/Thomson Learning. No warranty, guarantee, or representation is made by the American Chemical Society or Wadsworth/Thomson Learning as to the accuracy or sufficiency of the information contained herein, and the society and publisher assume no responsibility in connection therewith. This is intended to provide basic guidelines for safe practices. Therefore, it cannot be assumed that all necessary warning and precautionary measures are contained in this document and that other or additional information or measures may not be required. Users of this book should consult pertinent local, state, and federal laws and legal counsel prior to initiating any safety program.

ACTIVITY INDEX:
The Best of WonderScience, Volume I

Section 1: Science Process Skills

Unit 1: Estimating

Estimate—Investigate!   Investigate different methods of making an estimate   2–3

Quicker Than the Count   Discover a tool used by scientists to make estimates   4

How Many Books? Just Take a Look!   Practice estimating the number of books on a shelf and pages in a book   5

The Long and Short of It   Estimate the length of a shoelace when it is laced and tied   6

Time Flies—When You're Having Fun!   Estimate the time it takes you to lace your shoe   7

Picture-Perfect (Almost) Estimates   Discover another common method used to make estimates   8

Unit 2: Measuring

How Do You Measure Up?   Compare the accuracy of ancient measuring methods to today's method   10–11

Measurement Matters!   Learn about the modern metric system and how it was developed   12

Going Round in Circles   Discover a way to easily measure the distance of a crooked path   13

Measurement: The Long and Short of It!   Learn how to measure objects such as a skyscraper without a ruler   14–15

Picture Yourself a Ruler!   Try estimating a measurement and see how close you get   16

Unit 3: Designing Structures

WS Construction Challenge   Design and build your own model bridge   18–19

There's No Place Like Home!   Learn how climate and geography affect the design of a home   20

Reach for the Sky   Build a model skyscraper and then test it in a windstorm   21

Beam Me Up!   Investigate how beams are used in building to support the most weight   21

The Mighty Dome!   Test some eggshell domes for strength   22

An Unusual Home . . . A Geodesic Dome!   Construct a model geodesic dome, a lightweight but very strong structure   23

Animal Architects   Explore some animal architecture with three fun puzzles   24

Unit 4: Inventing

It's Time to Invent!   Make your own timer and plan how you could invent your own clock   26–27

Invention: What's New?   Learn about inventing and about some historical inventions   28

Invent-a-Jet   Use the hints given, then design your own jet propulsion vehicle   29

Let's Hear It for Inventions!   Create a device for communication and then see if you can invent one   30

Another Bright Idea   Devise your own electrical device and use it to make other inventions   31

Your Imagination Creation!   Study the examples given, then invent your own door knocker or pancake flipper   32

Unit 5: Investigating the Unseen

It's in the Bag!   Investigate things you can't see by hearing, touching, smelling, and tasting   34–35

Clue in to the Unknown   Discover how scientists learn about places and things they can't see   36

Probing Possibilities!   Observe an object by using a probe   37

Accelerators: They're Smashing!   Make your own accelerator to observe a hidden object   38–39

Quark Quest   Find out how a real accelerator studies the tiny particles of an atom   39

The Inside Story!   Use your senses to observe things you can't see   40

Section 2: Science and Recreation

Unit 6: Science of the Playground

WS Playground Challenge   Hypothesize and experiment with objects sliding down a sliding board   42–43

Playing with Physics!   Learn about physics on a playground   44

Spin Out!   Discover the force created by the circular motion of a merry-go-round   45

A Swinging Good Time!   Study the motion of a pendulum by using a swing   46

Oh Say Can You Seesaw!   Investigate balance using a seesaw   47

A New Twist!   Explore the motion of a spinning object using a swing   48

Unit 7: Physics of Baseball

A New Spin on Throwing a Curve!   Investigate how to make a spinning ball curve in different directions   50–51

Let's Play Ball!   Learn how much science there is in the sport of baseball   52

Batter Up!   Measure your reaction time to see if you are quick enough to be a batter   53

Catch That Fly!   Test your reaction time and see if you can shorten it with practice   54

Go the Distance   Discover why players crouch down, feet spread apart and knees bent   55

A Sports Spectacular!   Try creating a new and different sport   56

Unit 8: Chemistry in Art

The Dilution Solution!   Discover how the diluting and mixing of different paints affects them   58–59

Get Smart . . . With the Chemistry of Art!   Learn more about the chemicals   60
and chemistry used to create artwork

Become an Art Master . . . With the Power of Plaster!   Use some chemistry   61
to create a sculpture

Picture This!   See how photography uses chemistry   61

Vegetable Dyes—They're Hard to "Beet"!   Use the colorful chemicals in   62
vegetables as a fabric dye

WS Mystery Art!   Create some unique art using the properties of water and wax   63

Pick the Right Paint for your Palette   Experiment to find the best kind of   64
paint for the surface to be painted

Unit 9: Toys in Space

Space Hoppers   Make some toy grasshoppers and predict how they would hop   66–67
in space

That Freefall Feeling   Learn why astronauts and their objects float around in   68
space

The Astronauts' Toy Box   Predict how marbles, a ball and jacks, and yo-yos   69
would act in space

Cosmic Catch!   Create your own cosmic ball-and-cup toy   70

Out of This World Boomerang!   Explore flight patterns of a boomerang and   71
predict its flight without gravity

Space Waves?   Hypothesize about how liquids would behave in orbit   72

Section 3: Science and Technologies

Unit 10: Soaps and Detergents

If Cleaning is Urgent . . . Use Soap or Detergent   Compare the cleaning action   74–75
of some different soaps and detergents

Get the Real Dirt on Soap and Detergent   Learn how soap is made and why   76
it is such a good cleaner

Which Mixture is the Best Mixer?   Discover which soap or detergent allows   77
oil and water to mix the best

Totally Sudsational . . . Dude!   Experiment to see which soap or detergent is   78
the sudsiest

To Bubble or Not to Bubble, That is the Question   Investigate how added   79
chemicals can affect soaps and detergents

The Fate of Phosphate   Learn what phosphates are and why they were a   79
problem in detergents

A Total Washout?   Explore the effects of fresh water versus saltwater on soaps   80
and detergents

Unit 11: Bubbles

Bubbles Blowers   Blow bubbles through a variety of blowers   82–83

Bubble Mania!   Learn the answers to all of your questions about bubbles   84

It's a Frame-Up!   Discover a way to make bubbles shaped like a triangular   85
prism or a cube

Don't Burst My Bubble!   See how long different kinds of bubbles last   86

A Bagful of Bubbles!   Create some bubbles with an unusual shape   87

Double Bubbles   Try blowing a bubble inside a bubble   87

Hoop It Up!   Get inside a bubble yourself and see what its like   88

Bubbles Aloft!   See who can keep a soap bubble floating the longest without touching it   88

Unit 12: Lubricants

Let's Lube-a-Cube!   Race against time as you compare different lubricants   90–91

Slip Sliding Away!   Learn what makes a good lubricant and about the many uses of lubricants   92

Thick or Thin—Who Will Win?   Experiment to find out which lubricant is the most viscous   93

From Here to There . . .   Discover how air can be used as a lubricant   94

Test Your Aim . . . With a graphite Game!   Use a lubricant on your fingers to compete in this fun tossing game   95

Lip and Leafy Lubricants   Investigate how lubricants can prevent drying   96

Synovial Fluid—Your Super Lubricant!   Find out about a very special lubricant in your own body   96

Unit 13: Adhesives

Make Your Own Sticky-o-Meter!!   Construct a tool to measure the stickiness of a substance   98–99

Sticking to the Basics   Learn about adhesives and how they work   100

Today's Tape—Tremendous and Terrific, But Tacky   Test some different tapes to see which one is the stickiest   101

Adhesives   Create an adhesives poster with paste and glue you make   102

On Target with Adhesives!   Make a fun adhesives board game and challenge your partner to play   102

Make a Hit with Piñatas   Create a beautiful work of art with an adhesive you mix up   103

Tricky Sticky Riddles   Match up creatures that use adhesives with fun descriptive riddles   104

Unit 14: Fibers and Fabrics

Fibers to Thread—A New Twist!   Test different types of fibers to see which one makes the strongest thread   106–107

Fabulous Fibers Form Fantastic Fabrics   Learn about different types of fibers and their useful qualities   108

What a Mesh!   Discover how the weave of a fiber affects its qualities   109

Wear and Tear—The "Hole" Truth   Explore fabric durability by examining wear and tear of fabrics   110

Drip Busters!   Investigate the absorbency of different fibers   111

From Diapers . . . to Denim!   Predict which fabric would be best for a firefighter, football player, or baby   112

Section 4: Water

Unit 15: Properties of Water

Water Drops Unite!   Investigate how water sticks to itself and to other surfaces   114

Racedrop Raceway!   Race against time to see how skilled a water-drop driver you are   115

Water, Water Everywhere . . .   Learn all about the amazing properties of water   116

Solving Dissolving   Discover how the temperature of water affects its ability to dissolve sugar   117

Ice of a Different Color   See if water freezes the same way when salt or sugar is dissolved in it   118

Water: From H to O   Explore water's surface tension, capillarity, and electricity   119

Wondering about Water   Write a short story—Wandering in a Way-Out World of Whimsical Water   120

Unit 16: Surface Tension

Surfin' Surface Tension   Make some miniature water skiers that use surface tension to stay afloat   122–123

Water's Secret "Skin"   Learn what causes water's surface to form a "skin"   124

How to Give Pepper Some Pep!   Discover what detergent does to water's surface tension   125

Putting Your Two Cents In!   Challenge your partner to a water surface tension contest   125

Water Walking—They Take It In Stride   Read about amazing insects that walk on water   126

Dish Detergent Dynamos!   Explore the effects of detergent on surface tension   127

Great Strides in Poetry—Water Strider Limericks   Try a limerick puzzle about water striders   128

Unit 17: Capillarity

Soak Those Sharks!   Test the capillary action of different materials   130–131

What's Up with Capillarity   Find out how capillary action works   132

The Return of the Sharks!   Graph and compare the capillary action of materials   133

Celery Climb   Measure the capillary action in celery and graph your results   134

Soggy Socks!   Use capillary action to filter clear water from muddy water   135

A Day at Capillarity Park   Identify as many examples of capillary action as you can in the picture   136

Unit 18: Evaporation and Condensation

Water, Water, Everywhere   Use evaporation and condensation to make fresh water from salt water   138–139

Evaporation and Condensation—The Dynamic Duo!   Learn how and why liquids evaporate and condense   140

Lose Some Weight—Evaporate!   Test two liquids and see which one evaporates faster   141

Dew Drop Inn   Conduct an experiment to study a common problem—wet windows   142

Frosty the Snow Can   Observe the changing of a gas into a solid   143

Earth Day   Find out about the history of Earth Day and some ways to celebrate   143
it

Evaporation—A Paint Sensation!   Make two different kinds of paint and see   144
which one dries fastest

Section 5: Food Science

Unit 19: Food Nutrients

Get the Facts on Fats!   Experiment to learn about the properties of fats   146–147

Food: What's in It for You?   Learn how the important chemicals in food work   148
in your body

Starch Search!   Test for the presence of this major nutrient in food   149

Proteins: Your Pro Team!   Investigate the protein that makes up cartilage and   150–151
tendons

Fact or Fable? Read the Label!   Read food labels to see the nutrients contained   152
in the food you eat

Unit 20: Calcium

A Plaster Master or a Plaster Disaster?   Experiment with the hardening   154–155
quality of calcium in plaster of paris

Calcium—The Hard Facts   Learn about calcium's many different uses and   156
how it likes other chemicals

The Fate of Calcium Carbonate!   Discover what eggshells and bones would   157
be like without calcium

Calcium—The Game   Play this fun board game and learn all about calcium at   158–159
the same time

Hard Water—Bubble Trouble?   Investigate the properties of water that   160
contains lots of calcium

Unit 21: Food Additives

Through Thick or Thin   Compare two common food thickeners   162–163

Food Additives: Let's Sum It Up!   Learn about the history, purposes, and   164
health risks of food additives

A Coloring Conundrum   Experiment with adding color to food   165

Foiling Spoiling   Discover how some common chemicals can slow down food   166
spoilage

Flavorings: Let Your Taste Buds Blossom   Explore the effects of different   167
flavorings added to foods

WonderScience **Chef of the Future**   Combine all the different kinds of food   168
additives to make a tasty dessert

Unit 22: Soda Pop Science

Be A *WonderScience* **Fizz Whiz!**   Explore the fizzing phenomena of   170–171
carbonated soda

The Science of Soda!   Learn about the chemicals that go into carbonated soda   172

Racin' Raisins!   Challenge your partner to a raisin race through soda   173

All Shook Up!   Shake a soda and then measure the volume of gas given off   174

How Sweet It Is!   Perform a simple test to tell whether soda contains sugar or an artificial sweetener   175

Sour Power!   Investigate the chemicals in soda using an indicator   176

Section 6: Materials Science

Unit 23: Polymers

It's in the Bag!   Test and compare two types of bags, one natural and the other artificial   178–179

Surrounded by Polymers!   Everything you ever wanted to know about natural and artificial polymers   180

It's a Sticky Subject   Create glue from some food polymers   181

WonderScientist **Inventors**   Readers' solutions to the WonderScientist Challenge   182

The Recipe for a Great Inventor!   An interview with a chemist who invents new materials   182

From Moo to Glue   Make glue from a polymer (protein) found in milk   183

In Search of Polymers   See how many polymers you can spot in the picture   183

Polymer Triathlon   Experiment to see how natural and artificial polymers are alike/different   184

Unit 24: Plastics

Which Plastic Is Most Fantastic?   Test and compare three different kinds of plastic   186–187

Plastics: Breaking Out of the Mold   Learn how plastic is made and why it is so useful   188

A *WonderScience* **Incrediblob!**   Use chemistry to make your own plastic ball   189

Recycling: The Shape of Things to Come!   Recycle a plastic for another use   190–191

A Plastics Breakthrough!   Do this amazing trick using the flexibility and moldability of plastic   192

Unit 25: Rubber

Get a Grip!   Test the traction of different materials to find the best for a pair of shoes   194–195

Make Tracks with Rubber!   Learn about the different kinds of rubber and their many uses   196

A Stampede!   Investigate the properties of rubber that make it useful in printing   197

Rubber Band Racer!   Build a fun racing toy using the ability of rubber to store energy   198

A *WonderScience* **Boing Bat!**   Make a fun toy while exploring the bounciness of rubber   199

Rubber Is Amazing—Get the Point?   Experiment with rubber's amazing elastic qualities   200

Unit 26: Metals

Corrosion—Metals' Chemical Enemy!   Experiment to see which metals and what conditions cause rusting   202–203

You Deserve a Metal!   Read about the properties of metals that make them so useful   204

Shape Up with Metal Malleability! Be a sculptor of metals using their malleability — 205

Magnetism and Metals—Maybe Yes, Maybe No Test a variety of metal objects for magnetism — 206

Metals in Music—They're Instrumental! Make beautiful music with metals — 207

Metals Can Be Hot Stuff! Investigate the ability of a metal to conduct heat — 207

Metals Are Electrifying! Use metal as an electrical conductor to light up a bulb — 208

Unit 27: Insulation

Cold or Hot—Insulation Helps a Lot! Test different substances to see which one is the best insulator — 210–211

Insulation Learn all about the different kinds of insulators — 212

Heat's In—You Win! Use a model of a heated house to find out where heat is lost — 213

Cool Ways to Stay Warm! Discover how fat and air can serve as insulators — 214–215

Insulation: Nature's a Natural See how humans copy nature in this puzzle on insulation — 216

Unit 28: Recycling

The Great Divide! Use static electricity as a way to separate materials for recycling — 218–219

Be "Resource-Full": Recycle! Learn about the importance and methods of recycling — 220

Instant Re-Ply! Discover how to recycle paper — 221

Be a *WonderScience* Re-cycler! Think of some new uses for old things by playing this fun game — 222

Filtering: Slow and Steady wins the Rose Investigate ways that water can be purified for reuse — 223

The Truth about Trash Some interesting trash facts — 224

Recycling—It's a Natural Find out how nature recycles its resources — 224

Section 7: Physical Changes

Unit 29: Chemical Particles

Chemical Detectives Observe how different food chemicals dissolve in water — 226–227

Now You See Them . . . Now You Don't! Construct a balloon model to demonstrate dissolving — 228

Chem-Mystery Solve the case of the pooped balloons — 229

No Leaks Chemical engineer solves the problem of droopy helium balloons — 231

Particle Carnival A potpourri of particle activities — 232

Unit 30: Density

Density Dilemma Test different objects to see whether they will float or sink in water — 234–235

Dateline: Density Learn what density is and why some objects float while others sink — 236

Density Tower Experiment with liquids of different density — 237

How Dense Can It Be?   Calculate the density of a stick of butter   238

The Stubborn Aquarium   Use your knowledge of density to set up a new   239
aquarium

Density Dessert   Make and enjoy a delicious density treat   240

Unit 31: Mixtures

Master a Mixing Mystery!   Try mixing together a variety of different liquids   242–243

Get the Mixture Picture!   Learn what a mixture is and how scientists separate 244
them

Candy Chromatography!   Separate the substances used to color candy by   245
chromatography

A Soapy Separation!   Explore how some mixtures can be separated by adding   246
other chemicals

A *WonderScience* Centrifuge!   Discover another way to separate mixtures—by   247
spinning them

Inflate and Separate!   Separate the carbon dioxide gas from carbonated soda   248

Unit 32: More Mixtures

Mixable Unmixables   Experiment with liquids that don't mix   250–251

Detecting Dispersions   An explanation of how emulsions stay mixed   252

A Real Chemistry Brainteaser   Investigate the effects of detergent on mix-   253
tures of oil and water

Mix Tricks   Explore how stabilizers work on unmixable liquids   254

The Chemistry of Color Film   Learn how colors are produced in a color   255
photograph

The Search for Dispersions   A word search all about dispersions   255

Food for Thought   Recipes for some tasty emulsions in the kitchen   256

Unit 33: Diffusion

Molecules on the Move!   Observe the effects of temperature on the movement   258–259
of molecules

Diffusion: Movin' on Out!   Learn how odors move through the air in this   260
explanation of diffusion

Sweet, Sweeter, Sweetest . . .   Use your taste buds to test how fast sugar   261
diffuses in water

The Case of the Missing Bananas   Help find some missing bananas using   262
your knowledge of diffusion

Colliding Clouds of Color!   Compare the movement of food coloring   263
molecules in hot and cold water

What Is That Cologne You're Wearing?   Find out how perfumes are made   263
and why their scent doesn't last forever

Diffusion Designs   Use diffusion to make some pretty designs   264

Unit 34: Crystals

A Closer Look at Crystals   Observe shape and dissolving properties of some   266–267
common crystals

Let's Make This Crystal Clear!   Learn how crystals get their unique and   268
beautiful shapes

Table Salt Crystals   Construct a crystal model and then grow some real crystals   269

The Many Facets of Crystals   Discover the many different uses of crystals   270

Captain Ice . . . Commander Expander!   Investigate how ice is different   271
from other crystals

Crystals and Ice Cream Just Don't Mix   Make your own ice cream and taste   272
the difference crystals can make

Section 8: Chemical Changes

Unit 35: Chemicals and Chemical Reactions

Become a *WonderScience* Chemist . . .   Identify the chemical with the most   274–275
acid through chemical reactions

Celebrate National Chemistry Week!   Discover the many ways you can   276
celebrate National Chemistry Week

Solve a *WonderScience* Mix-Tery   Perform chromatography to separate   277
chemicals in a mixture

Chemistry Can Be Gobs Of Fun!   Mix up your own fun chemical gob   278

Carbon Dioxide . . . What a Gas!   Use an indicator solution to test for carbon   279
dioxide gas

Do These Liquids "Stack" Up?   Investigate a way to make water float on top   280
of water

Unit 36: More Chemical Reactions

Lose the Indicator Blues!   Use indicators to detect that a chemical reaction has   282–283
occurred

Chemical Reactions: The Main Attraction   Learn about some common   284
chemical reactions

Liquids to Lumps!   Observe a chemical reaction in which two liquids produce   285
a solid

Heat Up to Some Cool Reactions!   Experiment with chemical reactions that   286–287
absorb and release heat

A Gas Sudsation!   Discover a chemical reaction that produces a gas   288

Unit 37: Acids and Bases

Indicator Indi-gator   Observe chemicals that change color when other   290–291
chemicals are present

Plants with a Plus   Learn about chemical indicators found in plants   292

Inside Indicators   Use an acid and a base to test petals that contain chemical   293
indicators

ChemMystery   Solve the case of The Petal Puzzler   294

Lose the Red Cabbage Blues   Test for carbonic acid using cabbage leaves   295

Tim Clark—Water Analyst   Discover how one chemist uses indicators on the   296
job

Be an Investi-gator   Experiment with other flowers and juices that contain   296
indicators

Unit 38: Plant Chemistry

Be an Indicator Investigator!   Use plant chemicals to make indicators that   298–299
detect other chemicals

Plant Chemicals: They're Plantastic! Learn about the many uses for   300
chemicals found in plants

Starch: A Popular and Plentiful . . . Test for starch in various foods that   301
come from plants

Plant Parts: Common Scents . . . Experience the different scents and tastes   302
that come from plant parts

Plant Stems—Totally Tubular! Investigate the special way in which plants   303
drink water

A Plant Panorama! Identify all the things that come from plants in this typical   304
house

Unit 39: Carbon Dioxide

Fizz-Bubble Pop! Make carbon dioxide gas by mixing different substances   306–307

Seeing is Not Always Believing Learn how to detect the presence of carbon   308
dioxide

Out of Sight, But Not out Of . . . Brainstorming exercise: how to observe   308
something invisible

Fast Get-Aways Test the effects of temperature on carbon dioxide gas   309

Chem-Mystery Solve the case of the plastic that gives   310

Pumping Plastic Learn about a special plastic developed to hold carbon   311
dioxide

Gas Gallery Do some gas-boating, gas-painting, and gas dancing, all with CO_2 312

Section 9: Earth and Space Science

Unit 40: Rocks

Let's Rock! Compare different rock samples by performing some simple tests   314–315

Rocks around the Clock! Discover the many uses of rocks and the materials   316
that come from rocks

Panning for Gold! Try your hand at "panning" for gold like the miners did in   317
the gold rush

Japanese Garden! Use the beauty of rocks to create your own miniature   318
Japanese garden

Fabricate Some Fabulous Fossils! Investigate how fossils form by creating   319
your own

Rocks and Their Roles! Identify all the items made from rocks in the illustra-   320
tion

Unit 41: Earthquakes

Earthquake City! Design a city and then test its ability to withstand earth-   322–323
quakes

Curious about Quakes? Read up on earthquakes   324

Shake, Rattle . . . and Record! Make your own seismograph to detect earth-   325
quakes

Earthquakes: the Mercalli Tally Discover how earthquakes are rated on the   326
Mercalli scale

Quake Quest! Learn how scientists locate the epicenter of an earthquake   327

Earthquake Hazard Hunt   Identify the earthquake hazards present in a typical living room | 328

Unit 42: Weather

Be a Weather Watcher!   Make weather observations—measure rainfall, temperature, and windspeed | 330–331

Weather—You Like It or Not!   Learn all about meteorology, the study of weather | 332

Swirl & Twirl   Make your own model of a tornado | 333

Humidity—Don't Sweat It!   Measure relative humidity with a thermometer | 334

A Jarometer Barometer!   Explore atmospheric pressure with a barometer you make | 335

Wild Weather Wonders!   Enjoy some fascinating wild weather trivia | 336

Unit 43: Solar Energy

Warm Up to Your *WS* Solar Greenhouse   Build your own solar greenhouse and then test it | 338–339

Solar Energy   Discover how the sun's energy can be used in many different ways | 340

Soaking Up the Rays   Make a solar collector and see how well it soaks up the sun's energy | 341

Solar—Power Plants!   Use a solar greenhouse to see how plants use the sun's energy | 342

Be a Sun-Sational Chef!   Try cooking marshmallows using a solar cooker you make | 343

Solar Energy Maze   Trace the path of energy from the sun to a pencil | 344

Unit 44: Solar System

Scaling the Solar System!   Build model of the solar system to scale | 346

Planet Quest!   Use the clues given to identify the mystery planets | 347

Space Trek!   Travel the solar system with this fun board game | 348–349

Sun-Sational Shadows!   Track the rotation of the sun by observing shadows | 350

Moon Diary   Learn about the moon by keeping your own moon observation diary | 351

Space Voyager!   See how scientists use the space probe *Voyager II* to study the planets | 351

Be a *WS* Crater Creator!   Investigate how a crater forms by creating one yourself | 352

Unit 45: Stars and Constellations

Search for the Stars!   Discover the science of star gazing—try identifying some constellations | 354–355

Be a Backyard Astronomer!   Learn how to study the stars . . . without any equipment | 356

Canned Constellations   Make a set of constellation viewers to enjoy the stars any time of day | 357

Count Your Lucky Stars!   Approximate the number of stars in the sky using a method called sampling | 358

Constellations: Another Point of View   Build a 3-D model of a constellation   359
and see how it looks in space

Hercules: The Constellation and the Myth   Learn how constellations came   360
from myths and then create your own

Section 10: Energy

Unit 46: Energy

Energy to Go!   Discover and identify the different forms of energy   362–363

Go for the Glow!   Build a light bulb that uses electrical energy from a battery   364
to light up

The Hot Spot!   Observe an energy conversion—from mechanical to heat and   365
back again

Energy—It's All in the Cards!   Play an energy conversion card game   366–367

More Conversion Diversions!   Experiment with two more energy-converting   368
activities

Unit 47: Static Electricity

Make a Balloon Ec-Static Today!   Charge a balloon with static electricity and   370–371
see what happens

Static Electricity   Learn what causes static electricity   372

The Great Electron Rip-Off   Investigate the behavior of static electricity   373

Toe Dancing Tinsel!   Make some tinsel dance with static electricity   373

The Mysterious Moving Ping-Pong Ball   Charge up a couple of Ping-Pong   374
balls and challenge your partner to a race

Static Elec-Fish-Ity!   Go fishing using static electricity as your bait   375

Make a Lightning Safety Poster!   Learn about lightning and safety by creating   376
a poster to inform others

Unit 48: Electric Circuits

Get It Right and See the Light!   Build your own battery tester   378–379

Batteries and Bulbs—Get the Connection?   Learn how electricity travels in   380
a circuit to make electrical devices work

Fabulous Flashlights   Discover which kinds of materials allow electricity to   381
travel through them

WonderScience **Secret Circuits!**   Construct a Secret Circuit Board and try   382–383
predicting the path of electricity

Another Bright Idea!   Make your own flashlight   384

Unit 49: Heat

WonderScience **Balloon Bath**   Discover how a balloon's size is affected by   386–387
temperature

Warm Up and Cool Down   Learn why hot air rises and cool air falls   388

Full of Hot Air   See what can happen when air in a bottle is warmed   389

Warm Air Whizzers!   Create a fun toy that appears to move on its own   390

Up, Up, and Away!   Discover how a hot air balloon works   391

A Current Affair   Investigate how hot and cold liquids behave together   392

Unit 50: Magnetism

Electricity and Magnetism—A Powerful Pair!   Investigate how electricity   394–395
can be used to make a magnet

Magnets: What Makes Them So Attractive?   The most commonly asked   396
questions about magnets are answered

A *WonderScience* Magnetic Mystery Map!   A search for magnetic materials   397
in your own kitchen

Magnet-Making Marvels   Make your own magnet and test it for opposite   398
poles

Magnets Are Amazing Through and Through   Explore how magnets work   399
through gases, liquids, and solids

Pointing the Way . . . With a Compass   Use a magnet to make your own   400
compass, then use it to tell direction

Section 11: Motions and Forces

Unit 51: Forces

A *WonderScience* Bubble-O-Meter   Make an instrument to study balanced   402–403
and unbalanced forces

Forces   Learn what forces are and where forces occur   404

May the Force Be with You   Replace "push" and "pull" with more descriptive   405
terms for these actions

Science Friction   Compare the amount of friction between a rolling marble and   406
some surfaces

Gravity—It Can Really Get You Down   Investigate the interaction of different   407
objects with the Earth

The Great Tablecloth Trick!   Amaze both family and friends with this trick   408
that relies on inertia

Unit 52: Air Pressure

There's Air in There!   Observe some interesting effects of air pressure   410–411

Air Pressure Rules!   Explore the properties of air pressure   412

The Ins and Outs of Air Pressure!   Discover how air pressure differences can   413
create strong forces

The Difference Makes the Difference!   Use air pressure to inflate and deflate   414
a balloon inside a plastic bottle

Take the Plunge!   Investigate how a plunger works using air pressure   415
differences

Toying around with Air Pressure   Create and fly an air pressure rocket   416

Unit 53: Aerodynamics

***WonderScience* Flight School**   Use the science of aerodynamics to build and   418–419
fly your own airplane

It's a Bird, It's a Plane . . . It's Aerodynamics!   Learn all about aerodynamics   420
and do a crossword puzzle

Take A Whirl with a Wonderwhirler!   Make and fly an aerodynamically fun   421
  aircraft

3 . . . 2 . . . 1 . . . Lift Off!   Discover the importance of wing shape and angle in   422–423
  flying

Women on Wings!   Meet two women who have made aerodynamics their   423
  career

The Return of the Boomerang   Learn about boomerangs and then make one   424
  to throw4

Unit 54: Hovering

Hovercraft Test Pilots   Test-pilot your own hovercraft model   426–427

U.F.H.'s Sighted Racing on Kitchen Table   Learn how hovercrafts hover   428

Get a Better Feel for Air Pressure   Discover how trapped air allows a hover-   429
  craft to work

Its the Area That Counts   Predict and estimate the best shape to use in making   430
  a hovercraft

Fantastic Hover Voyage   Imagine a ride in your own hovercraft   430

Hovering Happenings   Learn the practical uses for hovercrafts (lawn mowers,   431
  trains)

Other Hovers   Design your own hovercraft model   432

Unit 55: Balance

Achieve the Power of Balance   Experiment with finding an object's center of   434–435
  gravity to keep it balanced

Bring Balance to Life!   Discover your own center of gravity and the cause of   436–437
  dizziness

Center of Gravity—On the Move!   Predict the location of an object's center   438
  of gravity

A *WonderScience* Balancing Act!   Investigate how weight distribution affects   439
  an object's balance

Balancing: Short & Simple   Discover how to make a short object easier to   440
  balance

Balancing Bernie   Balance Balancing Bernie and then create your own balanc-   440
  ing figure

Unit 56: Wheels

Round, Round Get A-Round   Experiment to learn about the behavior of a roll-   442–443
  ing wheel

Wheel Works   Discover the numerous uses of wheels   444

Merrily We Roll Along   Model the way the ancients used wheels and see how   445
  ball bearings work

Make a Wonder Wheel-a-Rang!   Construct a special wheel that will return to   446
  you like a boomerang

This Wheel Really Measures Up!   Measure distance using a wheel   447

Get a Lift with *WonderScience* Windlass   Build a special kind of wheel that   448
  will lift objects

Section 12: Sound

Unit 57: Sound and Hearing

Let Your Ears Be the Judge!   Use your ears to identify objects by the sound they make   450–451

Hear! Hear!   Learn how the parts of the ear allow us to hear   452

Good Vibrations!   Investigate how sound is produced and how it travels   453

Hearing in 3-D   Explore how you can identify the direction of a sound   454

A *WonderScience* Pitch Switcher   Create a sound instrument and use it to investigate pitch   455

The Many States of Hearing   Compare how sound travels through different types of materials   456

Unit 58: Physics of Music

Bottled Music!   Make beautiful music with just a bottle of water   458–459

Tune In!   Learn how sounds are created from instruments   460

Good Vibrations!   Investigate the sound that results when an object vibrates   461

What's All the Buzz About?   Interesting facts about insects and the sounds they make   461

Pluck-a-Cup Strummer   Construct your own string instrument   462

Singing Trees   See what causes the strange sounds that come from some trees   462–463

A Straw Whistle Symphony!   Make your own wind instrument to play   463

A Vibration Sensation!   Use a special detector to help you "see" musical vibrations from a radio   464

Unit 59: Echoes

Sounds Good to Me!   Experiment making echoes using a coffee can   466–467

Let's Hear It for Echoes!   Learn why echoes happen   468

Make an Echo . . . Echo . . . Echo!   Discover how to make sound bounce in a new direction   469–470

Echoes Are Everywhere!   Practice using longitude and latitude to learn more about echoes   471

Bats? We're All Ears!   Make some special ears to help you hear as well as a bat does   472

Section 13: Light

Unit 60: Vision

The Eyes Have It!   Investigate how your own eyes operate   474–475

Vision!   Learn how the parts of the eye make vision possible   476

Be a Receptor Detector!   Activate your retina's receptors for an interesting view   477

Letter-Perfect Vision   Test and compare your vision to your partner's vision   478

Two Eyes Are Better Than One!   Measure and compare the depth perception of your eyes   479

See a Sea in 3-D!   Focus your eyes to see a 3-D image in a 2-D picture   480

Unit 61: Colors

Making Rainbows!   Observe the colors present in light by making your own rainbow indoors   482–483

Color—What Goes In; What Comes Out   Learn what color is and what allows us to see it   484

Spin Those Colors!   Try a different way to mix colors   485

Break It Up!   Discover how to separate colors in a mixture   486

Make Your Own Color Mix Chart   Experiment by adding different colors together and see what you get   487

Color Haiku for You   Write a color-filled haiku   488

Prism in a Pan   Bend light to make a rainbow using a gelatin prism   488

Unit 62: Light

The Colors of Light—What a Sight!   Use the special *WS* diffraction slide to see the colors present in light   490–491

Seeing in a Whole New Light!   Learn about the colors in light and how light allows us to see colors   492

A Dot of a Different Color!   Discover how different-colored light can change the way colors appear   493

Inspect a Spectrum!   Create your own spectrum with things from around the house   494

Filter & Diffraction Action!   Use colored filters to see which colors the different filters let through   495

Your Own Rainbow Show!   Make a rainbow with your garden hose   496

Unit 63   Optical Illusions

Wonder Spinners   Make some fun and colorful optical illusions for yourself and friends   498–499

It's Fun to See in 3-D!   Use your special *WS* glasses to read this page in three dimensions   500

Ghostly Illusions   See how your eyes can play tricks on you   501

Mind and Line Benders   Discover that things are not always the way they appear   502

Illusions—A "Hole" New World!   Try this scary optical illusion   503

Can You Read This Title?   Some more fun optical illusions to figure out   504

Unit 64   Magnification

Magnificent Magnifiers!   Investigate the magnifying power of different materials   506–507

Lenses . . . Then and Now—Wow!   Learn about the earliest and the latest magnifiers   508

Magnifiers—How Do They Measure Up?   Measure the magnification of a lens   509

Say Cheese!   Discover how the lens in a camera produces an image   510

And Now for Something Really Big!   Make a simple projector with a flashlight and magnifying glass   511

What's for Lunch?   Identify foods magnified 200 to 5,000 times by an electron   512
microscope

Unit 65   Reflection

Be a Reflector Detector   Investigate how light bounces (reflects) off some   514–515
surfaces

Reflect on This . . .   Find out what causes a reflection to occur   516

There Are Two Sides to Everything!   Use your special *WonderScience* mirror   517
to test for symmetry

Mirror Myths   Tales and superstitions about reflections and mirrors   518

Fun House Mirrors   Discover how a mirror's shape affects reflection   519

Mirror Mania   A potpourri of fun mirror activities   520

ACTIVITY INDEX:
The Best of WonderScience, Volume II

Section 1: Science through Your Senses

Unit 1: Use Your Powers of Observation

Peanut Particulars   Know your peanut well enough to identify it in a group   6–7

Water—Watch and Wonder!   Food coloring shows how molecules move in hot and cold water   8

Chemistry and Colors—Mix and Match   Make an indicator solution and experiment to match colors   9

Food for Thought   Observe and record eating behaviors in the cafeteria   10

Think in a Wink!   See how much you can observe in three seconds   11

Unit 2: Smell and Taste

The Nose Knows!   Smell perfume, orange peel, and candy and make the scent stronger   18–19

Making Sense of Smell and Taste   Read about how your senses of smell and taste actually work   20

Sniffing Out Good Taste   Eat candy to experiment with your senses of smell and taste   21

How Sweet It Is!   Mix grape drink with different amounts of sugar and taste to identify them   22–23

Get the Skinny on Low-Fat Cookies!   Taste-test regular and low-fat cream-filled sandwich cookies   24

Unit 3: The Sense of Touch

Get in Touch with Your Feelings   Describe and identify objects in a box using only your sense of touch   30–31

A Touchy Subject   Read about the different receptors on our sensory nerves   32

Sandpaper Scraper   Differentiate between sandpaper using various parts of your hand   33

Temperature Touch-o-Meter   Compare the way fingers feel in different temperatures of water   34

Let's Give a Big Hand for the Sense of Touch!   Use a paper clip to find where your touch receptors are closer together   35

Read It with Feeling   Write your name in Braille using seeds and glue   36

Unit 4: Classification

Classification—All SORTS of Fun!   Use a flow chart to classify organisms   42–43

Periodic Table of the Elements   Table with drawings and common uses of each element   44–45

Start Your Own Rock Group!   Break, scratch, and observe rocks to classify them   46–47

A Periodic Table Game!   See who can find the most nearby elements with similar uses   48

Section 2: Chemical Tests

Unit 5: Chemistry and Color

Colors on the Moooove   Differentiate between three milks by adding food coloring and detergent — 54

Show Your True Colors   Mix two colors of food coloring and then separate them with chromatography — 55

Go for the Gold   Use special paper to test for pH differences in similar-looking substances — 56–57

Vitamin C Testing—Chemistry's Clear Solution!   Test for Vitamin C in Tang and orange juice iodine solutions — 58–59

Color & Chemistry—An Artful Solution!   "Paint" with different solutions on the special color-changing gold paper — 60

Unit 6: Investigating a Chemical Unknown!

A *WonderScience* Chem-Vestigation!   Make a chart, test six substances, and record your data — 66–67

Put Chemistry to the Test!   Gather information to help you identify mystery substances — 68

Dissolve It and Solve It!   Observe solubility of the six substances — 69

Color Clues You Can Use!   Use grape juice as an indicator — 70

Drop a Hint   Watch the behavior of food coloring on your solubility tests — 71

Discover the Unknown!   Use data from previous tests to identify a chemical unknown — 72

Unit 7: Chemistry Mystery Solvers

Solve a Powderful Mystery!   Conduct four tests on four different powders to help identify a mystery powder — 78–79

A Colorful Caper   Do a chromatography test for each of three candies to identify a smudge — 80–81

Soda Solutions   Use red cabbage juice to differentiate three clear liquids and identify a liquid — 82–83

Going, Going, Gone!   Use an evaporation test on three different liquids to identify a mystery liquid — 84

Section 3: Materials

Unit 8: Polymers

A Plastic Film Festival!   Do five tests on four types of plastic and record observations — 90–91

Pondering Polymers   Read about natural and synthetic polymers — 92

Goop to Go!   Make three polymers using glue, laundry detergent, and liquid starch — 93

Diapers—The Inside Story   Collect a polymer from a diaper and experiment with absorbency — 94–95

Poke But Don't Soak   Poke a pencil through a plastic bag full of water without spilling — 96

Unit 9: Parade of Paper

Tear ... and Compare!   Tear and pull three types of paper across the length and width 102–103

The Path to Paper   Read about the way paper is manufactured 104

Flex Finder   Measure the amount of bend in three different papers 105

Soak It Up!   Drop food coloring on paper to compare absorbency 106

Seeing Is Believing!   Hold paper up to the light and then try to read through it 106

The Art of Recycling   Make new paper from paper scraps and art materials 107

Unit 10: Materials: Test for the Best!

Get the Scoop on Goop!   Mix eighteen combinations of materials, place in a chart, and let dry 114–115

Test for the Best!   Run six tests on your eighteen substances to see which are best for building 116

Pasta Power!   Test the weight one piece of spaghetti can hold 117

Strength in Numbers?   Test how the number of spaghetti strands affects strength 118

Pile It On!   Glue layers of paper and wax paper and then test with pennies 119

The Ultimate Materials Challenge!   Build a bridge using only materials tested in this unit 120

Unit 11: Float and Sink

Water and Wax—The Sink-and-Float Facts!   Compare the weights of a candle and water to see if a candle floats 126–127

Float or Sink ... What Do You Think?   Compare the weights of clay and water to see if clay floats 128–129

Density Does It!   Use prior sink and float experiences to determine whether materials sink or float 130

Floating Fluids!   Compare weights of oil and water, then deduce the weight of candle wax 131

Go Nuts with Sink and Float!   Try floating a peanut in fresh water and salty water 132

Section 4: Measuring

Unit 12: Millimeters, Centimeters, and Beyond!

Measure Yourself in Metric!   Measure your height, hand, and jumps 138–139

English vs. Metric—And the Winner Is ...   Measure paper worms and find the best buy on a gold chain 140–141

Metric Map Maneuvers   Measure and use scale to find the distance between U.S. cities 142–143

Keep Metric in Mind!   Estimate length and then check 144

Unit 13: Measuring Time

It's Swing Time!   Record data from pendulum swings, weight, and length of string 150–151

Water Clock: Set It and Wet It!   Sink a cup in a bigger cup of water to tell time 152

Secondhand Sand!   Change the amount of sand and the hole to design a thirty-second timer 153

The Big Clock in the Sky!   Learn to tell time by observing shadows, moon 154–155
shapes, and star positions

Once upon a Time . . .   Read about ancient timepieces from around the world 156

Unit 14: Understanding Scale

On the Trail of the Wonders of Scale   Find the distance between two cities on 162–163
a map using a metric ruler

Design Your Own Scaled-Down Town!   Draw a map of a town using centi- 164
meters and millimeters

Scale-a-School!   Measure features of your school in metric and make a scale 165
drawing

One-to-One and Your Scale Is Done!   Read about actual-size drawings and 166
problems with scale

Up Close and Personal!   Measure a large and detailed drawing of an ant and 167
then find its actual size

Zooming In on Scale   Find the appropriate scale drawing to place several diff- 168
erent items

Unit 15: Finding Your Way with the Amazing Compass

Your Direction Connection   Find objects in your class that correspond with 174
north, south, east, and west

Do Your Degrees Agree?   Write the position of four objects in your room using 175
degrees

Earth—A Planet with Pull!   Read how a compass works and when it became 176
popular with sailors

Compass Making—Just Follow the Directions!   Make a floating compass 177
with a paper clip and bar magnet

Land Ho! Where'd You Go?   Plan a voyage and measure degrees to each 178–179
island on this map

Make a Compass Course . . . of Course!   Set up an outdoor course using your 180
compass and a meter stick

Section 5: Math Skills

Unit 16: Let's Graph It!

Graphing—It'll Grow on You!   Specific directions on how to plot a line graph 186–187
and what it means

Plot-a-Shot!   Make a toy with a plastic spoon and ball, and plot the distance the 188
ball traveled

Graphing—It's Gonna Be Big!   Graph breaths in a balloon versus its circum- 189
ference

Putting Time on the Line   Time a spool sliding down a thread from various 190
heights and graph your results

Stretching to Make a Point   Measure a rubber band weighted with pennies 191
and then make a line graph

Hot Plots!   Graph how peroxide and yeast heat up over time when combined 192

Unit 17: Volume: Full of Surprises!

Make Room for Volume   Cut three milk cartons at different heights and com- 198
pare their volumes

Looks Can Be Deceiving   Graduate a 2-liter bottle and a 1-liter bottle, then compare the markings   199

Down for the Count!   Use displacement to prove that different shapes can have the same volume   200

Measuring Volume the Handy Way!   Find the volume of your hand with your 2-liter bottle, water, and a film canister   201

The Cubic Centimeter: A Measure of Success!   Find volume with a formula, then by filling with centimeter cubes and counting   202–203

Spill and Fill!   Displace water and pour it into a beaker to discover that centimeters equal milliliters   204

Unit 18: Probability

Give Probability a Chance   Seek an eraser under a cup and record the number of times you find it   210–211

Hide and Seek!   Design an experiment with a 2/3 chance of finding an eraser   212

Probability—Give It a Whirl!   Make three paper spinners and record when they stop on the colored section   213–214

A Sure Thing!   Design spinners that will always or never stop on the colored part   215

What Are the Chances?   Estimate the likelihood of certain events and mark them on a number line   216

Unit 19: Symmetry: Two Sides to the Story

Symmetry—Two Sides to the Story   Use a small mirror to find lines of symmetry in capital letters   222–223

Fold and Behold!   Fold shapes along a line of symmetry, poke a hole, and measure findings   224

Reflect, Connect, Inspect!   Make a symmetrical drawing using a mirror and a ruler   225

A New Angle on Symmetry   Use a protractor and mirror to make a drawing with symmetrical angles   226

Imagine Your Image!   Take turns being the object and the reflection across lines of symmetry   227

Asymmetrical Spectacle!   View altered photos of normally symmetrical objects and find problems   228

Section 6: Physics

Unit 20: The Force of Friction!

Friction: More Than Just Scratching the Surface   Slide a lid across a table using the weight of washers; then add sandpaper   234

Friction: Just Weight and See!   Add weight to the lid and then graph the number of washers that move it   235

So What's the Rub?   Look at magnified photos and hypothesize about the amount of friction   236

Go with the Flow!   Drop pieces of clay in water to see friction in a liquid   237

Air Brakes   Make a paper airplane and drop balloons to investigate friction in air   238–239

Friction—Friend or Foe?   Think about ways friction is useful for items in the pictures   240

Unit 21: The Clever Lever

Never Say Never When It Comes to a LEVER!   Balance three pennies with only one on a ruler seesaw — 246–247

Hark: A Knock at the Lever!   Find the easiest way to open a door using only one finger — 248

Can a Lever Do It?—Yes it Can!   Position your hand to find the best way to open a can — 249

Something for Nothing?   Build a lever and compare pushing distances — 250–251

Living Lever-Limbs!   Lift a load with your own arm lever — 252

Unit 22: Structure and Function

Structure & Function Come in Handy!   Lose different features of your hands to see how useful they are — 258–259

The FUN in Structure and FUNction   Design a device to lift a marble out of a cup — 260

Structure with Some Stretch!   Cover a cup of water with plastic, poke a hole, and see why it doesn't leak — 261

Structured for Strength   Test the strength of corrugated cardboard by making cardboard shoes — 262–263

Structure & Function in Nature: We Imitate What's Great!   Look at pictures of human inventions and their counterparts in nature — 264

Unit 23: The Essence of Speed

Take the Lead—With Speed   Calculate your walking speed — 270–271

The Zip Line   Use a spool of thread and long string to investigate speed and acceleration — 272–273

Speed Sinking!   Predict relative speeds of sinking peanut parts — 274

Graphing to Go!   Read and then create a graph of a car's speed — 275

And You Thought You Were Fast!   Facts about speedy living and nonliving things — 276

Section 7: States of Matter

Unit 24: States of Matter

What's the Matter Anyway?   Discover that liquid in condensation comes from the air — 282–283

A Change in State Really Matters!   Read about the movement of atoms in solids, liquids, and gases — 284

Lose Some Mass—It's a Gas!   Compare evaporation rates of water and rubbing alcohol — 285

Salt and Water—No Easy Freeze   Melt an ice cube with salt and freeze waters with different salinities — 286

A *Wonder Science* State Debate!   Observe properties of shaving cream and identify its state of matter — 287

States of Matter Hall of Fame!   Read amazing facts about some unusual matter — 288

Unit 25: Gases

Air—It's Really There!   Prove that air exists by trapping it in a cup submerged in water — 294–295

Gases Galore!   Read about the characteristics of gases · 296

A Gas Bubble-ometer   Use a bottle dipped in soapy water and your warm hands to expand a gas · 297

Gas Pressure: It's in the Bag!   Blow a gas into a plastic bag and lift a book with the pressure · 298

Air Bags—Strong under Pressure!   Use a freezer bag and hard surface to model an inflated air bag · 299

Heat Up and Head Up!   Read about how hot air balloons work · 300

Unit 26: The Atmosphere

The Atmosphere: The Air We Share   Make different-sized parachutes and drop them · 306–307

Learn Not to Err When It Comes to Air!   Read about the main gases that make up air · 308

The No-Zone in the Ozone   Color globes showing the levels of concentration of ozone · 309

Don't Be Blue—Use CO_2   Pour carbon dioxide into indicator solution for a color change · 310

A *Wonder Science* Air Compare!   Collect three gases and see which has the most carbon dioxide · 311

A Water Uprising   Rust steel wool to use up oxygen gas and see what flows up in its place · 312

Section 8: Earth & Space Science

Unit 27: Erosion! Go with the Flow

Erosion: Going with the Flow   Compare erosion of sand, potting soil, and a mixture at different heights · 318–319

From Mountains to Molehills   Read about the power of erosion and view some examples · 320

Let's Settle the Matter   Observe a sand and soil mixture settling in water over time · 321

Caves: The "Hole" Story   Model the making of a cave with sugar cubes, clay, and a stream · 322

Waving Sand Goodbye   Test erosion on a model of a sand dune with plant roots and one without · 323

Erosion Spectacular!   View unusual rock formations and think about how erosion formed them · 324

Unit 28: Soil Science

Get the Dirt on Soil!   Closely examine characteristics of soil and sand · 330–331

Rain and Drain!   Find out whether soil or sand holds water better · 332–333

Soil Sizes—Some Surprises!   Separate soil particles in a bottle of water · 334

From Grass to Soil—Let Microbes Toil!   Compost grass clippings in a plastic bag · 335

Soak It Up!   Compare the capillary action of soil and sand · 336

Unit 29: Volcanoes: What a Blast!

Our Earth—From the Inside Out   Look at a scaled down cross-section of the   342–343
Earth and make a 3-D model

What on Earth Is a Volcano, Anyway?   Read about what volcanoes are made   344
of and what causes them to erupt

Convection: A Moving Experience   Food coloring in warm water models the   345
convection currents inside the Earth

Expanding Possibilities   Heat air in a bottle to show that gas expands when it   346
is heated

Magma—Gassed Up to Go!   Soda pop shows that pressure and heat cause the   347
gas in magma to expand

Mount Saint Helens—A Blast from the Past   Look at photographs to learn   348
about the 1980 explosion

Unit 30: Water: Clearly Wonderful!

Clump and Clean!   Add alum to dirty water and compare to untreated water   354–355
with a Secchi disk

Filters—Particularly Purifying   Make a toilet paper tube filter and try to clean   356
very dirty water with sand

Slow the Flow   Test materials for their ability to filter water   357

Testing the Waters   Use the color of the indicator solution to help neutralize an   358
acid with a base

Up, Up, and Away!   See how temperature affects gases in water   359

Hard Water Woes   Add soap to local, distilled, and hard water and compare   360
bubbles

Unit 31: Looking at the Moon

What's New in the Moon?   Record observations of the moon's shape and look   366–367
for patterns

Gaze-a-Phase!   Model positions of the Earth, sun, and moon and match to the   368–369
moon's phases

The Moon on the Move!   Observe the moon's movement in minutes   370

Craters—The Hole Story   Discover the sun's position in photos by making a   371
model moon and testing

A Moon Myth—Don't Let It Phase You!   Read a Native American folktale   372
about the moon

Unit 32: Shadows

Now Appearing: A Cast of Shadows!   Approximate the height of an object by   378–379
measuring shadows

Shifting Shadows!   Trace shadows outside every hour to identify the angle of   380–381
the sun

Sizing Up Shadows!   Graph shadow length at 10 cm intervals from a flashlight   382

Meet Some Shady Characters!   Create a play on the wall with transparency   383
film markers and a flashlight

Super-Size Shadows!   Read about both solar and lunar eclipses   384

NOTE: For page numbers, regular type refers to Volume 1. Boldface type refers to Volume 2.

A

adobe,
　　clay mixture, 20
absorbency,
　　of fabrics, 108
absorption of sound, 468
acetic acid, **66**
acid(s)
　　test for rocks, 315
　　in soda, 176
　　testing for, 274-275
　　indicator for, 292
　　in plants, 300
adhesion,
　　of water, 114
adhesives
　　testing different types, 98-101
　　in nature, 104
aerodynamics, 420
ailerons, 418
air
　　heating and cooling, 388, **296**
　　characteristics of, 410
　　in the atmosphere, **306**
　　gases in air, **308**
　　as an insulator, 214
air bags, **299**
air pressure
　　definition of, 428
　　principles, 412
　　activities, 409-416
air resistance, 420
air-cushioned vehicles, 428
airplanes
　　parts of, 418
　　design of, 418-420
Alcmene, and Hercules, 360
alcohol,
　　evaporation of, 144
algae,
　　affect of phosphate on, 79
alloys, 204
Alnilam, 359
Alnitak, 359
aluminum
　　as a rock, 316
　　as a metal, 202-203
amethyst, 316
ampulla, 437
animal homes, 24
antifreeze, 271
antioxidants,
　　to prevent color change in food, 166
anvil
　　of the ear, 452
appearance test,
　　for rocks, 315
Archimedes, 174
architecture, 20
argon, in air, **308**
arthritis, 96
art,
　　chemistry of, 58-59
assembly line, 28
asymetrical
　　versus symmetrical objects, **228**

B

bacteria
　　as natural recyclers, 224
　　and food spoilage, 164
bags,
　　paper vs. plastic, 178-179
balance, 402-403, 433-440
barometer,
　　how to make, 335
barometric pressure, 332
basalt, 316
baseball,
　　science of, 52
bases
　　indicator for, 294
　　in plants, 300
batik, 60
bats,
　　and echoes, 470-472
batteries,
　　testing, 378-379
beams,
　　in building, 21
Bellatrix, 359
Betelgeuse, 359
Big Dipper, 357
biology,
　　and classification systems, **42**
blind spot, 476
boomerang(s)
　　in space, 71
　　aerodynamics of, 424
bones,
　　and calcium, 156-159
Braille, **36**
brain,
　　and balancing, 437
brass, 204
break test,
　　for rocks, 315 and **47**
bridges,
　　design of, 19
broccoli,
　　and calcium, 158
bronze, 204
bubble blowers, 82-83
bubbles, 82-83
Burchette, Don
　　inventor of Hi-Float, 231

C

calcite, 315
calcium,
　　as a chemical, 154-155
　　in building materials, 154-156
　　in food, 156, 158-159
　　in bones and teeth, 156, 158-159
calcium carbonate
　　in chalk, 60
　　in plaster, 154-155
　　in cement, 156
calcium chloride, 156
calcium phosphate, 156
calcium sulfate
　　in plaster, 154-156
cameras, 508
capillarity
　　in different materials, 130-132
　　to filter liquids, 135
　　of water, 119
capillary action, 116
carbohydrates, 146-147, 152
carbon
　　in charcoal, 284
　　in steel, 204
　　in soda, 172
　　in rubber, 193
carbon dioxide
　　in bubbles, 84
　　in calcium carbonate, 157
　　in soda, 170-172, 248, 309
　　testing for, 279, **310-311**
　　production of, 308
　　in the atmosphere, **308**
　　and photosynthesis, **308**
carbonate, 154-155
carbonated soda
　　detection of carbon dioxide, 309
　　production of, 172
carbonation
　　in soda, 172
　　natural, 172
carbonic acid, 295
Cassiopeia, 354-355, 357
cast, fossil, 319
caves,
　　formation of, **322**
　　and erosion, **321-323**
CEBAF,
Continuous Electron Beam
Accelerator Facility, 38-39
cellulose, 148
Celsius temperature scale, 330-331
Celsius, Andes, 332
cement,
　　and calcium, 156-159
center of gravity, 434,436,438
centigrade, 332
centrifugation, 244
centimeter, **138**
chalk,
　　chemical found in, 60
　　and calcium, 158
charges,
　　positive and negative, 372
charcoal, 284

chemicals, 282
chemical bonds, 284
chemical energy, 362-363
chemical indicators,
    found in plants, 298-299
    and chemical reactions, 282-283
chemical reactions
    examples of, 274-275
    in metal, 202-203
    of indicators, 300
    in picture taking, 61
    of soap, 76
    of adhesives, 100
    of hair permanents, 284
    in rusting, 284
    in tanning, 284
    and burning of charcoal, 284
    in fireflies, 284
    and fireworks, 284
    and digestion, 284
    and temperature changes, 286-287
    and release of gas, 286-287
    and changes in state, 285
    to identify unknown substances, **66-72**
chemistry of art, **62**
chromatography
    separation of chemicals, 244, 277
    to separate colors, 486, **55**
circuit testers, 382-383
circuits, 380
circumference
    in wheels, 447
    how to measure, 13
    of a balloon and air temperature, 386-387
    graphing balloon circumference, **189**
Clark, Tim,
    water chemist, 296
classification, **42**
clay, 316
clouds,
    formation of, 140
cobalt, 396
cochlea, 452
Cockerell, Sir Christopher
    inventor of the first hovercraft, 431
cohesion
    in water, 114
    in soap bubbles, 82-83
collagen, 148, 150-151
cologne, 263
color
    complementary, 501
    in light, 490-491
    in rainbows, 484
    separation, 486, **55**
    and chemistry, **55-60**
color-changing paper, **56, 57-60**
color drop test,
    to identify unknown powders, **71**
color test,
    for rocks, **47**
colorings,
    in food, 165
communication,
    inventions in, 30
compass
    how to make, 400, **177**
    how they work, 396, **174-180**
    how to read, **174-180**
    history of, **176**
    and magnetic poles, 396, **176**
complementary colors, 501
compost, **335**
concave mirrors, 519

condensation,
    of water, 140
    and states of matter, **282-284**
conductors
    of heat, 207
    of electricity, 380
cones (of the eye)
    used to see color, 484
    effects of being tired, 501
constellations,
    identification of, 354-355
    using to tell time, **155**
contraction
    in frozen liquid molecules, 116
    of air in a balloon, 388
control,
    in an experiment, 275, 279, 298
convection current, 388
convex mirrors, 519
copper
    in batteries, 380
    in pure form, 316
    corrosion of, 202-203
    recycling of, 218-219
cornea, 476
corrosion, of metal, 202-203
cotton, 108
craters,
    from meteorites, 352
crystals
    dry or in solution, 226-227
    salt, 226-227, 266
    sugar, 226-227, 266-267
    Epsom salts, 266-267
    facets of, 268
    cube-shaped, 268-269
    Kool-Aid, 226-227
    metals as, 268
    to grow, 269
    quartz, 268
    uses of, 268
    and ice cream, 272
cubes, 85
cubic crystals, 268-269
cubit, 10-11
curve ball,
    and friction, 50-51

D
Dardin, Christine,
    aerodynamics engineer, 423
decomposers, **335**
density dessert, 240
density
    calculating, 238
    of materials compared with water, 234-235
    definition of, 236, **130**
    of water, 234-235, **130**
    of lead, **130**
    mineral oil, **130**
    oak, **130**
depth perception, 476
design,
    of structures, 18-19
detergent
    how it works, 76
    and phosphates, 79
    as a stabilizer, 252
    for cleaning, 74-75
    and surface tension, 122-124, 126-127, 253
dew,
    formation of, 140
diamonds,
    and other gems, 316

diffraction of light, 490
diffusion
    of odors, 260
    in art, 264
digestion
    and chemical reactions, 284
    and dissolving, 117
dilution,
    of paints, 58-59
dirt,
    removal with soap, 76
discovery,
    versus invention, 28
    dispersions,
    oil & water, 252
dissolving
    examples of, 228
    of substances in water, 117
    test, to identify unknown chemicals, **70**
distance
    measuring, 12
    and speed, **270**
distillation,
    to make wax, 63
domes, 22
drag,
    or air resistance, 420
dyes,
    in fabrics, 62

E
ear
    and dizziness, 437
    and hearing, 452
    canal, 452
    drum, 452
Earhart, Amelia, 423
earthquakes
    epicenter, 323-324
    how they occur, 324
    where the occur, 324
    and safety, 324
Earth Day activities, 143
earth,
    movement around sun, 350
echoes, 468
eclipses, **384**
eggshells,
    and calcium, 158
electrical energy, 362
elasticity,
    of fabric, 108
electric circuits, 378-379, 382-383
electric currents
    and magnetism, 396
electrical
    conductors, 380
    insulator, 212
    charges, 372
electricity
    static, 370-372
    and circuits, 380
    affect on water, 119
    and new inventions, 31
    produced by a quartz crystal, 270
electromagnet, 394-395
electron microscope, 508
electrons
    in atoms, 36
    in static electricity, 372
    in magnetism, 396
    in electric circuits, 380
    in metals, 204

emeralds,
 and other gems, 316
emulsifiers,
 types of, 252
emulsions
 in camara film, 61
energy
 forms of, 362
 in rubber, 198
 solar, 340
 conversions, 362-368
enzymes, 151
epicenter,
 of an earthquake, 323-324
equator, 470
erosion,
 activities, **318-324**
 and speed of moving, **319**
 and land formations, **320, 322, 324**
Esposito, Christine,
 chemist, 255
essential oils, 263
estimating
 numbers of objects, 2-3, 5, 8
 using a grid, 4
 distance or length, 7, 8
 time, 7
 size, 263
evaporation
 of a crystal solution, 266-267
 of water, 140
 of water from bubbles, 82-83
 to produce crystals, 227
 of water from our bodies, 334
 of humidity, 334
 and states of matter, **284, 285**
 test, to identify unknown, **70**
expansion
 in frozen water molecules, 116
 of air in a balloon, 388
eye structures
 to see colors, 484
 and vision, 476

F

fabrics
 cotton, 108
 silk, 108
 wool, 108
 weaving, 108
 durability in, 108
 elasticity in, 108
 absorbency of, 108
 strength of, 108
 insulating quality of, 108
 water resistance of, 108
 flame resistance of, 108
 how to dye, 62
facets,
 sides of crystals, 268
Fahrenheit scale, 330-331
Fahrenheit, Gabriel, 332
fat
 as an insulator, 214-215
 in food, 146-147
FDA,
 and food labeling, 152
fibers,
 in fabrics, 108
film negatives, 61
filtration,
 to separate mixtures, 244
fireflies,
 and chemical reactions, 284

fireworks,
 and chemical reactions, 284
Fitzgerald, Chris
 hovercraft designer, 431
flame resistance,
 of fabrics, 108
flashlights,
 how to make, 384
flavorings,
 of food, 164
floating,
 and density, 234-235
 and sinking, **126, 132**
 fluids, **131**
flowers,
 as indicators, 296
 used for scent, 302
flow chart, **42**
flow test,
 for thickness, 163
food additives, 161-168
 chemicals, 227
 labeling, 152
 nutrients, 148
 spoilage, 166
foot,
 as a unit of measurement, 10-11
forces, 404
fossil
 formation of, 319
 types, 319
freefall, 68
freezing, **284**
friction
 and rubber, 194-195
 ways to reduce, 92
 force of, 404
 in baseball, 51
 static, **236**
 sliding, **236**
 of objects through liquids, **237**
 of objects through a gas, **238-239**
frost,
 formation of, 140
fructose
 as a food additive, 167
 as a carbohydrate, 145
fulcrum,
 of a lever, **246-248, 250-252**
function,
 and structure, **258-264**

G

garden,
 Japanese rock, 318
gas(es)
 activities, 312
 and evaporation, 140
 in magnetism, 399
 in mixtures, 242
 production of, 309
 and chemical reactions, 288
 as a state of matter, **282-285, 287-288**
 in air, **294, 295**
 characteristics of, **294-300**
 under pressure, **298, 299**
 in a hot-air balloon, **300**
gelatin,
 chemicals in, 150-151
gems, 316
geodesic dome, 23
geologists, **46**
geology, **46**

glasses,
 history of, 508
glue
 from egg whites, 181
 from flour, 181
 from different foods, 98-99
 made from milk, 183
gold
 mines, 317
 panning activity, 317
 in pure form, 316
 as a metal, 204
Goodyear, Charles, 196
granite, 316
graphs,
 defined, **186**
 how to make, **186-192**
 and slopes, **187**
graphing exercises, 186-192
graphite
 as a lubricant, 95
 in pencils, 60
gravitational pull, 407
gravity, 404
Guericke, Otto von, 415
gypsum, 156

H

hailstorms, 336
hammer,
 of the ear, 452
hard water, 160
hardness test,
 for rocks, 315, **47**
Hazlitt, Andrea
 plastics inventor, 192
hearing,
 and observation, 34-35
 and sound, 450-456
heat energy, 362-363, 365-367
heat insulator, 212
heliostats, 340
helium, 231
hematite, 316
Hercules
 the constellation, 360
 the myth, 360
Hi-Float
 coating for helium balloons, 231
homes, of animals, 24
homogenized milk, 252
hot air balloons,
 short history of, 391
 parts of, 391
 how they work, 391, **300**
hourglass,
 to keep time, **153**
hovercraft(s)
 test models, 426-427
 in Disney World, 431
Hubble space telescope
 and solar energy, 340
 as a magnifier, 508
humidity
 definition, 332
 relative, 332
 and evaporation, 334
humus, 316
hydrogen
 to make water, 116
 in charcoal, 284
 atoms, 194-195

I

ice
  and insulation, 214-215
  water molecules in, 116
igloos, 20
illusions, optical, 498-499
IMAX projector, 508
indicators
  in plants, 294, 298-299
  uses in industry, 296
  for acids, 176, 274-275, 279
  to observe color reactions, **9**
  to test for carbon dioxide, **310, 311**
  to identify unknown substances, **69-71**
inertia, 408
inner ear, 437
insects, 126
insulating quality, of fabrics, 108
insulation, 210-211
insulators
  examples of, 212
  how they work, 212
  in nature, 216
intraocular lens, 508
International System of Units, 12
inventions
  in transportation, 29
  in communication, 29
  and electricity, 31
inventory, vs. estimates, 509
iodine test
  for starch, **68**
iris, 476
iron
  as a magnet, 396
  in pure form, 316
  in metal, 202-203
  and rusting, 284
iron oxide, 284

J

joints,
  In the body, 96

K

key,
  classification, **43**
kilometer, **142**
kinetic energy, 42-43

L

laboratory safety
  smelling chemicals, 307
  cleaning equipment, 250
lamination
  process to strengthen material, **119**
land formations,
  and erosion, **320**
latex,
  in rubber, 196
latitude, 470
laundry detergent
  for cleaning, 74-75
lead, 316
Leeuwenhoek, Antonie van, 508
length, 12
lens,
  of the eye, 476
lenses
  history of, 508
  intraocular, 508
Leo, 357
levers, **246-252**

lift,
  an upward push, 420
light
  bulbs, 380
  spectrum, 484
  and color, 492
  receptors, 476-477
  energy, 362-363, 366-368
lightning
  trivia, 336
  safety, 376
lignin, **104**
limestone
  uses of, 316
  calcium carbonate in, 60
liquid(s)
  nitrogen, **288**
  lubricants, 92
  molecules of, 140
  in magnetism, 399
  in mixtures, 242
  as a state of matter, **282-288**
Little Bear constellation, 354
Little Dipper, 356
longitude, 470
lubricants, 92
lunar eclipses, **384**
Lyra, 357

M

Magdeburg, Germany
  air pressure experiment, 415
magnetic poles
  defined, 396
  of a compass, 396, **176**
magnets,
  how they work, 396
  compasses, and the Earth, **176**
magnesium, 204
magnetism,
  and metals, 206
magnification
  testing for, 506-507
  calculating, 509
magnifiers
  testing different types, 506
  history of, 508
magnitude,
  of an earthquake, 327
malleability, 205
maltose, 146
marble
  and calcium, 158
  used in building, 316
materials,
  development and testing, **114-120**
matter, states of, **282-288**
measurement
  units of, 10-11
  rules for accuracy, 12
  history of, 12
  in metric system, **138-144**
  in English system, **138-144**
medicines, from plants, 301
Meissa, 358
melanin, 284
melting, **284**
Mercalli scale, 326
mercury
  in thermometers, 332
  at room temperature, **288**
metals
  as crystals, 268
  as musical instruments, 207

as magnets, 396
  corrosion of, 202-203
  as heat conductors, 207
  and rust, 284
meteor, 352
meteorites, 35
meteorology, 332
metric system,
  measuring in, 12, **138**
  units, **138**
  comparing with English system, **140, 141**
  and map scales, **142**
  estimating in, **144**
microorganisms,
  in soil, **335**
  as decomposers, **335**
microscope
  first model, 508
  scanning electron, 508
microgravity, 68
milk
  and calcium, 159
  and detergent reaction, 253
  as a mixture, 252
  making glue from, 183
Milky Way Galaxy, 356
millimeter, **138**
Mintaka, 359
mirrors
  how they work, 516
  images in, 516
  and light, 516
  and myths, 516
mixtures
  definition of, 244
  examples of, 244
  separation of, 277
  of oil and water, 77, 254
  molecules in, 244
milk, 252
molds, made from plaster, 61
molecules
  of water, 140
  production of, 116
  in mixtures, 244
  in plastic, 188
  in soda, 172
  in crystals, 268
  diffusion of, 258
  study of, 276
  in air, 410
  in matter, **282**
moon
  cycles, 351, **367, 155**
  phases, **366-369**
  craters, **371**
  folklore, **372**
  eclipses, **384**
  to tell time, **155**
Morse code, 208
motion, 52
music, 458-459
musical instruments, 460
mylar balloons, 231
myths,
  and constellations, 354

N

natural resources, 220
negative charges, 372
negatives
  from picture taking, 61
neutrons, 36
Newton, Sir Isaac
  and early telescopes, 508

nickel,
    as a magnet, 396
nitrogen,
    in air, **308**
North Star, 356
nova, 360
nutrients
    labeling, 152
    in food, 108, 146
    in soil, 22

O

observation
    direct, **6-7**
    indirect observation, **8**
    of human behavior, **10**
    of chemical reactions, **9**
    in a short period of time, **9**
    of human behavior, **10**
obsidian, 316
ocean in a bottle, 72
ocean currents, 392
odometer
    definition of, 447
    make your own, 13
oil, and water
    dispersions, 252
olfactory,
    bulb, **20**
    nerve, **20**
    tract, **20**
optical illusions, 497-504
optic nerve, 476
ores, 317
organisms,
    classification of, **42**
Orion, 354-355, 357
outer ear,
    and balance, 437
    and hearing, 452
oval window,
    in the ear, 452
oxidation
    and color changes in food, 166
oxygen
    in soda, 172
    in water, 116
    in charcoal, 284
    in air, **308, 312**
    and rusting, **312**
ozone, **309**

P

pagodas, 20
paint,
    how to make, 64
paper
    as a natural polymer, 184
    recycling of, 221, **107**
    comparing different types, **102, 103**
    making of, **104**
    characteristics of, **102-108**
particle accelerators, 36
Pegasus, 354-355
pencils,
    chemicals in, 60
pendulum,
    motion, 44
    used to keep time, **150,151**
percent daily value, 152
perfume,
    chemicals in, 263
periodic table game, **48**
permanents,
    and chemical reactions, 284

persistence of vision, 500
PET-Polyethylene terephthalate
    as soda bottles, 311
petroleum
    in crayons, 60
    to make detergent, 76
    to make synthetic fibers, 108
    used to make wax, 63
petroleum jelly
    as a lubricant, 96
phosphates
    in detergents, 79
photography
    chemistry of, 61
photosynthesis, 340, **308**
photovoltaic cells, 270
pigments, 62
pitch
    in echoes, 470-471
    in music, 460
plane,
    make your own, 422
planets
    facts about, 347
    distance from sun, 346
    distance in scale, 346
    diameters of, 346
plants
    medicines from, 300
    food from, 300
    parts of, 300
    and water transport, 303
    as chemical indicators, 292-299
    used in scents and flavorings, 302
plasma,
    as a state of matter, **288**
plaster of paris
    making of, 156
    and calcium, 157
    to make molds, 61
plastic
    testing different types, 186-187, **90, 91**
    uses of, 188
    dissolving, 188
    soda bottles, 311
    an artificial polymer, 184
    recycling of, 191, 311
playground,
    physics of, 44
Polaris, 354
polarity, 113
polymers
    natural, 180, **92**
    artificial, 180, **92**
    structure of, **261, 92**
    characteristics of, **90-96**
    make your own, **93**
polyvinyl alcohol, **92**
polyvinyl acetate, **92**
positive charges, 372
positive terminals,
    in batteries, 380
potassium, 204
precipitate
    in a mixture, 244
    in chemical reactions, 284
precipitation
    to separate mixtures, 244
preservatives, 164
pressure,
    of gases in soda, 172
    of gases, **298**
Priestley, Joseph,
    discoverer of rubber, 196

prism,
    made from gelatin, 488
probes
    used to investigate, 36
projector,
    early movie, 508
    IMAX, 508
    make your own, 511
protein
    as a polymer, 181, **92**
    as a stabilizer, 252
    in food, 152
    in hair, 284
protons
    study of, 36
    in static electricity, 372
Proxima Centauri, 356
pull force, 404
pulp,
    paper, **104**
pupil, 476
purification,
    of water, 223
push force, 404

Q

quarks, 38-39
quartz, as a crystal, 268
quinine, 300

R

Rain
    gauge, 330-331
    formation of rain drops, 332
    and condensation, 140
rainbow
    colors in a, 484
    how to make, 482-483, 496
reaction time,
    in baseball, 53-54
receptors, ST, 4
recycling
    types of, 220
    paper, 220-221, **107**
    plastics, 311
red cabbage as in indicator 295, 298-299
reflected sound, 468
reflections,
    and light, 514-515
    and symmetry, 517, **225, 226**
reflector, 514-515
relative humidity, 332
repulsion,
    of magnets, 396
retina
    in seeing color, 501
    and vision, 476
Rigel, 359
rocks
    testing , 314-315
    and, **47**
    uses of, 316
rubber
    natural, 196
    synthetic, 196
    uses of, 196
    characteristics of, 196, 199
    and printing, 197
    and stored energy, 198
    as a natural polymer, 184
    versus plastic, 184
    recycling of, 218-219
rudders,
    on airplanes, 418-419

rust, 202-203
rusting,
    chemical reaction of, 284
    role of oxygen in, **312**

S

Saiph, 359
salt
    water, 138
    to make crystals, 232
    dissolved in water, 226-227
    frozen in water, 118
    as a crystal, 266-267
sampling, 358
sand,
    comparing with soil, **330, 319, 321**
    dunes and erosion, **323**
sandstone, 316
sapphires, 316
saturated fats, 145
scale
    of maps in metric, **142**
    interpreting scale, **150-156**
scales,
    temperature, 330-331
scanning electron microscope
    history of, 508
    photos from, 512
seashells,
    and calcium, 159
sedimentation, 244
seesaws
    and balance, 47
seismic focus, 324
seismograph,
    to detect earthquakes, 324
semicircular canals,
    of the ear, 437
senses,
    smell, **12-24**
    touch, **30-36**
sensory nerves,
    and sense of touch, **32**
    and sense of taste, **20**
separating a mixture, 277, 244
sextant, 14-15
shadows,
    to track the sun, 350
    length of, **378, 379, 382**
    and the sun, **380, 381**
    eclipses, **384**
silicon, 316
silver, 204
sinking,
    and floating, **126-132**
Sirius, 354-355
sizing,
    in paper making, **104**
skyscrapers, 21
slope
    of a graph, **187**
smell,
    sense of, **18-24**
    receptors, **20**
    and observation, 34-35
    and taste, **20-21**
soap
    bubble film, 84
    for cleaning, 74-75
    history of, 76
    how it works, 76
soda
    ingredients in, 172
    bottling, 170-171

gases in, 311
sodium polyacrylate,
    polymer in diapers, **92, 94-95**
soil,
    comparing with sand, **330, 331**
    size of particles, **330, 331**
    type and erosion, **318, 319, 321, 323**
    nutrients, 224
    science, **330-336**
Solar Thermal Energy Conversion, 340
solar,
    cells, 340
    collector, 340
    cooker, 343
    eclipses, **384**
    energy, 340
    greenhouse, 338-339
    system, 347
    power plants, 342
solids
    in magnetism, 399
    in mixtures, 242
    as a state of matter, **282-284, 286-288**
solvents,
    in markers, 60
solubility, **69**
sonogram, 470-471
sonar, 470-471
sound
    stereo, 452
    and echoes, 468
    materials that absorb, 468
    materials that reflect, 468
    energy, 362-368
    and hearing, 449-456
space
    toys in, 69
    shuttle, 68
spectrum,
    light, 484, 492-496
speed
    measuring, **270**
    formula for, **270**
    units used to express, **270**
    through water, **274**
    graphing, **275**
    trivia facts, **276**
    of sound, **276**
    of light, **276**
speedometer, **270**
spider webs, 24
stabilizer
    in milk, 252
    examples of, 254
standards,
    in experiments, 167
stars,
    to tell time, **155**
starch
    testing for, 149
    as a polymer, 180
    in food, 148
    in plants, 301
static electricity, 370-371
steel, 204
stirrup,
    of the ear, 452
streak test,
    for rocks, 315, **47**
structure,
    in building, 18-19
    and function, **258-264**
sugar
    crystals, 266-67

as a food additive, 167
    dissolved in water, 226
    frozen in water, 118
    diffusion of, 261
    in food, 148
    as a crystal, 266-267
sulfate, 154-155
sulfur,
    in vulcanization, 196
    sulfur, 202-203
sun,
    as an energy source, 340
    and shadows, **378-380, 384**
    eclipses of,
    to tell time, **154**
supporting cell,
    and sense of smell, **20**
surface tension
    of water, 119
    affects from detergent, 122
sweeteners
    in sodas, 175
    as food additives, 167
swing,
    as a pendulum, 46
symmetry,
    testing for, 517, Sy, 2
    line of, 517, Sy, 2-8
synovial
    fluid, 96
    membrane, 96
synthetic rubber, 196

T

tanning,
    chemical reaction of, 284
tarnish, 203
taste,
    sense of, **18-24**
    and observation, 34-35
    and smell, **20-21**
    receptors, **20**
    buds, **20**
    cell, **20**
Teflon, 182
telegraph, 208
telescope
    early models, 508
    Hubble Space, 508
temperature
    scales, 330-331
    effect on gases, 309
    taking readings, 330-331
teepees, 20
teeth,
    and calcium, 156
terminals,
    in batteries, 380
texture test,
    for rocks, **47**
thatch huts, 20
thermometer, 330-331
thickeners,
    in food, 162-163
thread, 108
3-D images, 480
time,
    and speed, **270**
    measuring, **150-156**
timing devices,
    inventing, 26-27
tin, 204
toilet water,
    chemistry of, 263

tongue,
    and tasting, **20**
tornadoes
    causes, 332
    make your own model, 333
touch,
    sense of, **30-36**
touching,
    and observation, 34-35
toys,
    in space, 65-72
transportation,
    inventions in, 29
trash,
    facts about, 224
trees that sing, 462
triangular prisms, 85
triangulation
    to locate earthquakes, 327

U

ultrasonic sounds, 462
unbalanced forces, 402-403
uncia, 10-11
units,
    of measurement, 10-11
unlike poles,
    in magnets, 398
uranium ore, 316
Ursa Minor, 354-355, 357
utricle, 437

V

vanilla ice cream,
    made in a bag, 256
variable,
    of an experiment, **186**
vibrations
    in musical instruments, 460

from earthquakes, 322-323
vinegar
    used to curdle milk, 183
    as an acid, 291
    mixed with baking soda, 306
    test, to identify unknowns, CU, 3
Vitamin C,
    testing for, **59-60**
viscosity, 93
vision
    seeing colors, 501
    persistence of, 500
    testing, 478
volume,
    or loudness, 466-467
    measuring volume, **198-204**
    calculating volume, **202, 203**
vortex, 333
vulcanization,
    for car tires, 196

W

water,
    clock, **152**
    molecules, 124
    of fabrics, 108
    water treatment plant, 223
    as a lubricant, 90-91
    and cohesion, 114
    mixed with baking soda, 306
    mixed with salt, 280
    purification, 223
    freezing of, 116
    and stalagmite formation, 117
    and stalactite formation, 117
    to dissolve things, 116-117
    atoms and molecules of, 116
    recycled, 224
    and capillarity, 132

striders, 126
    surface tension of, 124
wave bottle, 252
weaving, 108
weight,
    affects on hovering, 426
weightlessness in space, 68
wheels
    history of, 444
    uses in machines, 444
wigwams, 20
Winged Horse constellation, 354
wind
    measuring speed, 330-331
windlass, 448
wood, 218-219
wool, 218-219
Wright, Orville and Wilbur, 419
Wyeth, Nathaniel
    inventor of PET, 311

X

x-rays,
    as probes, 37

Y

yaks, 20
yard,
    unit to measure distance, 10-11
yo-yo,
    played in space, 69

Z

zinc, 204